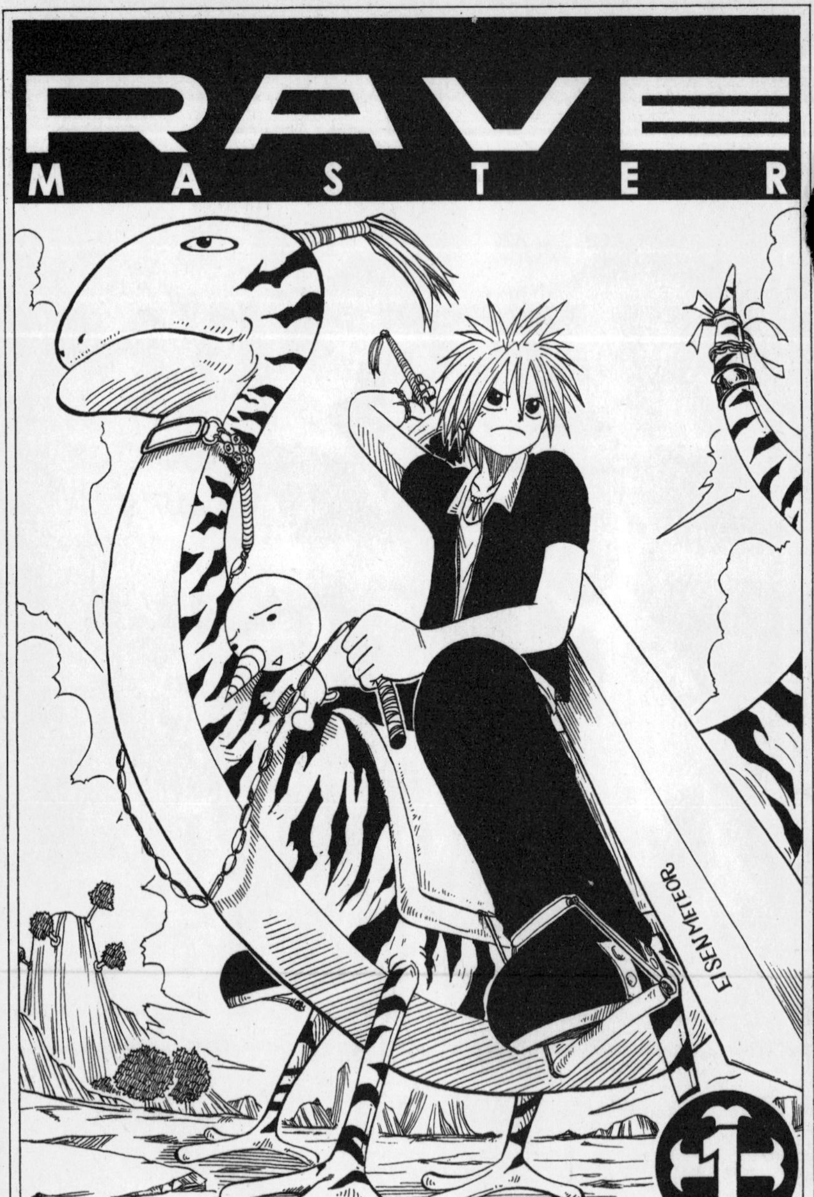
RAVE
MASTER
EISENMETEOR
1

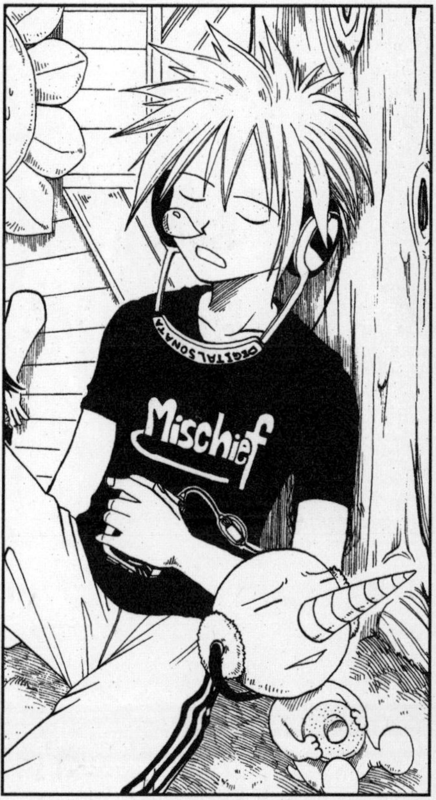
DIGITALSONATA
Mischief

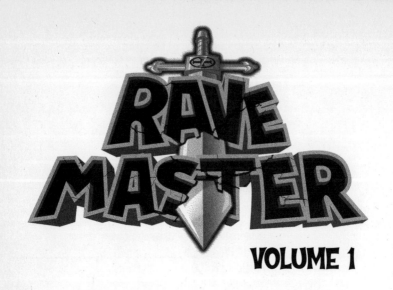

VOLUME 1

Story and Art by
HIRO MASHIMA

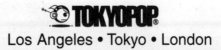

Los Angeles • Tokyo • London

Translator - Amy Forsyth
English Adaption - James Lucas Jones
Copy Editor - Amy Kaemon
Retouch & Lettering - Krystal Dawson
Cover Colors - Pauline Sim
Cover Layout - Raymond Makowski

Senior Editor - Jake Forbes
Managing Editor - Jill Freshney
Production Coordinator - Antonio DePietro
Production Manager - Jennifer Miller, Mutsumi Miyazaki
Art Director - Matt Alford
Editorial Director - Jeremy Ross
VP of Production - Ron Klamert
President & C.O.O. - John Parker
Publisher & C.E.O. - Stuart Levy

Email: editor@TOKYOPOP.com
Come visit us online at www.TOKYOPOP.com

A 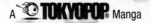 Manga

TOKYOPOP Inc.
5900 Wilshire Blvd. Suite 2000
Los Angeles, CA 90036

ISBN: 1-59182-064-2

First TOKYOPOP® printing: February 2003

11 10 9 8 7
Printed in the USA

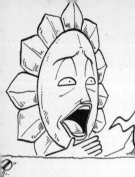

CONTENTS

RAVE: 1 Opened Map ▶▶ 10

RAVE: 2 Guiding Bell ▶▶ 81

RAVE: 3 Red Signal ▶▶ 137

RAVE: 4 Stairway to the Unknown ▶▶ 167

BONUS COMIC:
RAVE0077 ▶▶ 193

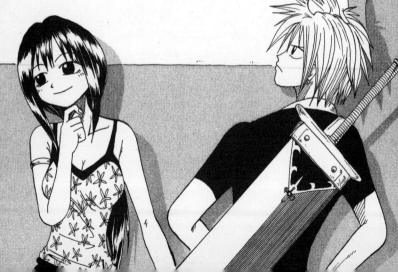

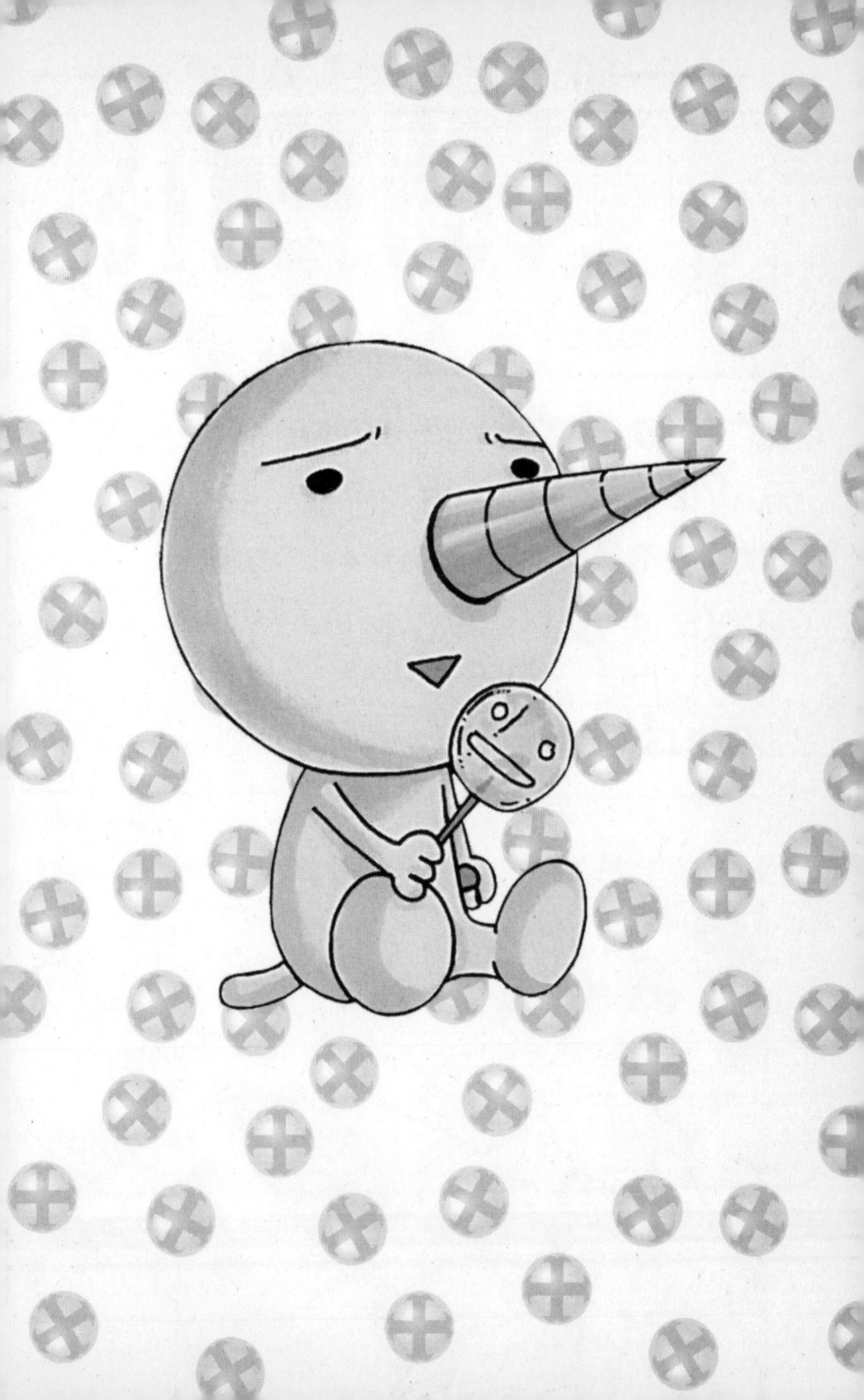

—50 YEARS AGO—

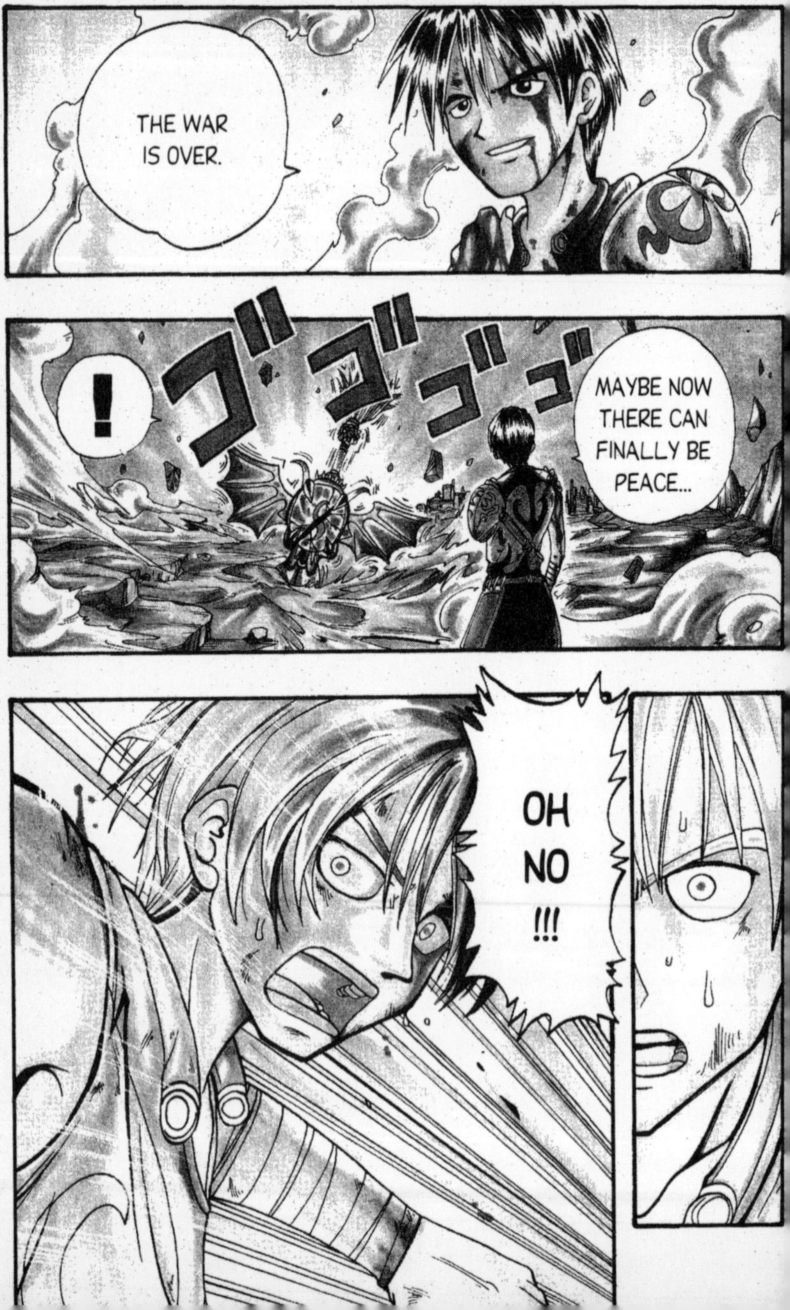
THE WAR IS OVER.
MAYBE NOW THERE CAN FINALLY BE PEACE...
ゴゴゴ
!
OH NO !!!

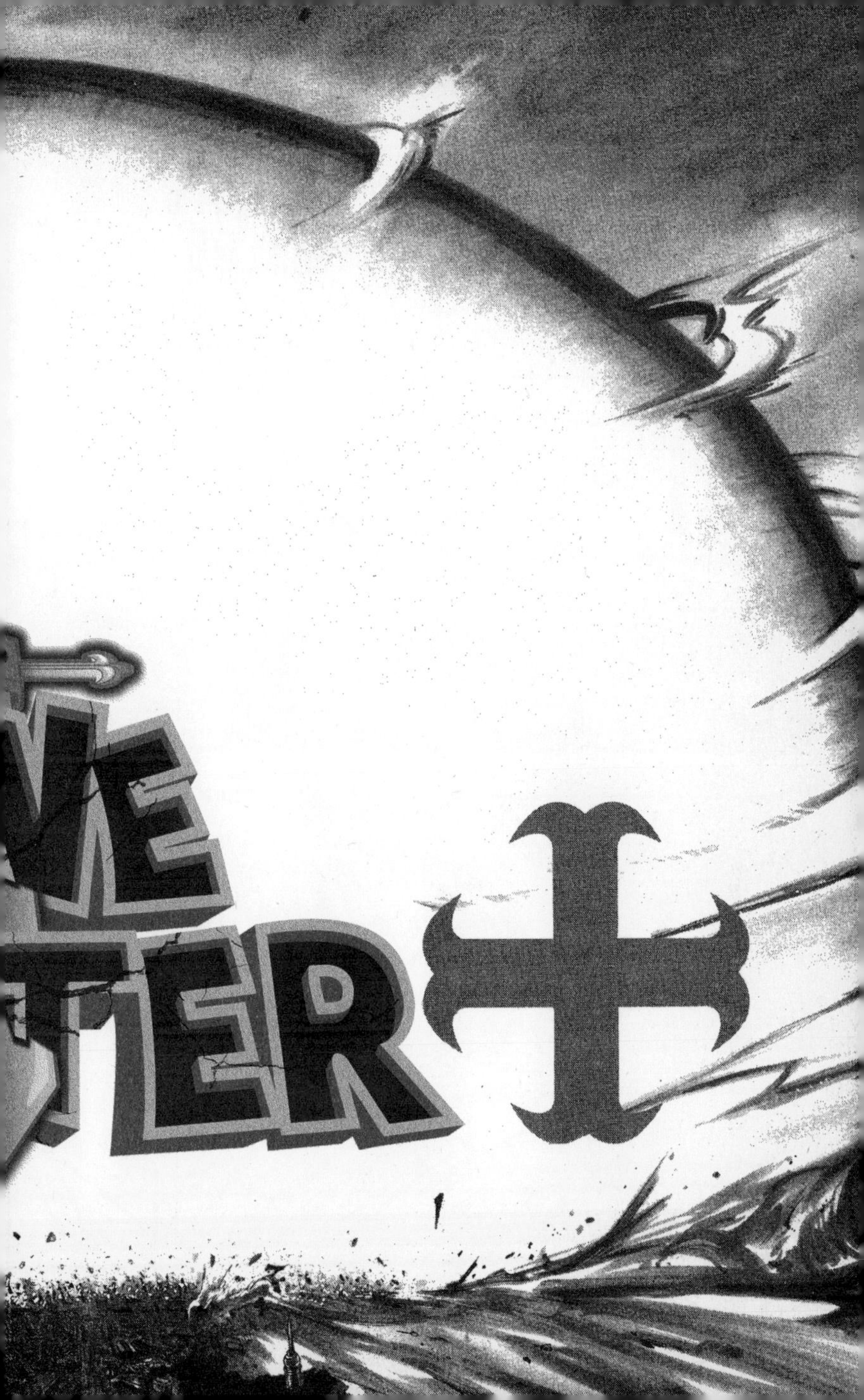
VE
TER

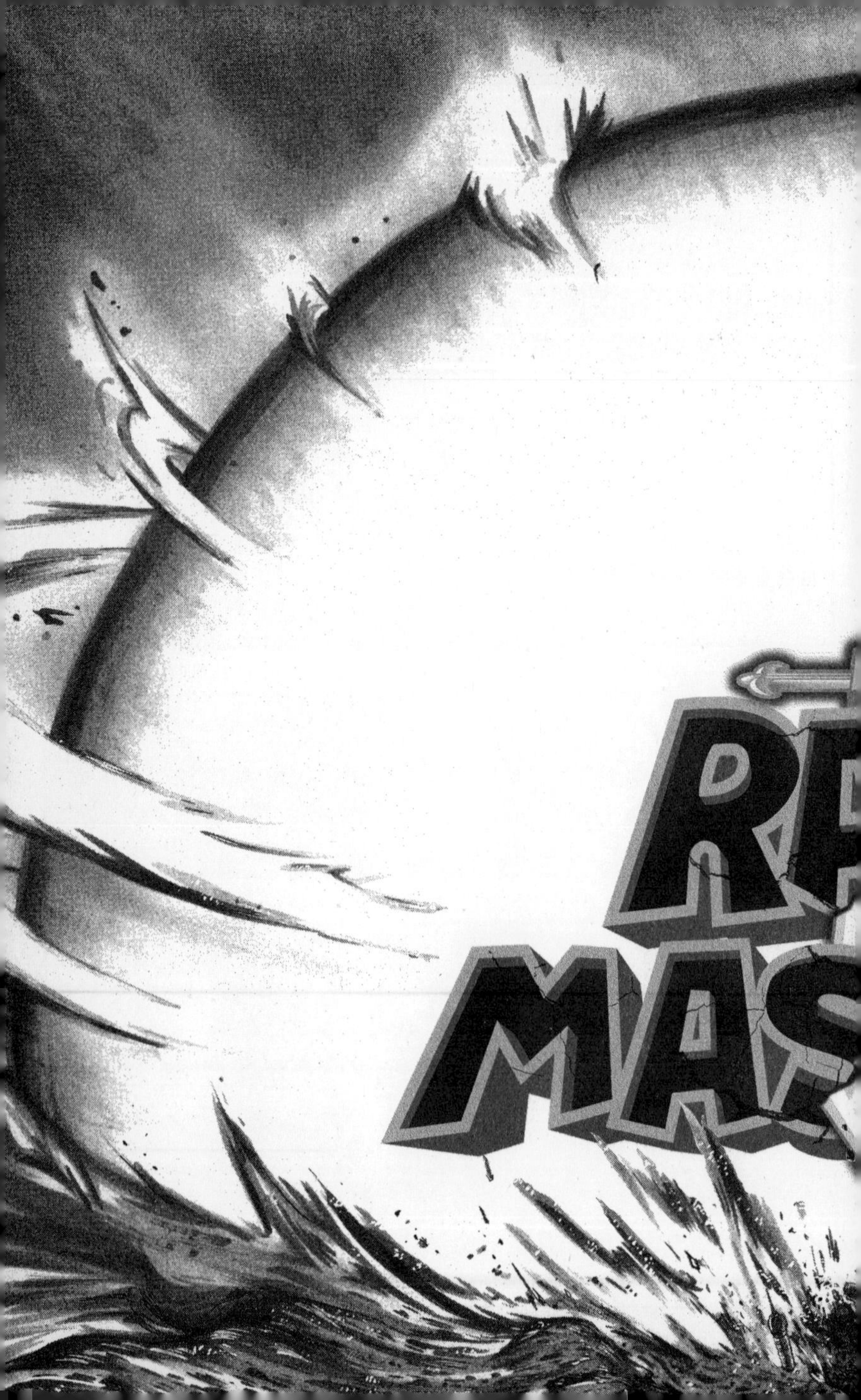

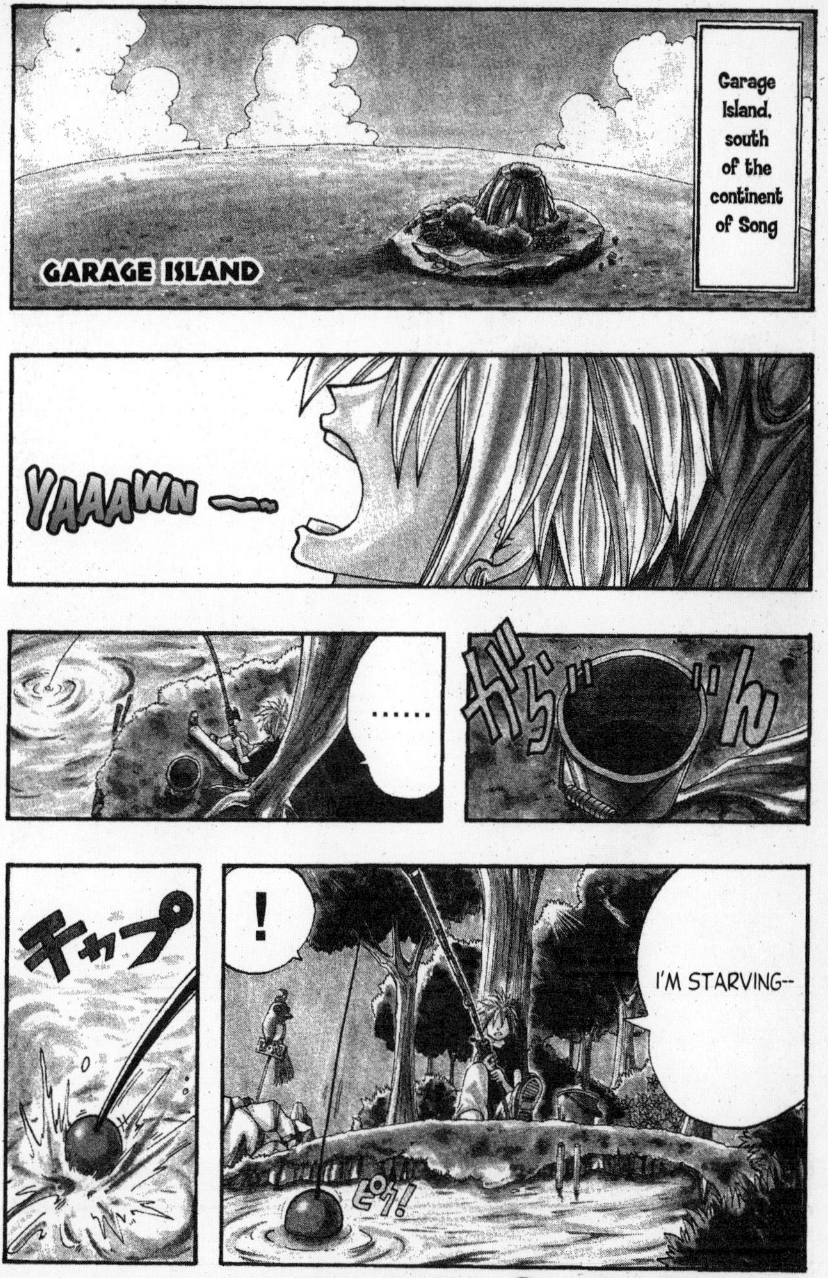
Garage Island, south of the continent of Song
GARAGE ISLAND
YAAAWN ~~
がらーん
......
I'M STARVING--
!
チャプ

RAVE: 1 ✠ OPENED MAP

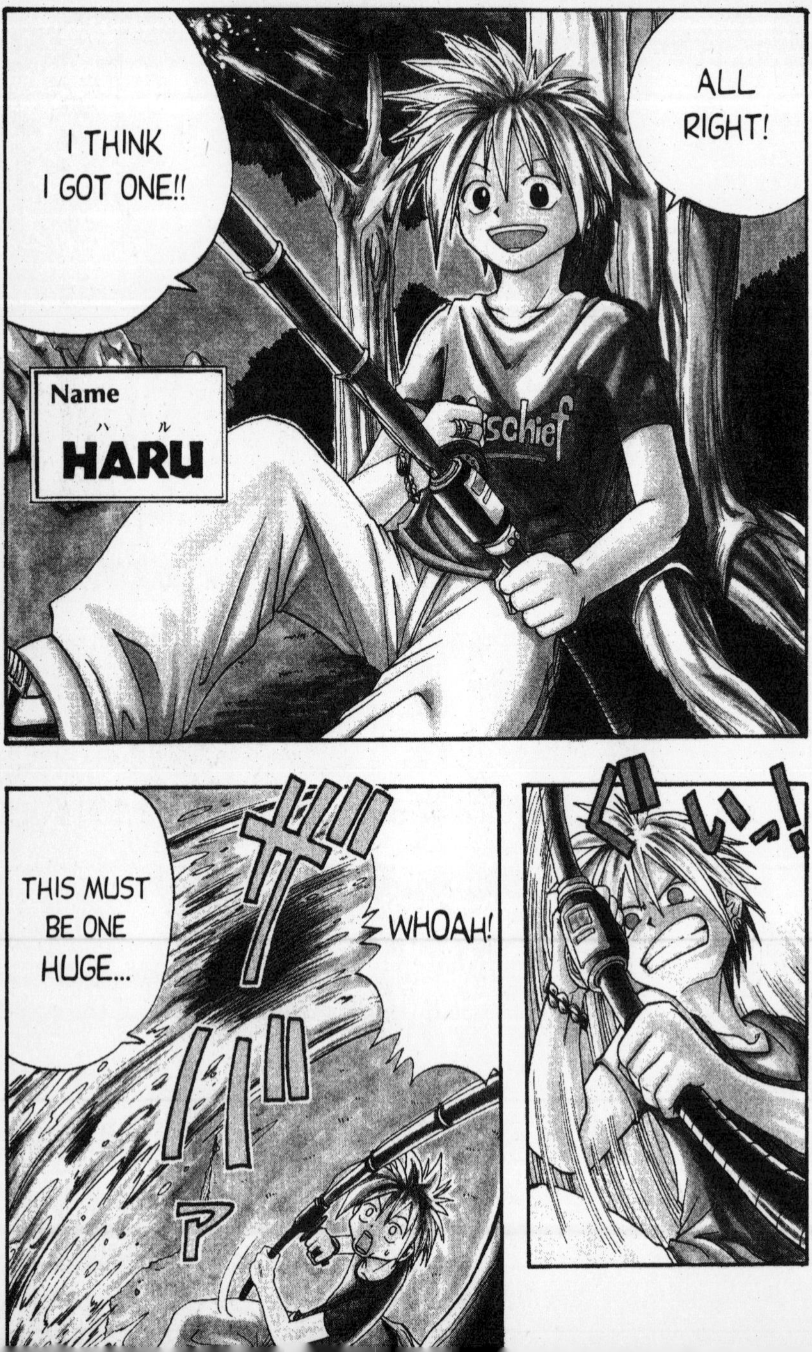
ALL RIGHT!
I THINK I GOT ONE!!
Name
ハル
HARU
THIS MUST BE ONE HUGE...
WHOAH!

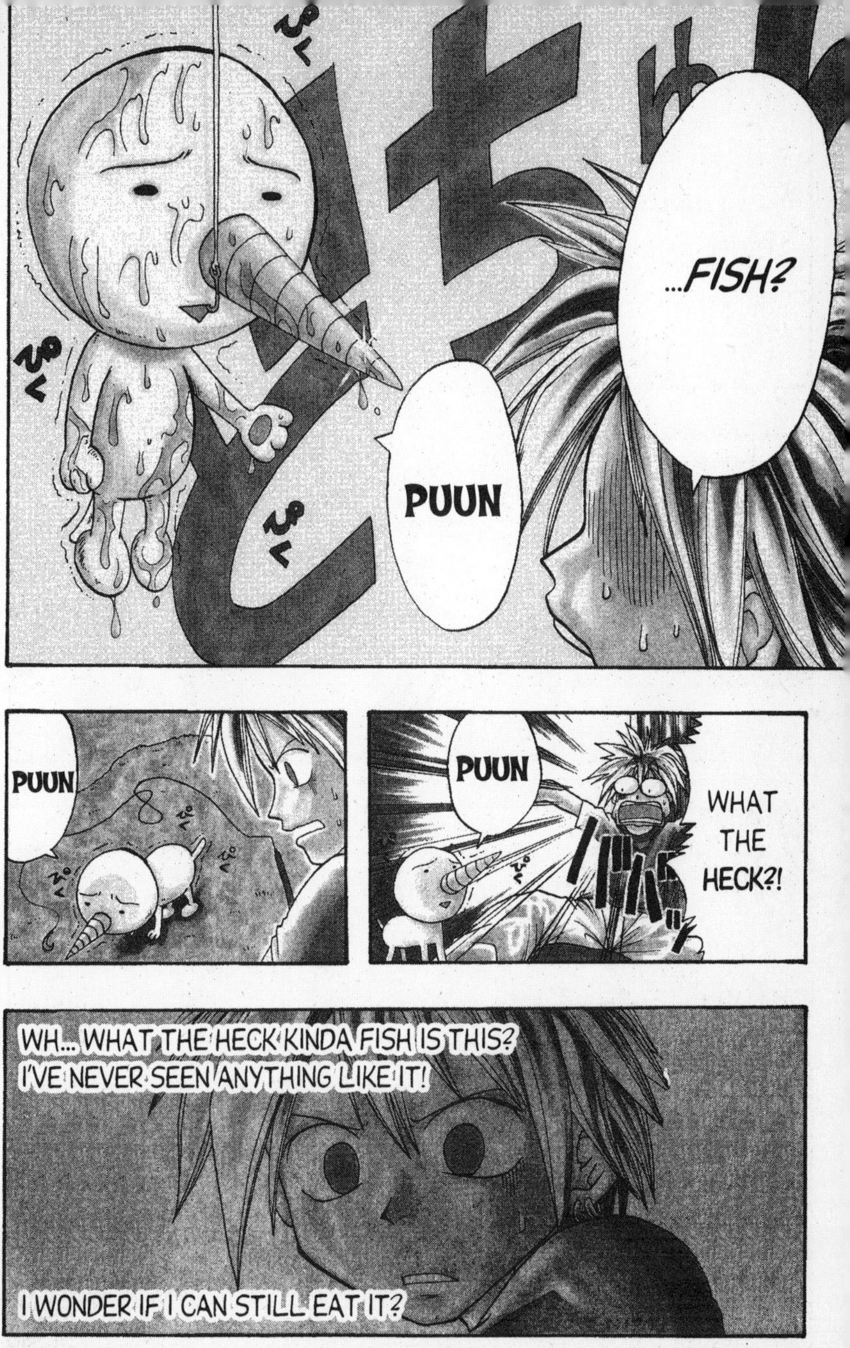
...FISH?
PUUN
PUUN
WHAT THE HECK?!
PUUN
WH... WHAT THE HECK KINDA FISH IS THIS? I'VE NEVER SEEN ANYTHING LIKE IT!
I WONDER IF I CAN STILL EAT IT?

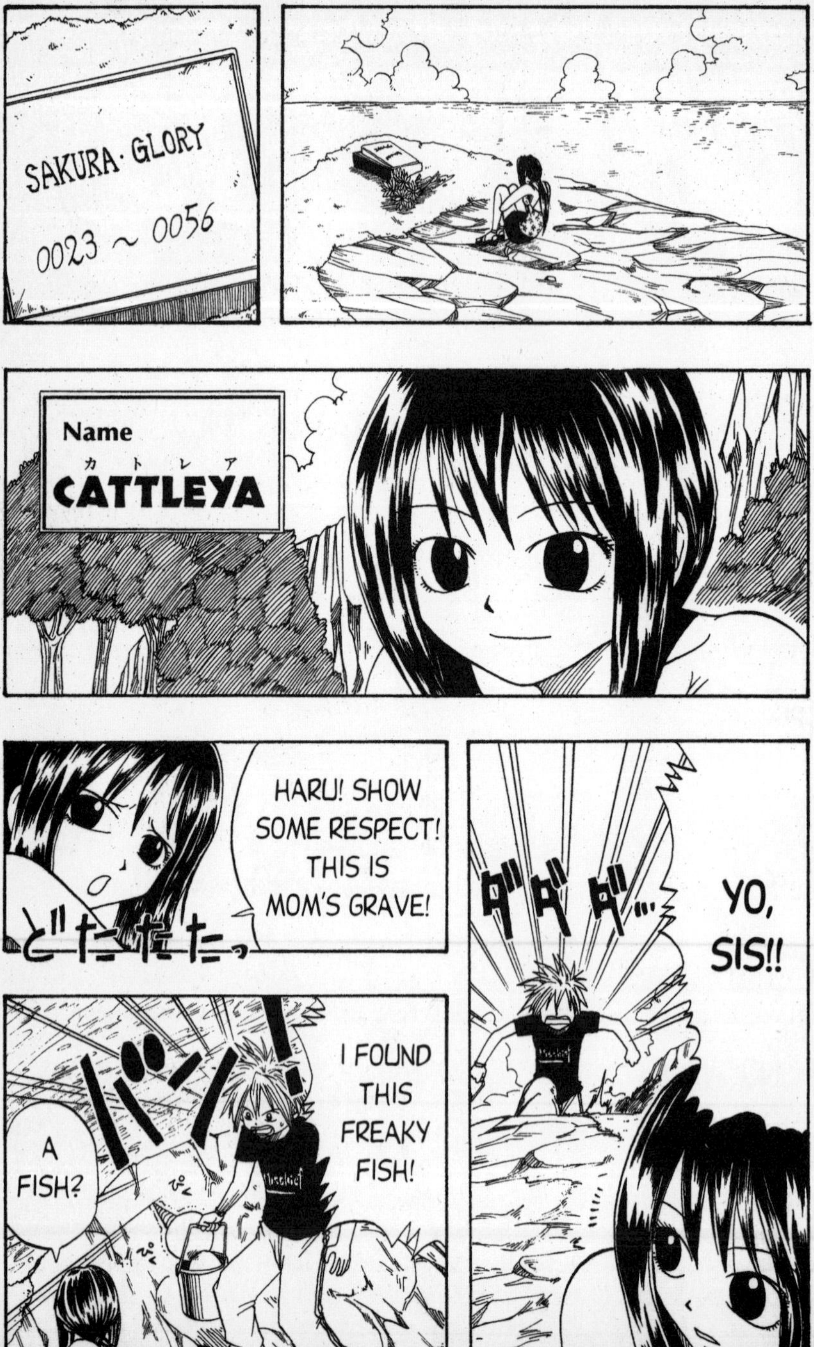
SAKURA · GLORY
0023 ~ 0056
Name
カトレア
CATTLEYA
ダダダ…
YO, SIS!!
HARU! SHOW SOME RESPECT! THIS IS MOM'S GRAVE!
どたたたっ
バン!!
I FOUND THIS FREAKY FISH!
A FISH?

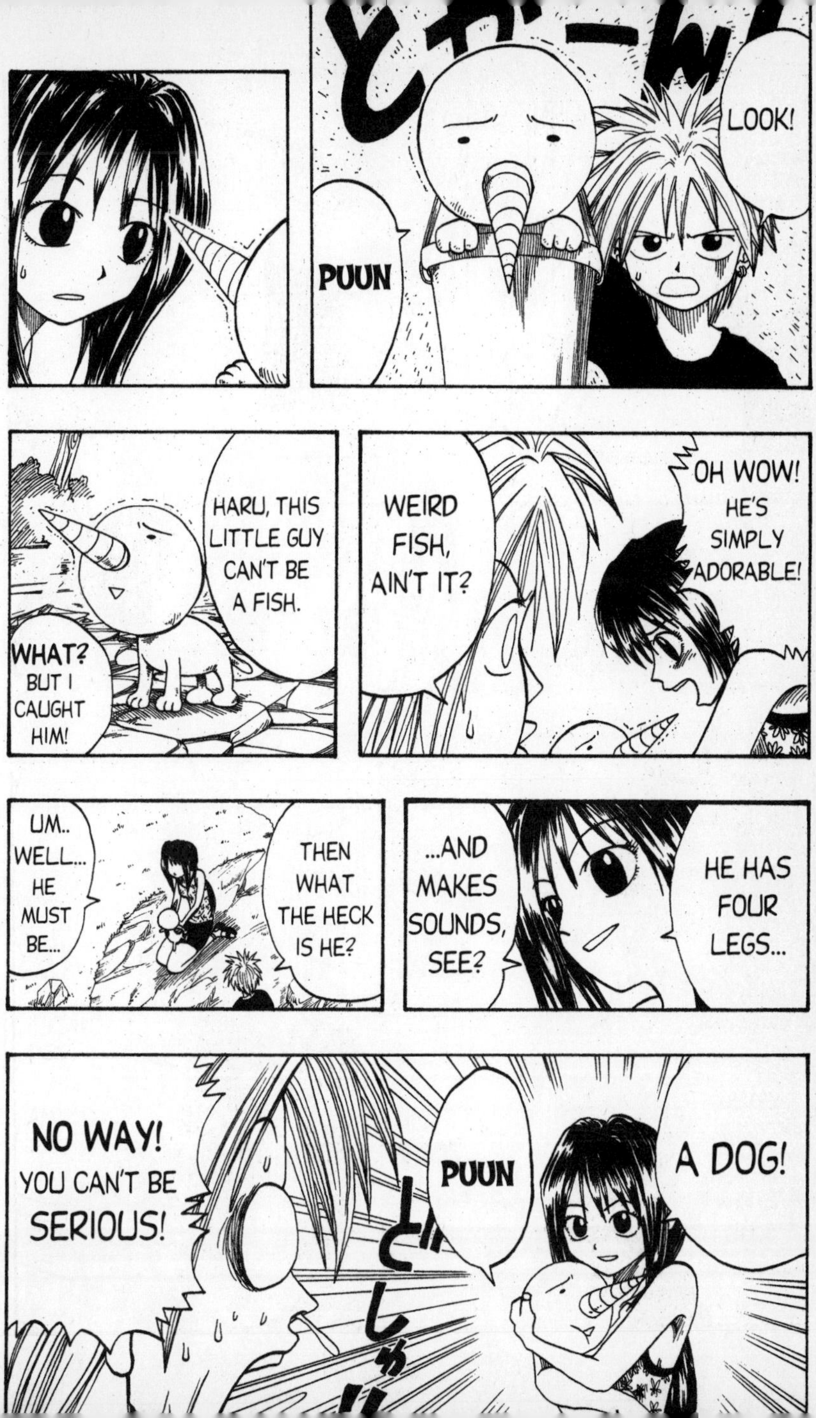
LOOK!
PUUN
OH WOW! HE'S SIMPLY ADORABLE!
WEIRD FISH, AIN'T IT?
HARU, THIS LITTLE GUY CAN'T BE A FISH.
WHAT? BUT I CAUGHT HIM!
HE HAS FOUR LEGS...
...AND MAKES SOUNDS, SEE?
THEN WHAT THE HECK IS HE?
UM.. WELL... HE MUST BE...
A DOG!
PUUN
NO WAY! YOU CAN'T BE SERIOUS!

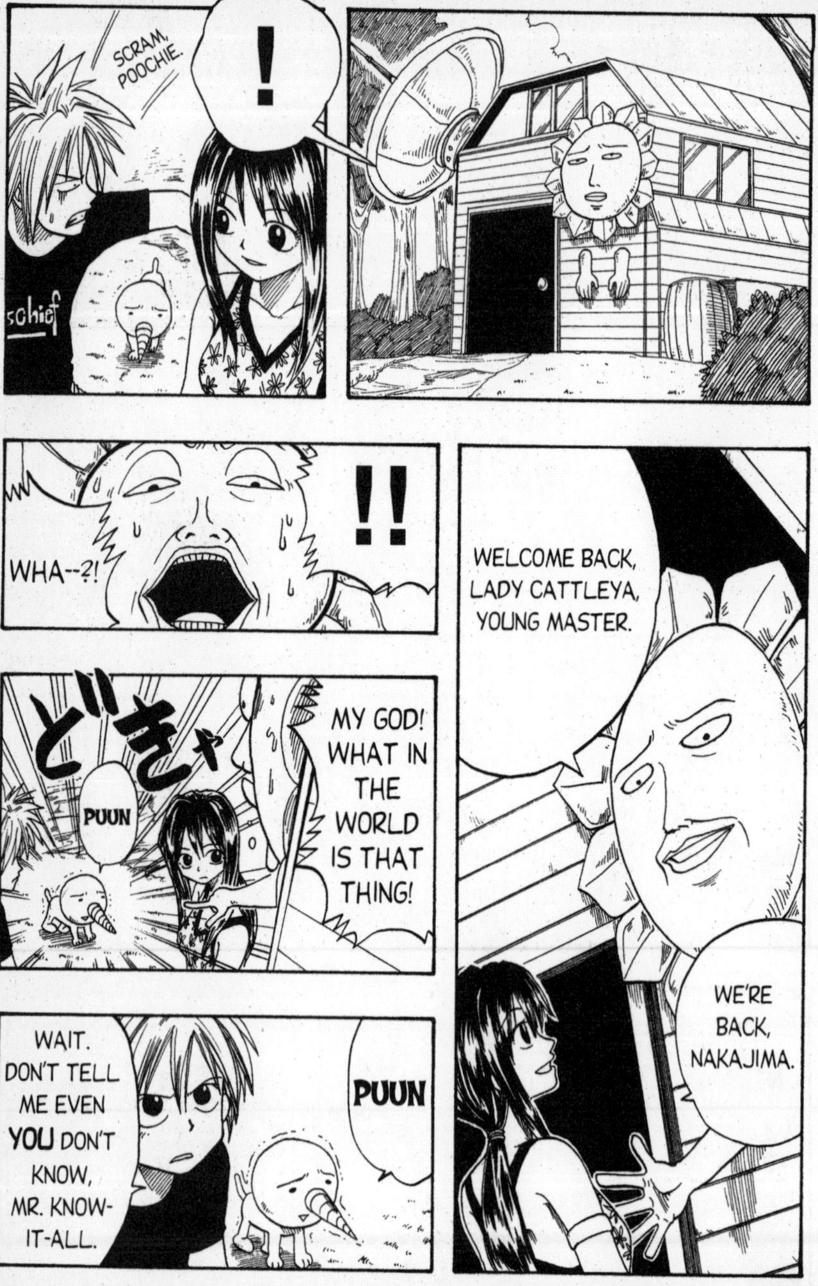
SCRAM, POOCHIE.
!
WELCOME BACK, LADY CATTLEYA, YOUNG MASTER.
WE'RE BACK, NAKAJIMA.
!!
WHA--?!
MY GOD! WHAT IN THE WORLD IS THAT THING!
どぎゃ
PUUN
WAIT. DON'T TELL ME EVEN **YOU** DON'T KNOW, MR. KNOW-IT-ALL.
PUUN

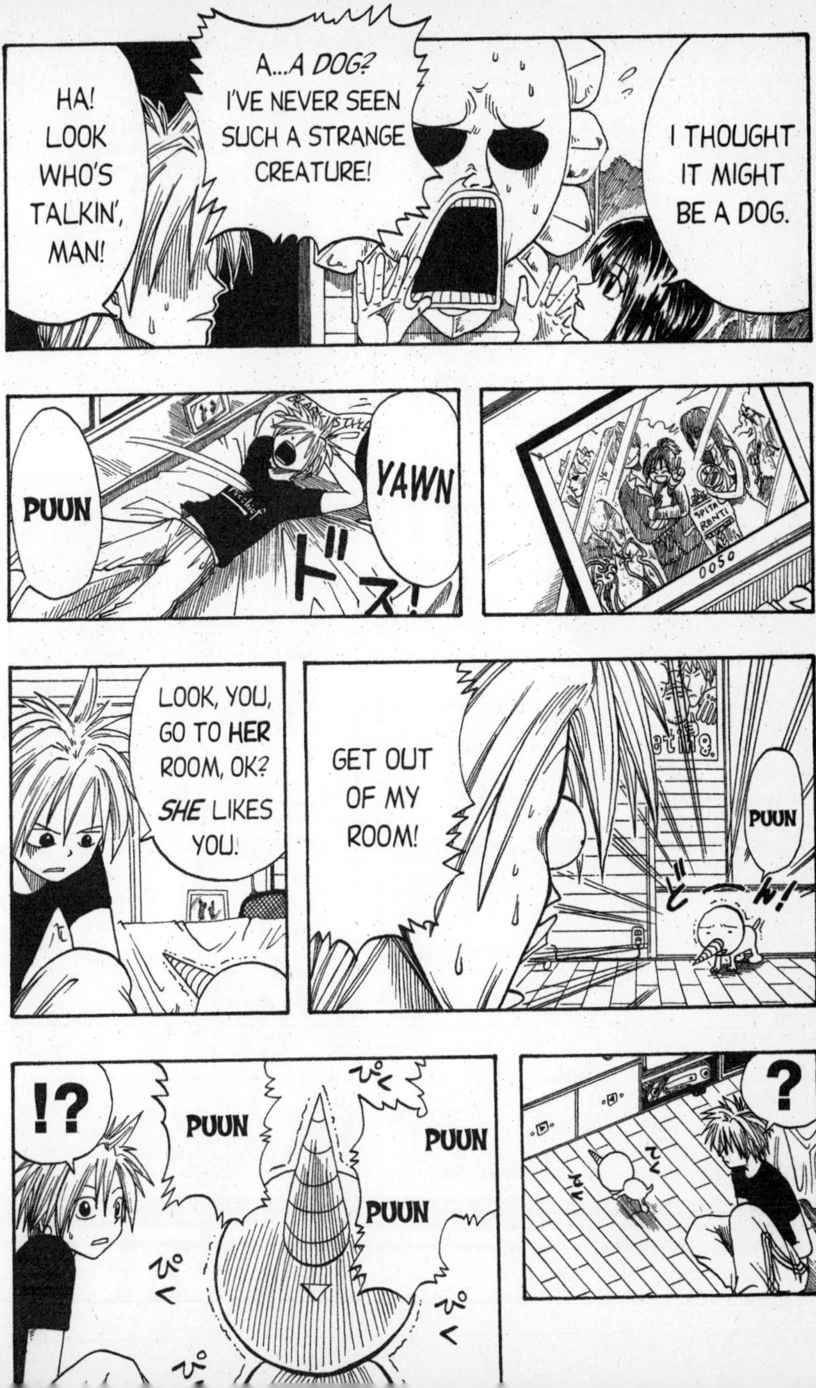
I THOUGHT IT MIGHT BE A DOG.
A...*A DOG?* I'VE NEVER SEEN SUCH A STRANGE CREATURE!
HA! LOOK WHO'S TALKIN', MAN!
YAWN
ドス!
PUUN
PUUN
どーん!
GET OUT OF MY ROOM!
LOOK, YOU, GO TO **HER** ROOM, OK? *SHE* LIKES YOU.
?
ぴく
ぴく
ぴく
PUUN
PUUN
PUUN
!?
ぴく
ぴく
ぴ

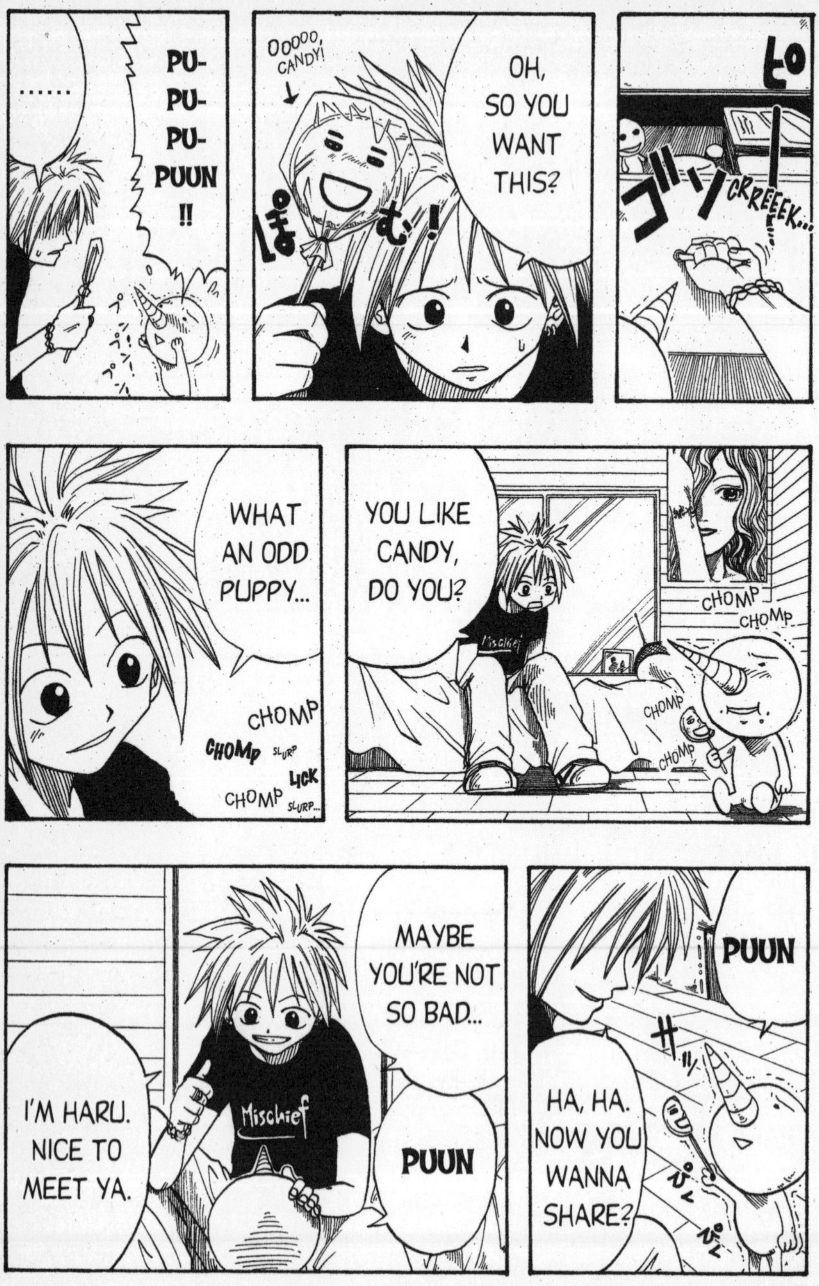
CREEEK...
OOOOO, CANDY!
OH, SO YOU WANT THIS?
......
PU-PU-PU-PUUN!!
YOU LIKE CANDY, DO YOU?
CHOMP CHOMP
CHOMP
CHOMP
WHAT AN ODD PUPPY...
CHOMP
CHOMP SLURP
LICK
CHOMP SLURP...
PUUN
HA, HA. NOW YOU WANNA SHARE?
MAYBE YOU'RE NOT SO BAD...
PUUN
I'M HARU. NICE TO MEET YA.

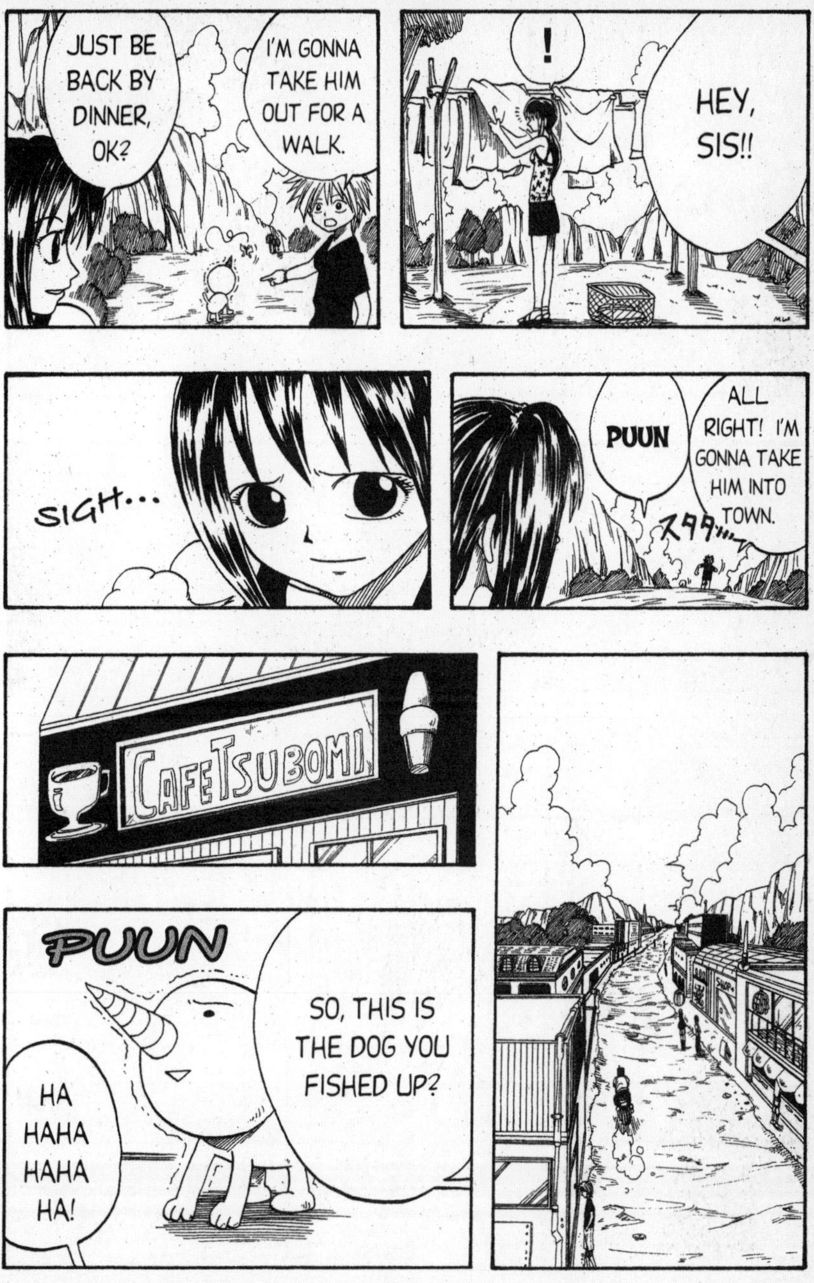
!
HEY, SIS!!
I'M GONNA TAKE HIM OUT FOR A WALK.
JUST BE BACK BY DINNER, OK?
ALL RIGHT! I'M GONNA TAKE HIM INTO TOWN.
PUUN
スタタッ
SIGH...
CAFE TSUBOMI
SHOP
SO, THIS IS THE DOG YOU FISHED UP?
PUUN
HA HAHA HAHA HA!

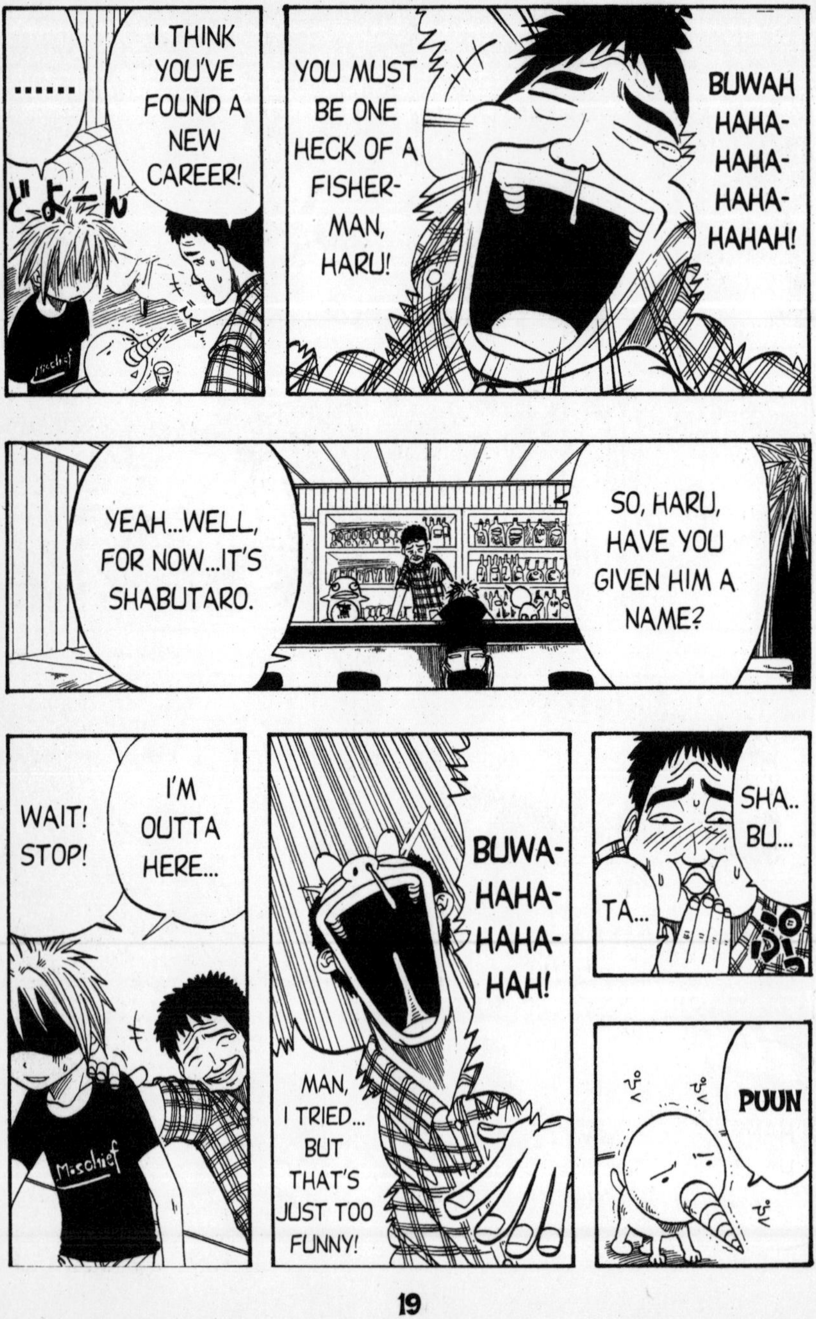
BUWAH HAHA-HAHA-HAHA-HAHAH!
YOU MUST BE ONE HECK OF A FISHER-MAN, HARU!
I THINK YOU'VE FOUND A NEW CAREER!
......
どよ〜ん
SO, HARU, HAVE YOU GIVEN HIM A NAME?
YEAH...WELL, FOR NOW...IT'S SHABUTARO.
SHA.. BU...
TA...
PUUN
BUWA-HAHA-HAHA-HAH!
MAN, I TRIED... BUT THAT'S JUST TOO FUNNY!
I'M OUTTA HERE...
WAIT! STOP!

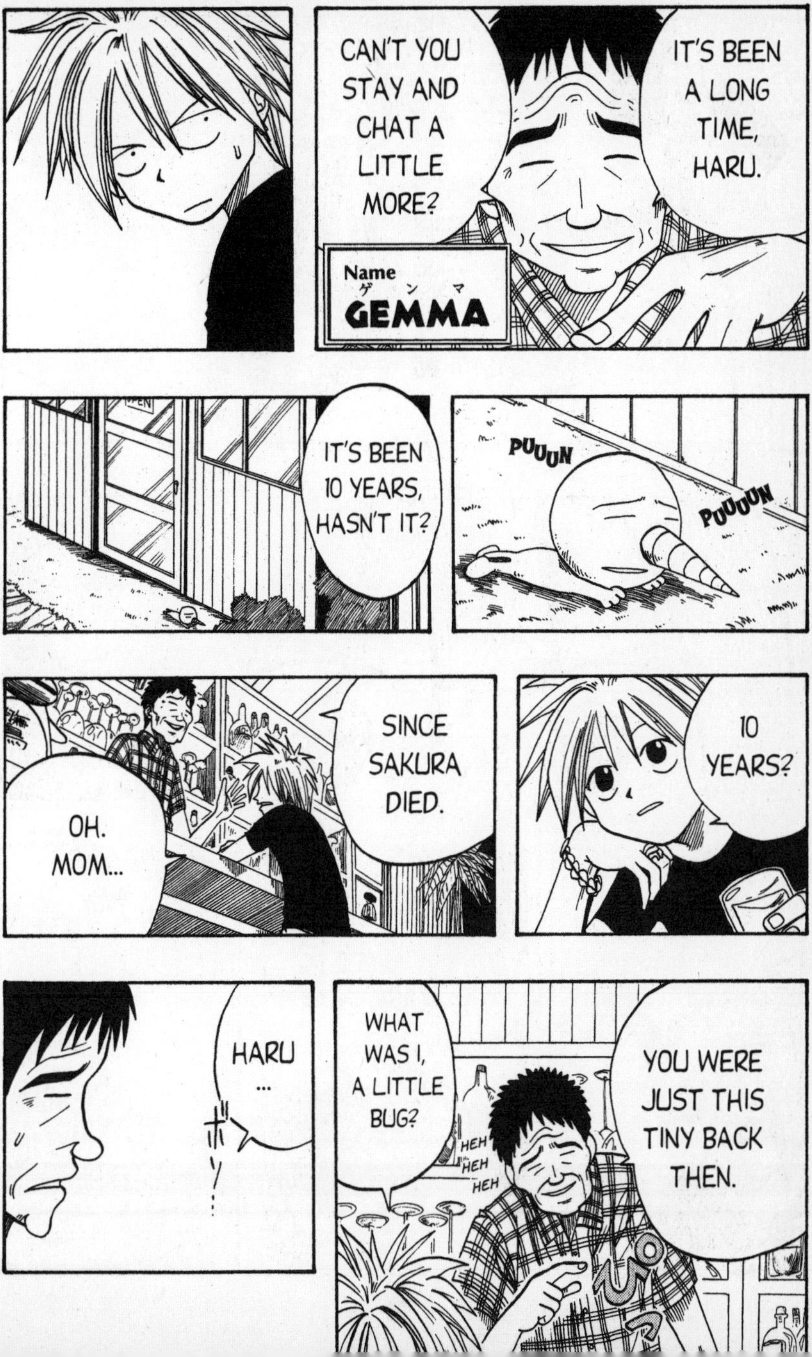
IT'S BEEN A LONG TIME, HARU.
CAN'T YOU STAY AND CHAT A LITTLE MORE?
Name ゲンマ GEMMA
PUUUN
PUUUUN
IT'S BEEN 10 YEARS, HASN'T IT?
10 YEARS?
SINCE SAKURA DIED.
OH. MOM...
YOU WERE JUST THIS TINY BACK THEN.
HEH HEH HEH
WHAT WAS I, A LITTLE BUG?
HARU ...
ボソッ…

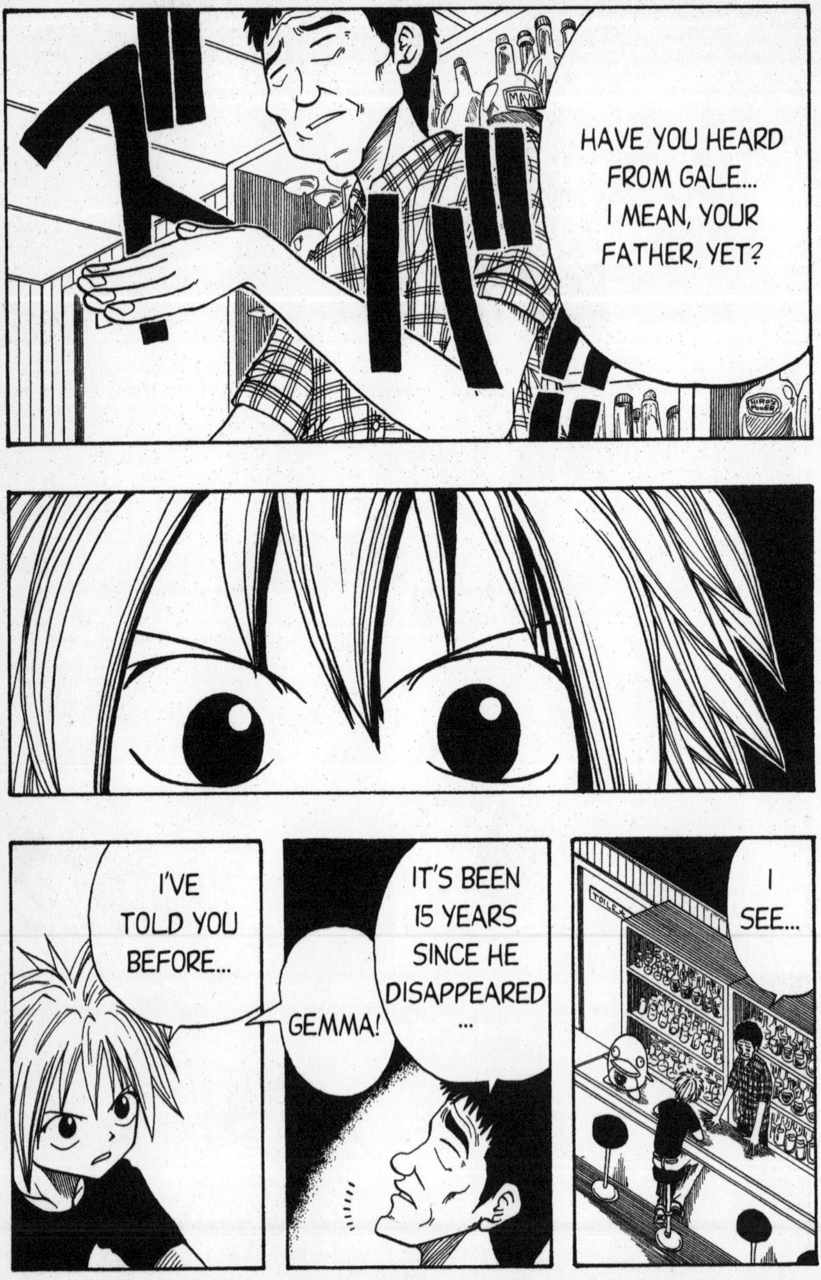
HAVE YOU HEARD FROM GALE... I MEAN, YOUR FATHER, YET?
I SEE...
IT'S BEEN 15 YEARS SINCE HE DISAPPEARED ...
GEMMA!
I'VE TOLD YOU BEFORE...

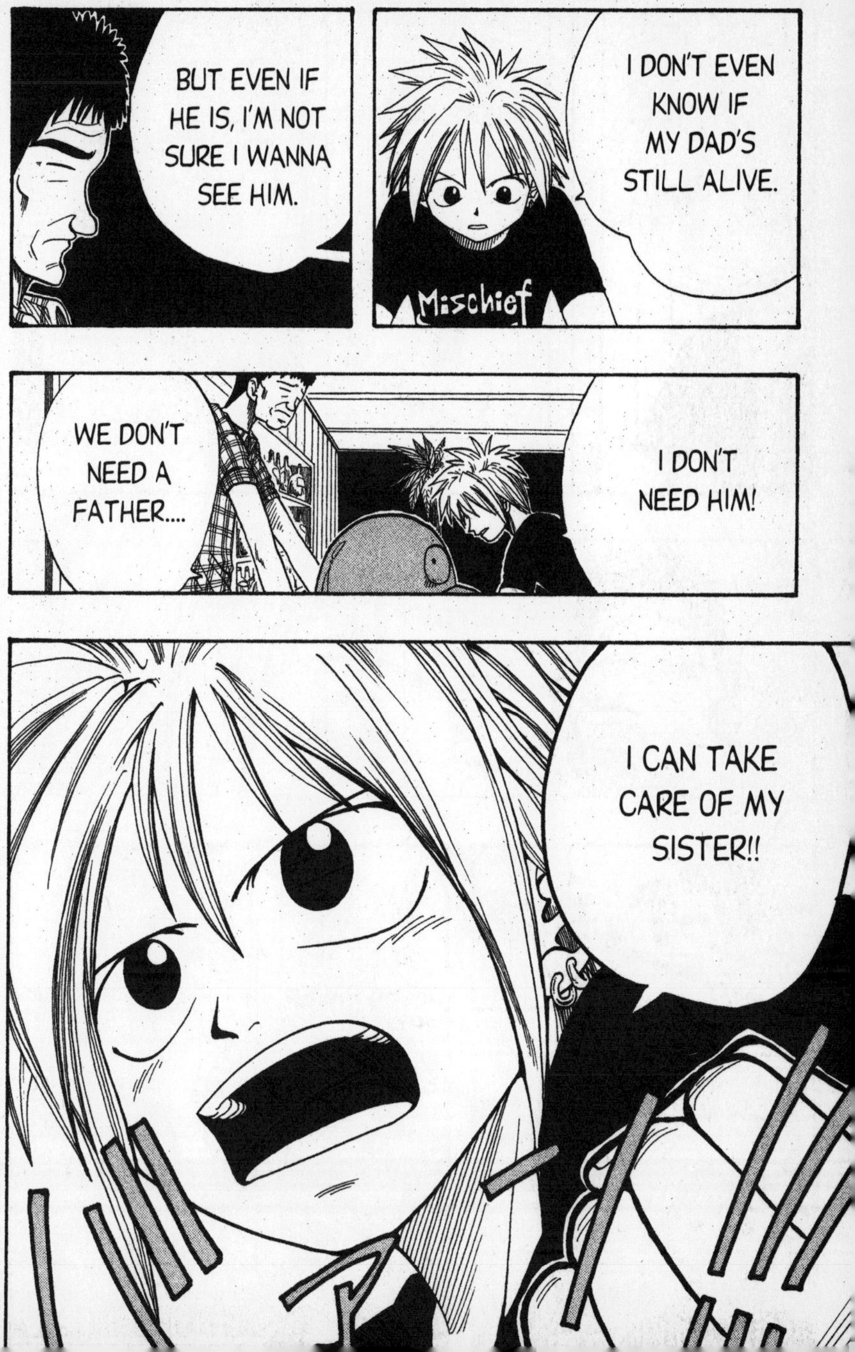
I DON'T EVEN KNOW IF MY DAD'S STILL ALIVE.
Mischief
BUT EVEN IF HE IS, I'M NOT SURE I WANNA SEE HIM.
I DON'T NEED HIM!
WE DON'T NEED A FATHER....
I CAN TAKE CARE OF MY SISTER!!

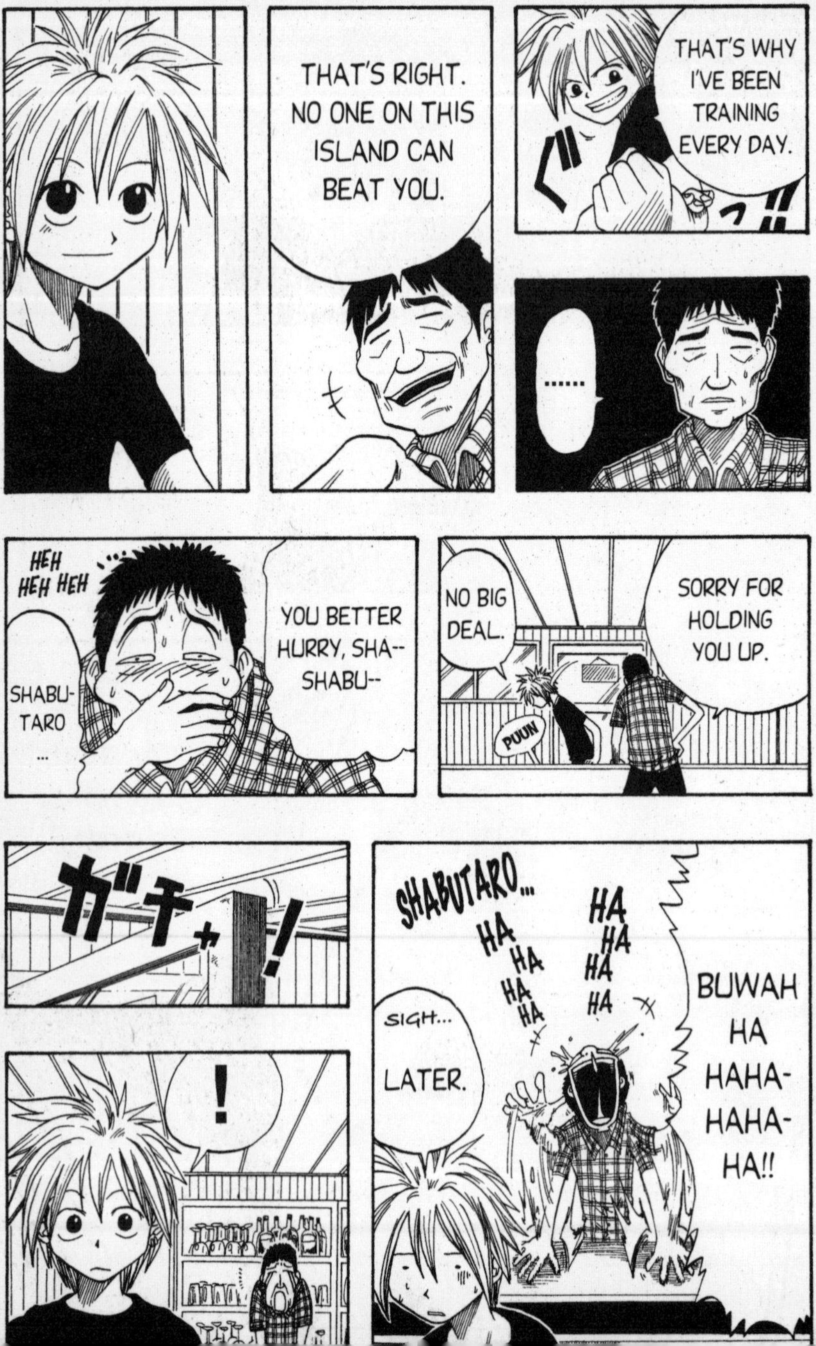
THAT'S RIGHT. NO ONE ON THIS ISLAND CAN BEAT YOU.
THAT'S WHY I'VE BEEN TRAINING EVERY DAY.
......
HEH HEH HEH
SHABU-TARO ...
YOU BETTER HURRY, SHA-- SHABU--
NO BIG DEAL.
PUUN
SORRY FOR HOLDING YOU UP.
ガチャ!
!
SHABUTARO...
HA HA HA HA HA HA HA HA HA
SIGH...
LATER.
BUWAH HA HAHA-HAHA-HA!!

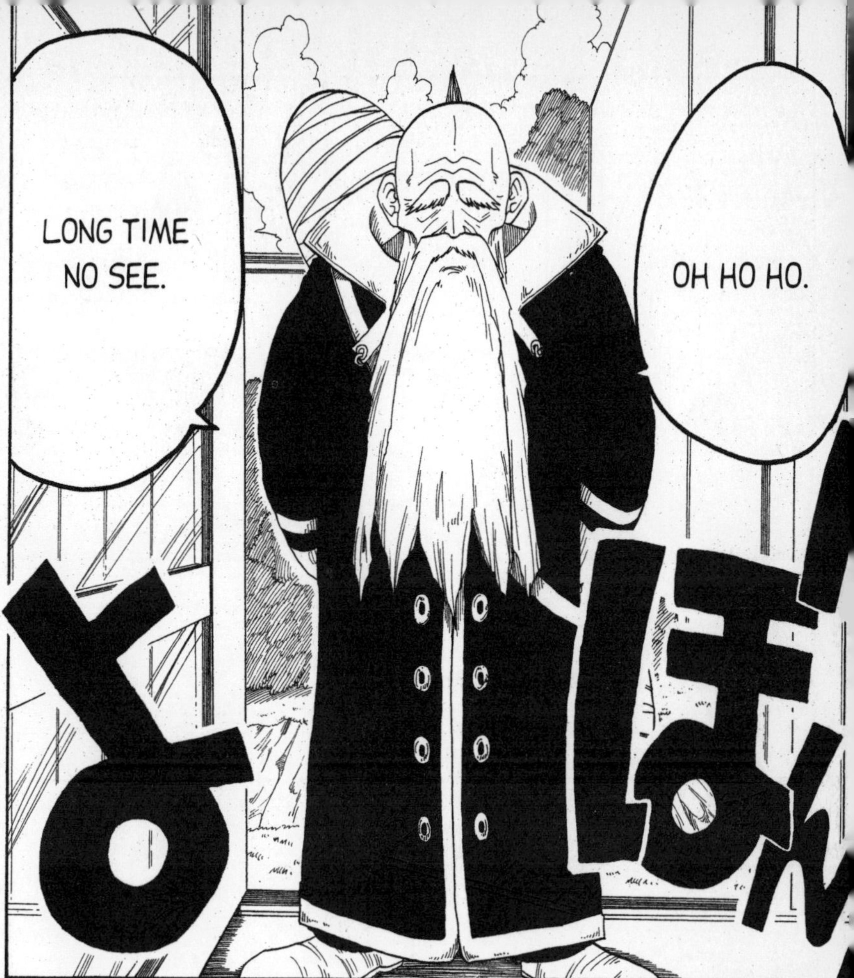
OH HO HO.
LONG TIME NO SEE.

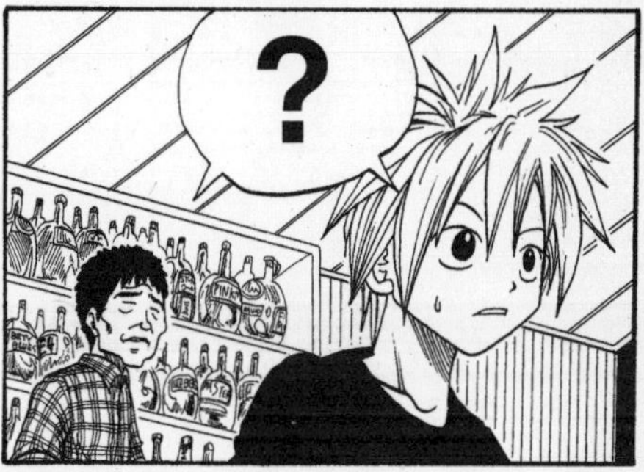
?

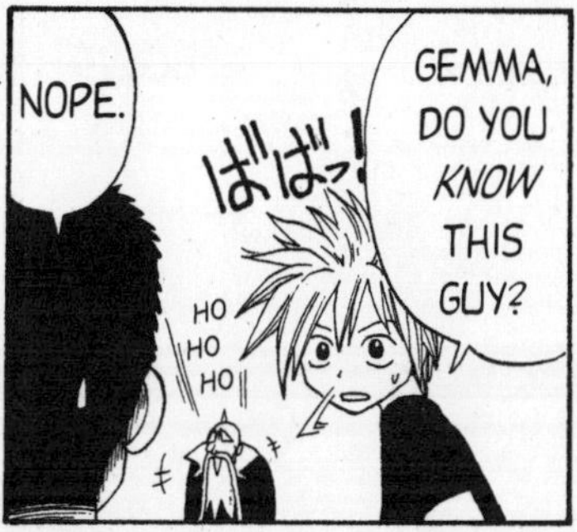
GEMMA, DO YOU *KNOW* THIS GUY?
ばばっ!
NOPE.
HO HO HO

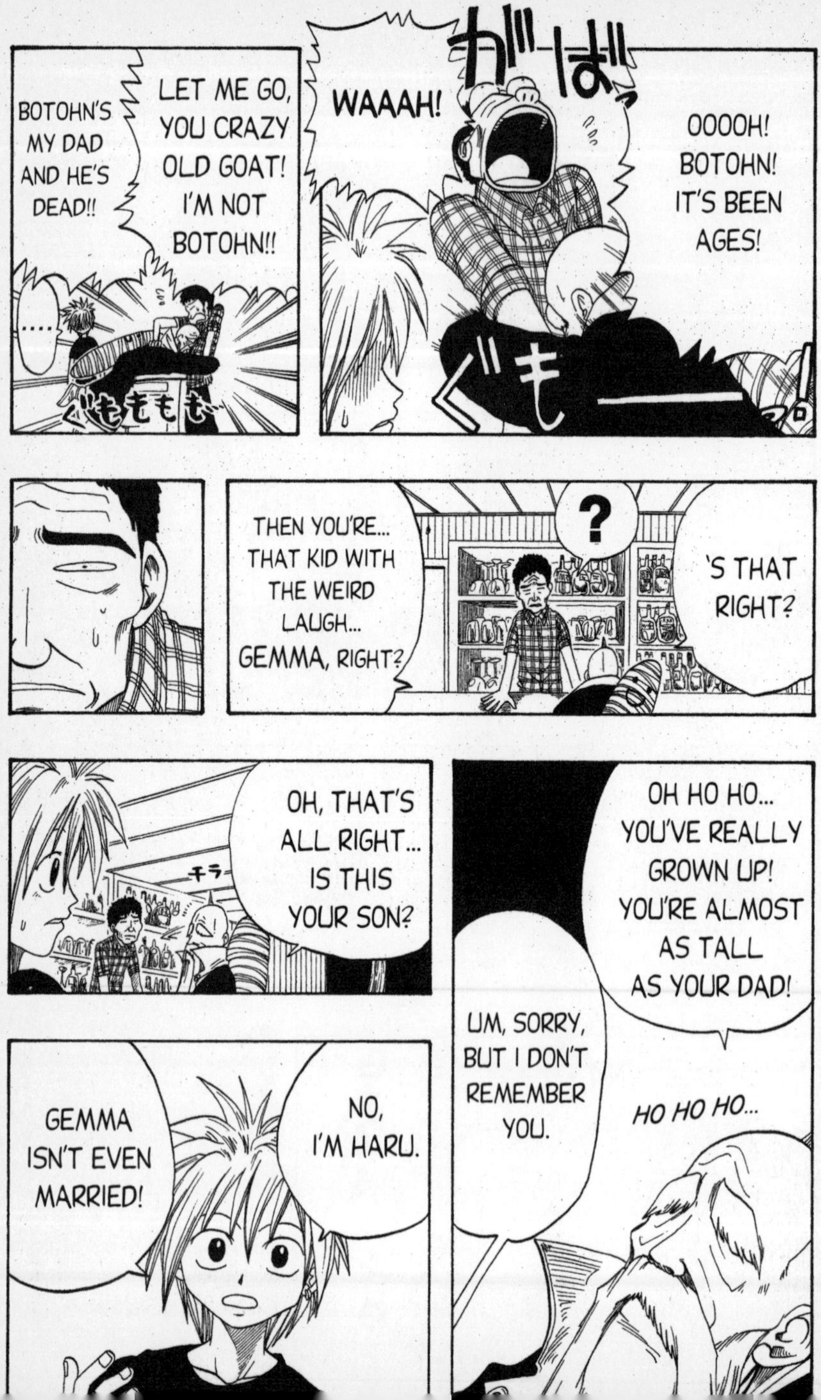
OOOOH! BOTOHN! IT'S BEEN AGES!
WAAAH!
LET ME GO, YOU CRAZY OLD GOAT! I'M NOT BOTOHN!!
BOTOHN'S MY DAD AND HE'S DEAD!!
.....
THEN YOU'RE... THAT KID WITH THE WEIRD LAUGH... GEMMA, RIGHT?
?
'S THAT RIGHT?
OH HO HO... YOU'VE REALLY GROWN UP! YOU'RE ALMOST AS TALL AS YOUR DAD!
UM, SORRY, BUT I DON'T REMEMBER YOU.
HO HO HO...
OH, THAT'S ALL RIGHT... IS THIS YOUR SON?
NO, I'M HARU.
GEMMA ISN'T EVEN MARRIED!

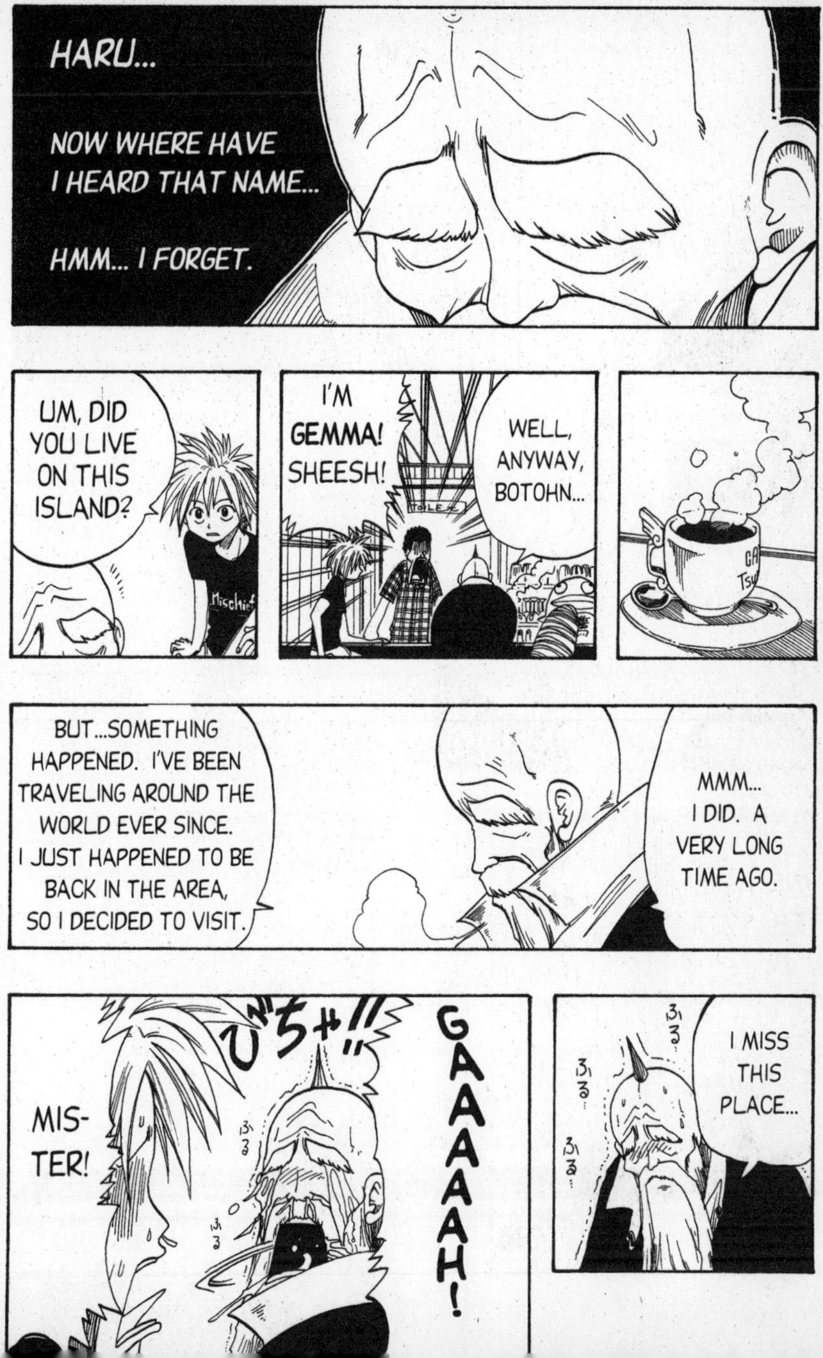
HARU...
NOW WHERE HAVE I HEARD THAT NAME...
HMM... I FORGET.
WELL, ANYWAY, BOTOHN...
I'M GEMMA! SHEESH!
UM, DID YOU LIVE ON THIS ISLAND?
MMM... I DID. A VERY LONG TIME AGO.
BUT...SOMETHING HAPPENED. I'VE BEEN TRAVELING AROUND THE WORLD EVER SINCE. I JUST HAPPENED TO BE BACK IN THE AREA, SO I DECIDED TO VISIT.
I MISS THIS PLACE...
ふる
ふる...
ふる...
GAAAAAH!
びちゃ!!
ふる
ふる
MIS-TER!

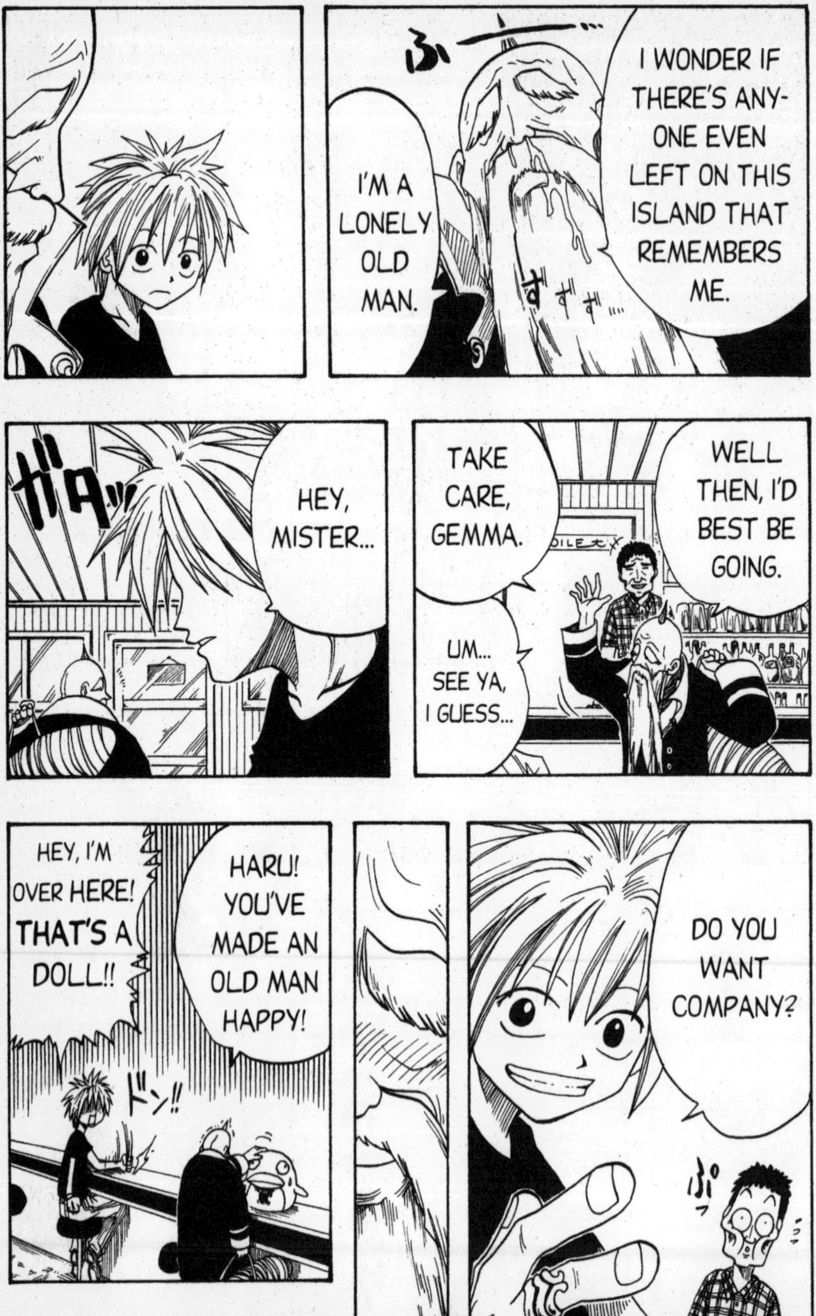
ふー…
I WONDER IF THERE'S ANY-ONE EVEN LEFT ON THIS ISLAND THAT REMEMBERS ME.
I'M A LONELY OLD MAN.
ずずず…
WELL THEN, I'D BEST BE GOING.
TAKE CARE, GEMMA.
UM... SEE YA, I GUESS...
ガタッ
HEY, MISTER...
DO YOU WANT COMPANY?
ぷっ
HARU! YOU'VE MADE AN OLD MAN HAPPY!
HEY, I'M OVER HERE! THAT'S A DOLL!!
ドン!!

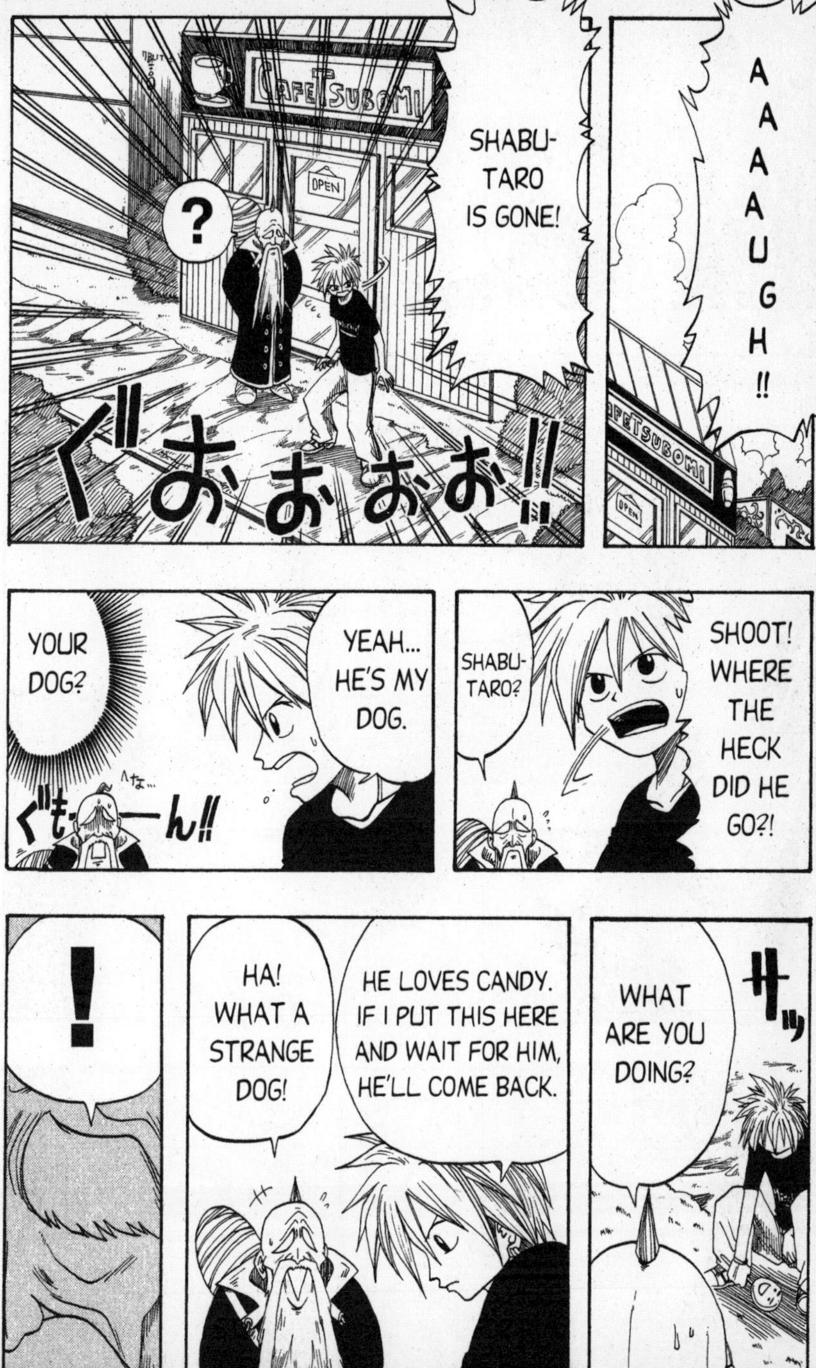
AAAAUGH!!
CAFE TSUBOMI
SHABU-TARO IS GONE!
CAFE TSUBOMI
OPEN
?
ぐおおおお!!
SHOOT! WHERE THE HECK DID HE GO?!
SHABU-TARO?
YEAH... HE'S MY DOG.
YOUR DOG?
ぐも～ん!!
サッ
WHAT ARE YOU DOING?
HE LOVES CANDY. IF I PUT THIS HERE AND WAIT FOR HIM, HE'LL COME BACK.
HA! WHAT A STRANGE DOG!
!

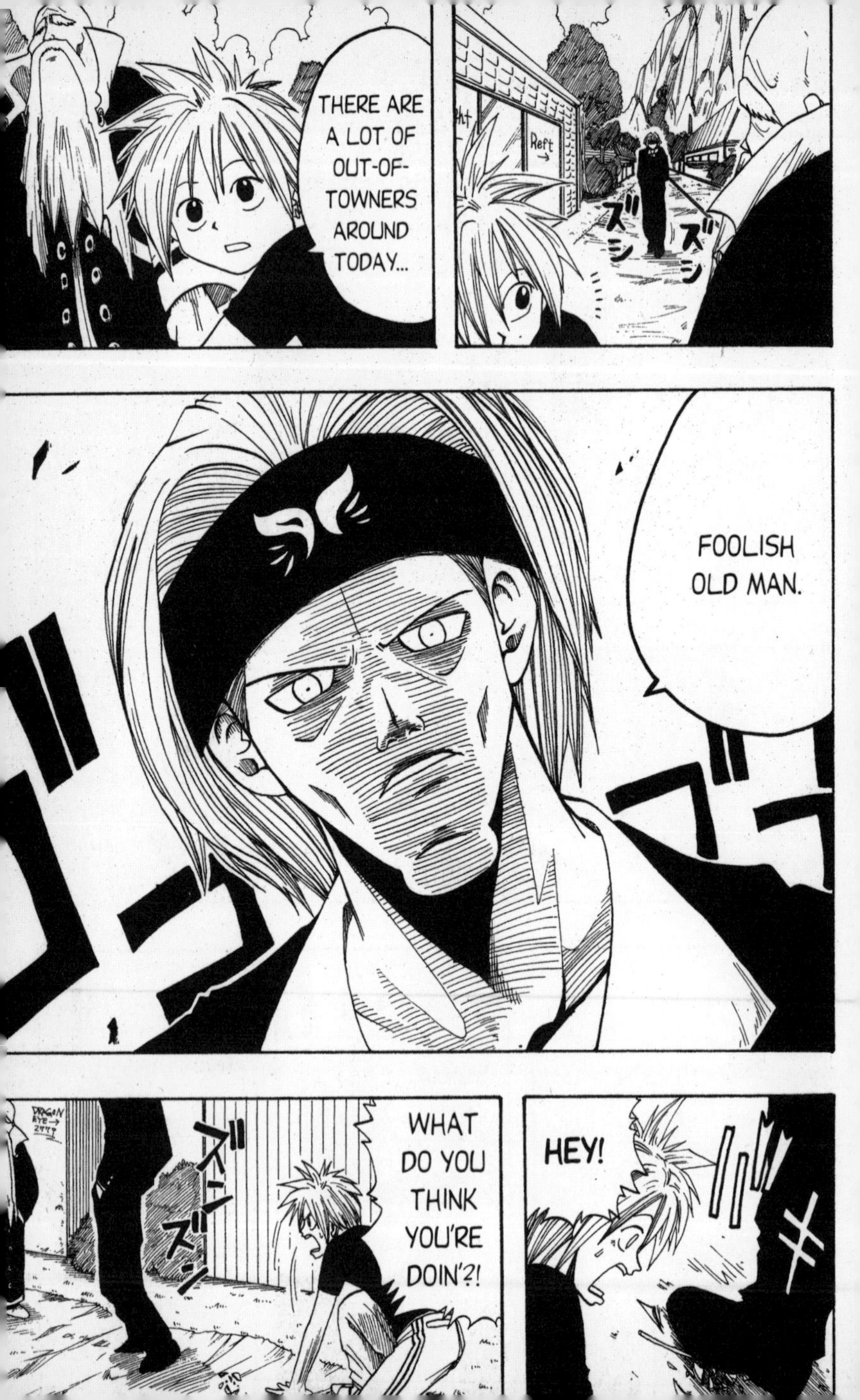
Reft →
ズシ
ズシ
THERE ARE A LOT OF OUT-OF-TOWNERS AROUND TODAY...
FOOLISH OLD MAN.
HEY!
WHAT DO YOU THINK YOU'RE DOIN'?!

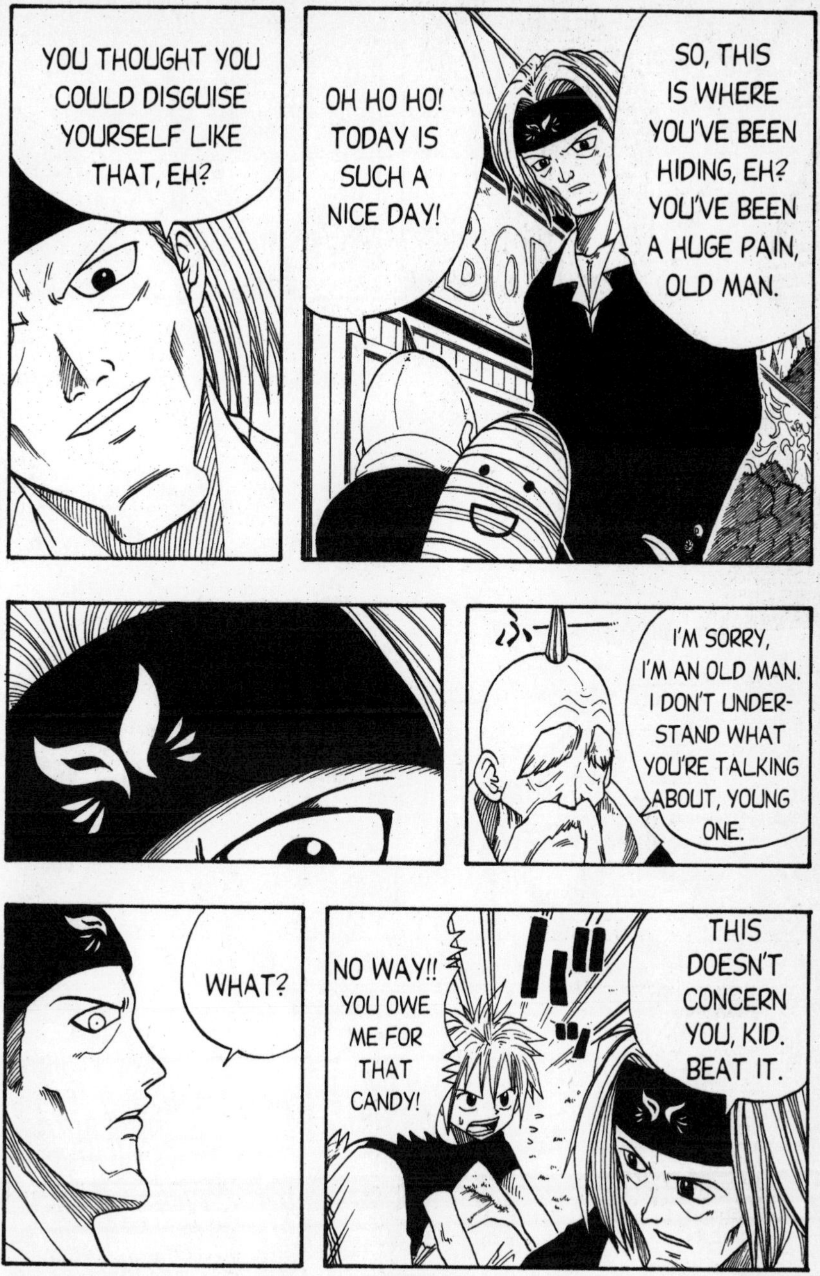
SO, THIS IS WHERE YOU'VE BEEN HIDING, EH? YOU'VE BEEN A HUGE PAIN, OLD MAN.
OH HO HO! TODAY IS SUCH A NICE DAY!
YOU THOUGHT YOU COULD DISGUISE YOURSELF LIKE THAT, EH?
ふー
I'M SORRY, I'M AN OLD MAN. I DON'T UNDER-STAND WHAT YOU'RE TALKING ABOUT, YOUNG ONE.
THIS DOESN'T CONCERN YOU, KID. BEAT IT.
NO WAY!! YOU OWE ME FOR THAT CANDY!
WHAT?

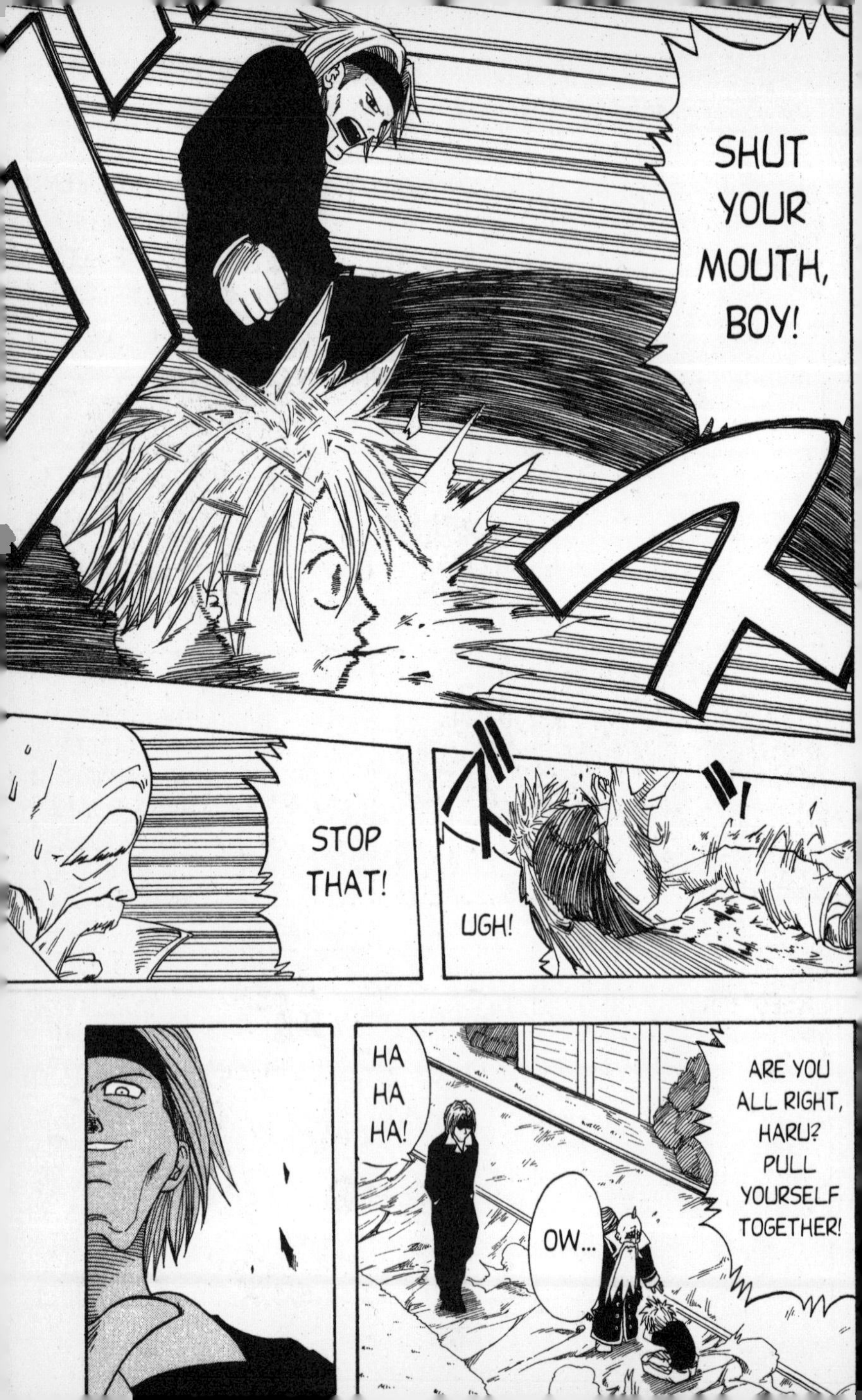
SHUT YOUR MOUTH, BOY!
UGH!
STOP THAT!
ARE YOU ALL RIGHT, HARU? PULL YOURSELF TOGETHER!
OW...
HA HA HA!

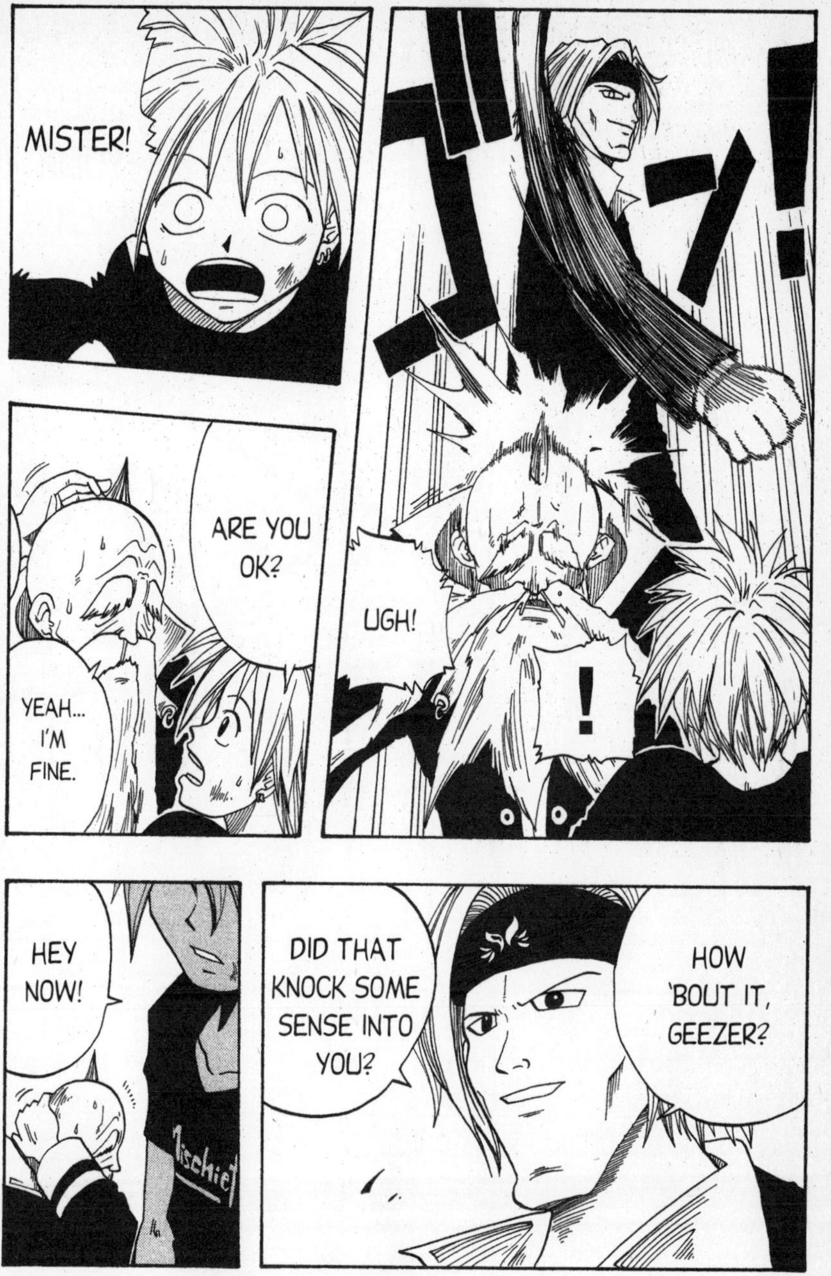
UGH!
!
MISTER!
ARE YOU OK?
YEAH... I'M FINE.
HOW 'BOUT IT, GEEZER?
DID THAT KNOCK SOME SENSE INTO YOU?
HEY NOW!

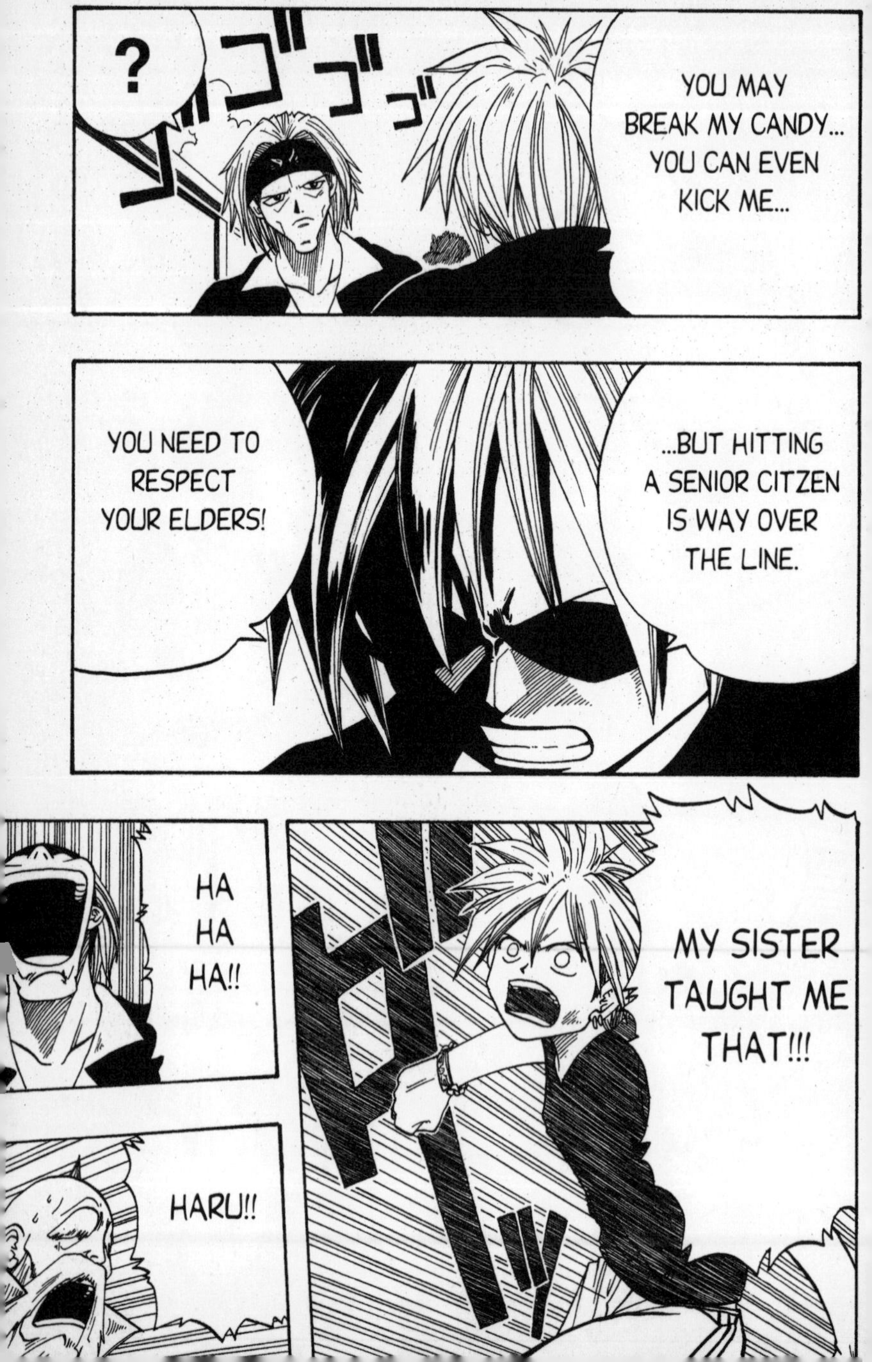
YOU MAY BREAK MY CANDY... YOU CAN EVEN KICK ME...
?
...BUT HITTING A SENIOR CITZEN IS WAY OVER THE LINE.
YOU NEED TO RESPECT YOUR ELDERS!
MY SISTER TAUGHT ME THAT!!!
HA HA HA!!
HARU!!

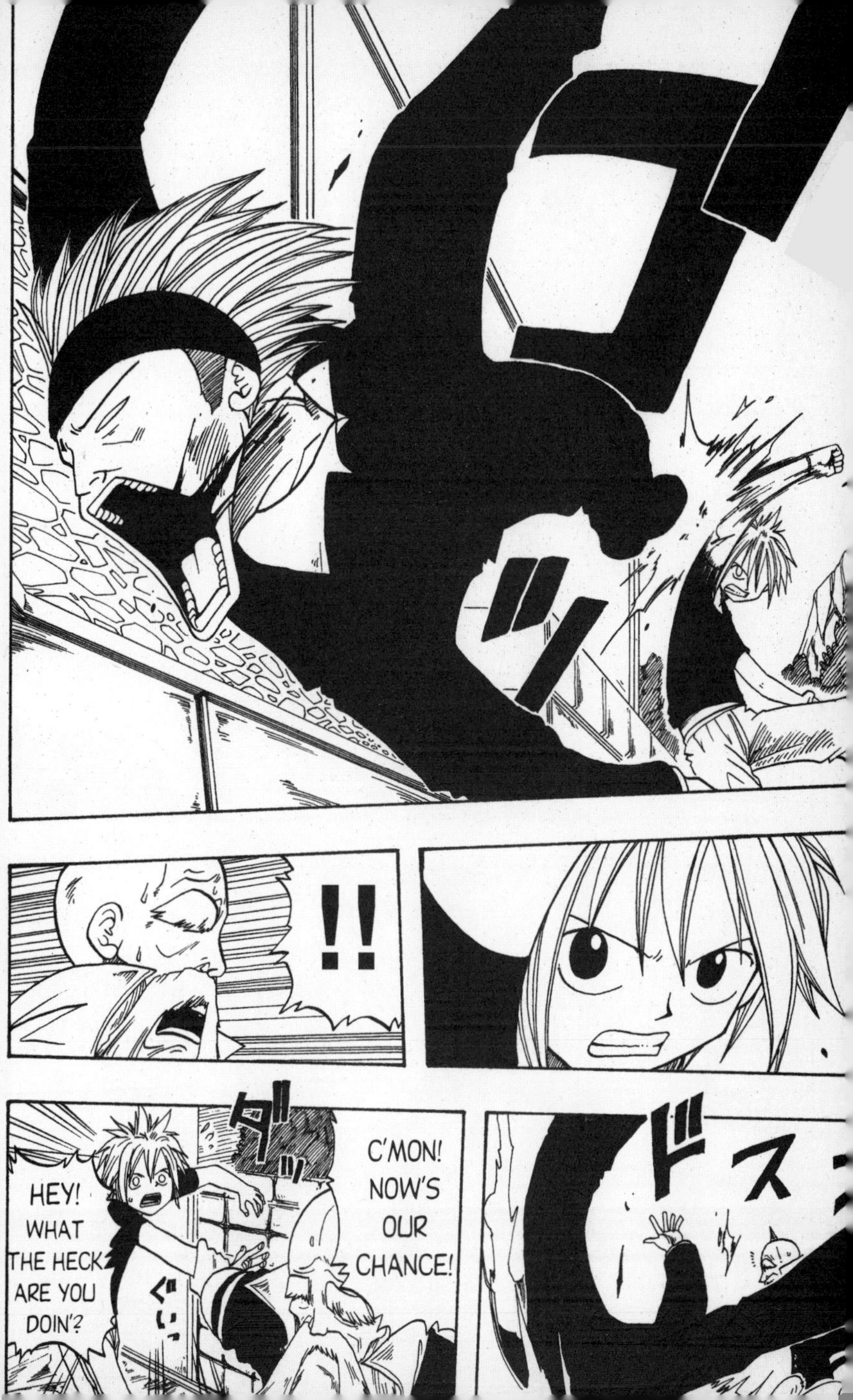
!!
ドス
C'MON! NOW'S OUR CHANCE!
HEY! WHAT THE HECK ARE YOU DOIN'?

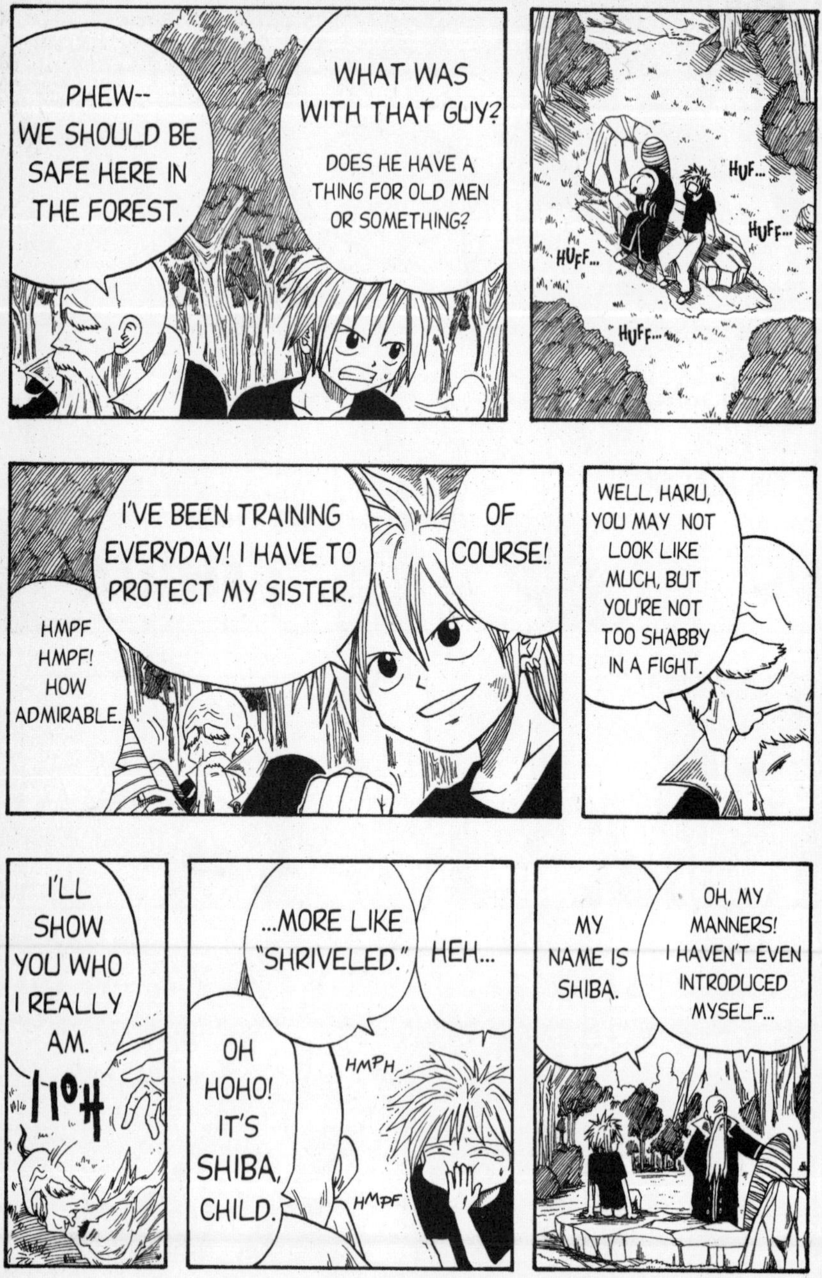
HUF...
HUFF...
HUFF...
HUFF...
WHAT WAS WITH THAT GUY?
DOES HE HAVE A THING FOR OLD MEN OR SOMETHING?
PHEW-- WE SHOULD BE SAFE HERE IN THE FOREST.
WELL, HARU, YOU MAY NOT LOOK LIKE MUCH, BUT YOU'RE NOT TOO SHABBY IN A FIGHT.
OF COURSE!
I'VE BEEN TRAINING EVERYDAY! I HAVE TO PROTECT MY SISTER.
HMPF HMPF! HOW ADMIRABLE.
OH, MY MANNERS! I HAVEN'T EVEN INTRODUCED MYSELF...
MY NAME IS SHIBA.
HEH...
...MORE LIKE "SHRIVELED."
HMPH
HMPF
OH HOHO! IT'S SHIBA, CHILD.
I'LL SHOW YOU WHO I REALLY AM.

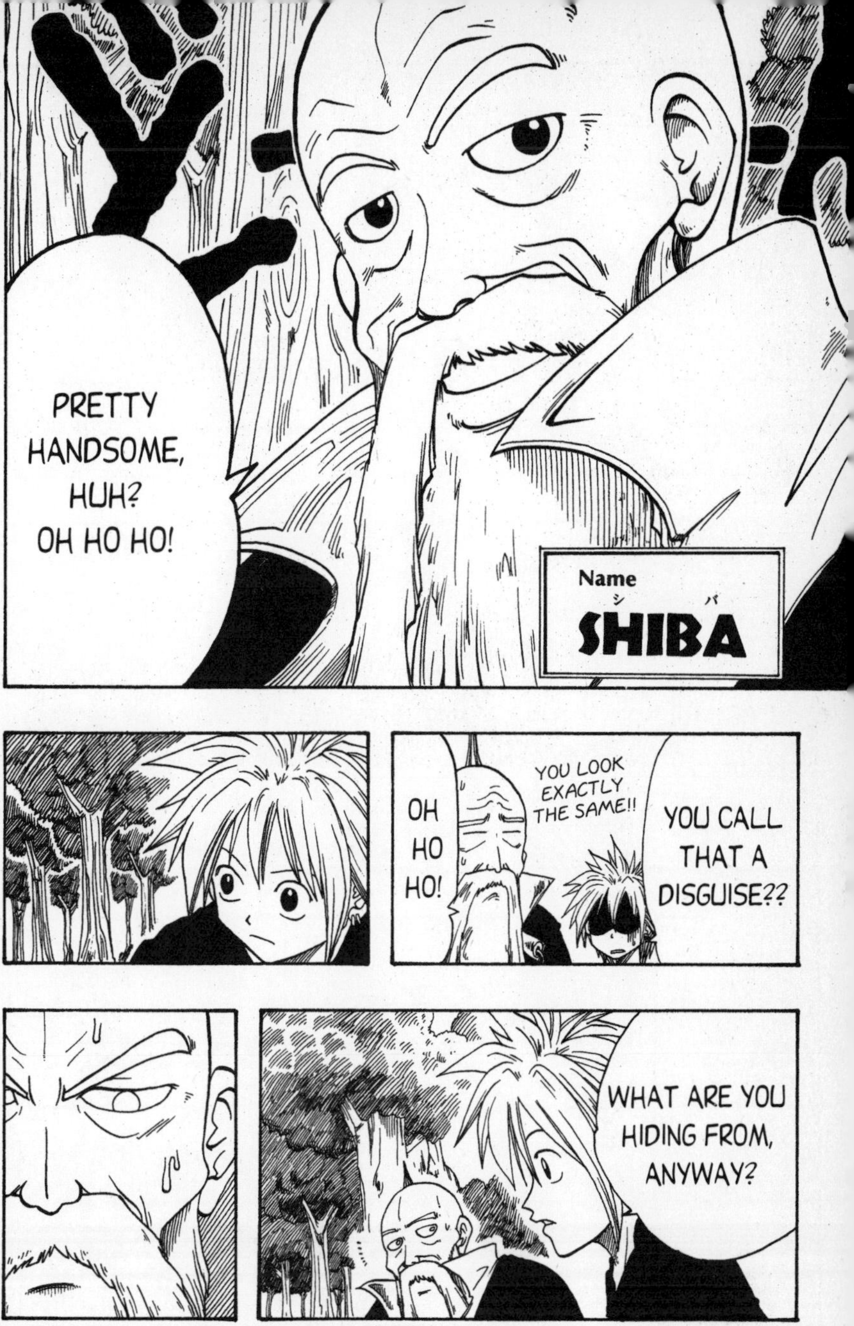
PRETTY HANDSOME, HUH? OH HO HO!
Name
シ バ
SHIBA
YOU CALL THAT A DISGUISE??
YOU LOOK EXACTLY THE SAME!!
OH HO HO!
WHAT ARE YOU HIDING FROM, ANYWAY?

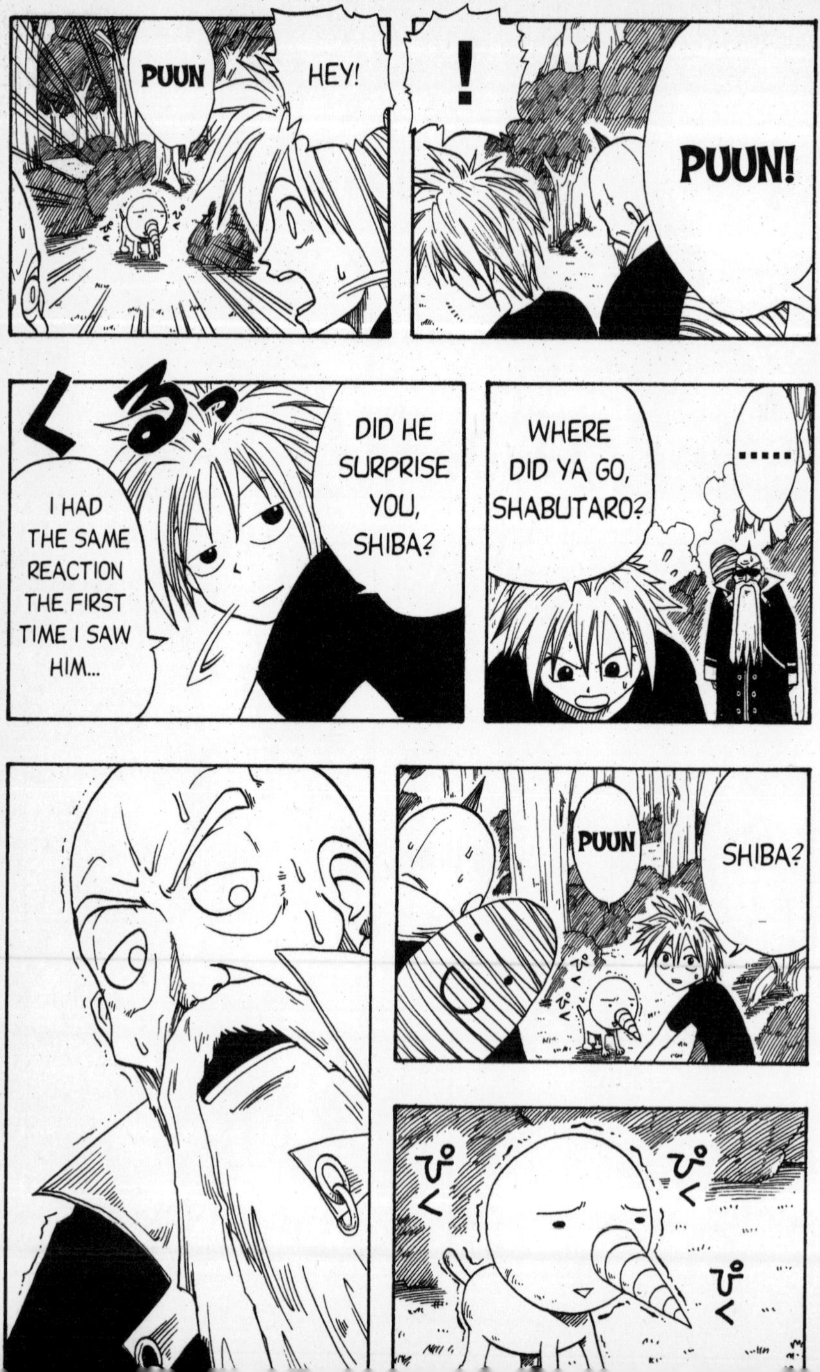
PUUN!
!
HEY!
PUUN
.....
WHERE DID YA GO, SHABUTARO?
DID HE SURPRISE YOU, SHIBA?
くるっ
I HAD THE SAME REACTION THE FIRST TIME I SAW HIM...
SHIBA?
PUUN
ぴく
ぴく
ぴく
ぴく

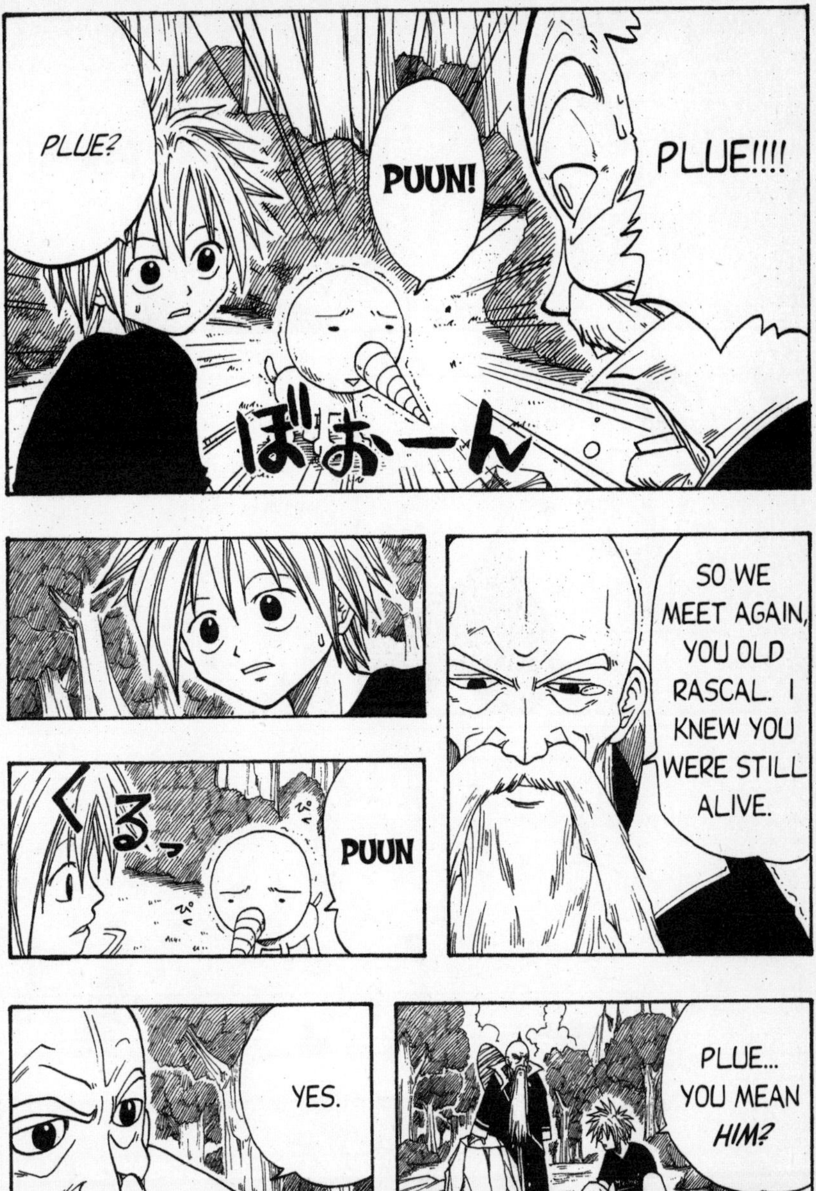
PLUE!!!!
PUUN!
PLUE?
ぼぉーん
SO WE MEET AGAIN, YOU OLD RASCAL. I KNEW YOU WERE STILL ALIVE.
くるっ
PUUN
PLUE... YOU MEAN *HIM?*
YES.

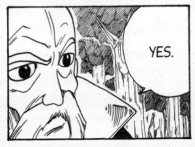

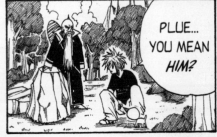

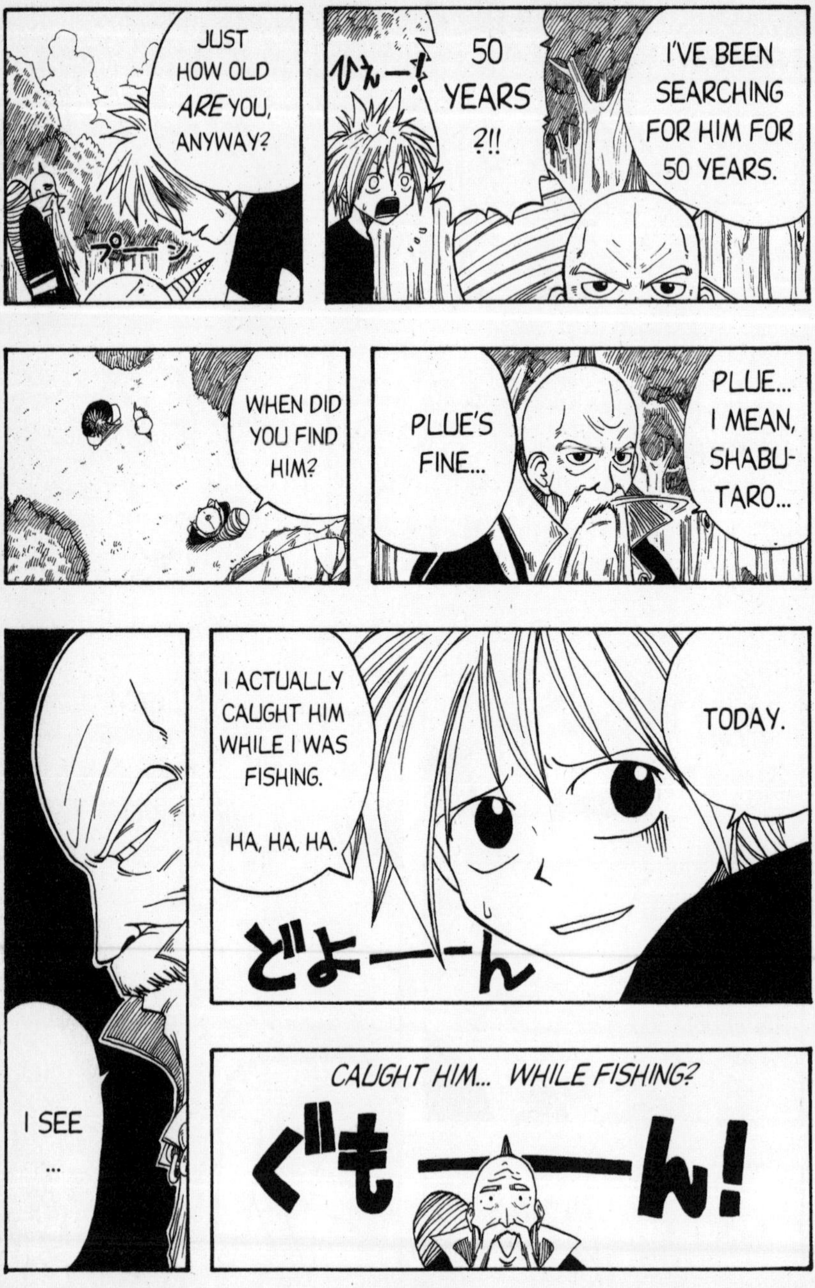
I'VE BEEN SEARCHING FOR HIM FOR 50 YEARS.
50 YEARS ?!!
ひえー!
JUST HOW OLD ARE YOU, ANYWAY?
PLUE... I MEAN, SHABU-TARO...
PLUE'S FINE...
WHEN DID YOU FIND HIM?
TODAY.
I ACTUALLY CAUGHT HIM WHILE I WAS FISHING.
HA, HA, HA.
どよーーん
CAUGHT HIM... WHILE FISHING?
ぐもーーん!
I SEE ...

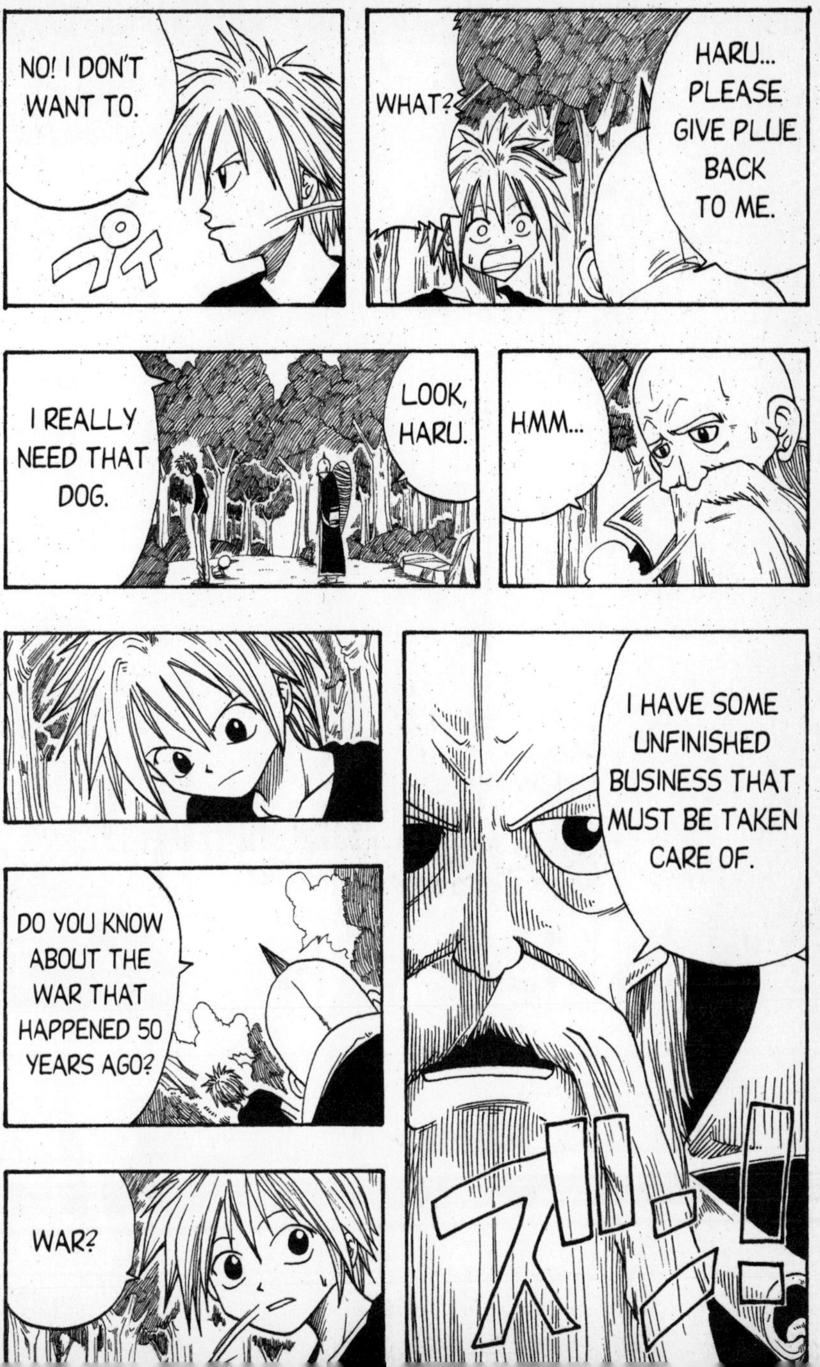
HARU... PLEASE GIVE PLUE BACK TO ME.
WHAT?
NO! I DON'T WANT TO.
HMM...
LOOK, HARU.
I REALLY NEED THAT DOG.
I HAVE SOME UNFINISHED BUSINESS THAT MUST BE TAKEN CARE OF.
DO YOU KNOW ABOUT THE WAR THAT HAPPENED 50 YEARS AGO?
WAR?

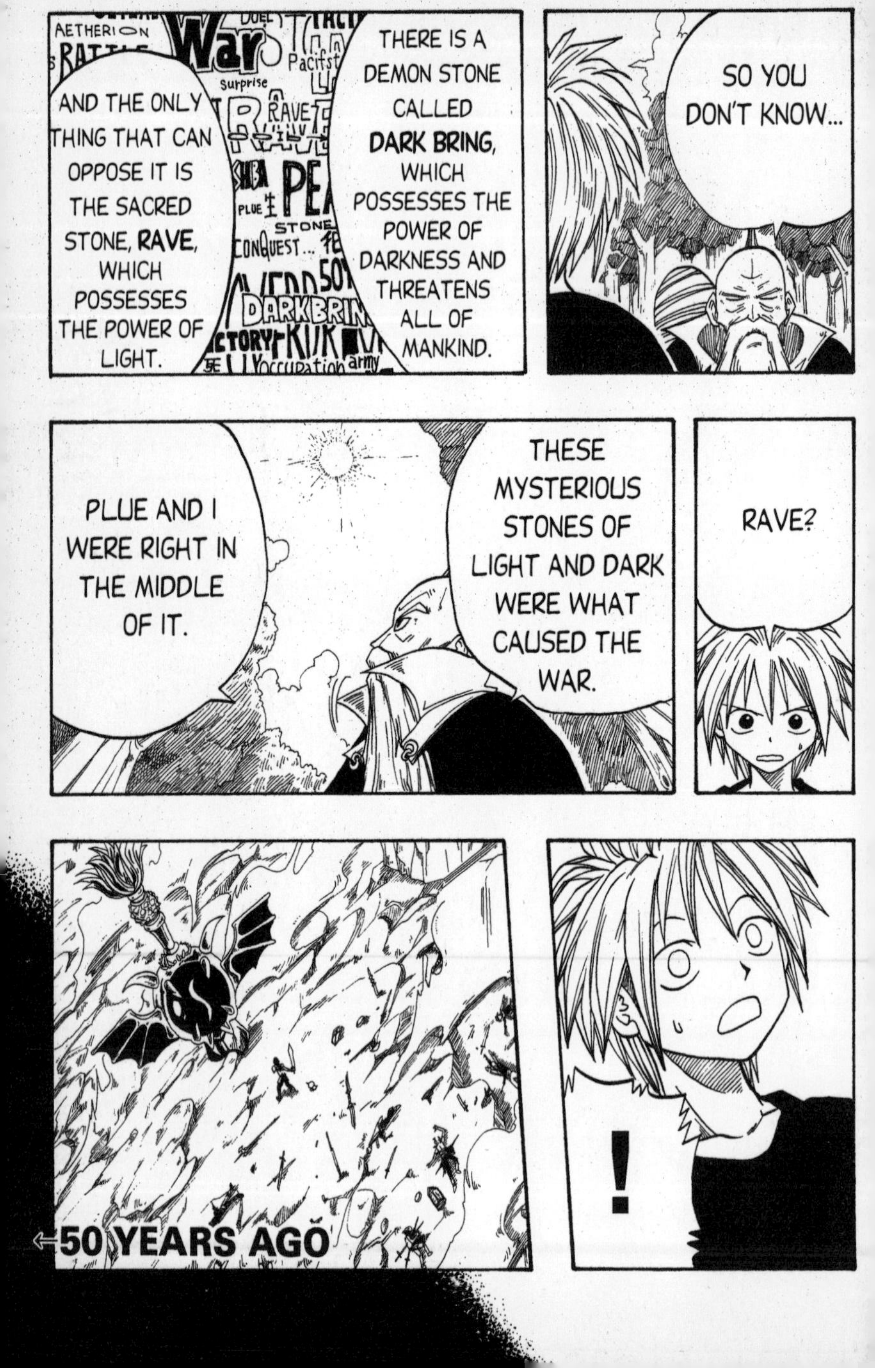

SO YOU DON'T KNOW...
THERE IS A DEMON STONE CALLED **DARK BRING**, WHICH POSSESSES THE POWER OF DARKNESS AND THREATENS ALL OF MANKIND.
War
DUEL
AETHERION
Surprise
RAVE
PLUE
STONE
CONQUEST...
Occupation
army
AND THE ONLY THING THAT CAN OPPOSE IT IS THE SACRED STONE, **RAVE**, WHICH POSSESSES THE POWER OF LIGHT.
RAVE?
THESE MYSTERIOUS STONES OF LIGHT AND DARK WERE WHAT CAUSED THE WAR.
PLUE AND I WERE RIGHT IN THE MIDDLE OF IT.
!
⇦50 YEARS AGO

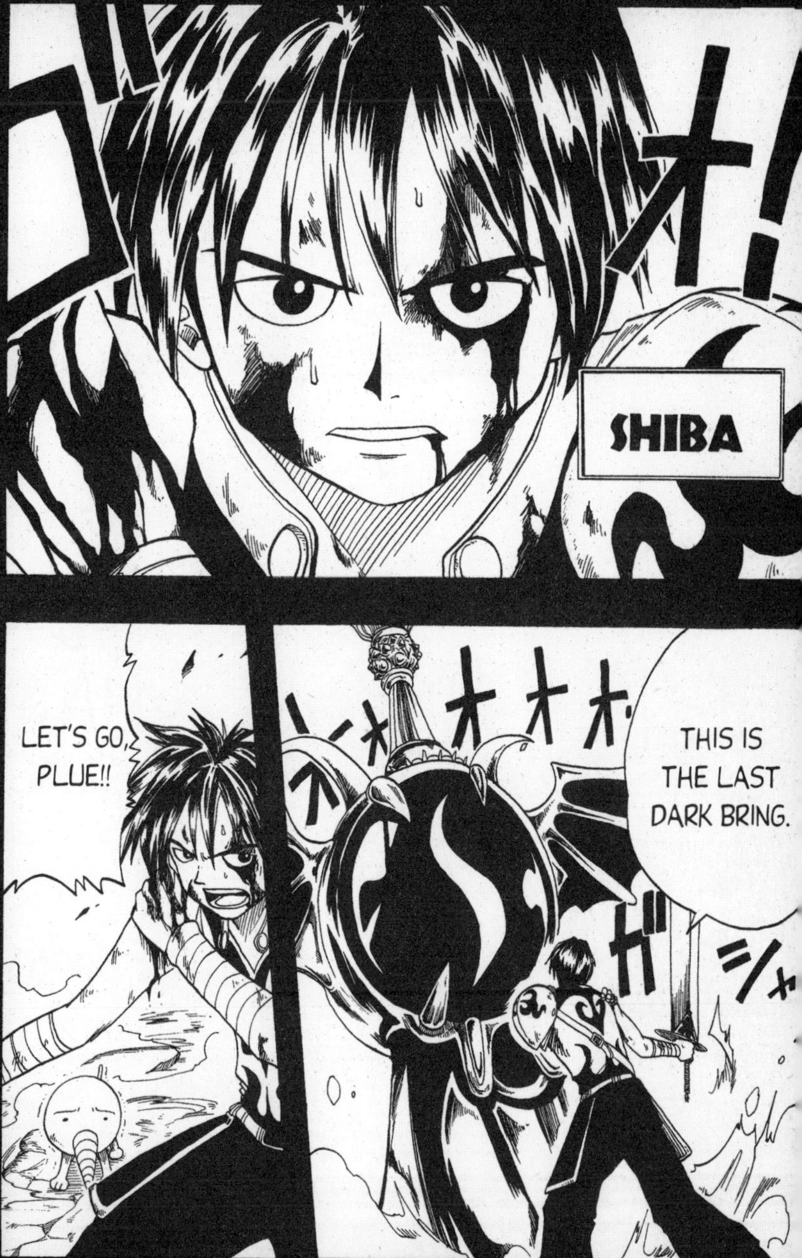
SHIBA
THIS IS THE LAST DARK BRING.
LET'S GO, PLUE!!

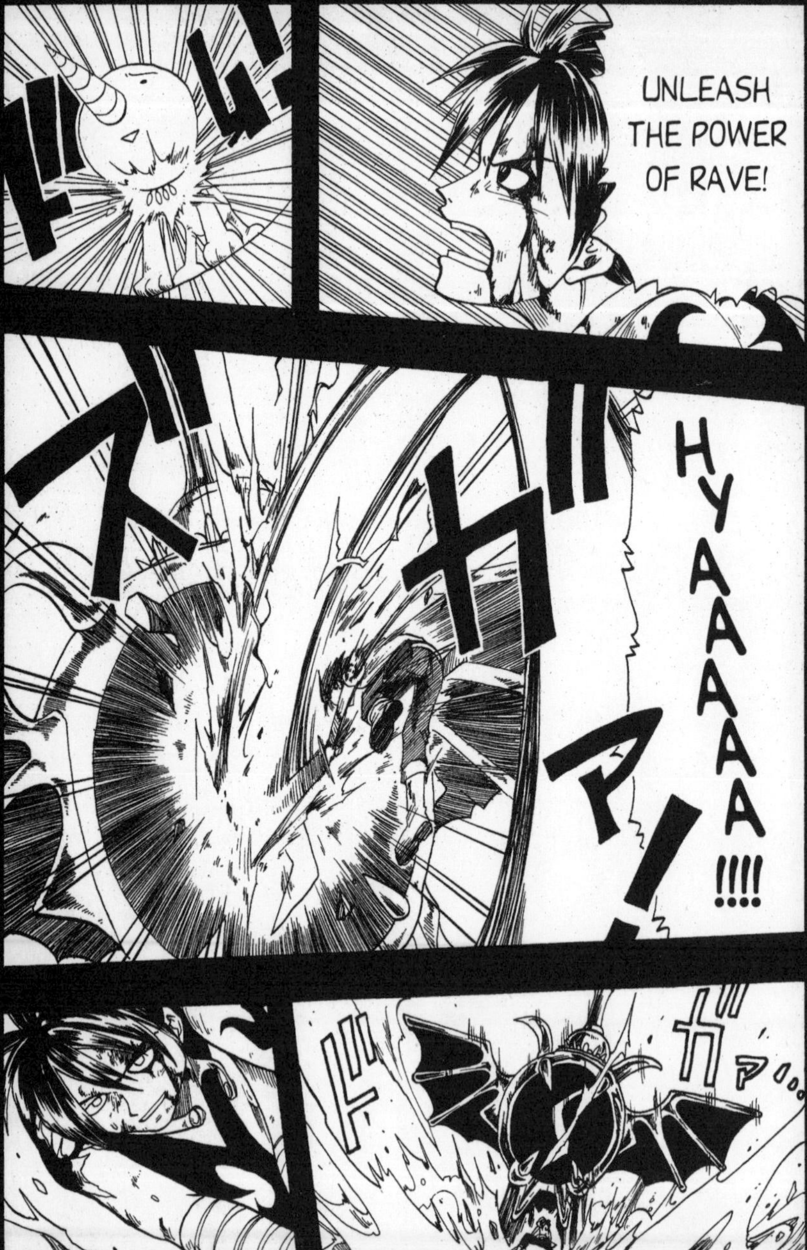
UNLEASH THE POWER OF RAVE!
HYAAAAA!!!!

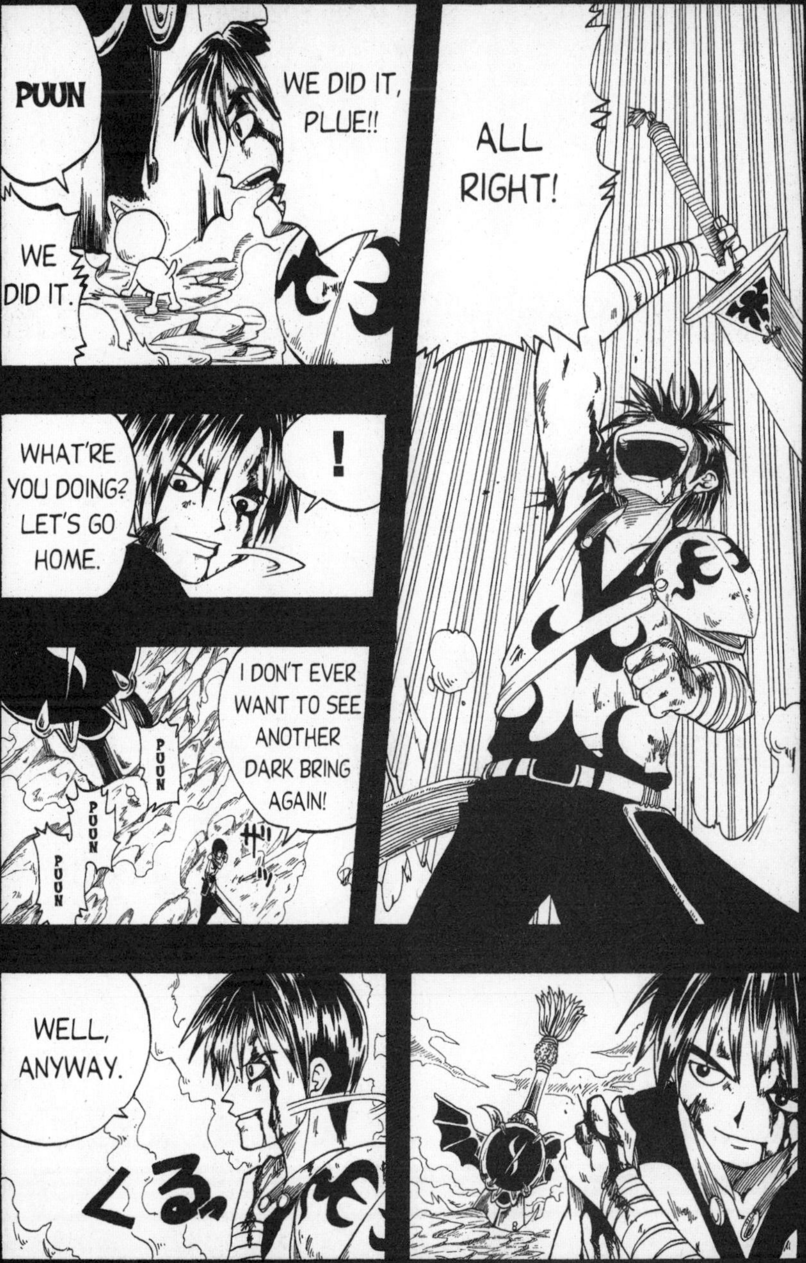
WE DID IT, PLUE!!
PUUN
WE DID IT.
ALL RIGHT!
WHAT'RE YOU DOING? LET'S GO HOME.
!
I DON'T EVER WANT TO SEE ANOTHER DARK BRING AGAIN!
PUUN
PUUN
PUUN
WELL, ANYWAY.
くるっ

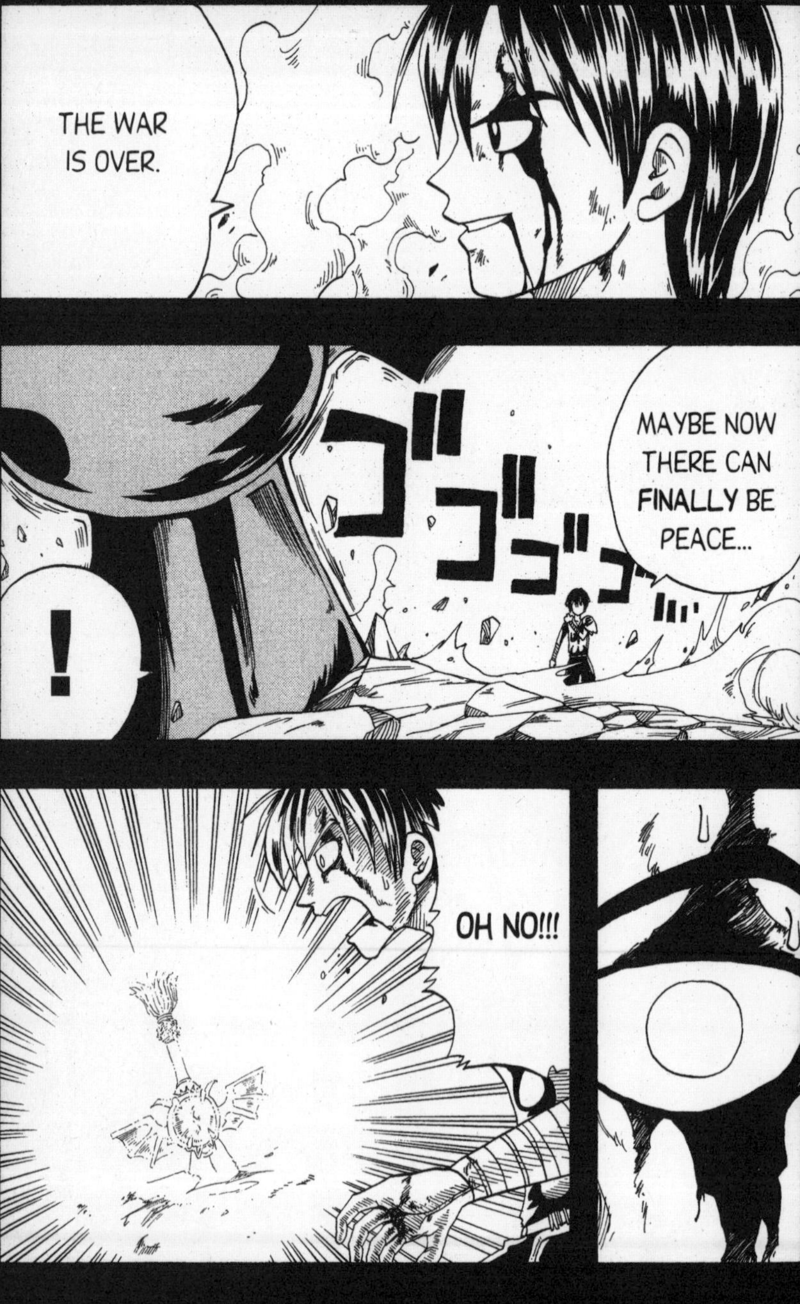
THE WAR IS OVER.
MAYBE NOW THERE CAN FINALLY BE PEACE...
ゴゴゴゴ
!
OH NO!!!

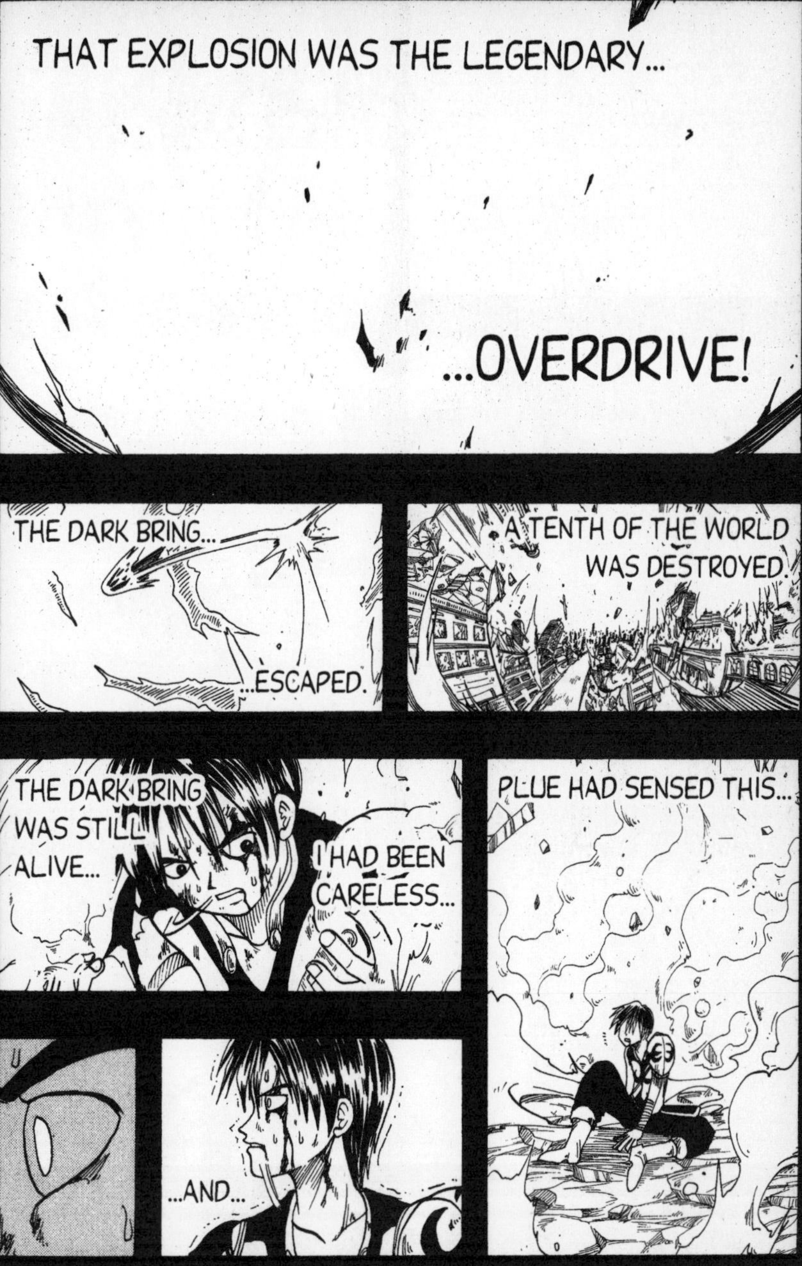
THAT EXPLOSION WAS THE LEGENDARY...
...OVERDRIVE!
THE DARK BRING...
...ESCAPED.
A TENTH OF THE WORLD WAS DESTROYED.
THE DARK BRING WAS STILL ALIVE...
I HAD BEEN CARELESS...
...AND...
PLUE HAD SENSED THIS...

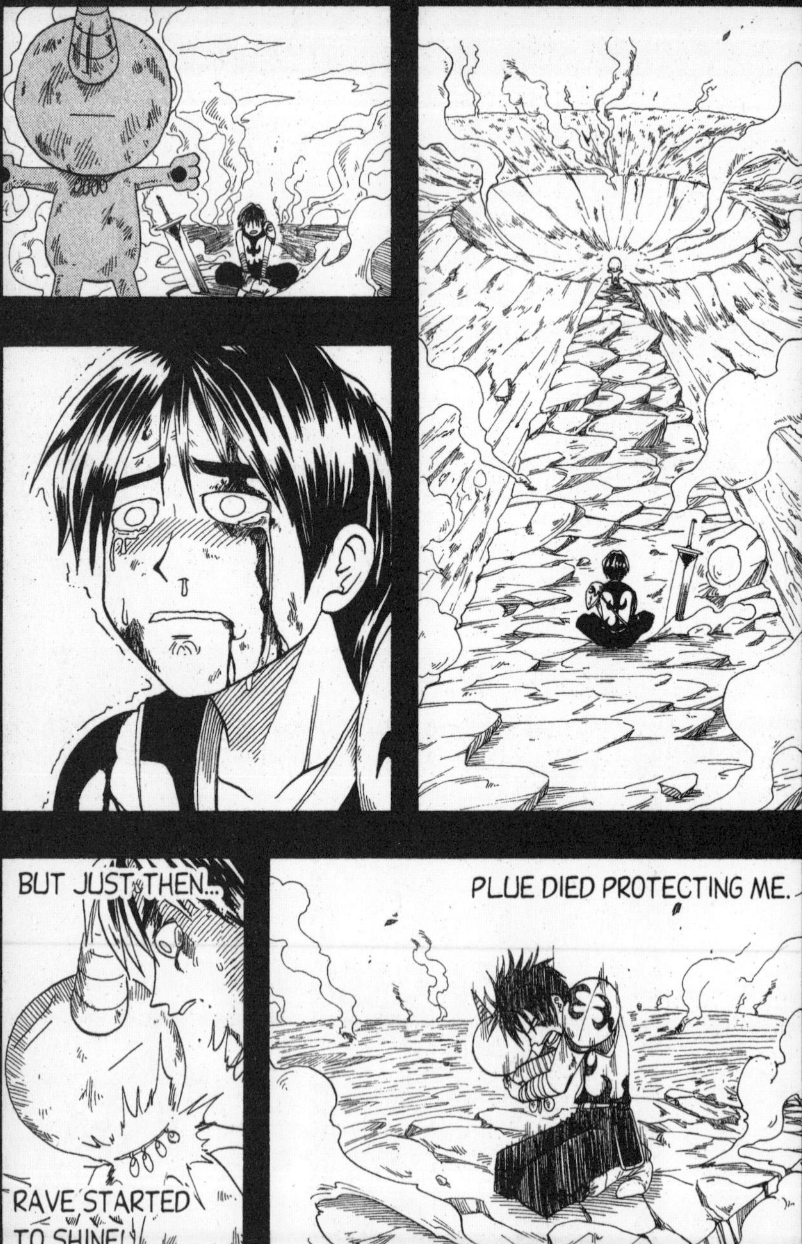
PLUE DIED PROTECTING ME.
BUT JUST THEN...
RAVE STARTED TO SHINE!

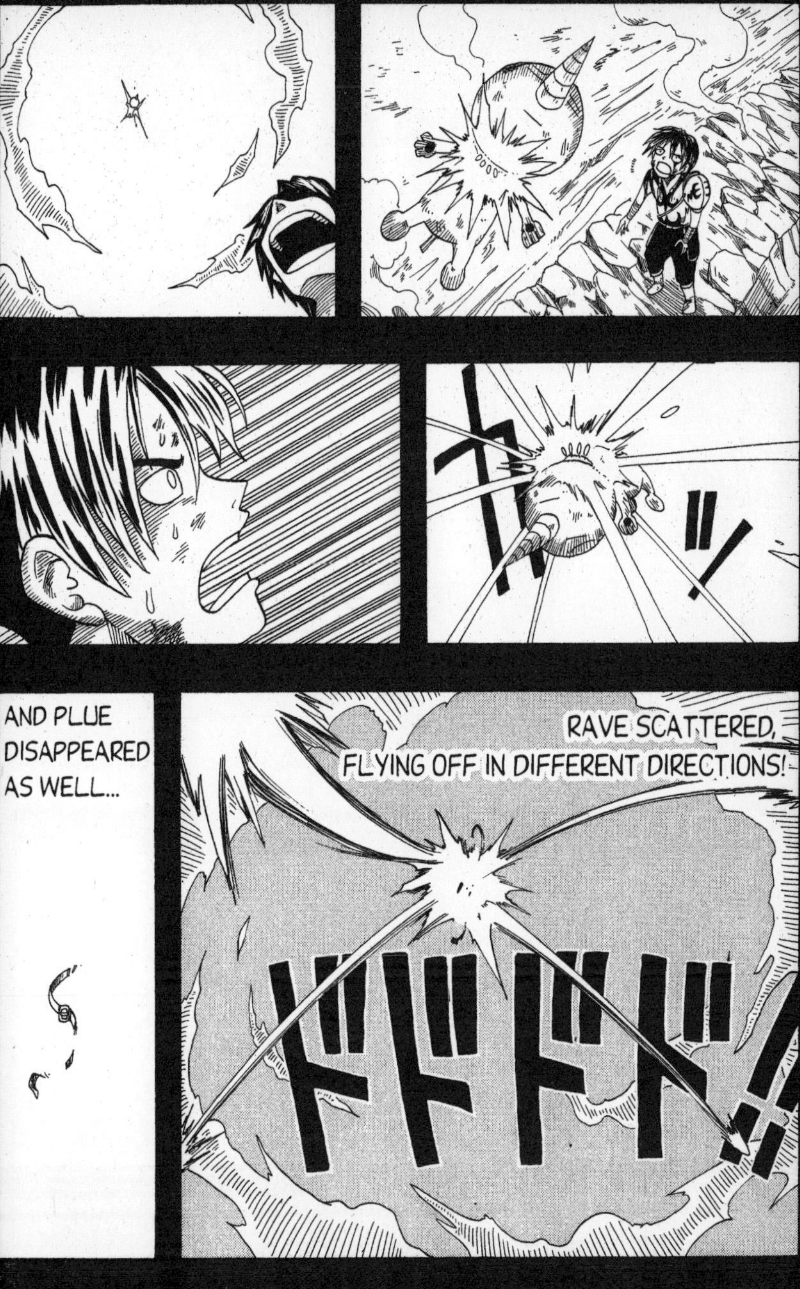
RAVE SCATTERED,
FLYING OFF IN DIFFERENT DIRECTIONS!
AND PLUE DISAPPEARED AS WELL...

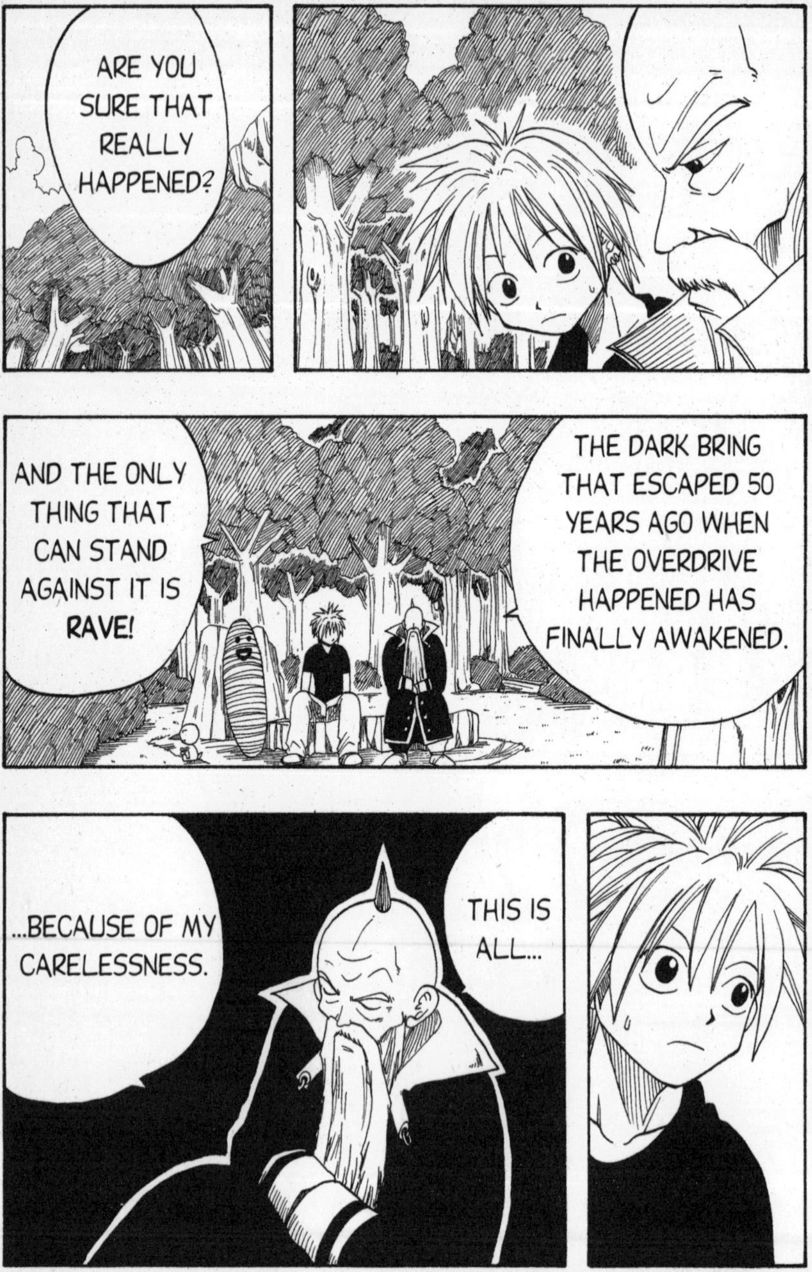
ARE YOU SURE THAT REALLY HAPPENED?
THE DARK BRING THAT ESCAPED 50 YEARS AGO WHEN THE OVERDRIVE HAPPENED HAS FINALLY AWAKENED.
AND THE ONLY THING THAT CAN STAND AGAINST IT IS RAVE!
THIS IS ALL...
...BECAUSE OF MY CARELESSNESS.

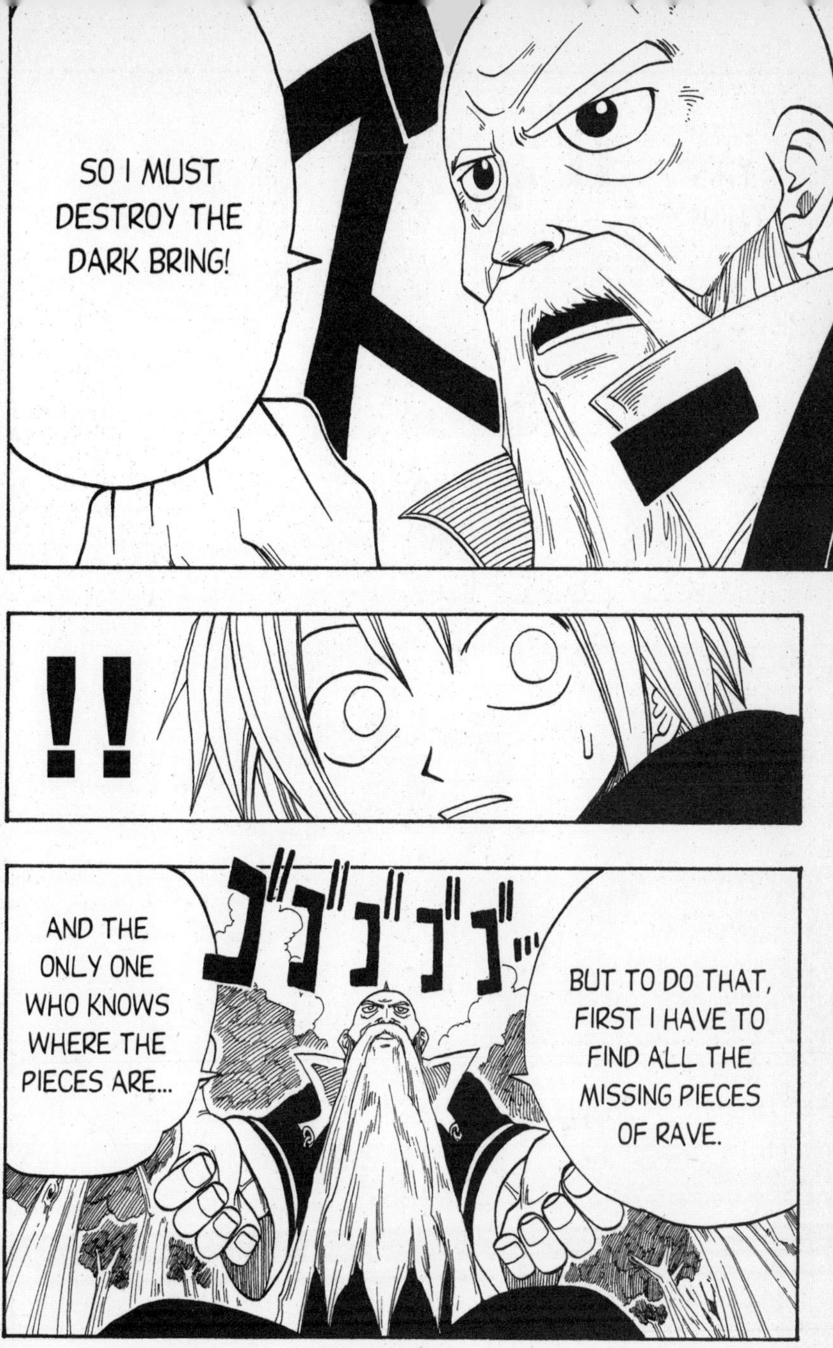
SO I MUST DESTROY THE DARK BRING!
!!
ゴゴゴゴ
BUT TO DO THAT, FIRST I HAVE TO FIND ALL THE MISSING PIECES OF RAVE.
AND THE ONLY ONE WHO KNOWS WHERE THE PIECES ARE...

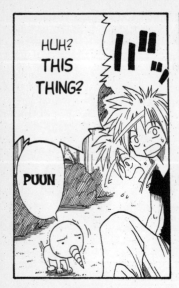

HUH? THIS THING?

PUUN

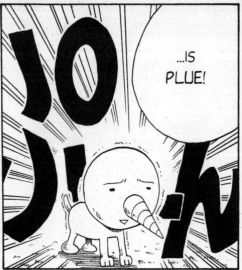

...IS PLUE!

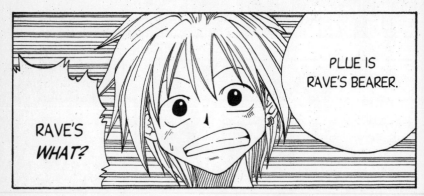

PLUE IS RAVE'S BEARER.

RAVE'S *WHAT?*

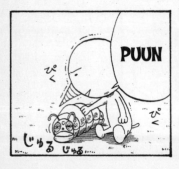

PUUN

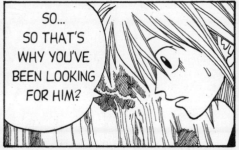

SO... SO THAT'S WHY YOU'VE BEEN LOOKING FOR HIM?

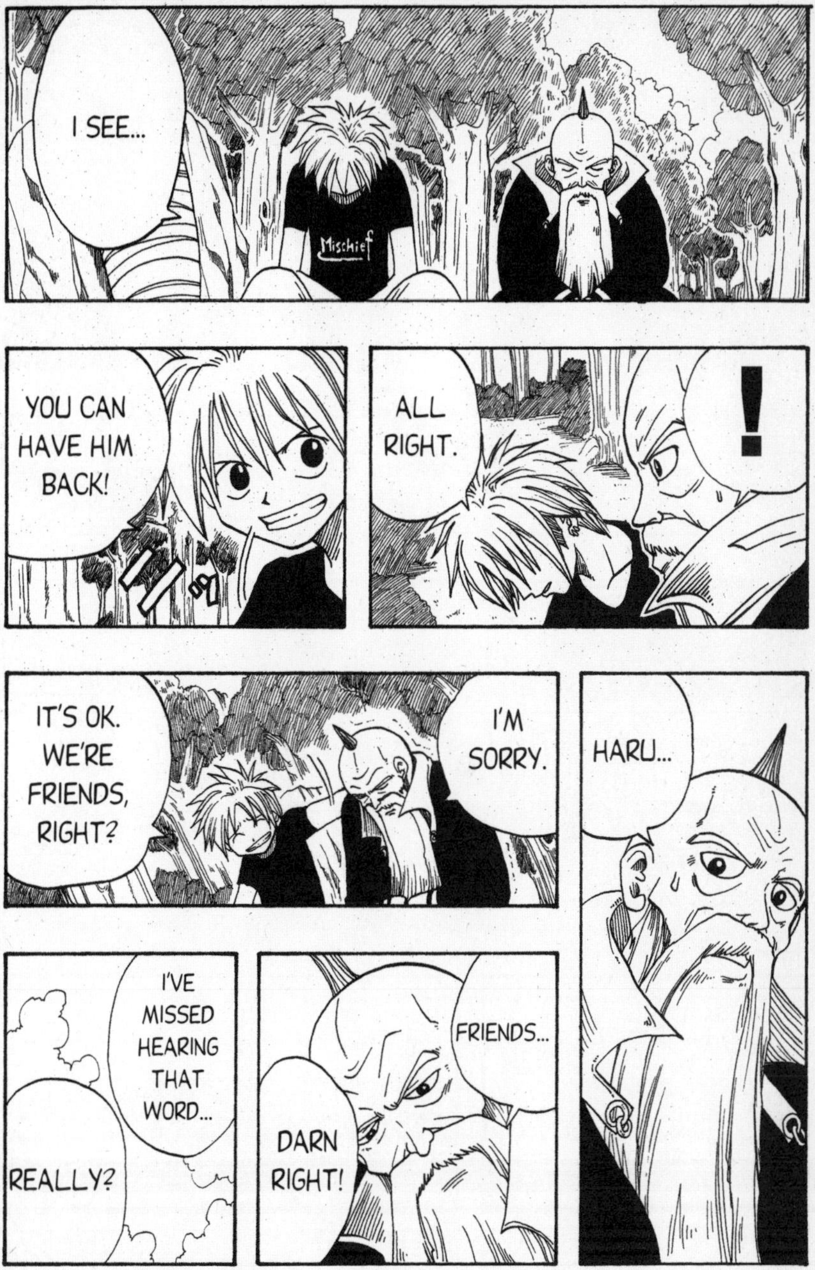
I SEE...
ALL RIGHT.
!
YOU CAN HAVE HIM BACK!
HARU...
I'M SORRY.
IT'S OK. WE'RE FRIENDS, RIGHT?
FRIENDS...
DARN RIGHT!
I'VE MISSED HEARING THAT WORD...
REALLY?

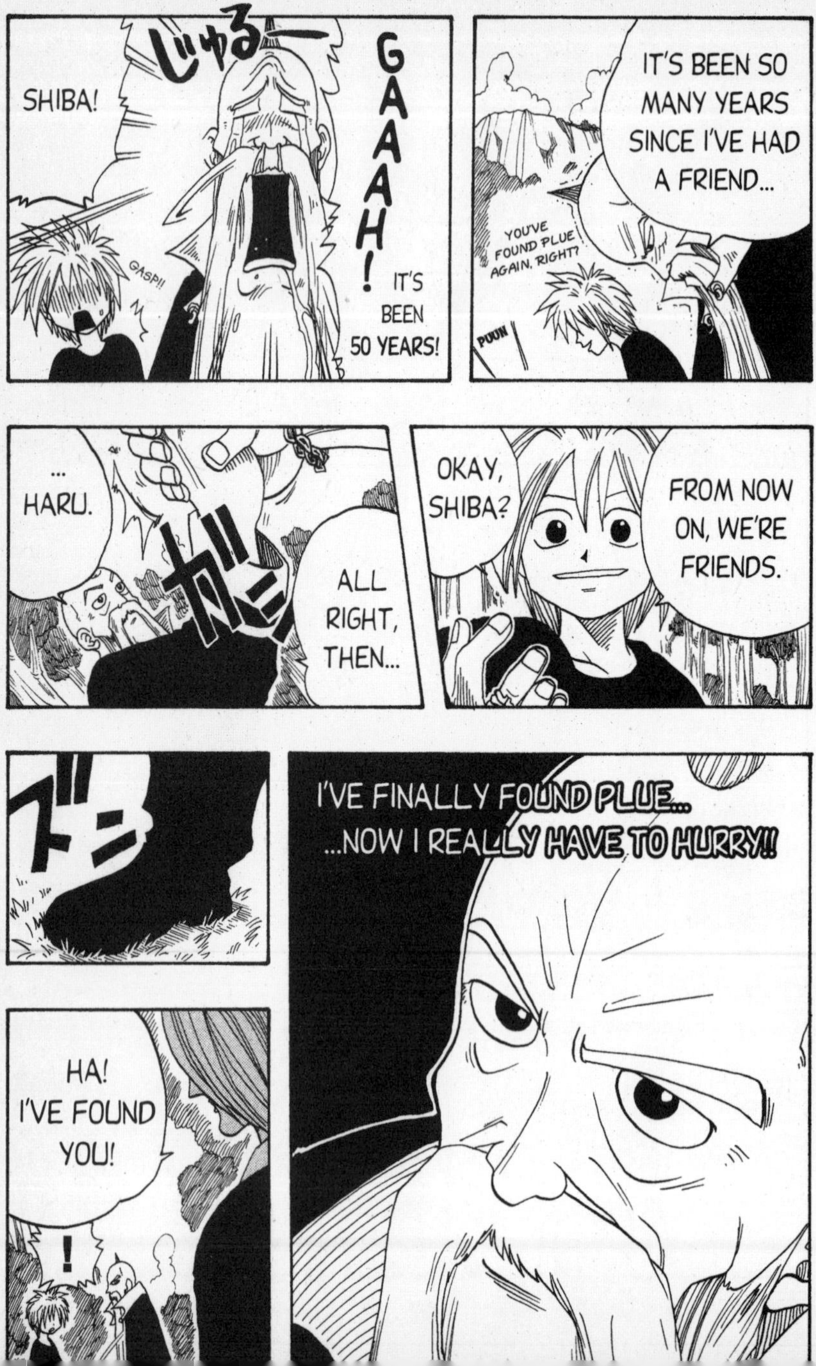
IT'S BEEN SO MANY YEARS SINCE I'VE HAD A FRIEND...
YOU'VE FOUND PLUE AGAIN, RIGHT?
PUUN
じゅるー
GAAAAH!
SHIBA!
GASP!!
IT'S BEEN 50 YEARS!
FROM NOW ON, WE'RE FRIENDS.
OKAY, SHIBA?
... HARU.
ALL RIGHT, THEN...
I'VE FINALLY FOUND PLUE...
...NOW I REALLY HAVE TO HURRY!!
HA! I'VE FOUND YOU!
!

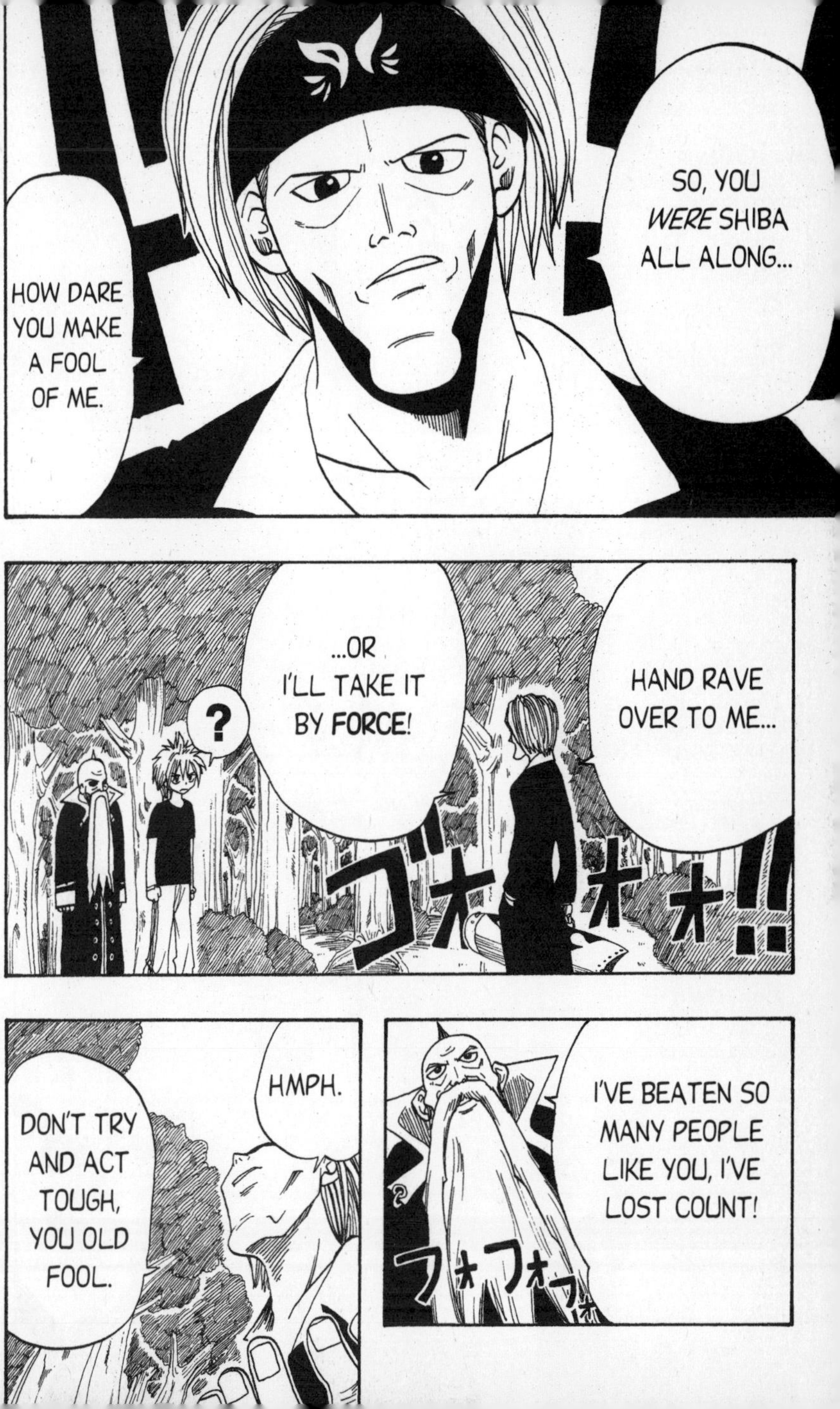
SO, YOU *WERE* SHIBA ALL ALONG...
HOW DARE YOU MAKE A FOOL OF ME.
HAND RAVE OVER TO ME...
...OR I'LL TAKE IT BY **FORCE!**
?
ゴォォォ!!
I'VE BEATEN SO MANY PEOPLE LIKE YOU, I'VE LOST COUNT!
フォフォフォ
HMPH.
DON'T TRY AND ACT TOUGH, YOU OLD FOOL.

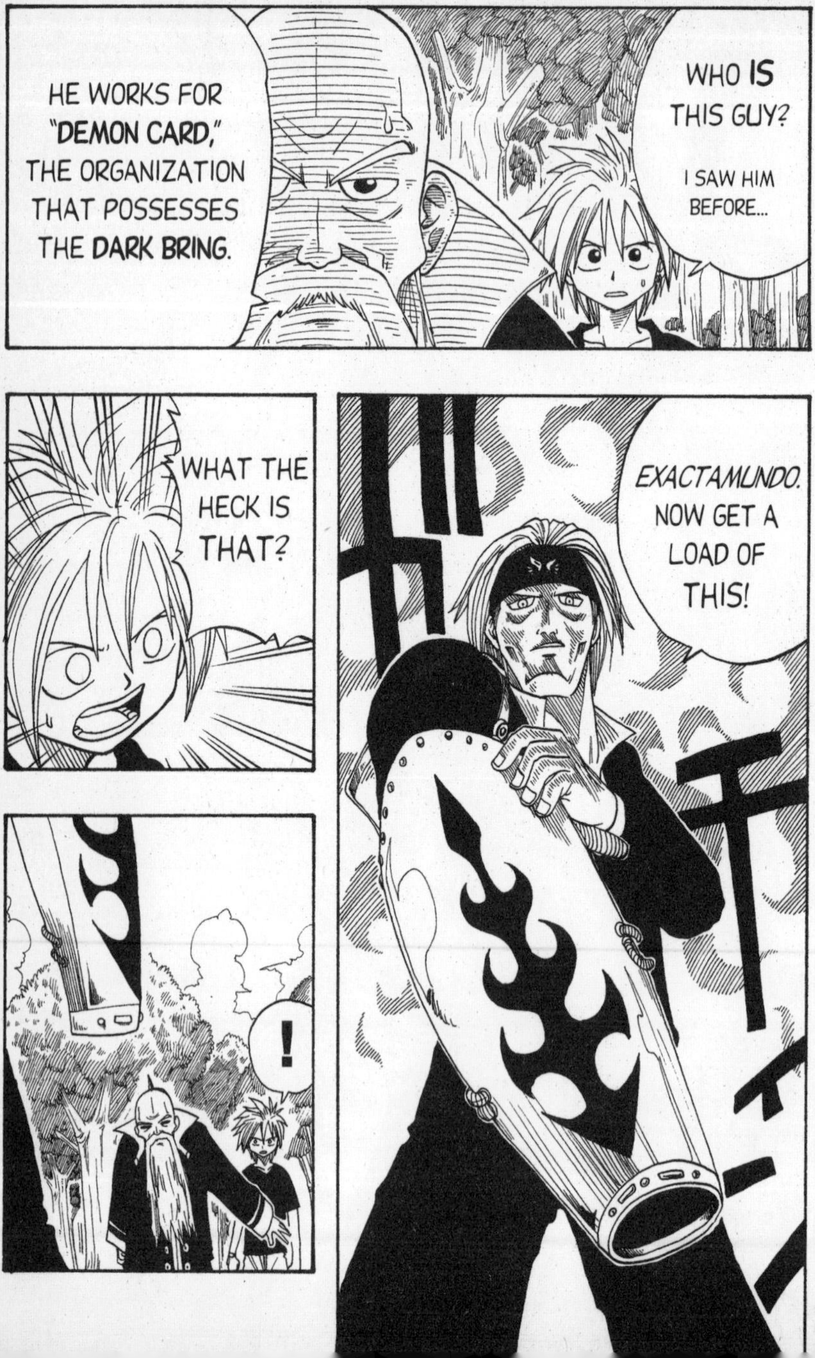
WHO IS THIS GUY?
I SAW HIM BEFORE...
HE WORKS FOR "DEMON CARD," THE ORGANIZATION THAT POSSESSES THE DARK BRING.
EXACTAMUNDO. NOW GET A LOAD OF THIS!
WHAT THE HECK IS THAT?
!

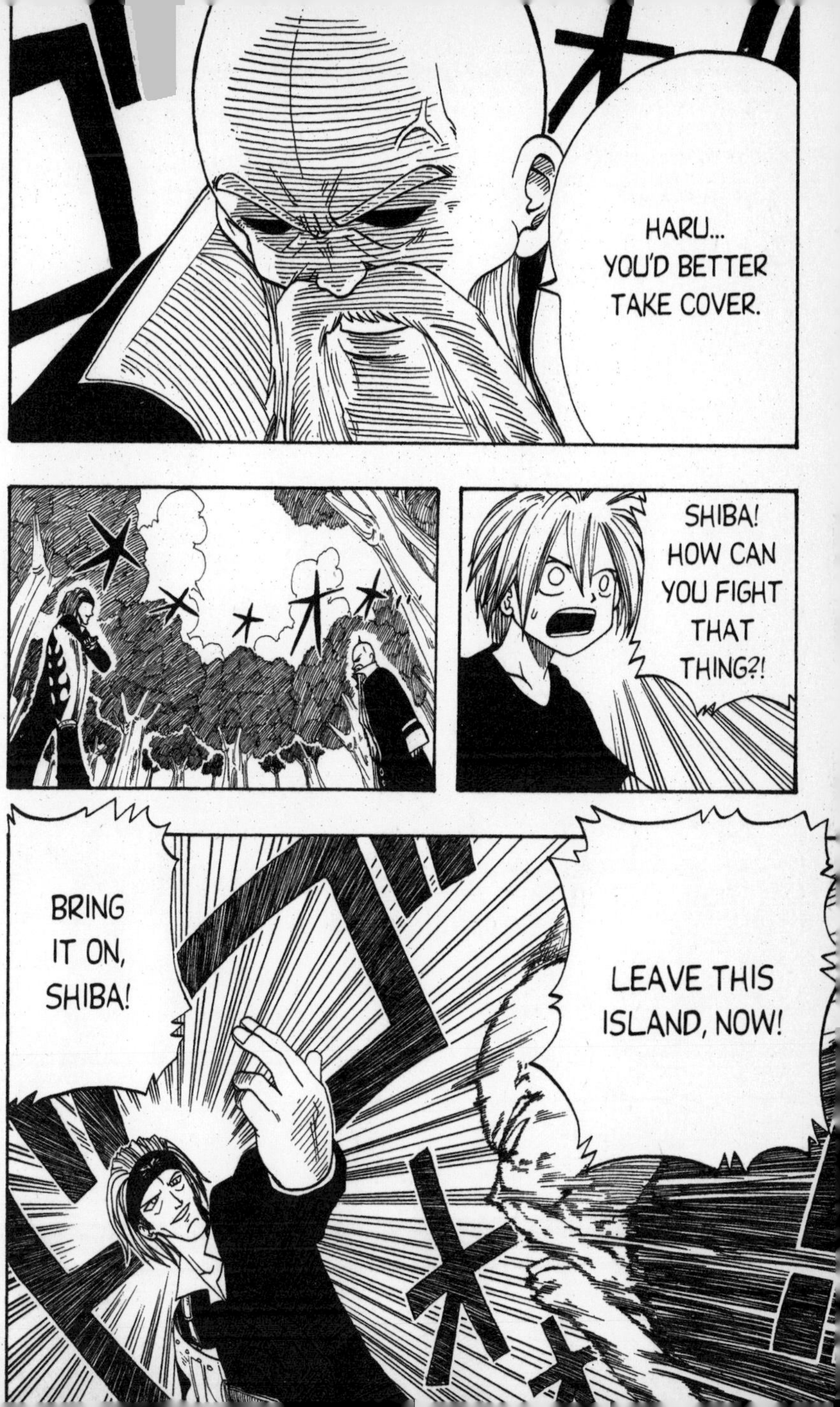
HARU... YOU'D BETTER TAKE COVER.
SHIBA! HOW CAN YOU FIGHT THAT THING?!
LEAVE THIS ISLAND, NOW!
BRING IT ON, SHIBA!

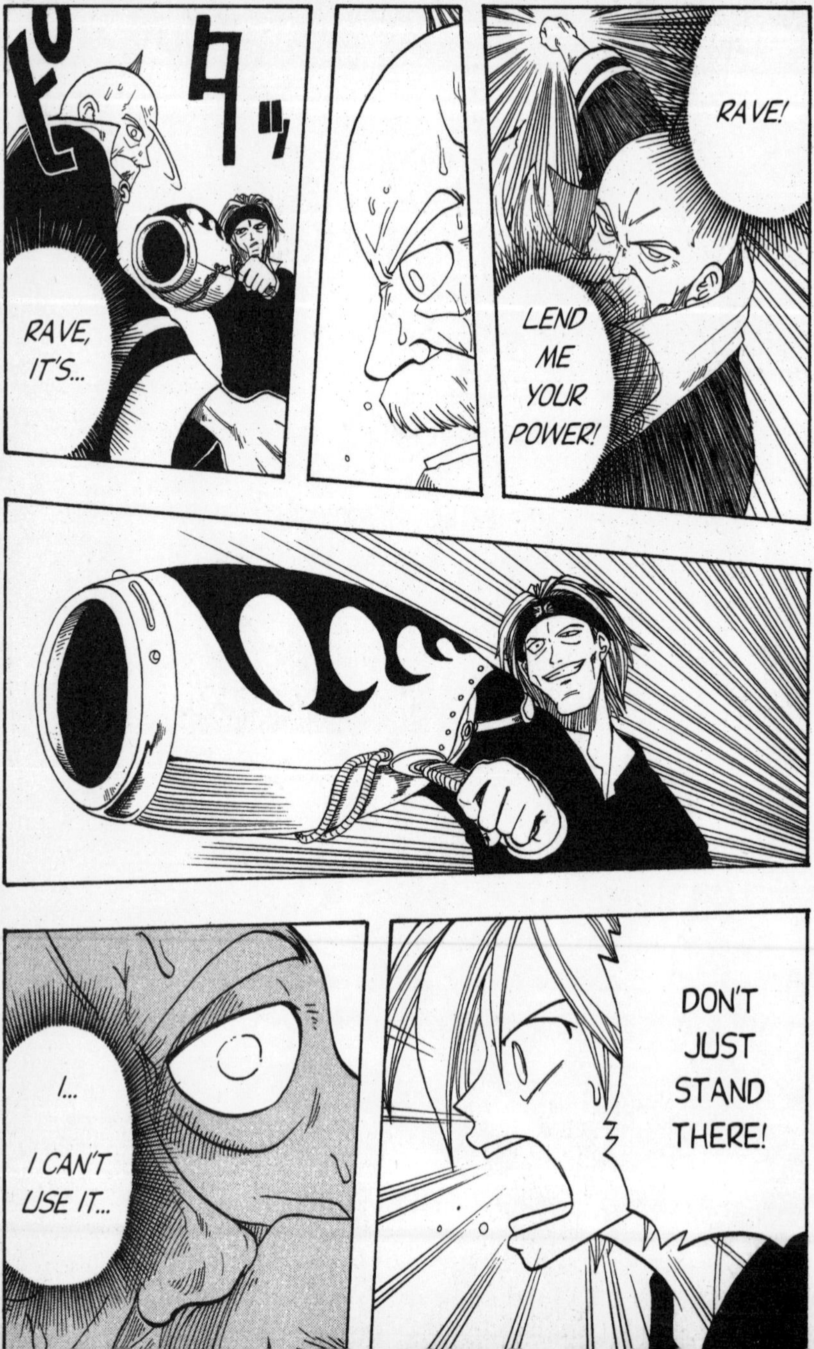
RAVE!
LEND ME YOUR POWER!
タッ
RAVE, IT'S...
DON'T JUST STAND THERE!
I...
I CAN'T USE IT...

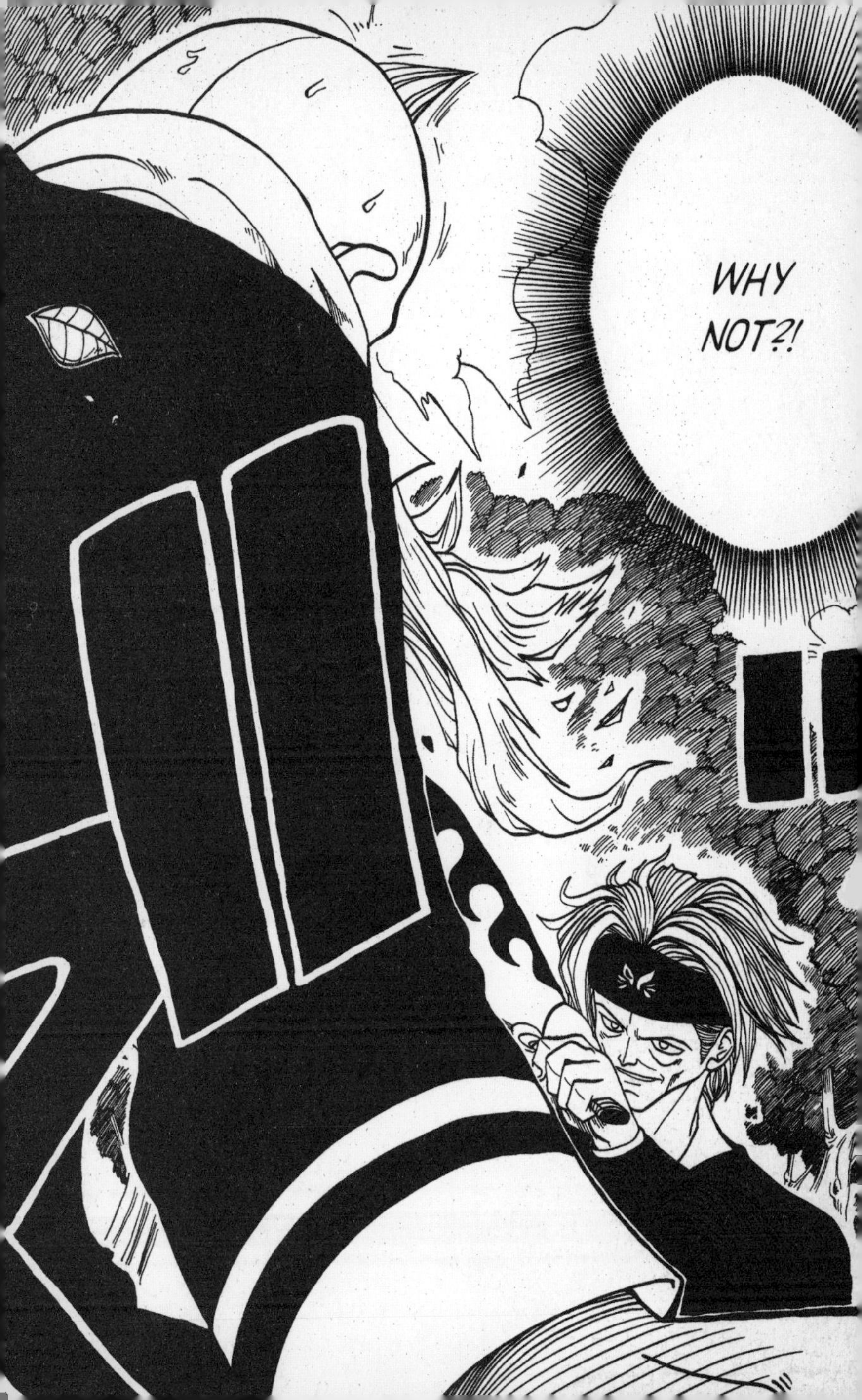
WHY NOT?!

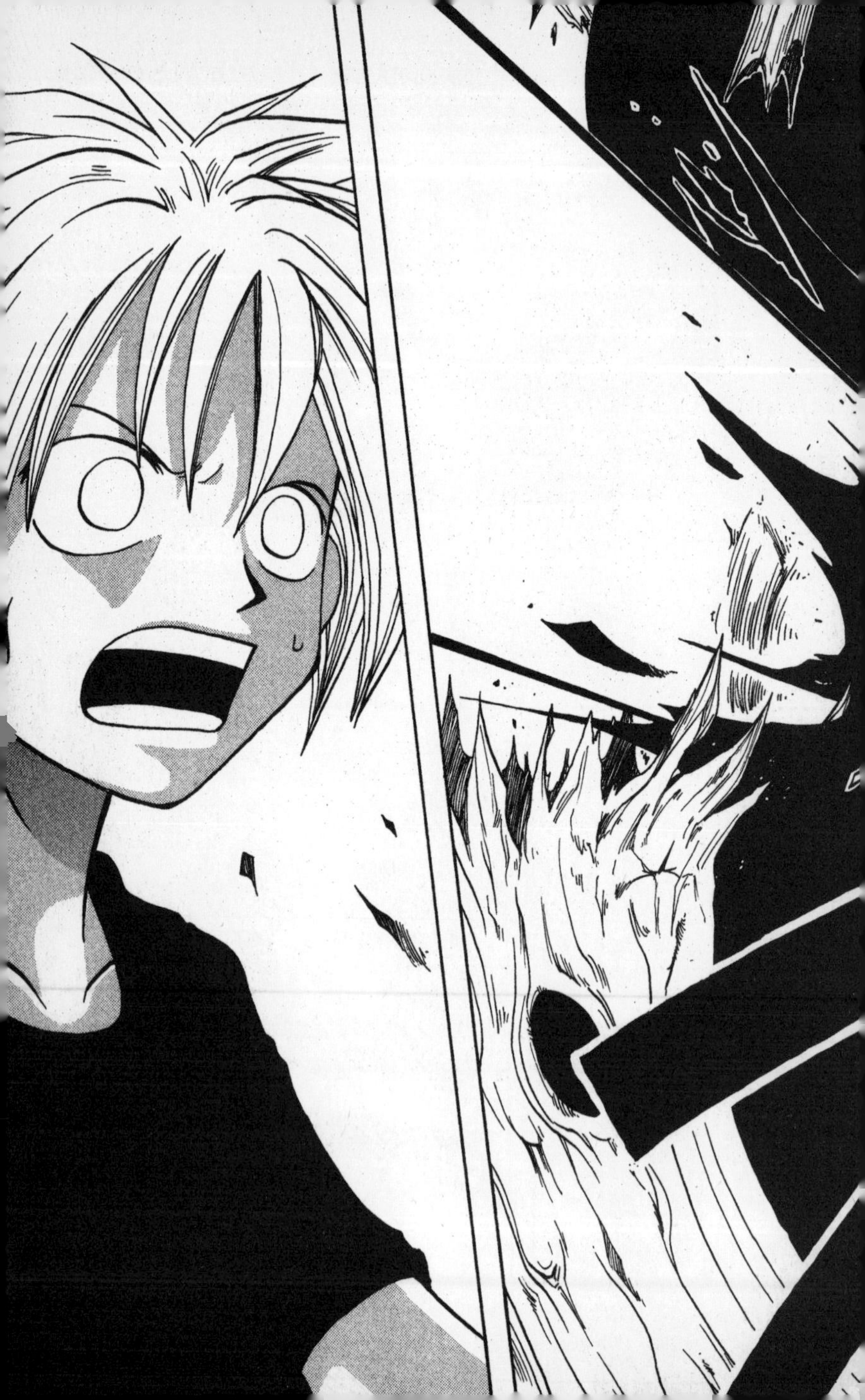

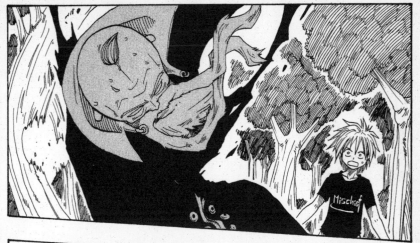

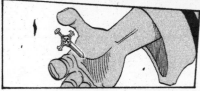
IT'S...
...OVER.
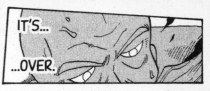

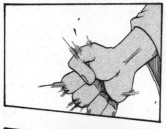
WHAT ELSE DID YOU EXPECT FROM THIS FINE WEAPON?

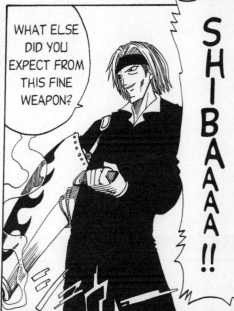
SHIBAAAA!!

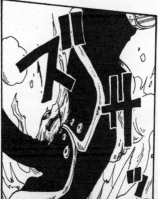

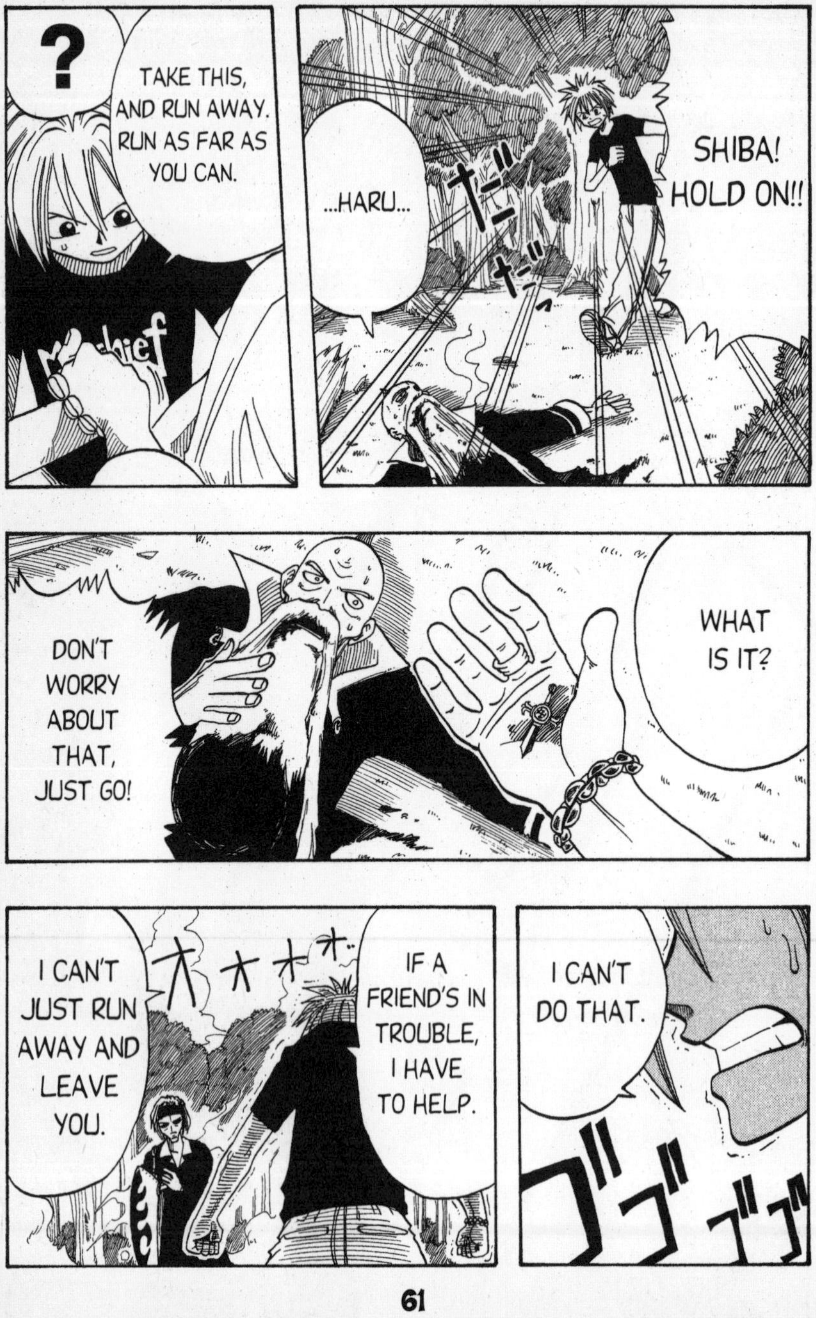
SHIBA! HOLD ON!!
...HARU...
TAKE THIS, AND RUN AWAY. RUN AS FAR AS YOU CAN.
?
WHAT IS IT?
DON'T WORRY ABOUT THAT, JUST GO!
I CAN'T DO THAT.
IF A FRIEND'S IN TROUBLE, I HAVE TO HELP.
I CAN'T JUST RUN AWAY AND LEAVE YOU.

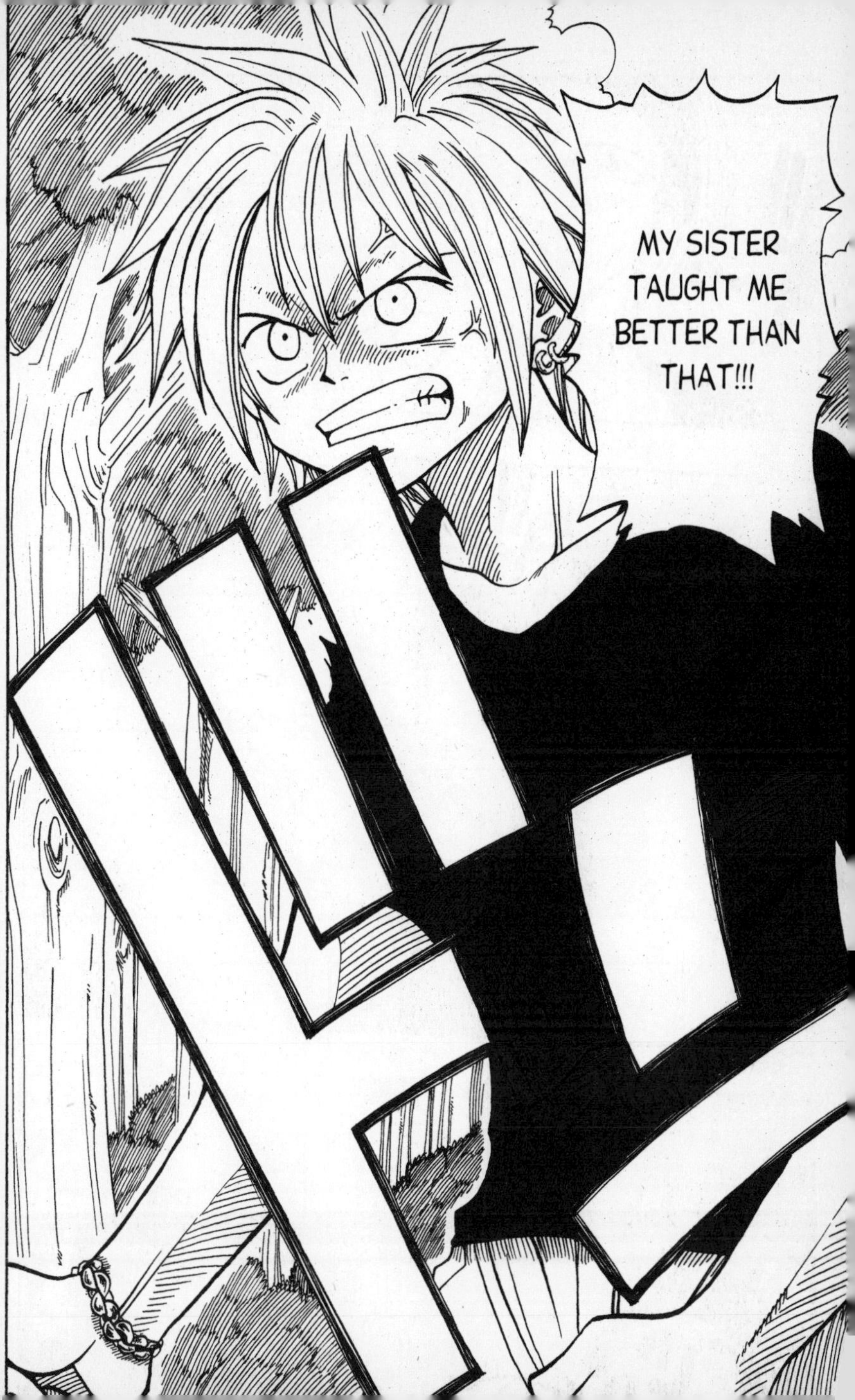
MY SISTER TAUGHT ME BETTER THAN THAT!!!

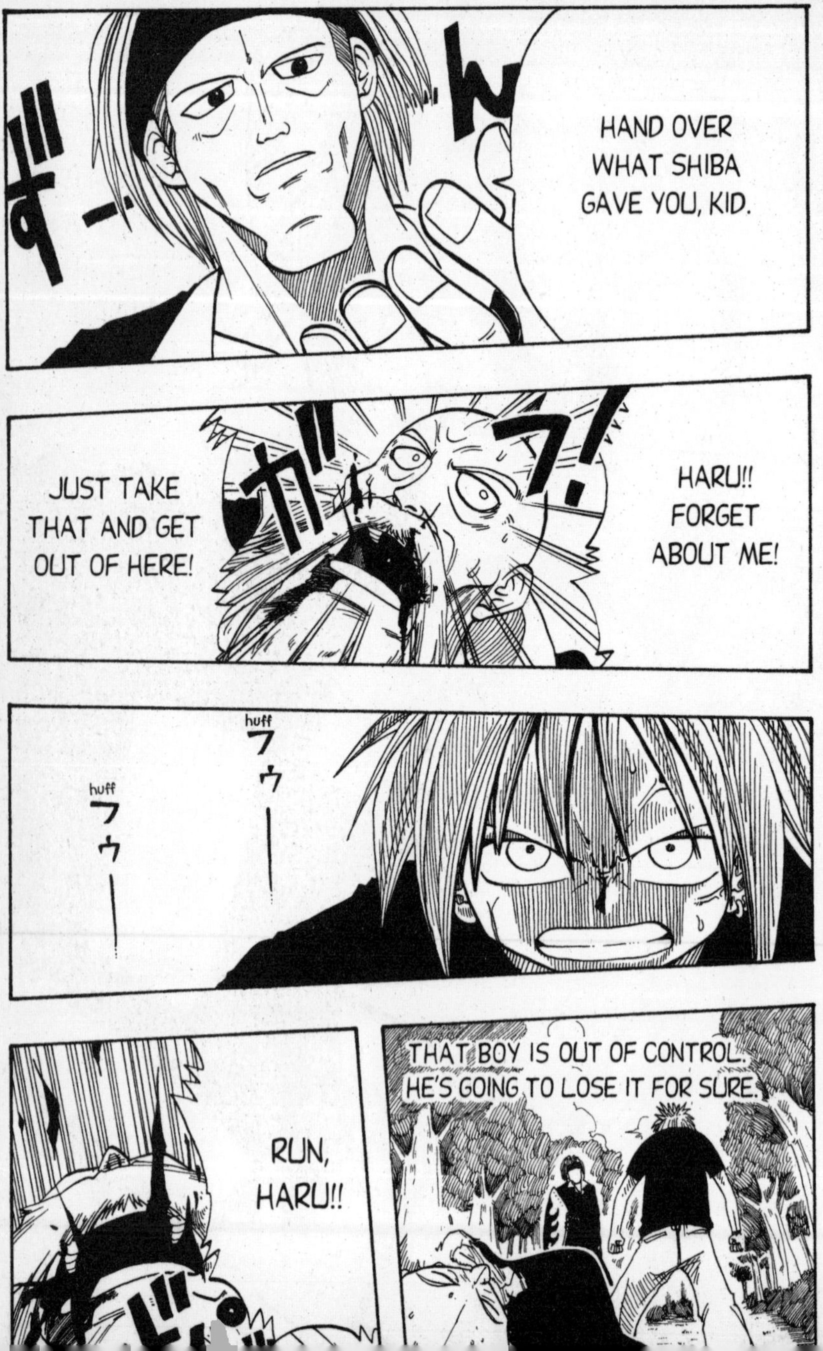
HAND OVER WHAT SHIBA GAVE YOU, KID.
HARU!! FORGET ABOUT ME!
JUST TAKE THAT AND GET OUT OF HERE!
huff
huff
THAT BOY IS OUT OF CONTROL. HE'S GOING TO LOSE IT FOR SURE.
RUN, HARU!!

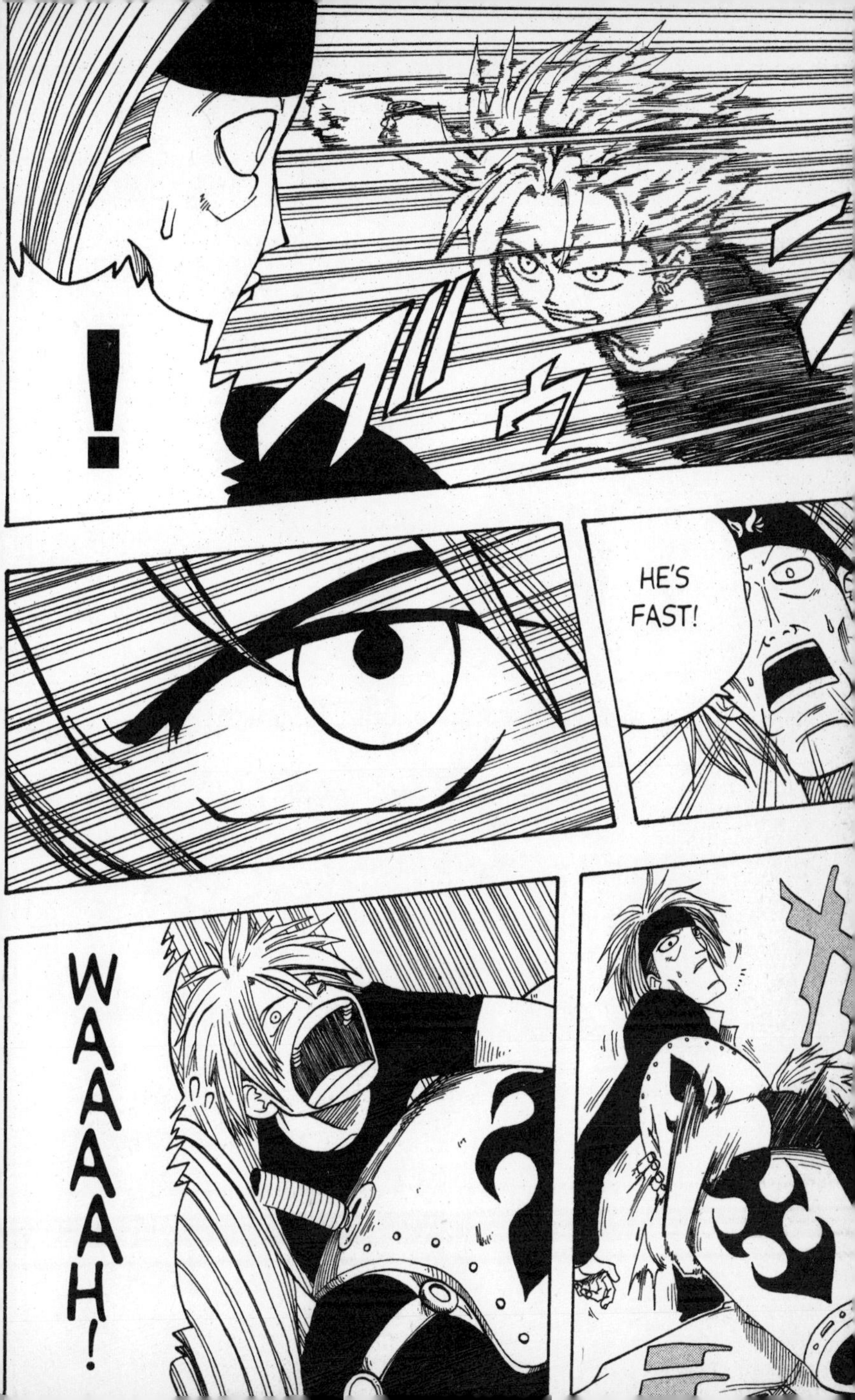
!
HE'S
FAST!
WAAAAAH!

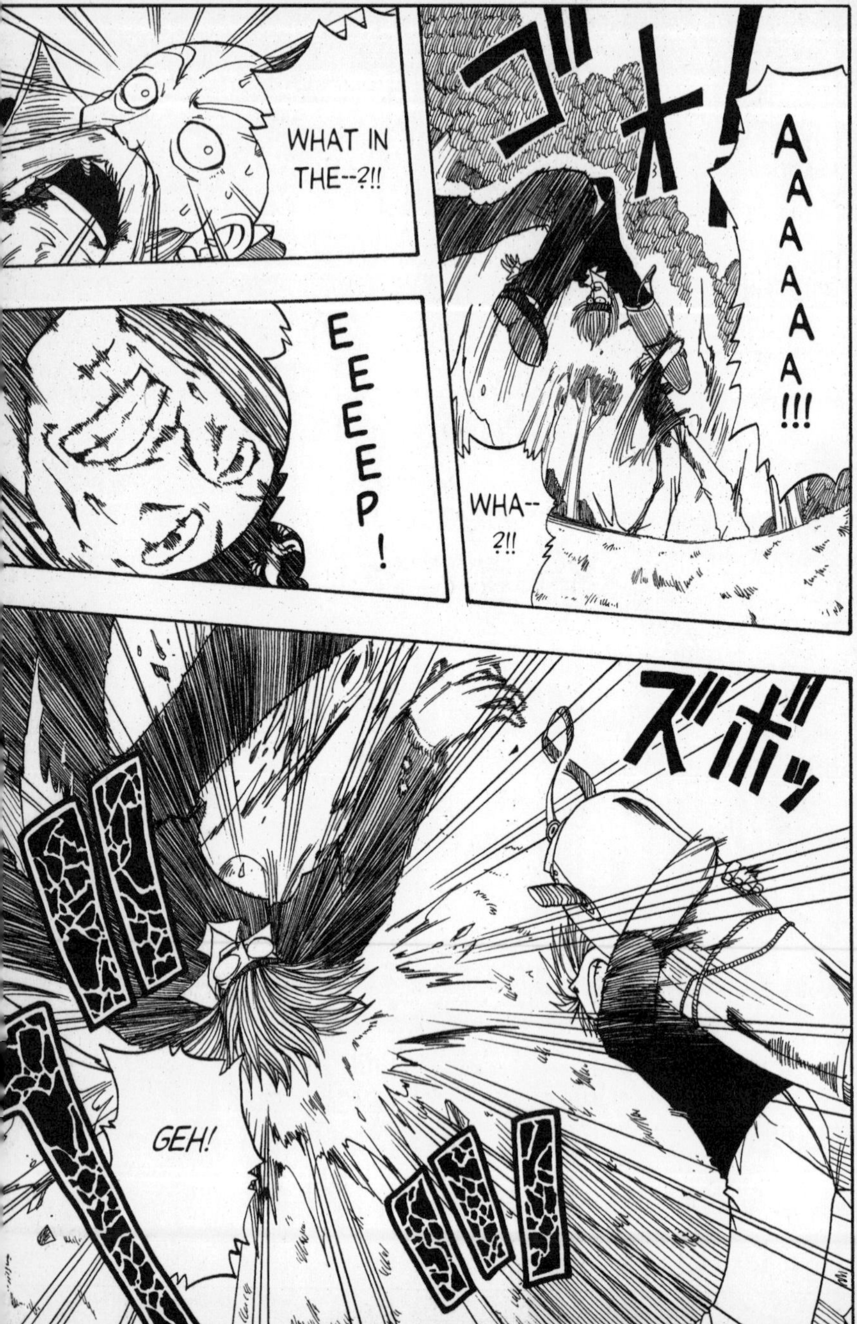
ゴオ!
AAAAAAA!!!
WHA--?!!
WHAT IN THE--?!!
EEEEP!
ズボッ
GEH!

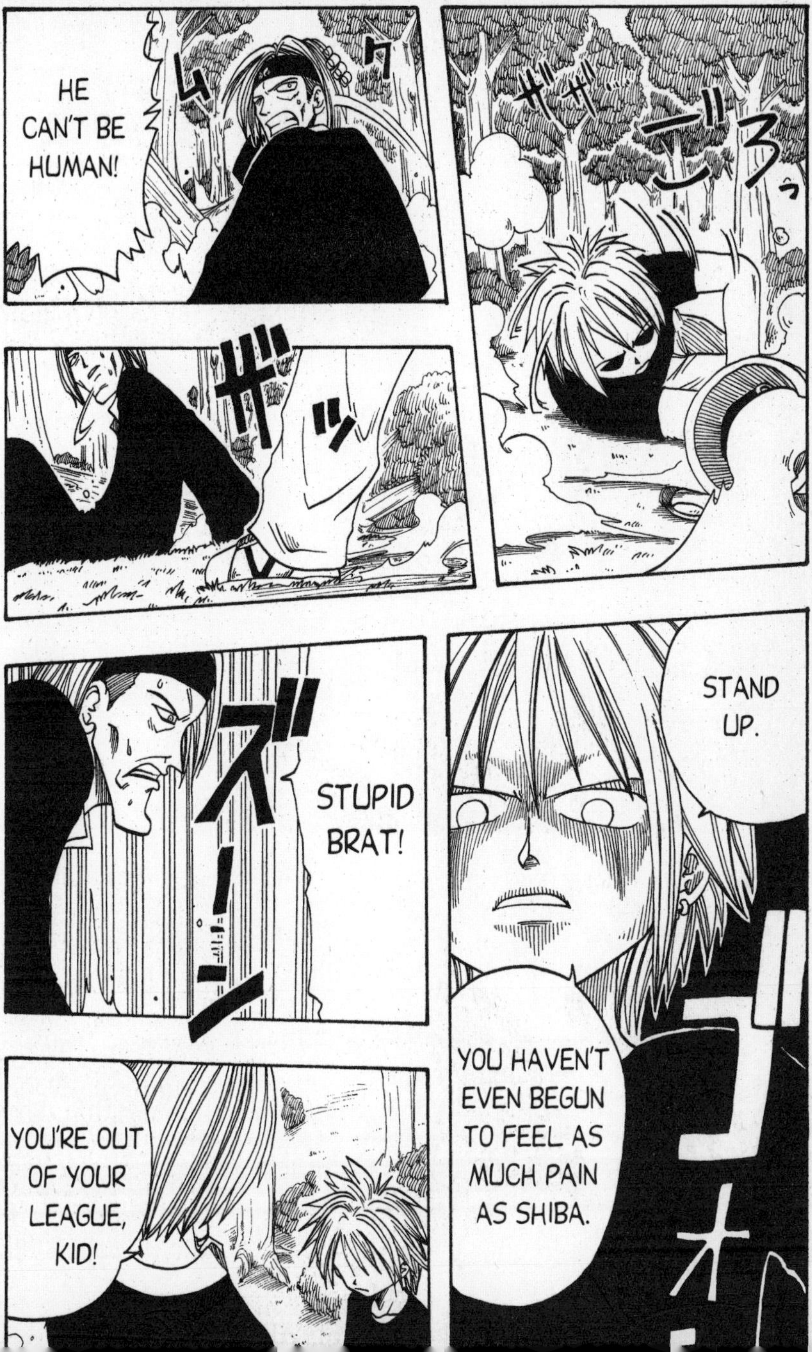
ザザ
ごろっ
HE CAN'T BE HUMAN!
ムク
ザッ
STAND UP.
YOU HAVEN'T EVEN BEGUN TO FEEL AS MUCH PAIN AS SHIBA.
ズ
STUPID BRAT!
YOU'RE OUT OF YOUR LEAGUE, KID!

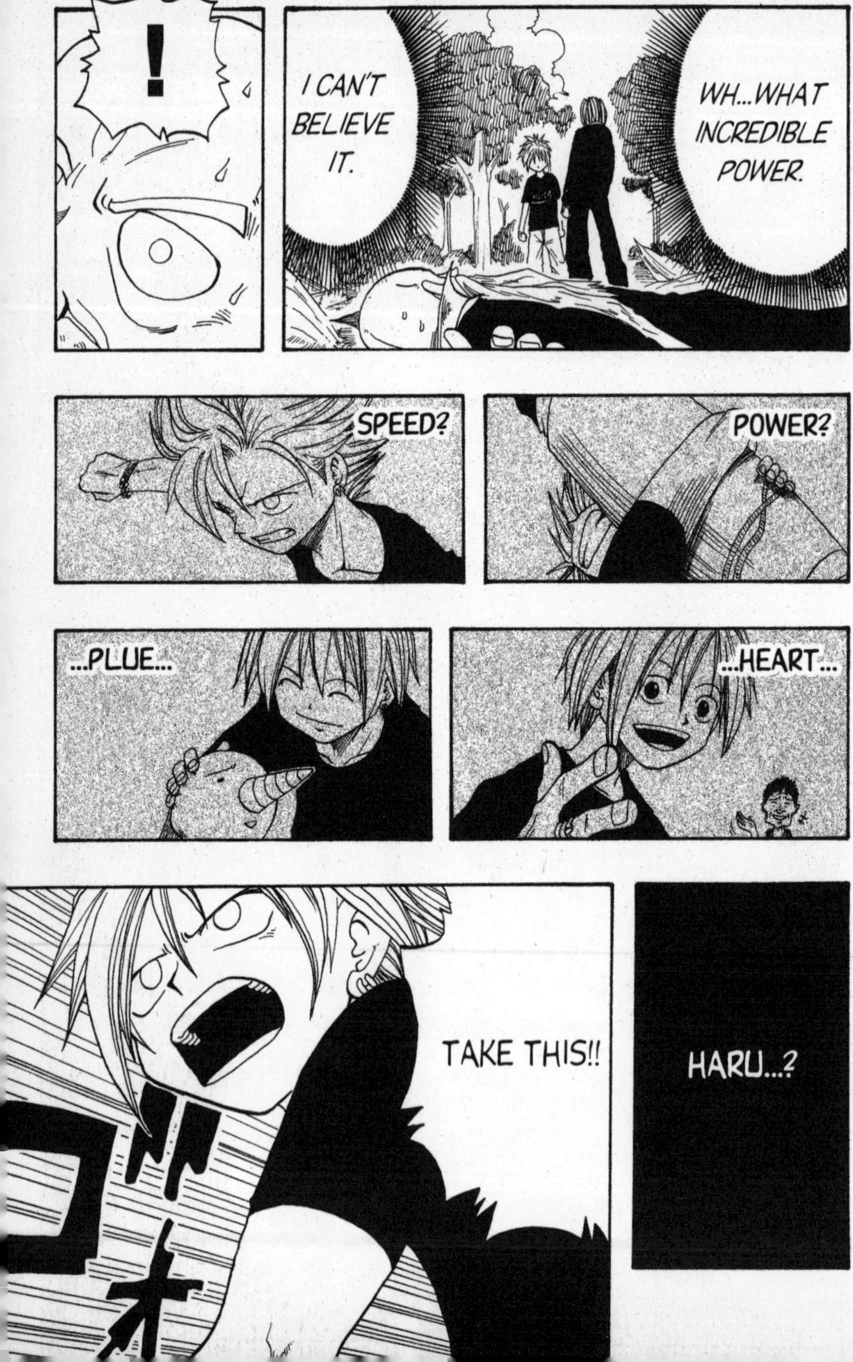
WH...WHAT INCREDIBLE POWER.
I CAN'T BELIEVE IT.
!
POWER?
SPEED?
...HEART...
...PLUE...
HARU...?
TAKE THIS!!

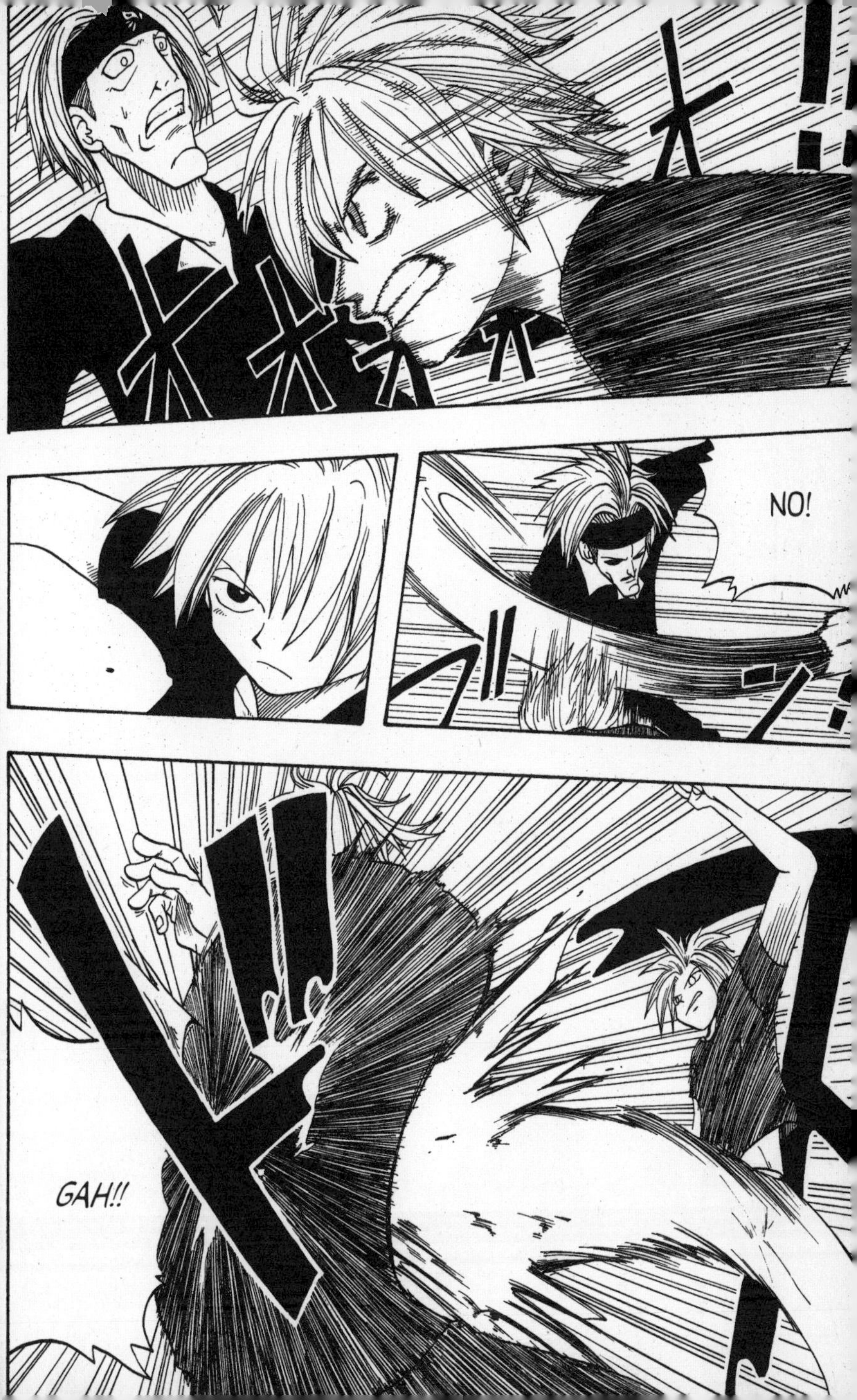
NO!
GAH!!

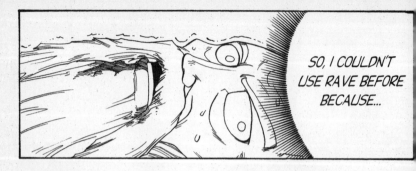

SO, I COULDN'T USE RAVE BEFORE BECAUSE...

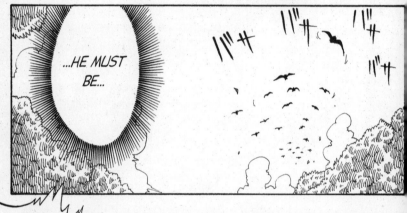

...HE MUST BE...

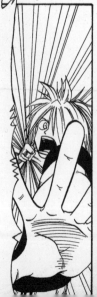

WAAAH!!!

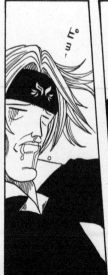

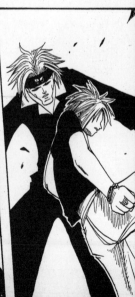

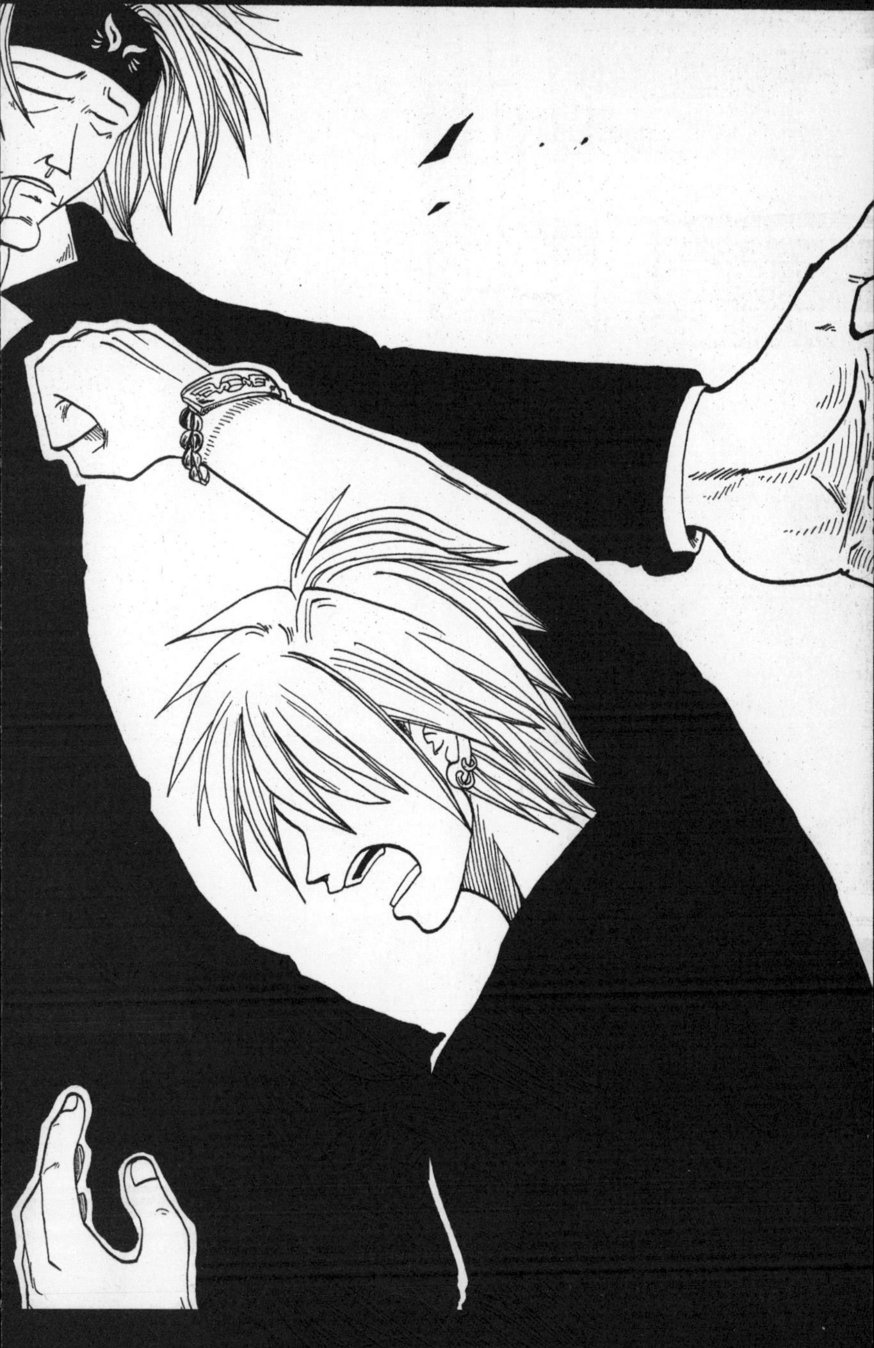

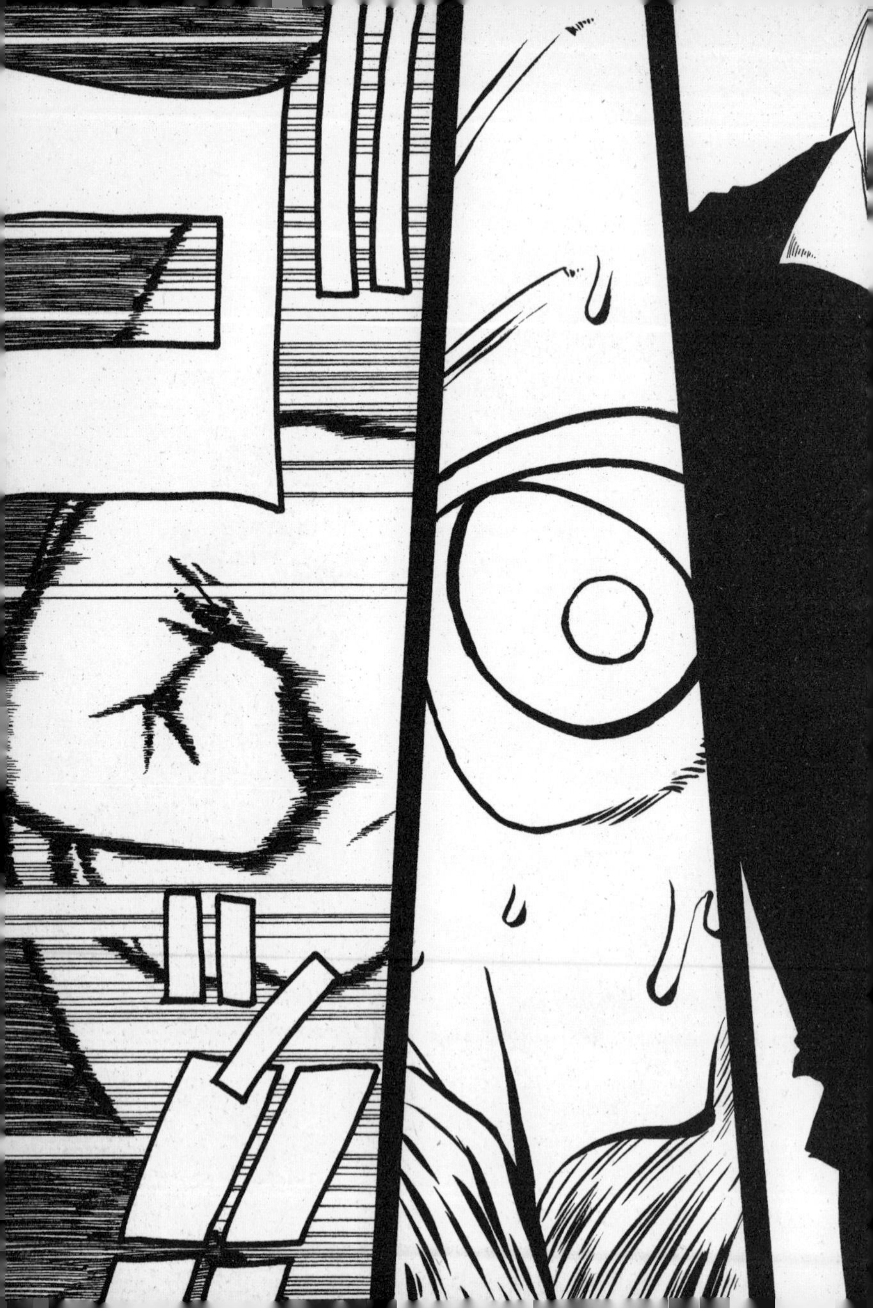

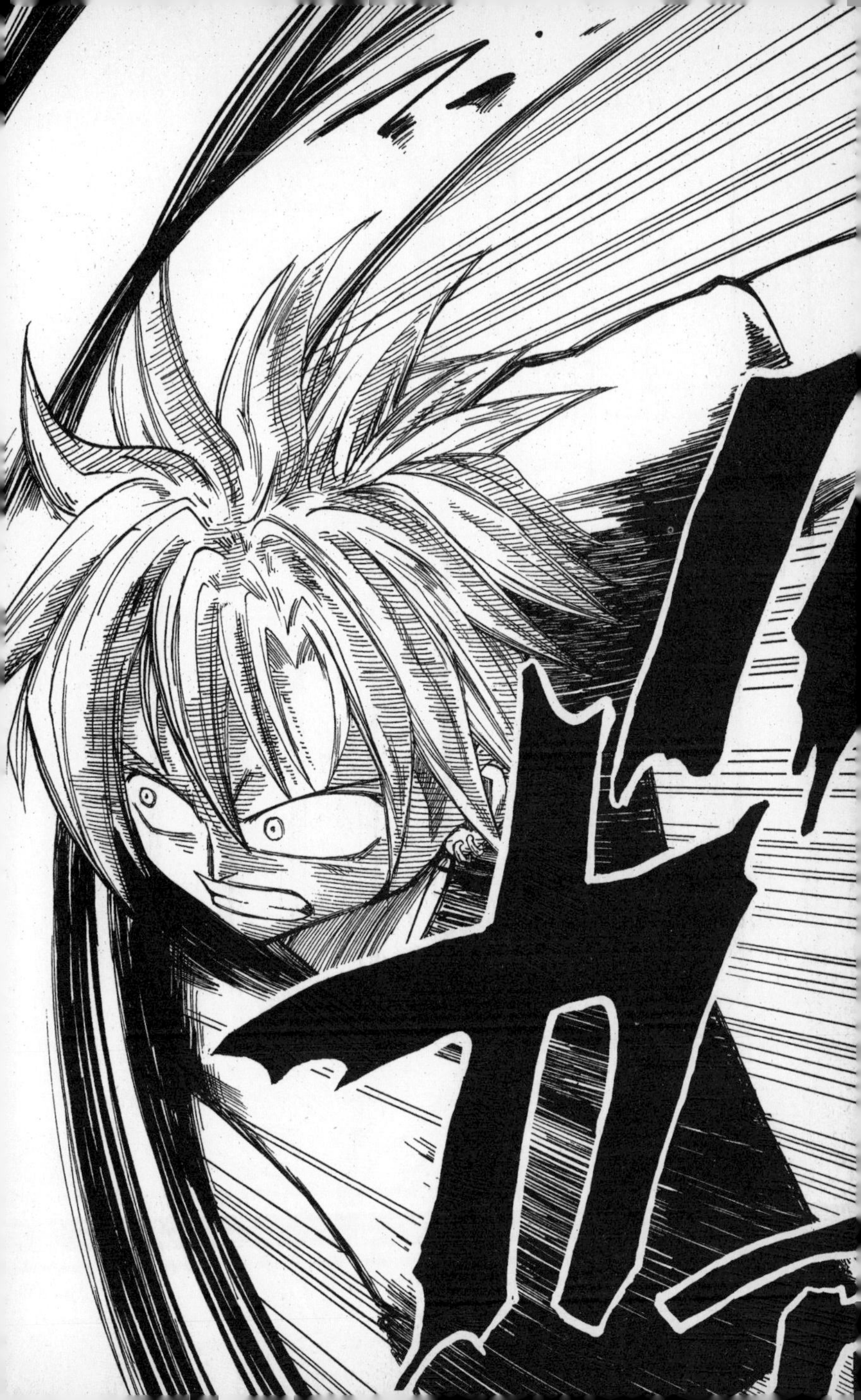

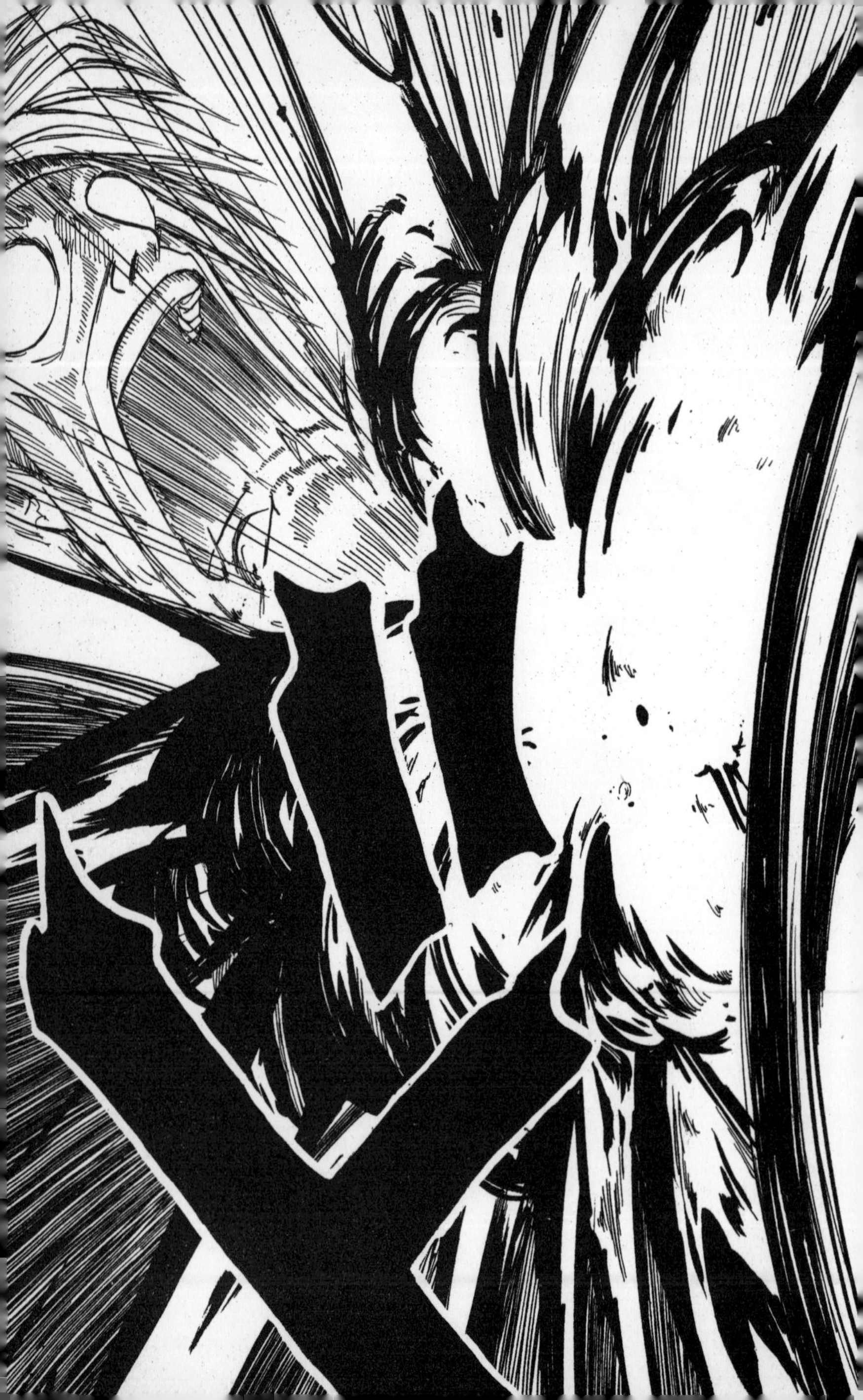

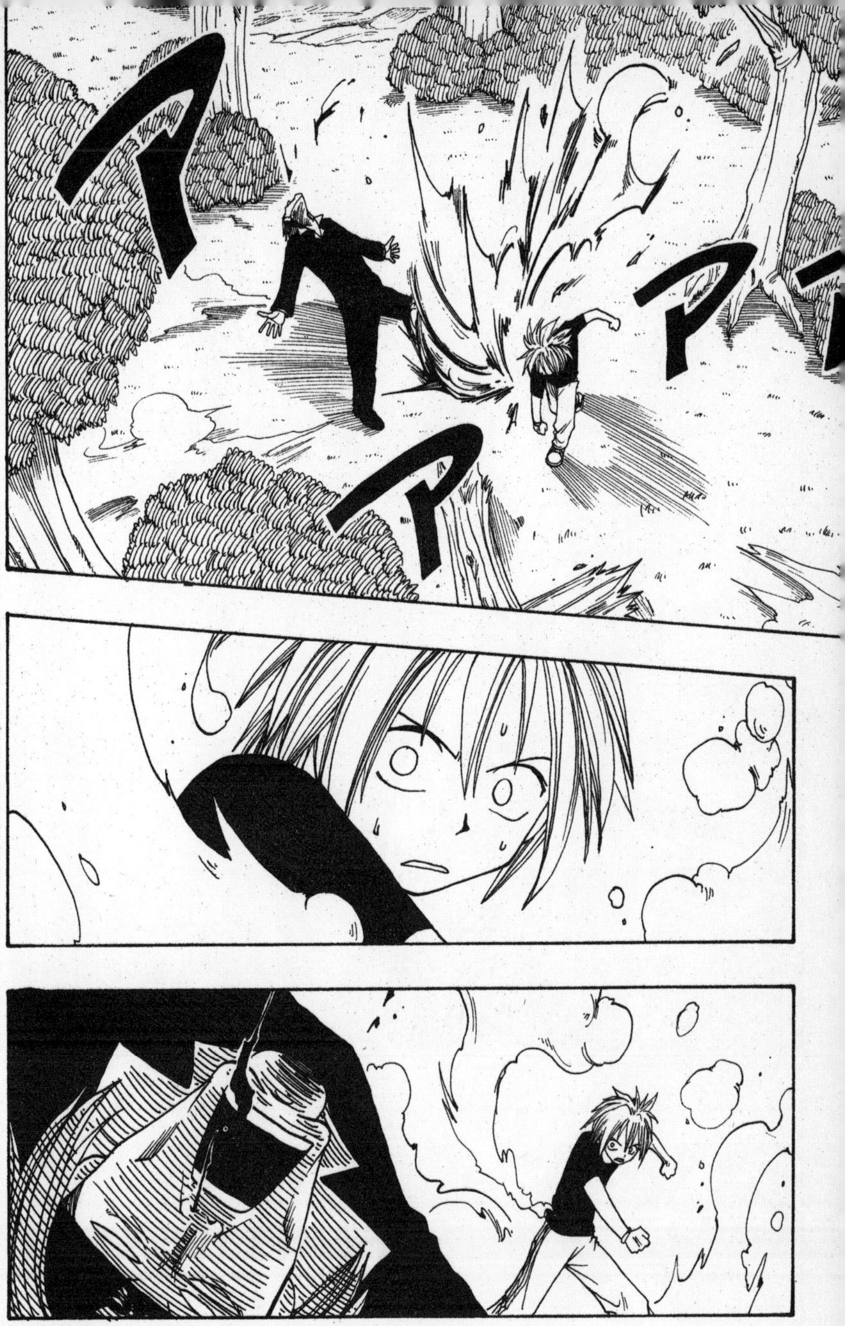

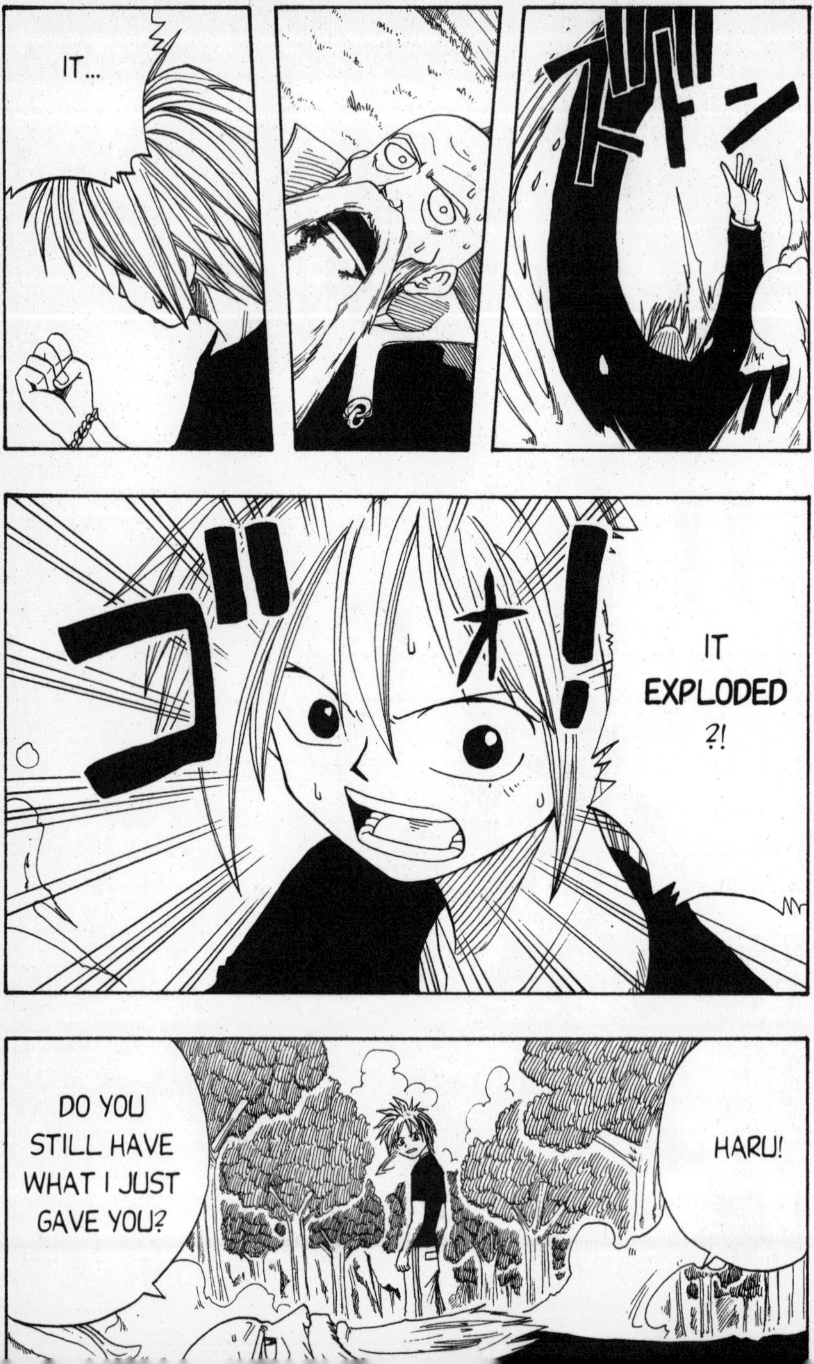
ズドン
IT...
IT EXPLODED ?!
ゴオ!
HARU!
DO YOU STILL HAVE WHAT I JUST GAVE YOU?

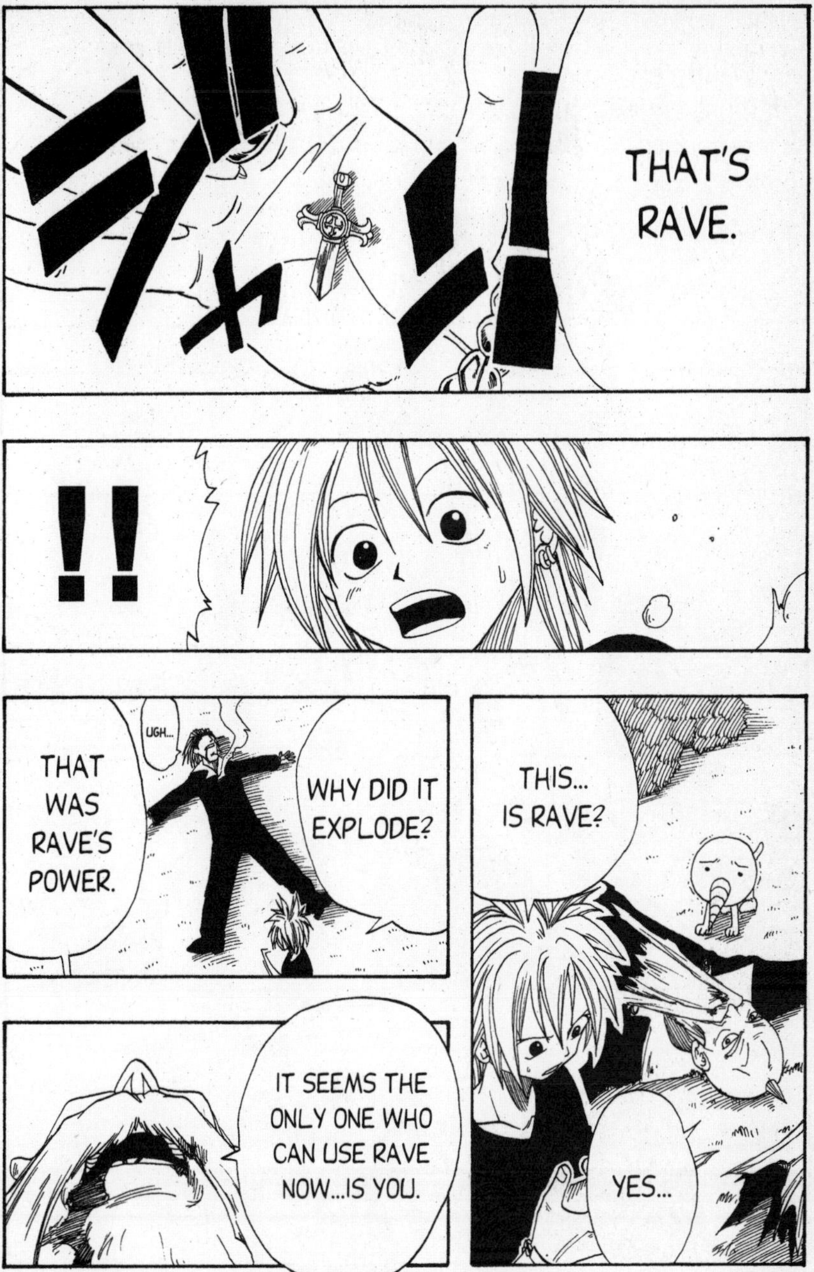
THAT'S RAVE.
!!
THIS... IS RAVE?
YES...
WHY DID IT EXPLODE?
UGH...
THAT WAS RAVE'S POWER.
IT SEEMS THE ONLY ONE WHO CAN USE RAVE NOW...IS YOU.

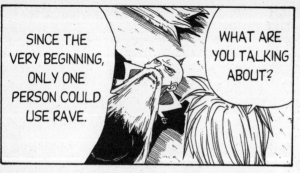

SINCE THE VERY BEGINNING, ONLY ONE PERSON COULD USE RAVE.

WHAT ARE YOU TALKING ABOUT?

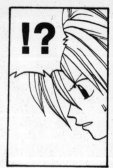

!?

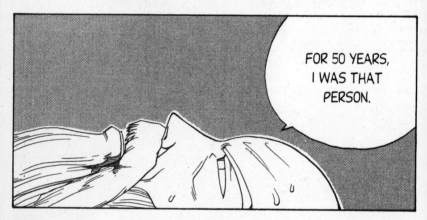

FOR 50 YEARS, I WAS THAT PERSON.

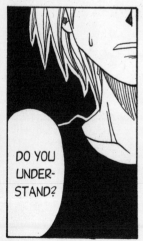

DO YOU UNDER-STAND?

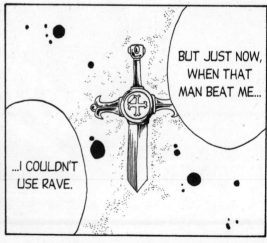

BUT JUST NOW, WHEN THAT MAN BEAT ME...

...I COULDN'T USE RAVE.

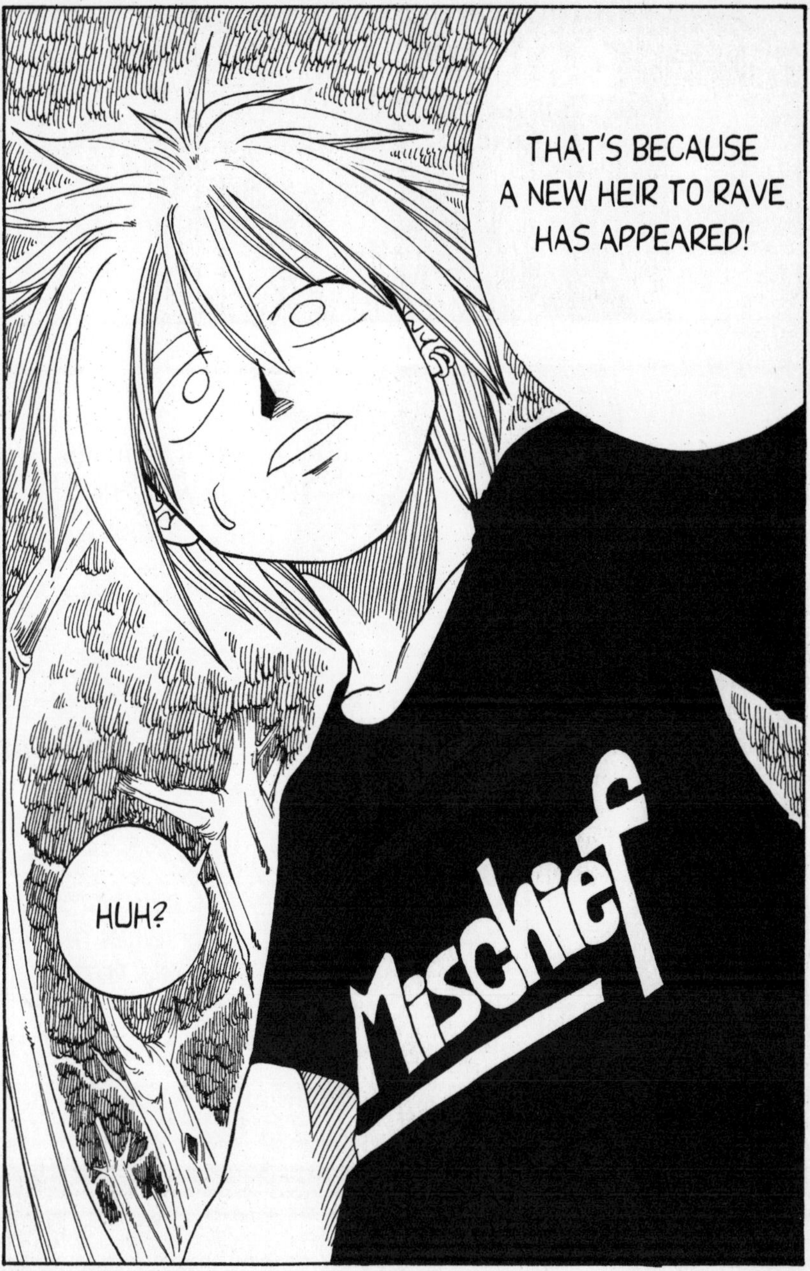
THAT'S BECAUSE A NEW HEIR TO RAVE HAS APPEARED!
HUH?
Mischief

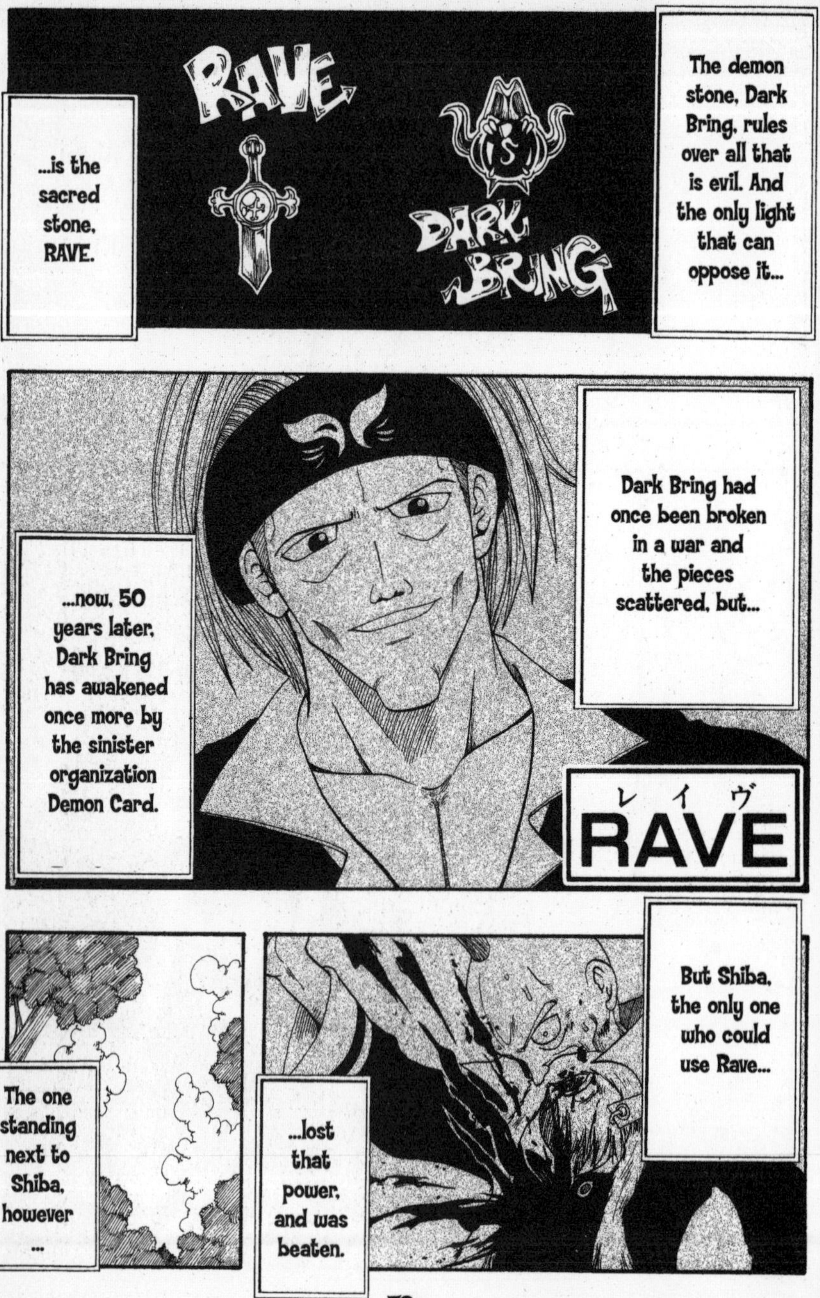
The demon stone, Dark Bring, rules over all that is evil. And the only light that can oppose it...
RAVE
DARK BRING
...is the sacred stone, RAVE.
Dark Bring had once been broken in a war and the pieces scattered, but...
レイヴ
RAVE
...now, 50 years later, Dark Bring has awakened once more by the sinister organization Demon Card.
But Shiba, the only one who could use Rave...
...lost that power, and was beaten.
The one standing next to Shiba, however ...

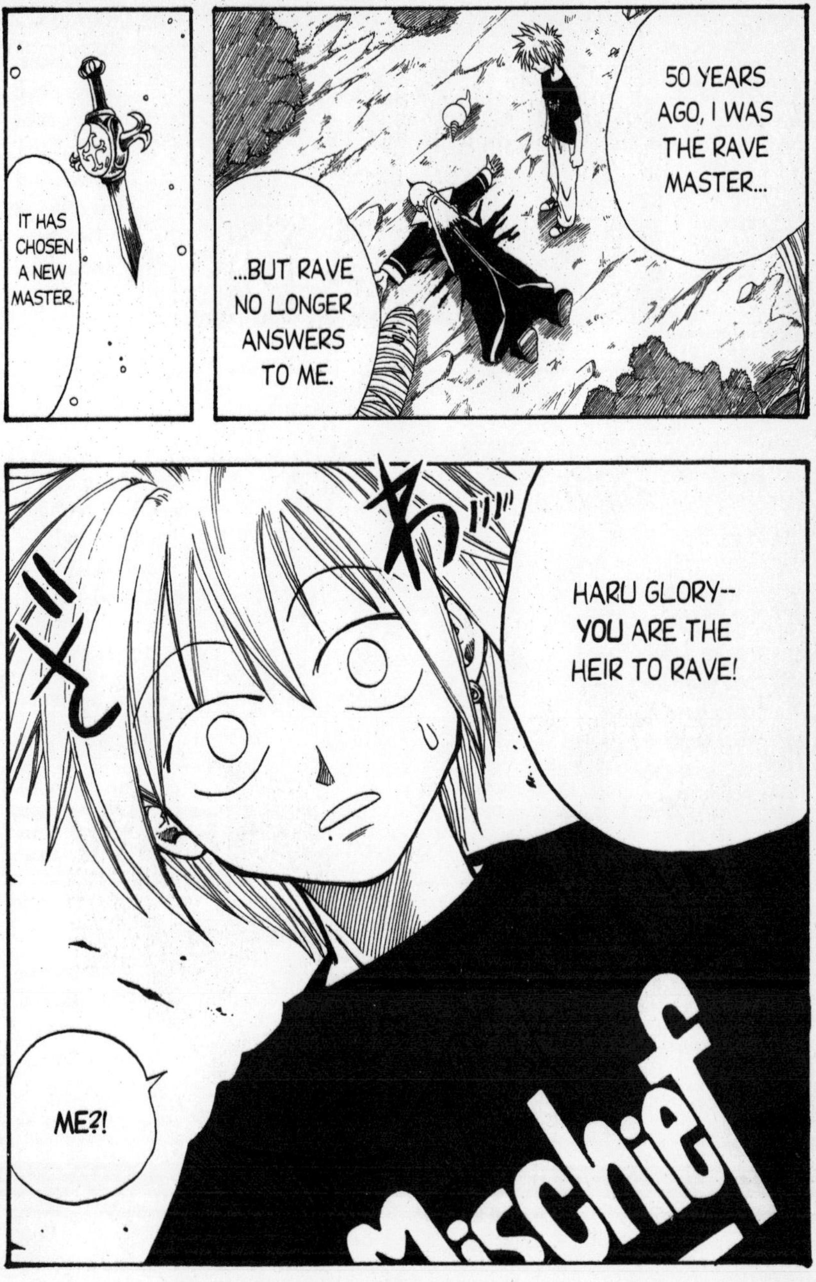
50 YEARS AGO, I WAS THE RAVE MASTER...
...BUT RAVE NO LONGER ANSWERS TO ME.
IT HAS CHOSEN A NEW MASTER.
HARU GLORY-- YOU ARE THE HEIR TO RAVE!
ME?!
Mischief

RAVE MASTER

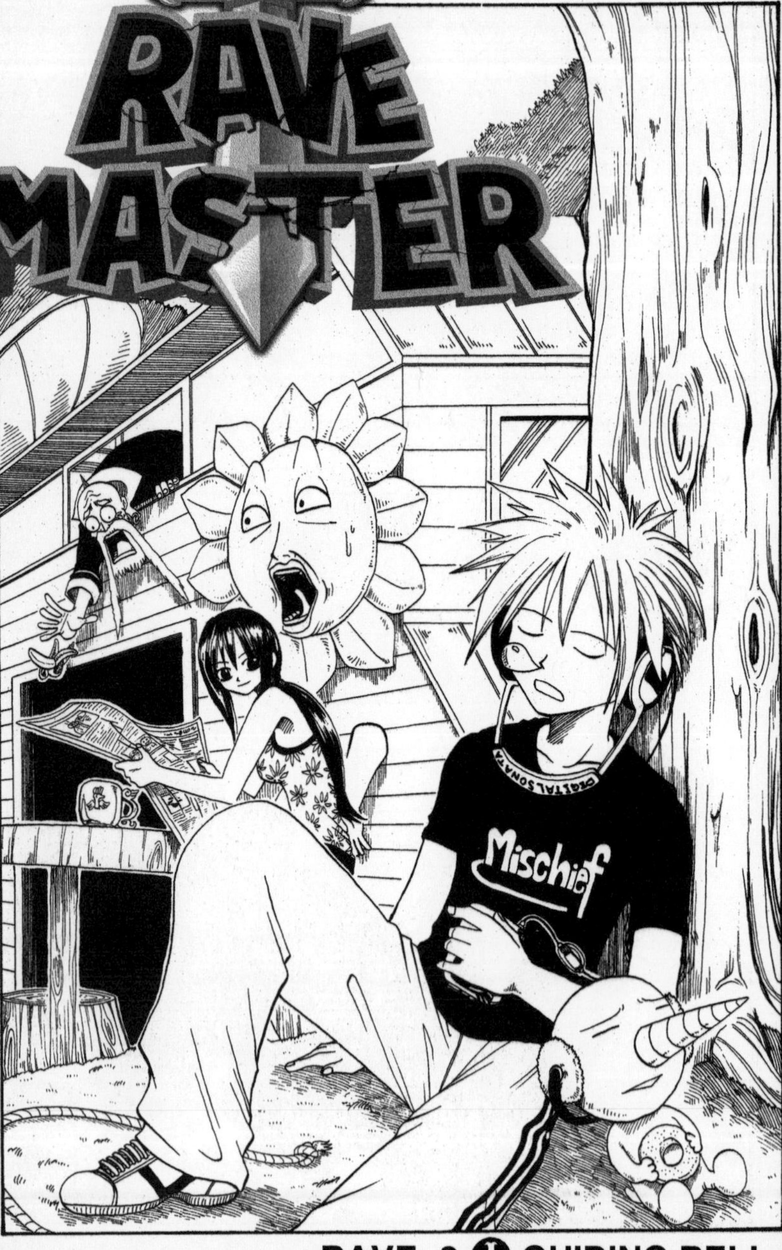
Mischief

RAVE: 2 ✠ GUIDING BELL

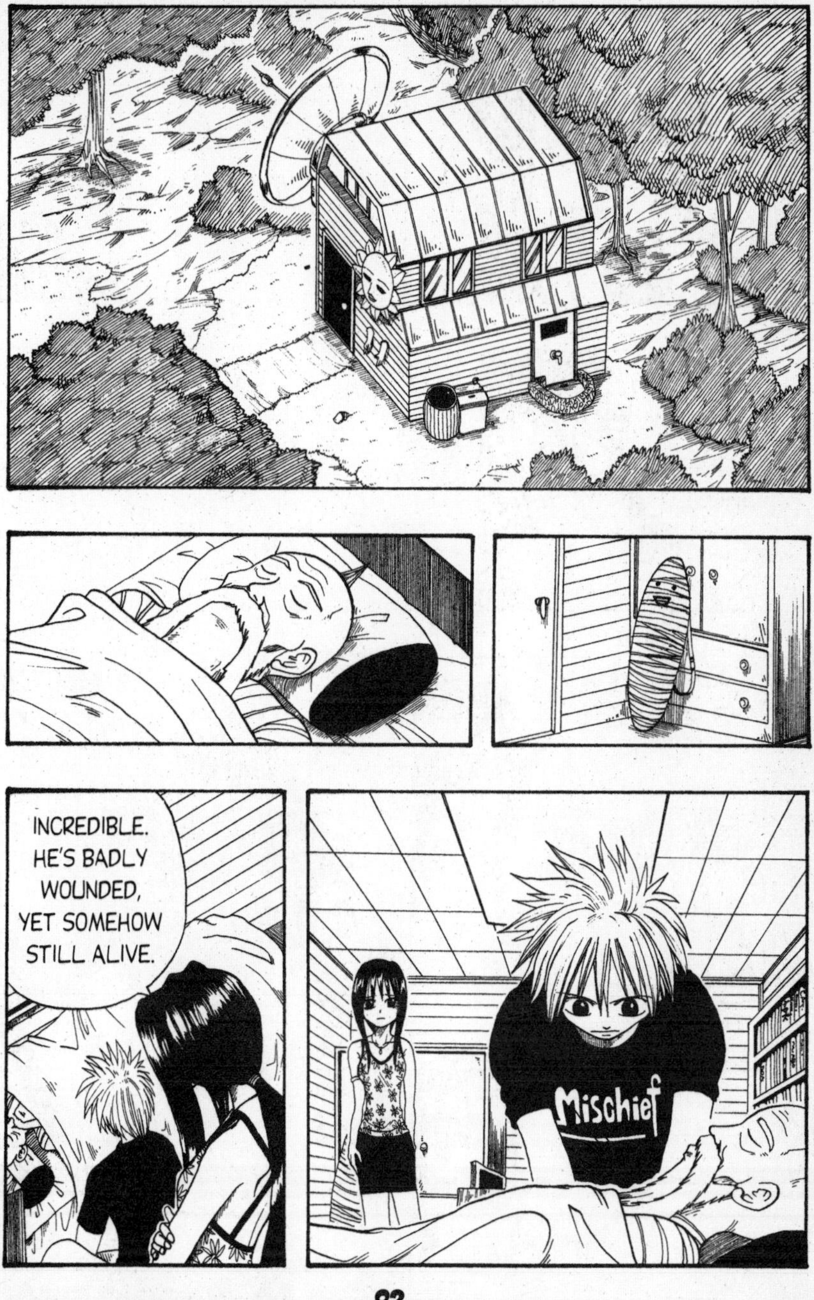
Mischief
INCREDIBLE. HE'S BADLY WOUNDED, YET SOMEHOW STILL ALIVE.

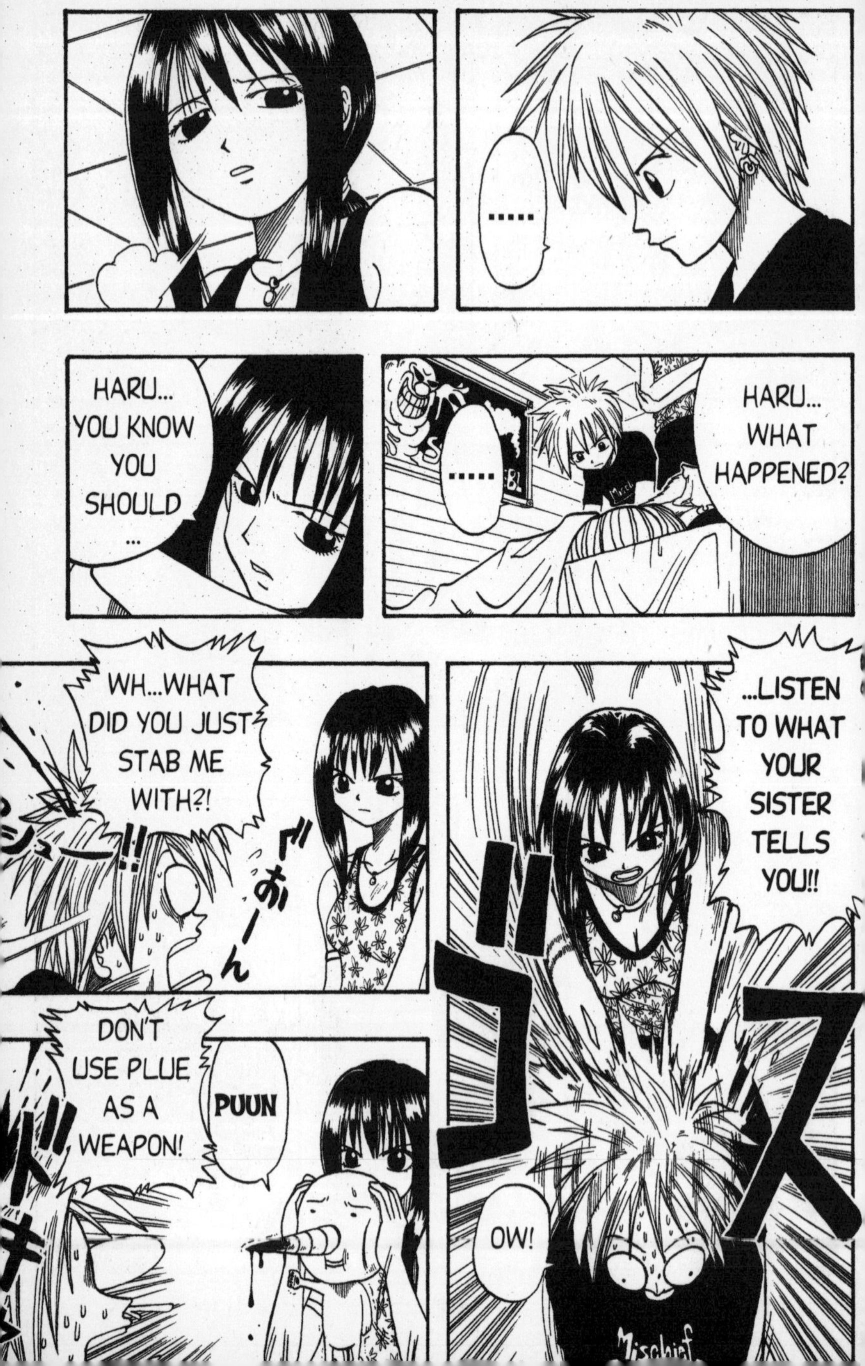
.....
HARU... WHAT HAPPENED?
.....
HARU... YOU KNOW YOU SHOULD ...
...LISTEN TO WHAT YOUR SISTER TELLS YOU!!
OW!
WH...WHAT DID YOU JUST STAB ME WITH?!
DON'T USE PLUE AS A WEAPON!
PUUN

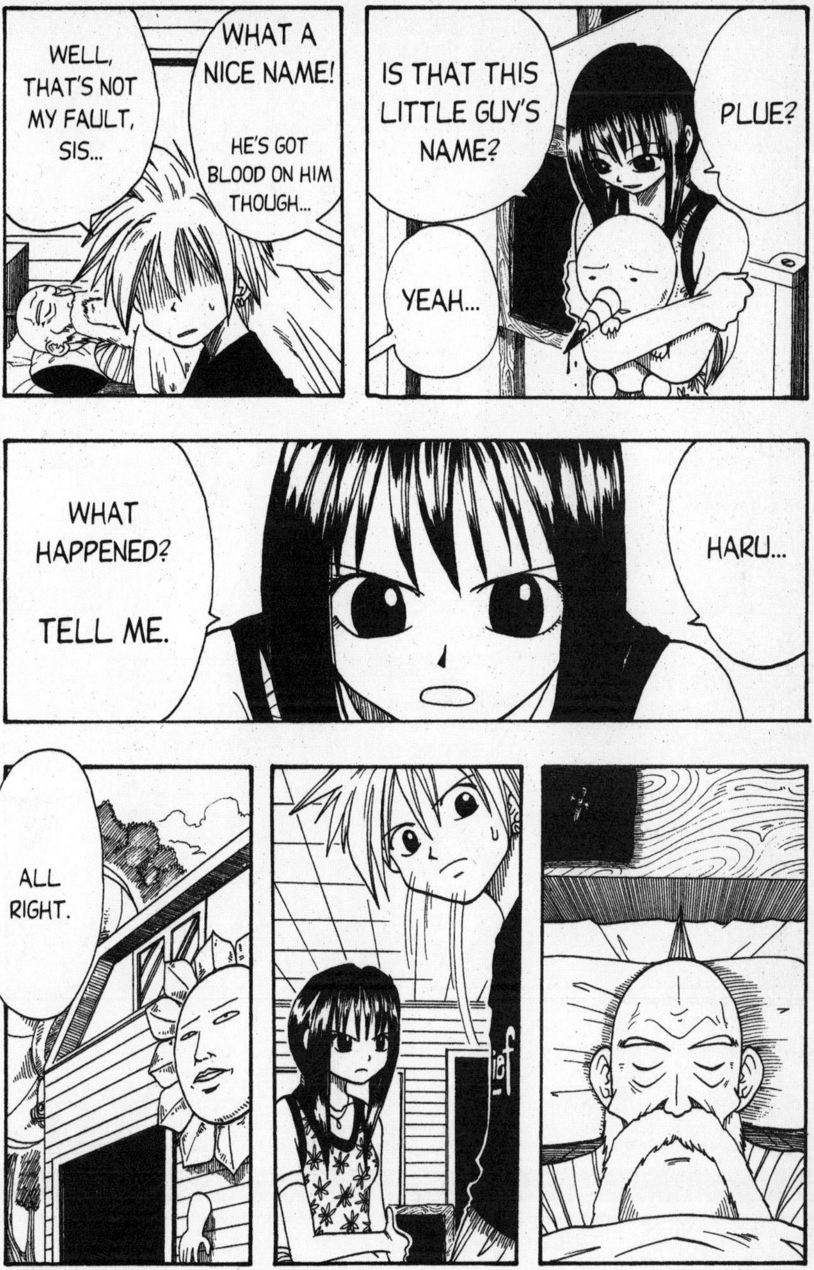
PLUE?
IS THAT THIS LITTLE GUY'S NAME?
YEAH...
WHAT A NICE NAME!
HE'S GOT BLOOD ON HIM THOUGH...
WELL, THAT'S NOT MY FAULT, SIS...
HARU...
WHAT HAPPENED?
TELL ME.
ALL RIGHT.

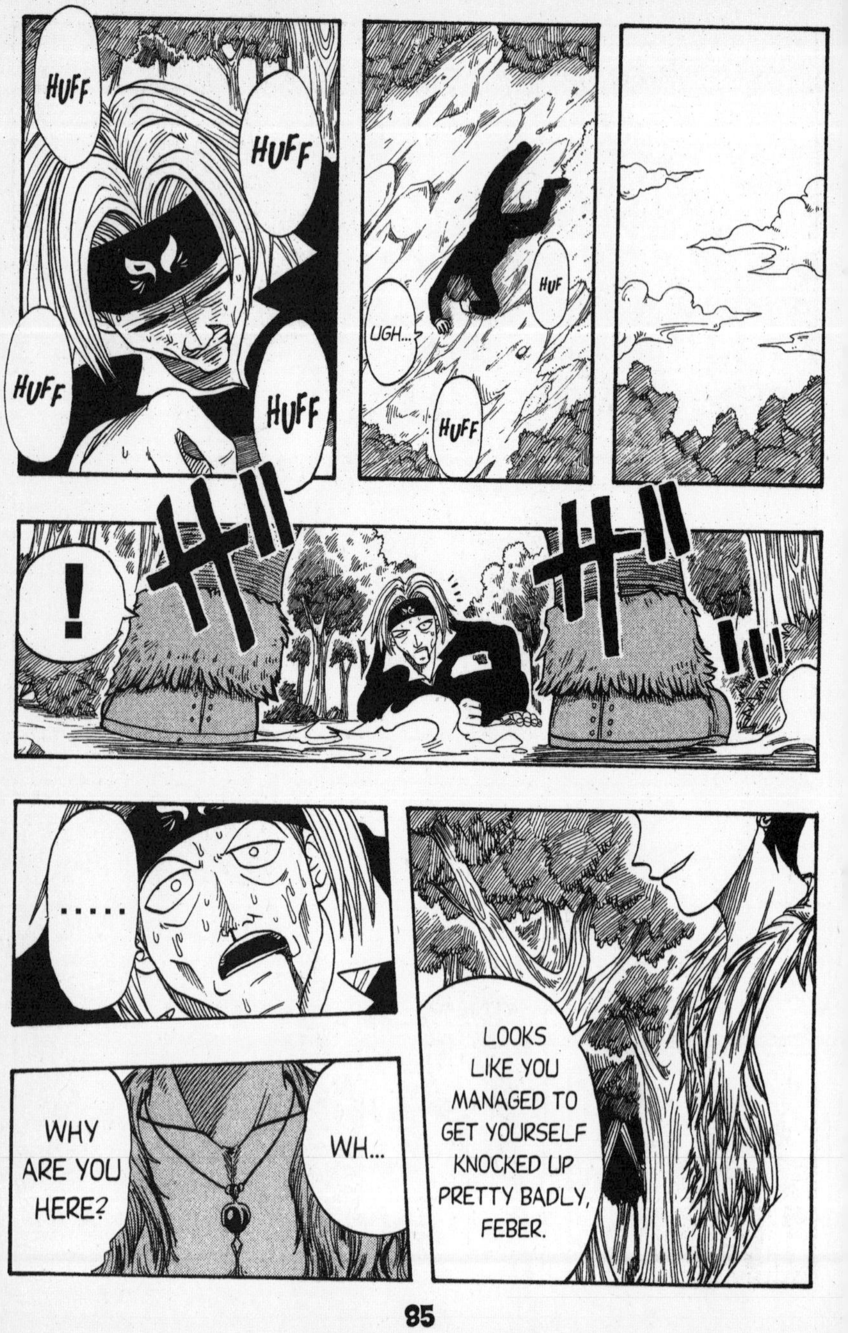
HUF
UGH...
HUFF
HUFF
HUFF
HUFF
HUFF
!
LOOKS LIKE YOU MANAGED TO GET YOURSELF KNOCKED UP PRETTY BADLY, FEBER.
.....
WH...
WHY ARE YOU HERE?

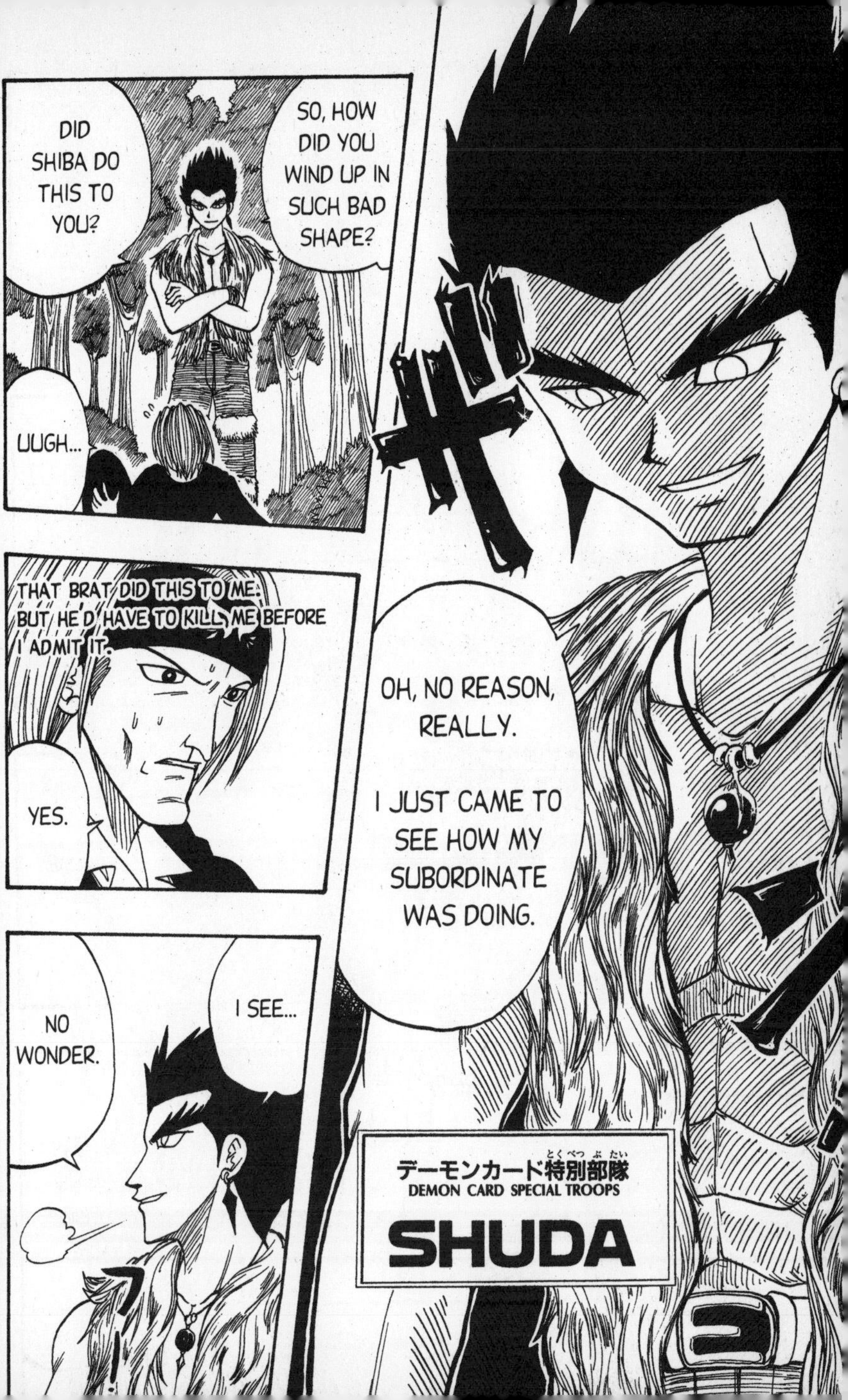
OH, NO REASON, REALLY.
I JUST CAME TO SEE HOW MY SUBORDINATE WAS DOING.
デーモンカード特別部隊
DEMON CARD SPECIAL TROOPS
SHUDA
SO, HOW DID YOU WIND UP IN SUCH BAD SHAPE?
DID SHIBA DO THIS TO YOU?
UUGH...
THAT BRAT DID THIS TO ME. BUT HE'D HAVE TO KILL ME BEFORE I ADMIT IT.
YES.
I SEE...
NO WONDER.

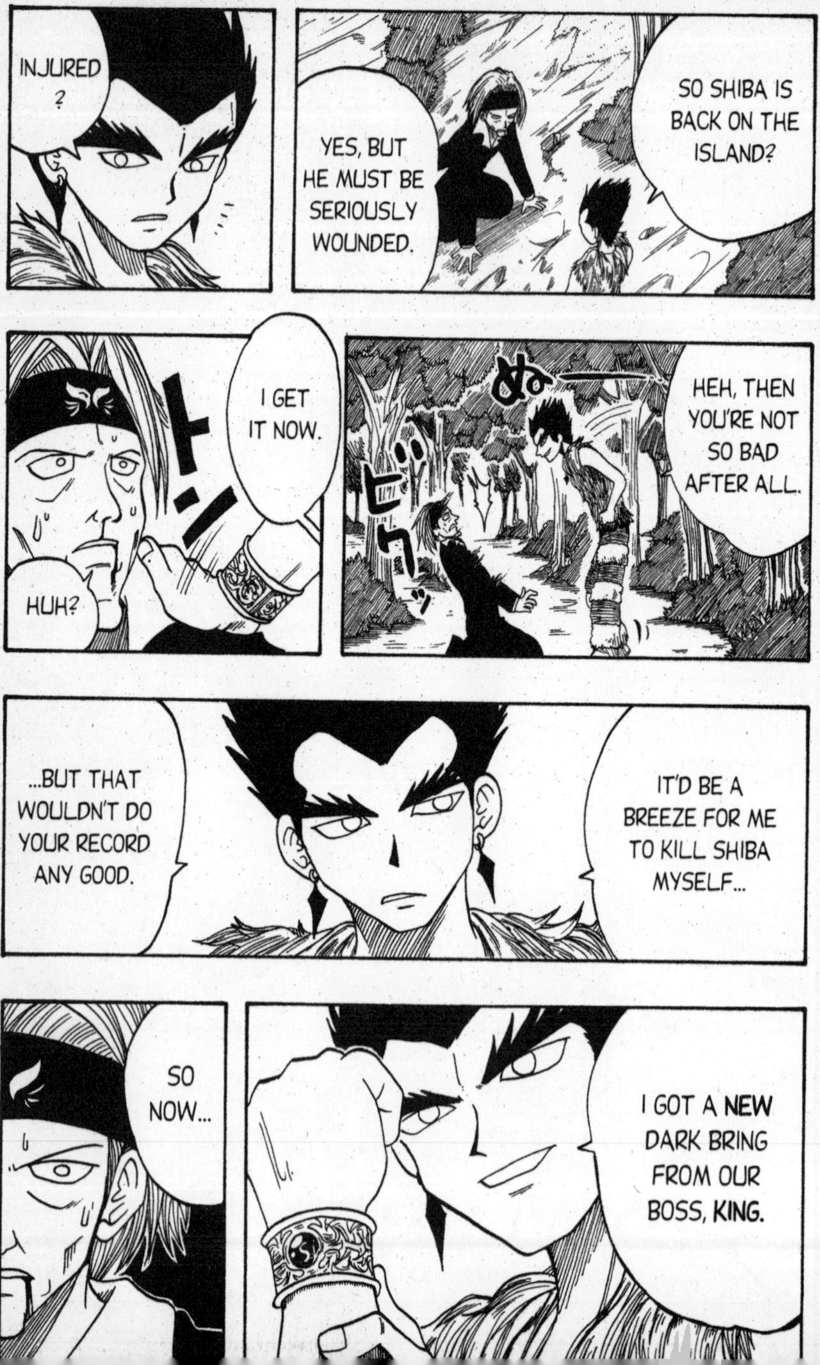
SO SHIBA IS BACK ON THE ISLAND?
YES, BUT HE MUST BE SERIOUSLY WOUNDED.
INJURED?
ぬ
HEH, THEN YOU'RE NOT SO BAD AFTER ALL.
I GET IT NOW.
HUH?
IT'D BE A BREEZE FOR ME TO KILL SHIBA MYSELF...
...BUT THAT WOULDN'T DO YOUR RECORD ANY GOOD.
I GOT A **NEW DARK BRING** FROM OUR BOSS, **KING**.
SO NOW...

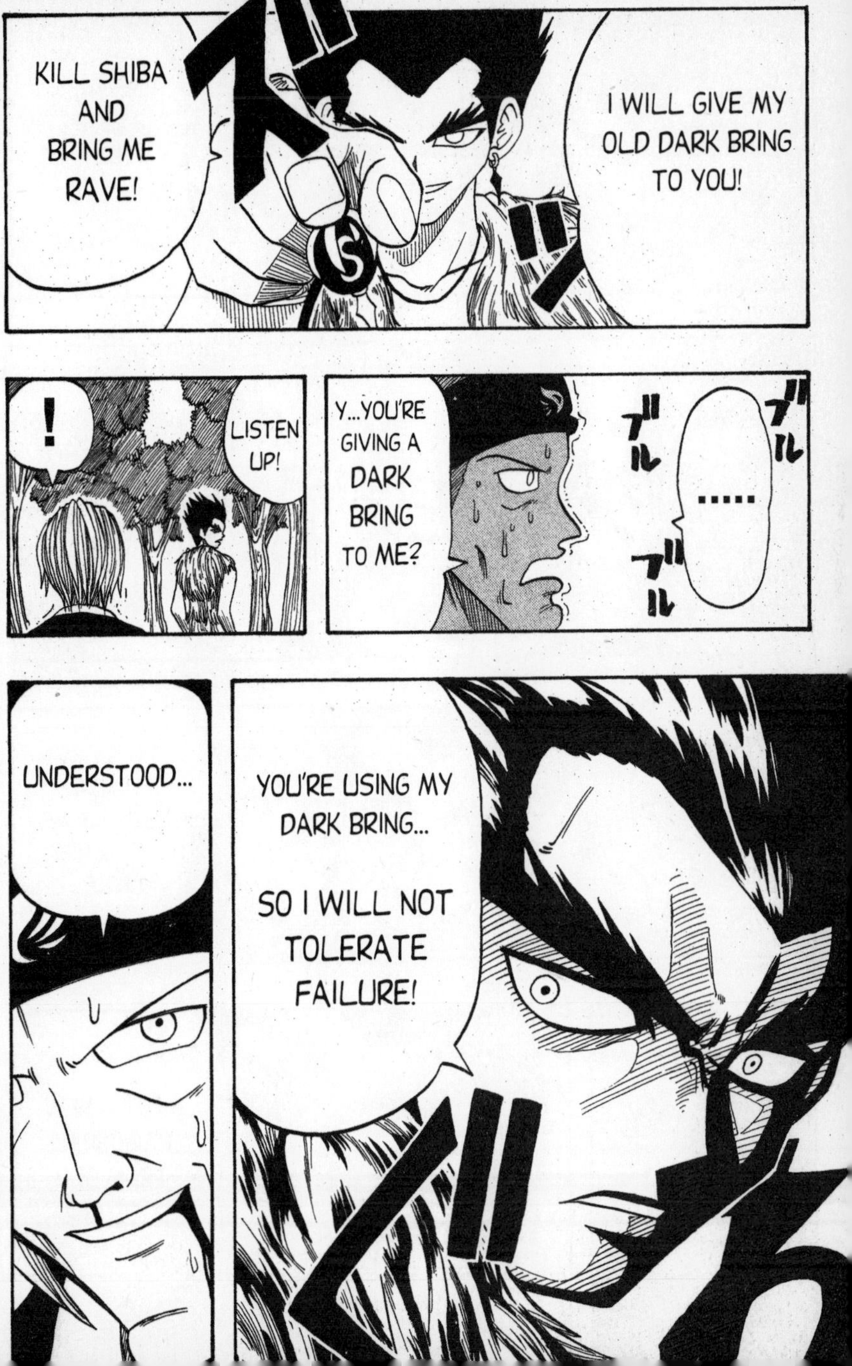
I WILL GIVE MY OLD DARK BRING TO YOU!
KILL SHIBA AND BRING ME RAVE!
ブル
ブル
.....
ブル
Y...YOU'RE GIVING A DARK BRING TO ME?
LISTEN UP!
!
YOU'RE USING MY DARK BRING...
SO I WILL NOT TOLERATE FAILURE!
UNDERSTOOD...

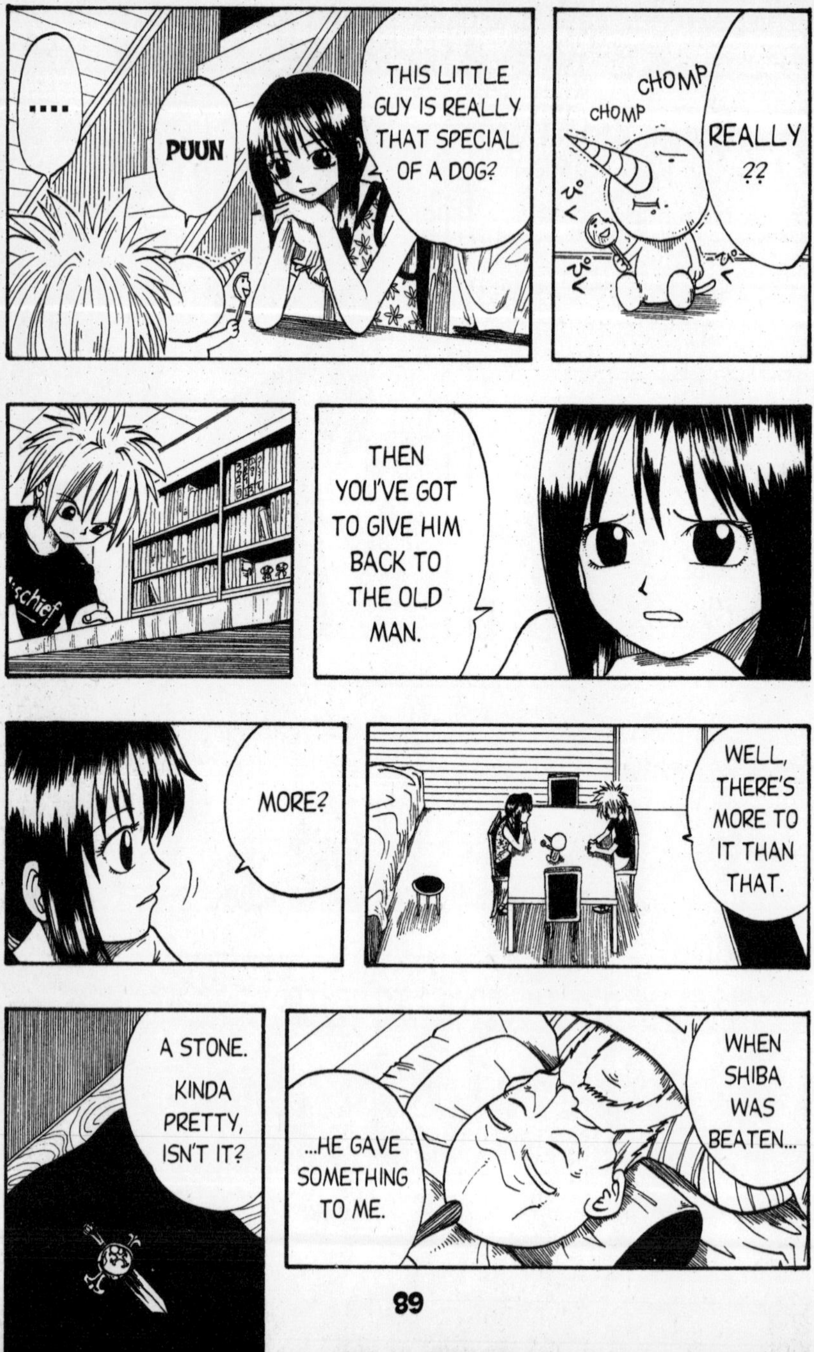
CHOMP
CHOMP
REALLY ??
THIS LITTLE GUY IS REALLY THAT SPECIAL OF A DOG?
PUUN
....
THEN YOU'VE GOT TO GIVE HIM BACK TO THE OLD MAN.
WELL, THERE'S MORE TO IT THAN THAT.
MORE?
WHEN SHIBA WAS BEATEN...
...HE GAVE SOMETHING TO ME.
A STONE.
KINDA PRETTY, ISN'T IT?

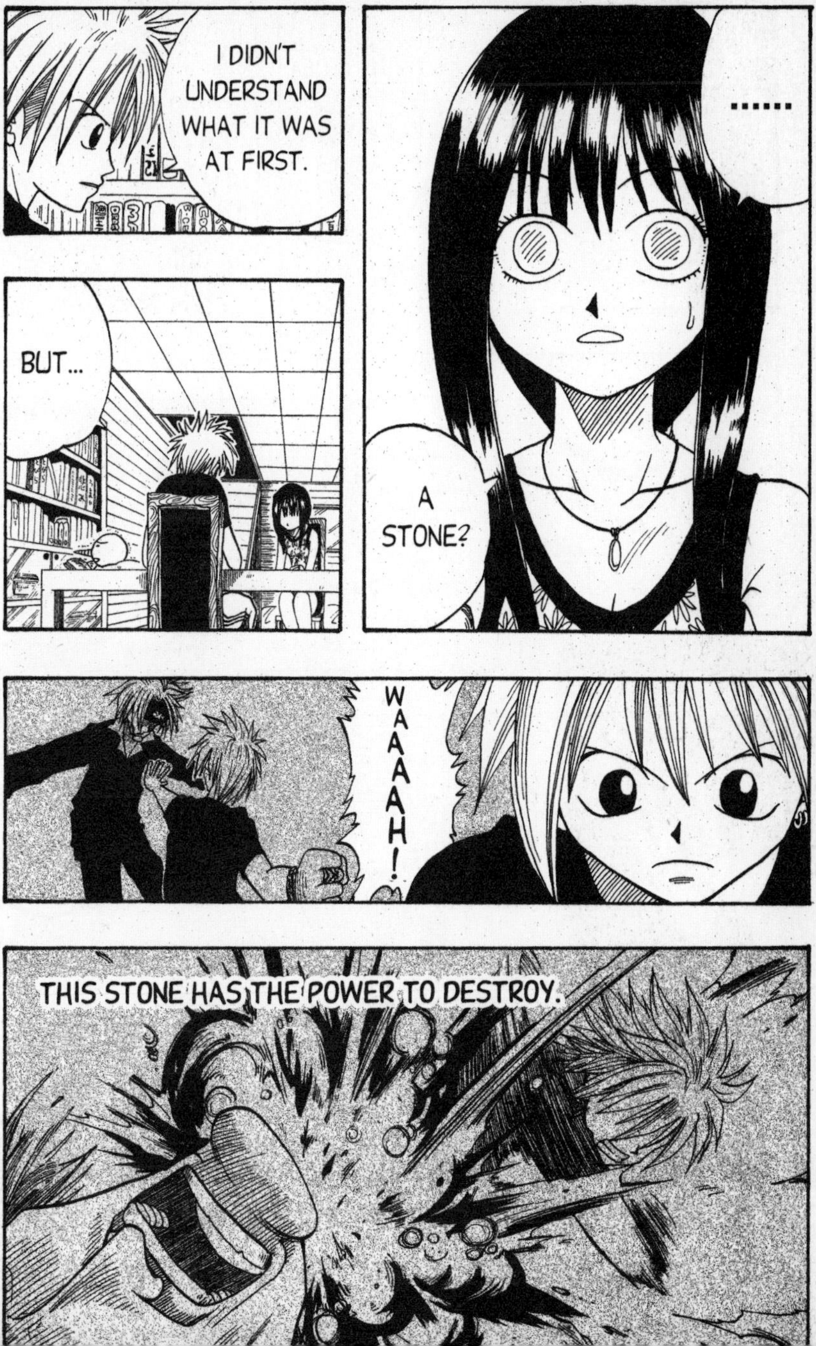
......
A STONE?
I DIDN'T UNDERSTAND WHAT IT WAS AT FIRST.
BUT...
WAAAAAH!
THIS STONE HAS THE POWER TO DESTROY.

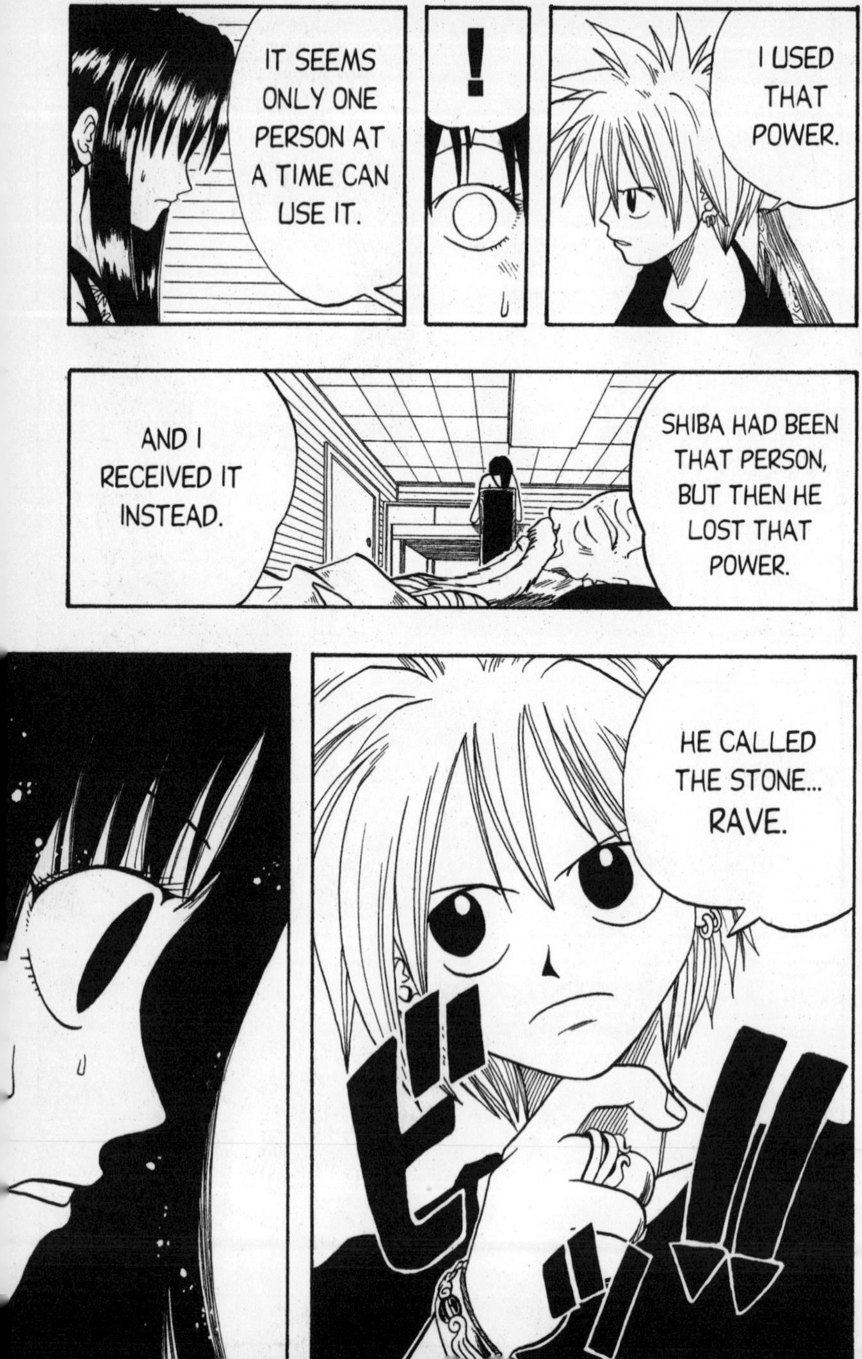
I USED THAT POWER.
!
IT SEEMS ONLY ONE PERSON AT A TIME CAN USE IT.
SHIBA HAD BEEN THAT PERSON, BUT THEN HE LOST THAT POWER.
AND I RECEIVED IT INSTEAD.
HE CALLED THE STONE... RAVE.

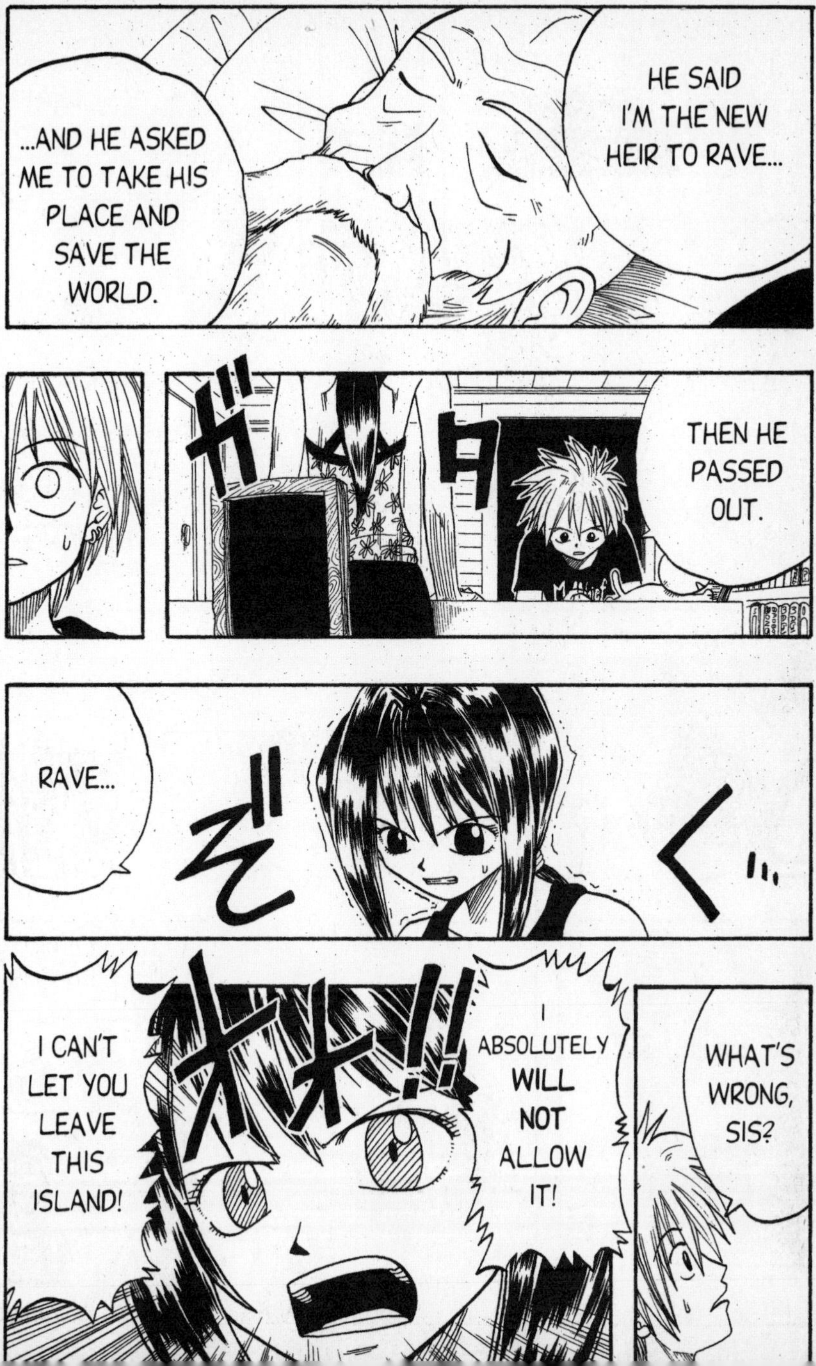
HE SAID I'M THE NEW HEIR TO RAVE...
...AND HE ASKED ME TO TAKE HIS PLACE AND SAVE THE WORLD.
ガタ
THEN HE PASSED OUT.
RAVE...
ぞく
WHAT'S WRONG, SIS?
オオ!!
I ABSOLUTELY WILL NOT ALLOW IT!
I CAN'T LET YOU LEAVE THIS ISLAND!

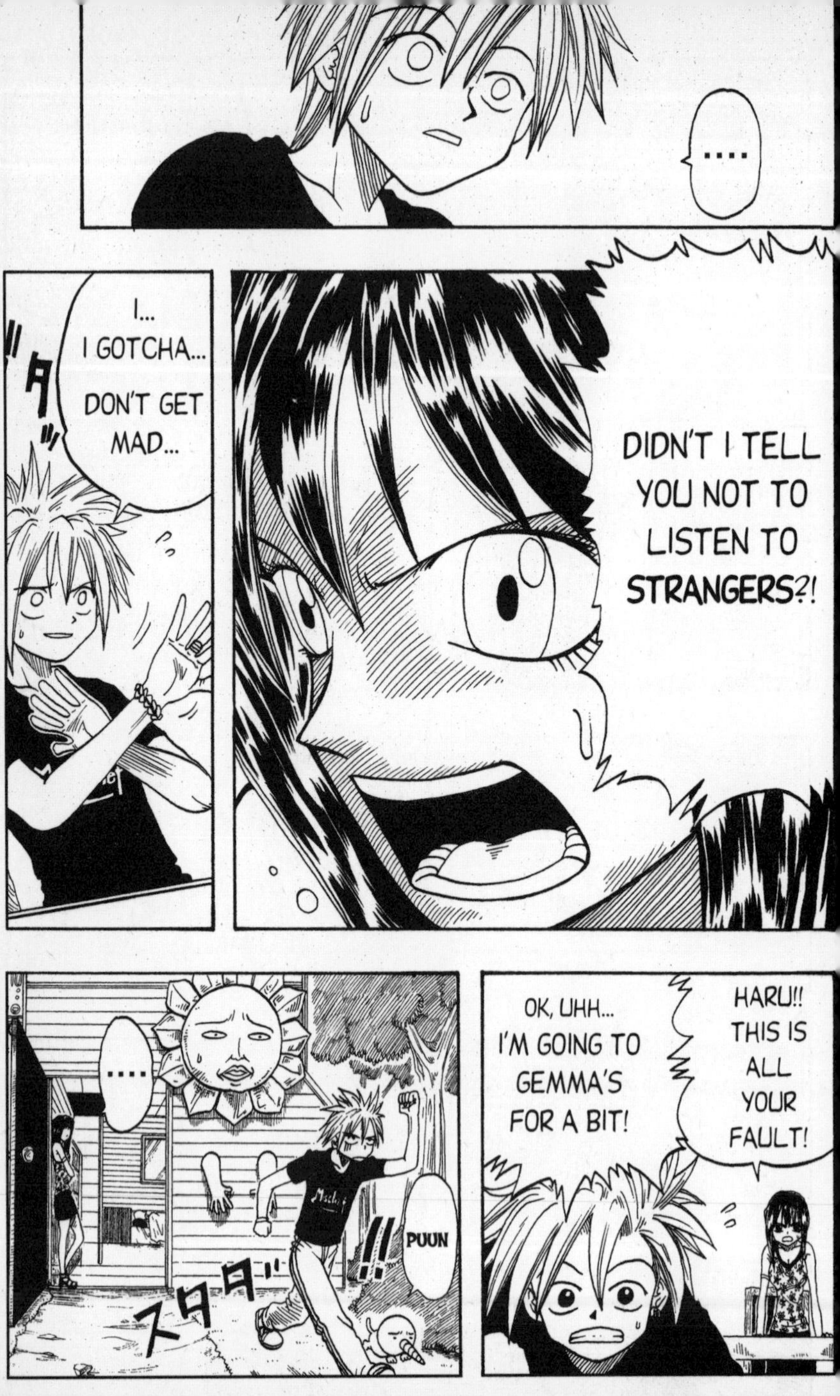
....
DIDN'T I TELL YOU NOT TO LISTEN TO **STRANGERS?!**
I... I GOTCHA... DON'T GET MAD...
HARU!! THIS IS ALL YOUR FAULT!
OK, UHH... I'M GOING TO GEMMA'S FOR A BIT!
....
PUUN

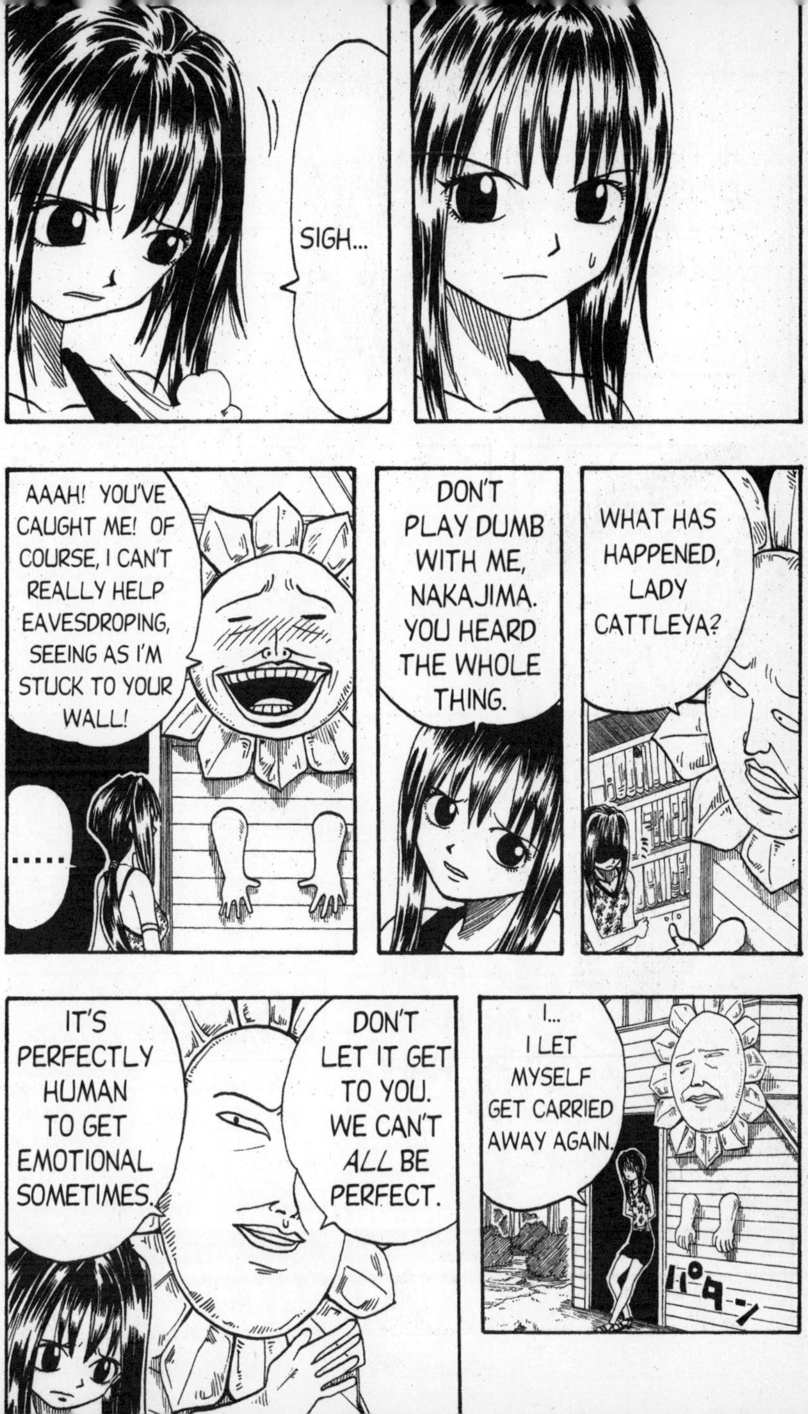
SIGH...
WHAT HAS HAPPENED, LADY CATTLEYA?
DON'T PLAY DUMB WITH ME, NAKAJIMA. YOU HEARD THE WHOLE THING.
AAAH! YOU'VE CAUGHT ME! OF COURSE, I CAN'T REALLY HELP EAVESDROPING, SEEING AS I'M STUCK TO YOUR WALL!
......
I... I LET MYSELF GET CARRIED AWAY AGAIN.
パターン
DON'T LET IT GET TO YOU. WE CAN'T ALL BE PERFECT.
IT'S PERFECTLY HUMAN TO GET EMOTIONAL SOMETIMES.

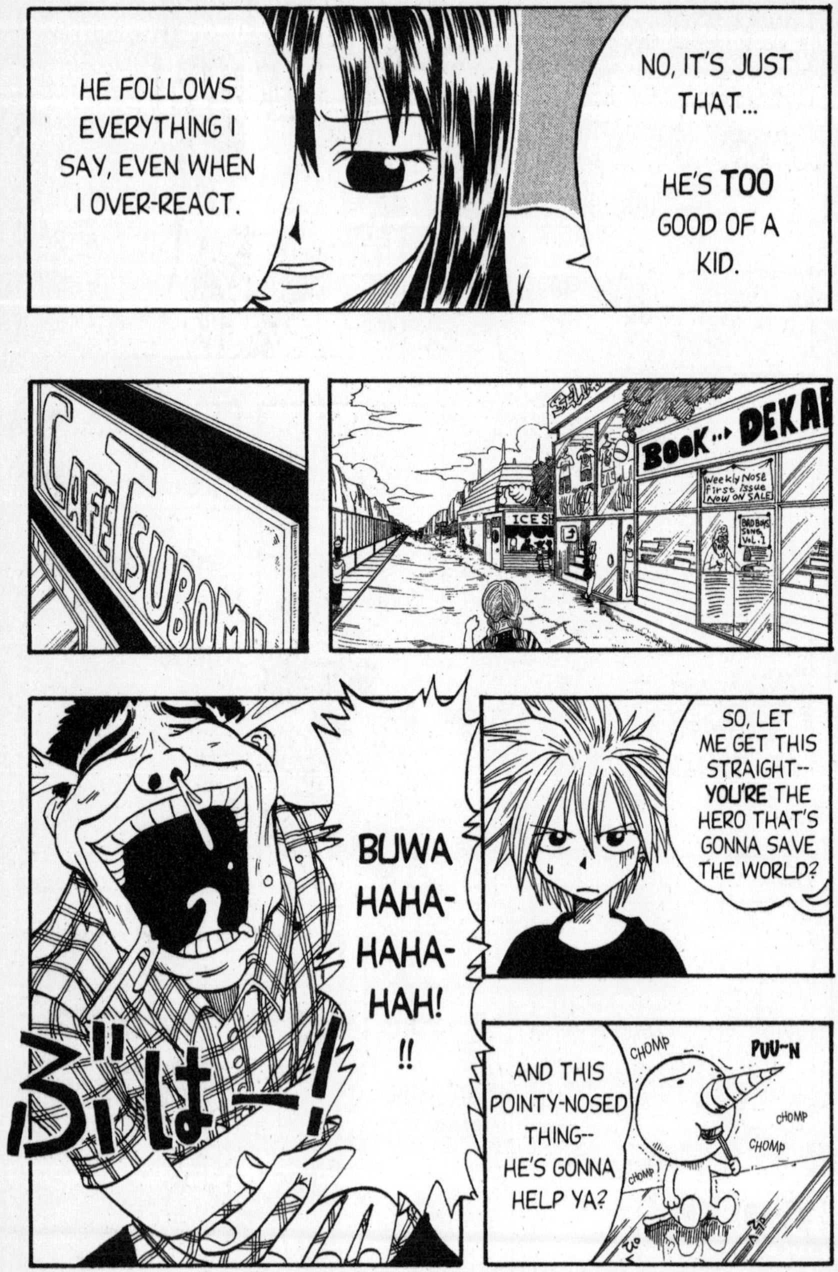
NO, IT'S JUST THAT... HE'S **TOO** GOOD OF A KID.
HE FOLLOWS EVERYTHING I SAY, EVEN WHEN I OVER-REACT.
BOOK ··› DEKA
Weekly Nose First Issue NOW ON SALE!
BAD BOYS SONG Vol.1
ICE SH
CAFE TSUBOM
SO, LET ME GET THIS STRAIGHT-- **YOU'RE** THE HERO THAT'S GONNA SAVE THE WORLD?
CHOMP
PUU~N
CHOMP
CHOMP
CHOMP
AND THIS POINTY-NOSED THING-- HE'S GONNA HELP YA?
BUWA HAHA-HAHA-HAH!!!
ぶはー！

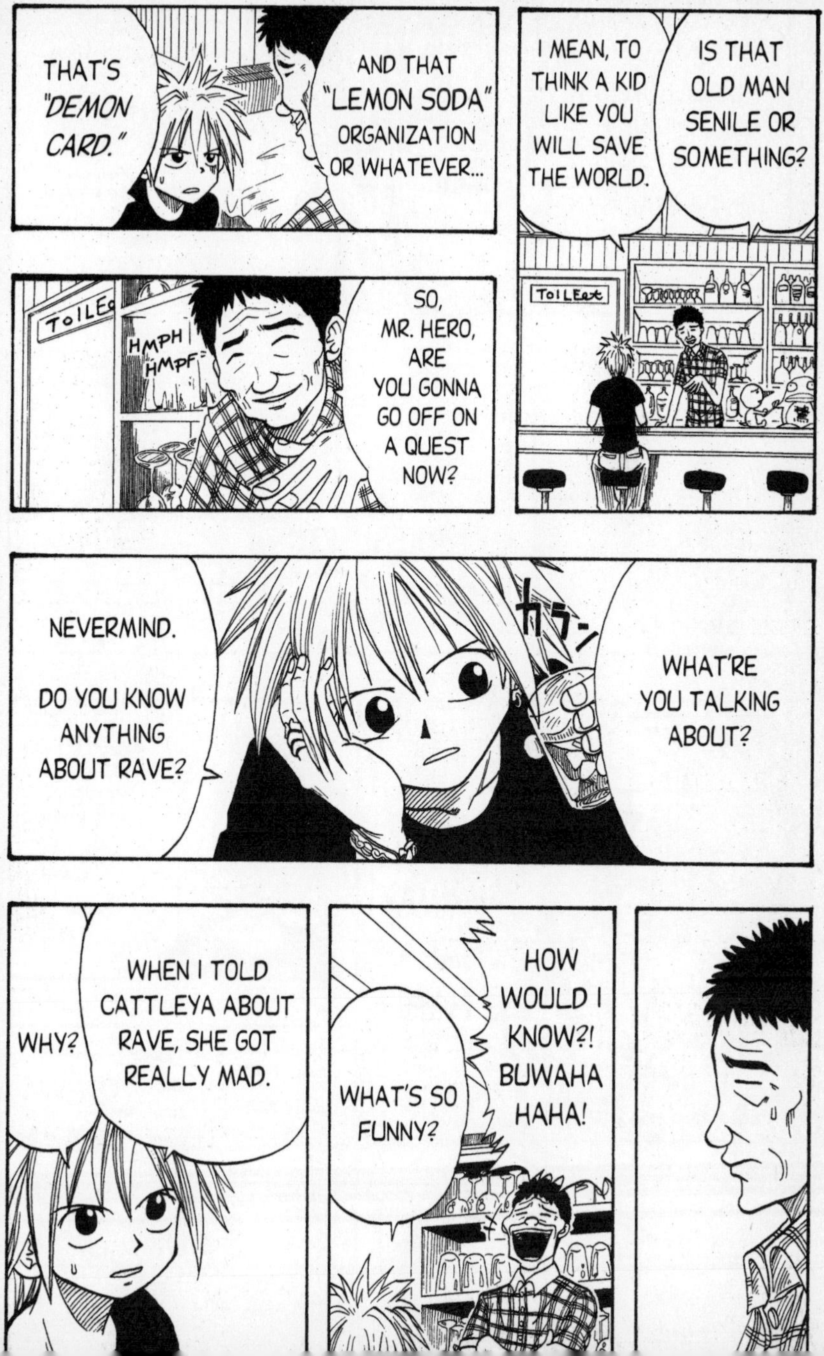
THAT'S "DEMON CARD."
AND THAT "LEMON SODA" ORGANIZATION OR WHATEVER...
IS THAT OLD MAN SENILE OR SOMETHING?
I MEAN, TO THINK A KID LIKE YOU WILL SAVE THE WORLD.
HMPH HMPF
SO, MR. HERO, ARE YOU GONNA GO OFF ON A QUEST NOW?
カラン
WHAT'RE YOU TALKING ABOUT?
NEVERMIND.
DO YOU KNOW ANYTHING ABOUT RAVE?
WHY?
WHEN I TOLD CATTLEYA ABOUT RAVE, SHE GOT REALLY MAD.
HOW WOULD I KNOW?! BUWAHA HAHA!
WHAT'S SO FUNNY?

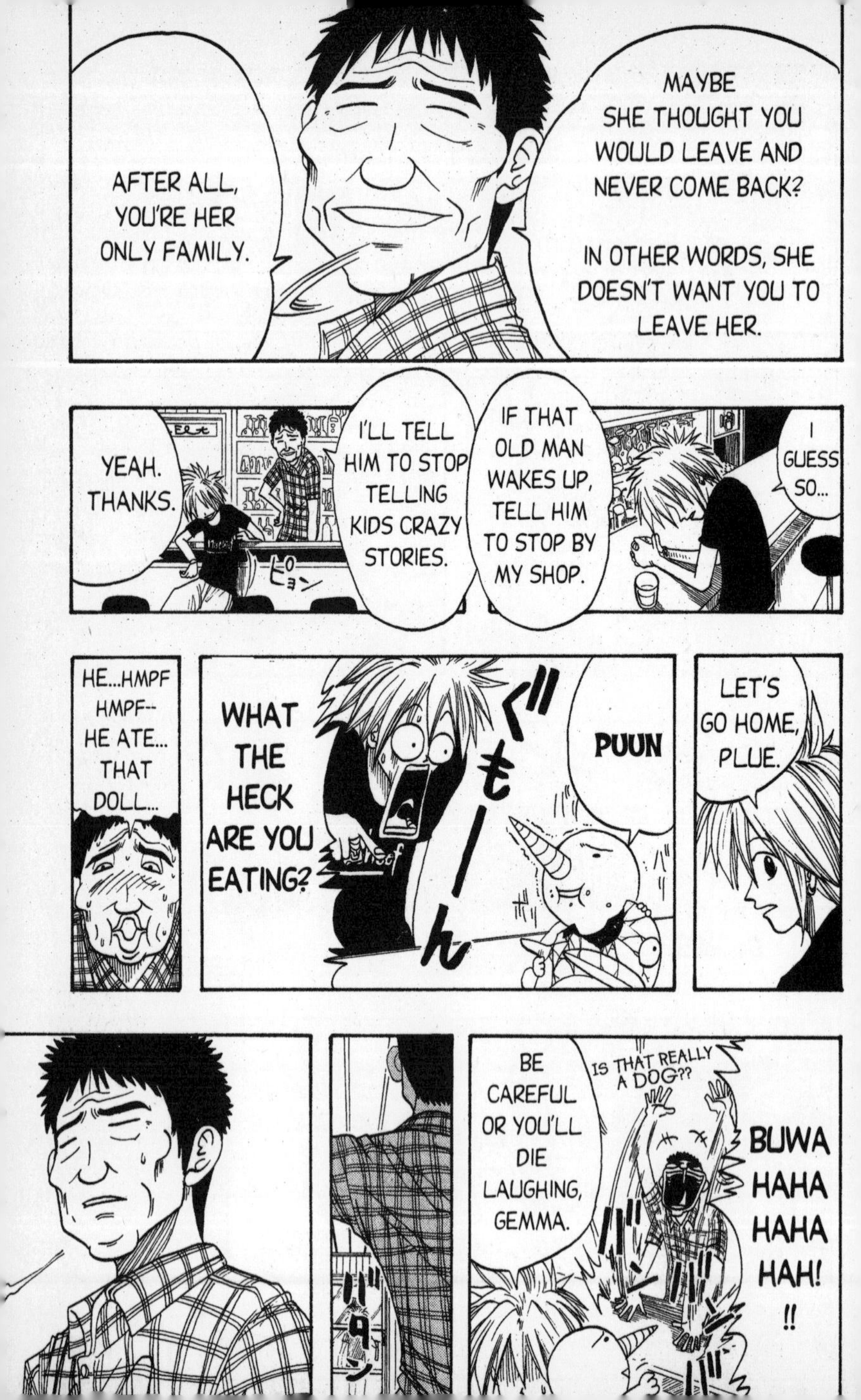
MAYBE SHE THOUGHT YOU WOULD LEAVE AND NEVER COME BACK?
IN OTHER WORDS, SHE DOESN'T WANT YOU TO LEAVE HER.
AFTER ALL, YOU'RE HER ONLY FAMILY.
I GUESS SO...
IF THAT OLD MAN WAKES UP, TELL HIM TO STOP BY MY SHOP.
I'LL TELL HIM TO STOP TELLING KIDS CRAZY STORIES.
YEAH. THANKS.
ピョン
LET'S GO HOME, PLUE.
PUUN
ぐもーん
WHAT THE HECK ARE YOU EATING?
HE...HMPF HMPF-- HE ATE... THAT DOLL...
IS THAT REALLY A DOG??
BUWA HAHA HAHA HAH!!!
BE CAREFUL OR YOU'LL DIE LAUGHING, GEMMA.

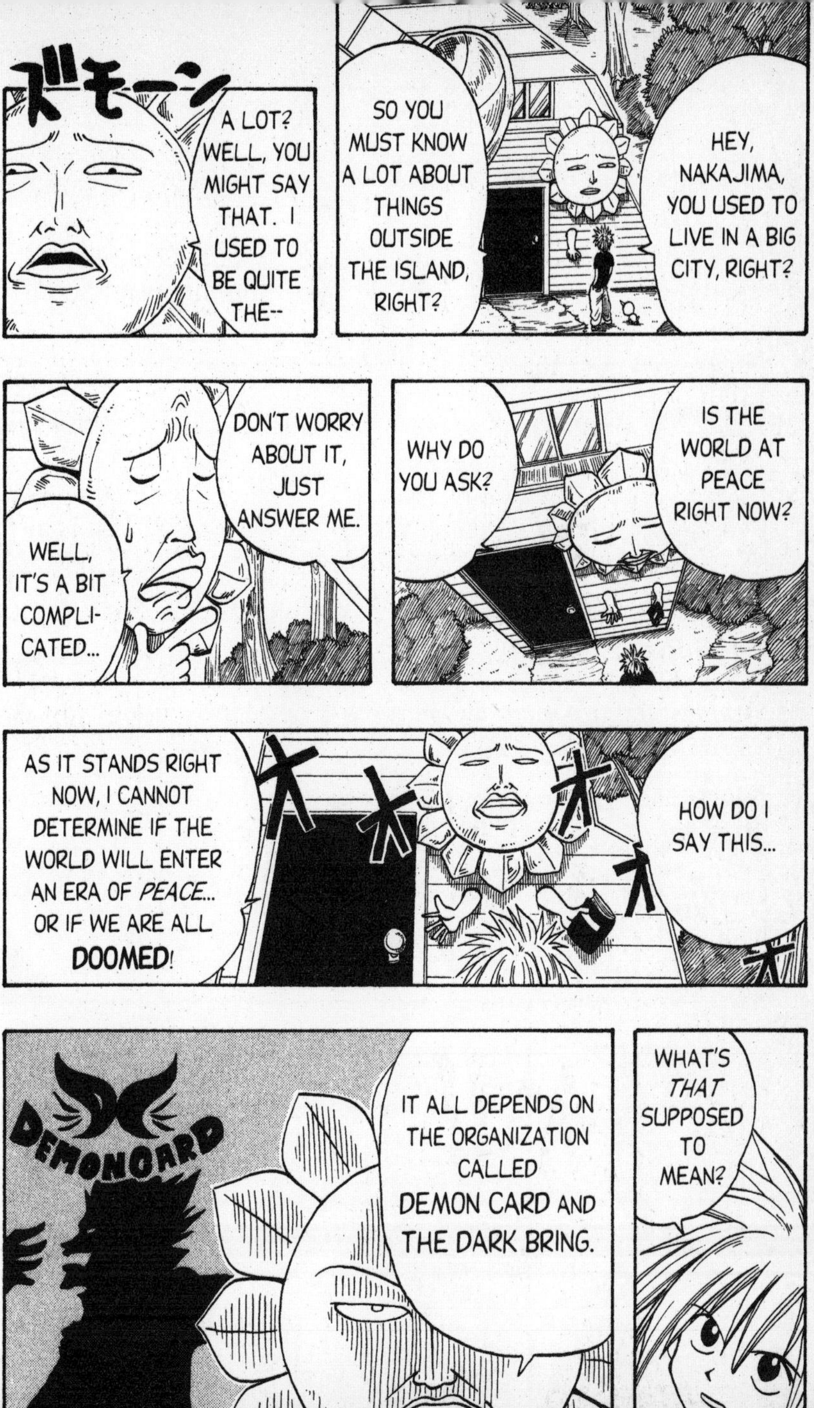
HEY, NAKAJIMA, YOU USED TO LIVE IN A BIG CITY, RIGHT?
SO YOU MUST KNOW A LOT ABOUT THINGS OUTSIDE THE ISLAND, RIGHT?
ズモーン
A LOT? WELL, YOU MIGHT SAY THAT. I USED TO BE QUITE THE--
IS THE WORLD AT PEACE RIGHT NOW?
WHY DO YOU ASK?
DON'T WORRY ABOUT IT, JUST ANSWER ME.
WELL, IT'S A BIT COMPLI-CATED...
HOW DO I SAY THIS...
AS IT STANDS RIGHT NOW, I CANNOT DETERMINE IF THE WORLD WILL ENTER AN ERA OF *PEACE*... OR IF WE ARE ALL **DOOMED**!
WHAT'S *THAT* SUPPOSED TO MEAN?
IT ALL DEPENDS ON THE ORGANIZATION CALLED DEMON CARD AND THE DARK BRING.
DEMONCARD

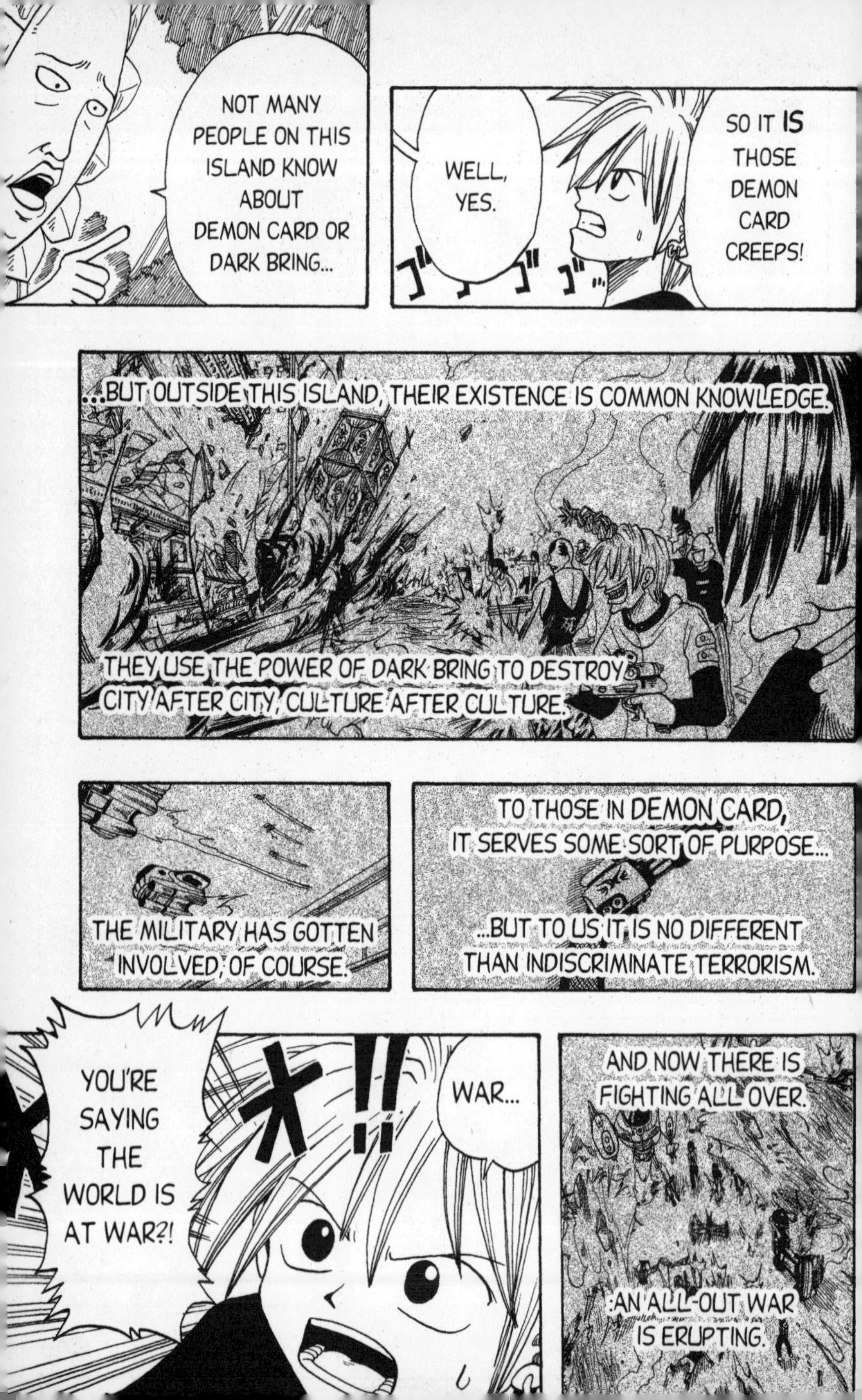
SO IT IS THOSE DEMON CARD CREEPS!
WELL, YES.
NOT MANY PEOPLE ON THIS ISLAND KNOW ABOUT DEMON CARD OR DARK BRING...
...BUT OUTSIDE THIS ISLAND, THEIR EXISTENCE IS COMMON KNOWLEDGE.
THEY USE THE POWER OF DARK BRING TO DESTROY CITY AFTER CITY, CULTURE AFTER CULTURE.
TO THOSE IN DEMON CARD, IT SERVES SOME SORT OF PURPOSE...
...BUT TO US IT IS NO DIFFERENT THAN INDISCRIMINATE TERRORISM.
THE MILITARY HAS GOTTEN INVOLVED, OF COURSE.
AND NOW THERE IS FIGHTING ALL OVER.
AN ALL-OUT WAR IS ERUPTING.
WAR...
YOU'RE SAYING THE WORLD IS AT WAR?!

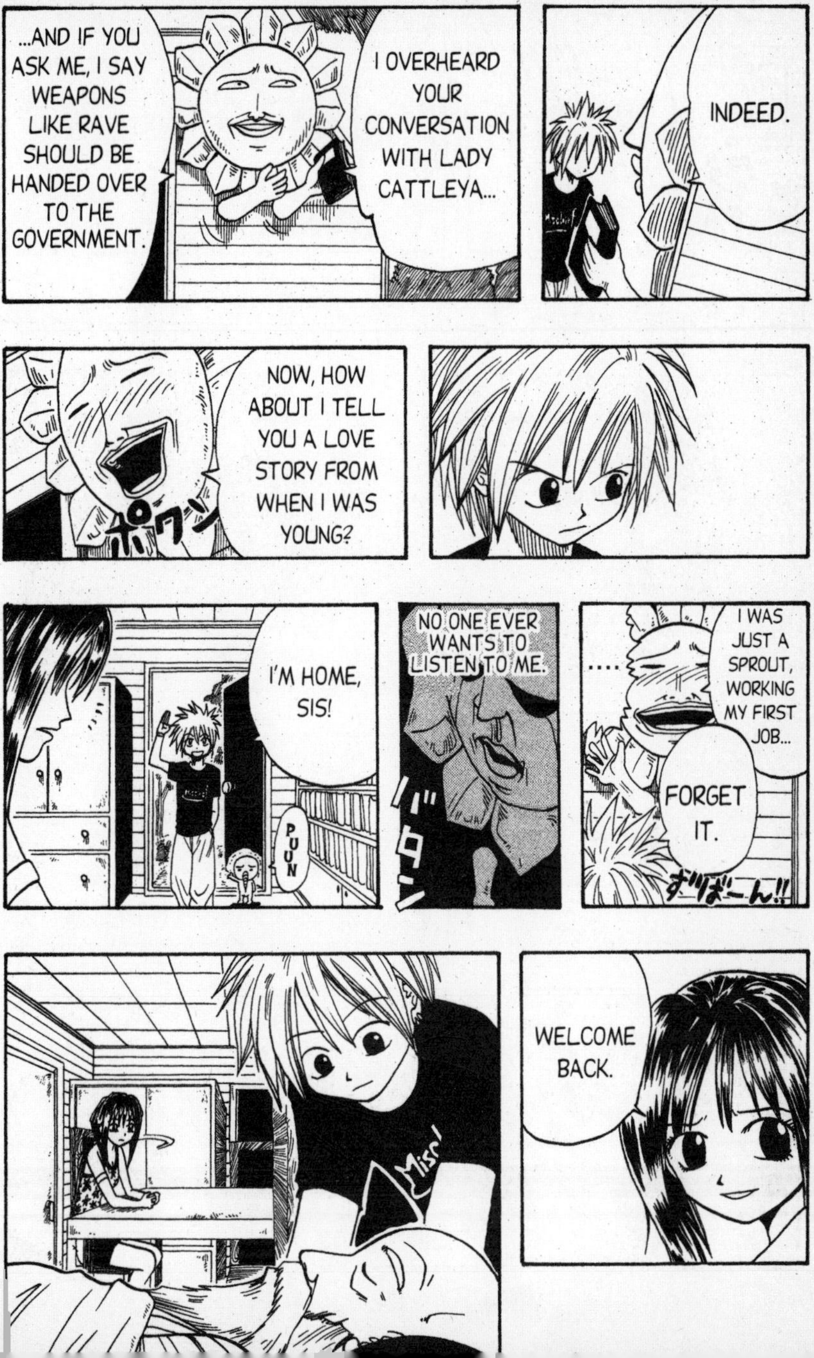
INDEED.
I OVERHEARD YOUR CONVERSATION WITH LADY CATTLEYA...
...AND IF YOU ASK ME, I SAY WEAPONS LIKE RAVE SHOULD BE HANDED OVER TO THE GOVERNMENT.
NOW, HOW ABOUT I TELL YOU A LOVE STORY FROM WHEN I WAS YOUNG?
ポワン
I WAS JUST A SPROUT, WORKING MY FIRST JOB...
....
FORGET IT.
ずりばーん!!
NO ONE EVER WANTS TO LISTEN TO ME.
バタン
I'M HOME, SIS!
PUUN
WELCOME BACK.

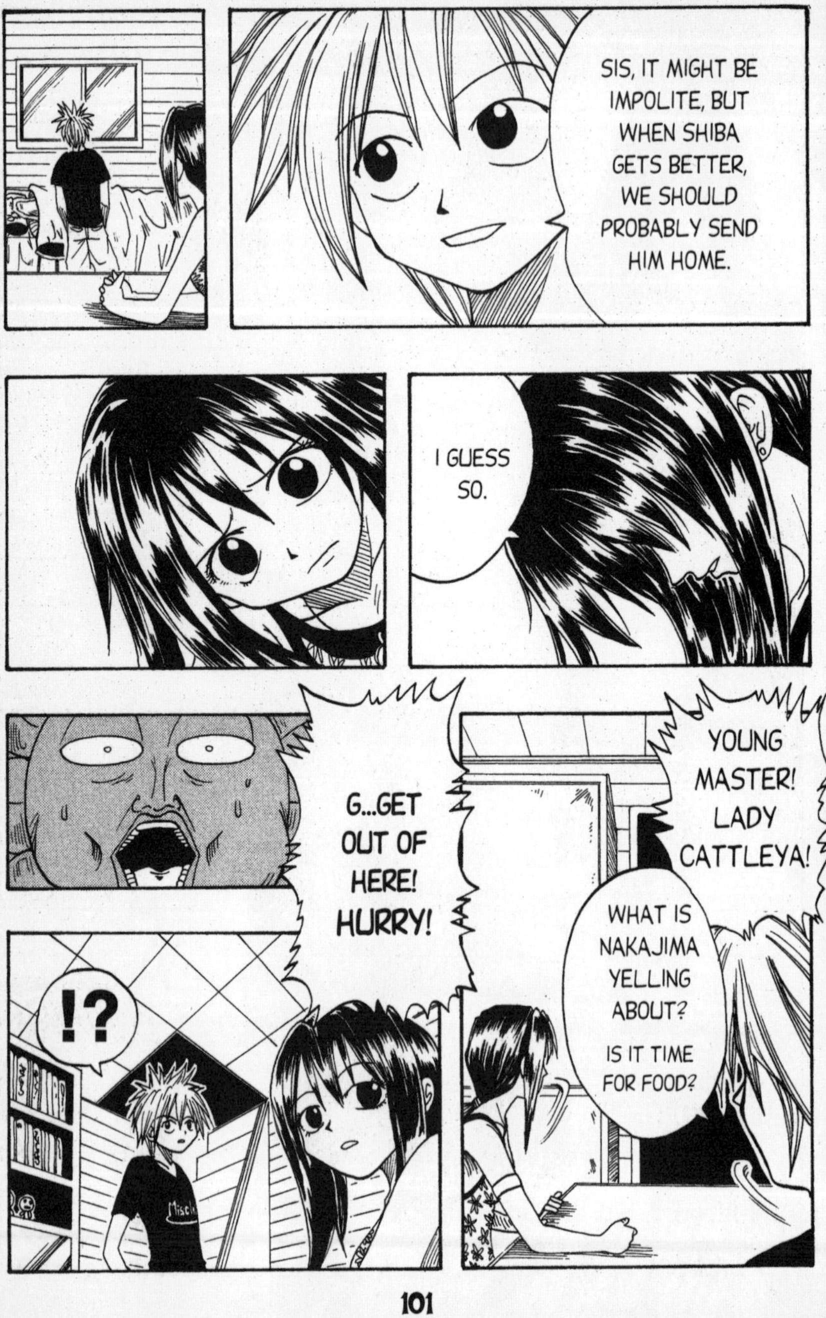
SIS, IT MIGHT BE IMPOLITE, BUT WHEN SHIBA GETS BETTER, WE SHOULD PROBABLY SEND HIM HOME.
I GUESS SO.
YOUNG MASTER! LADY CATTLEYA!
G...GET OUT OF HERE! HURRY!
WHAT IS NAKAJIMA YELLING ABOUT?
IS IT TIME FOR FOOD?
!?

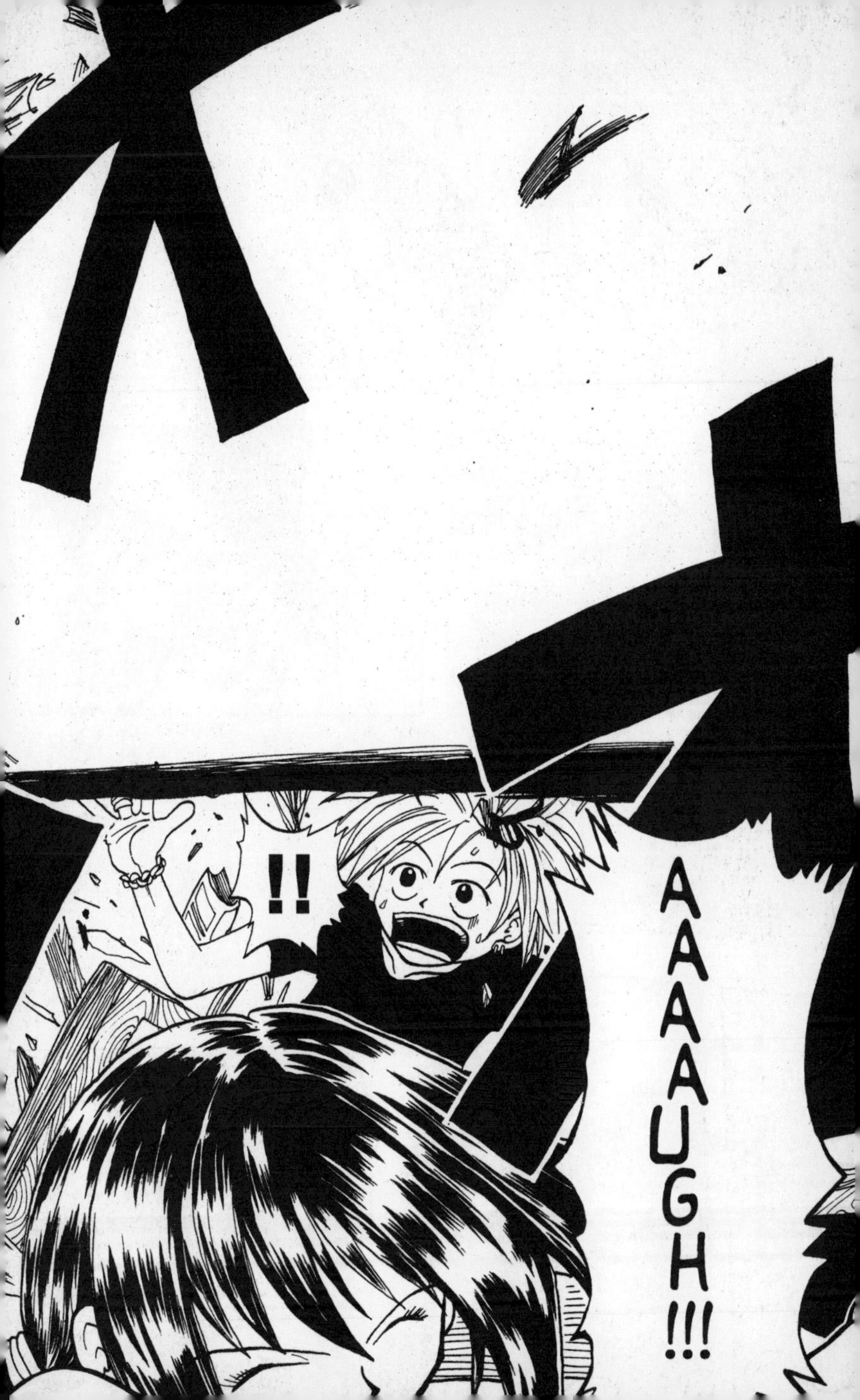
!!
AAAAUGH!!!

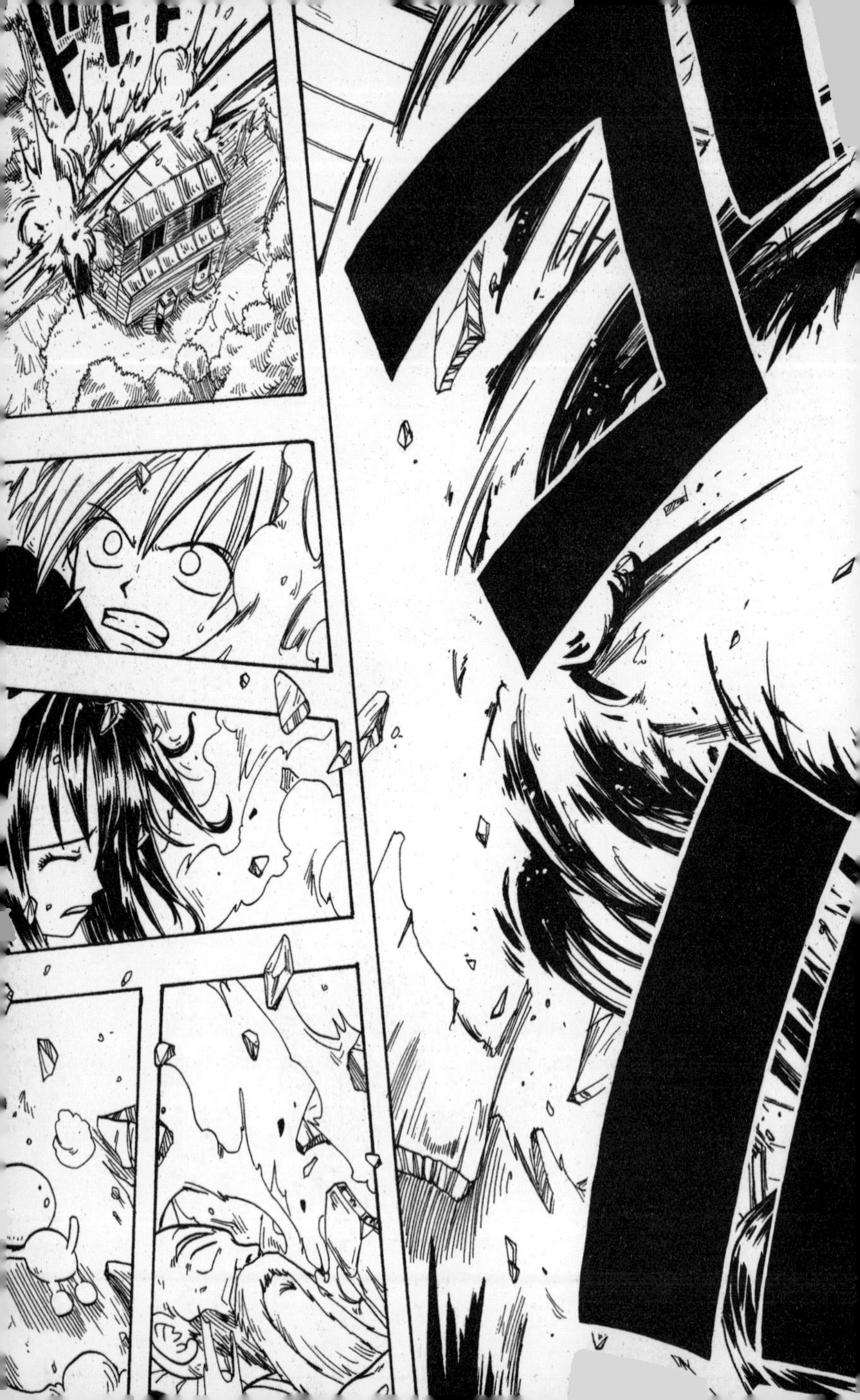

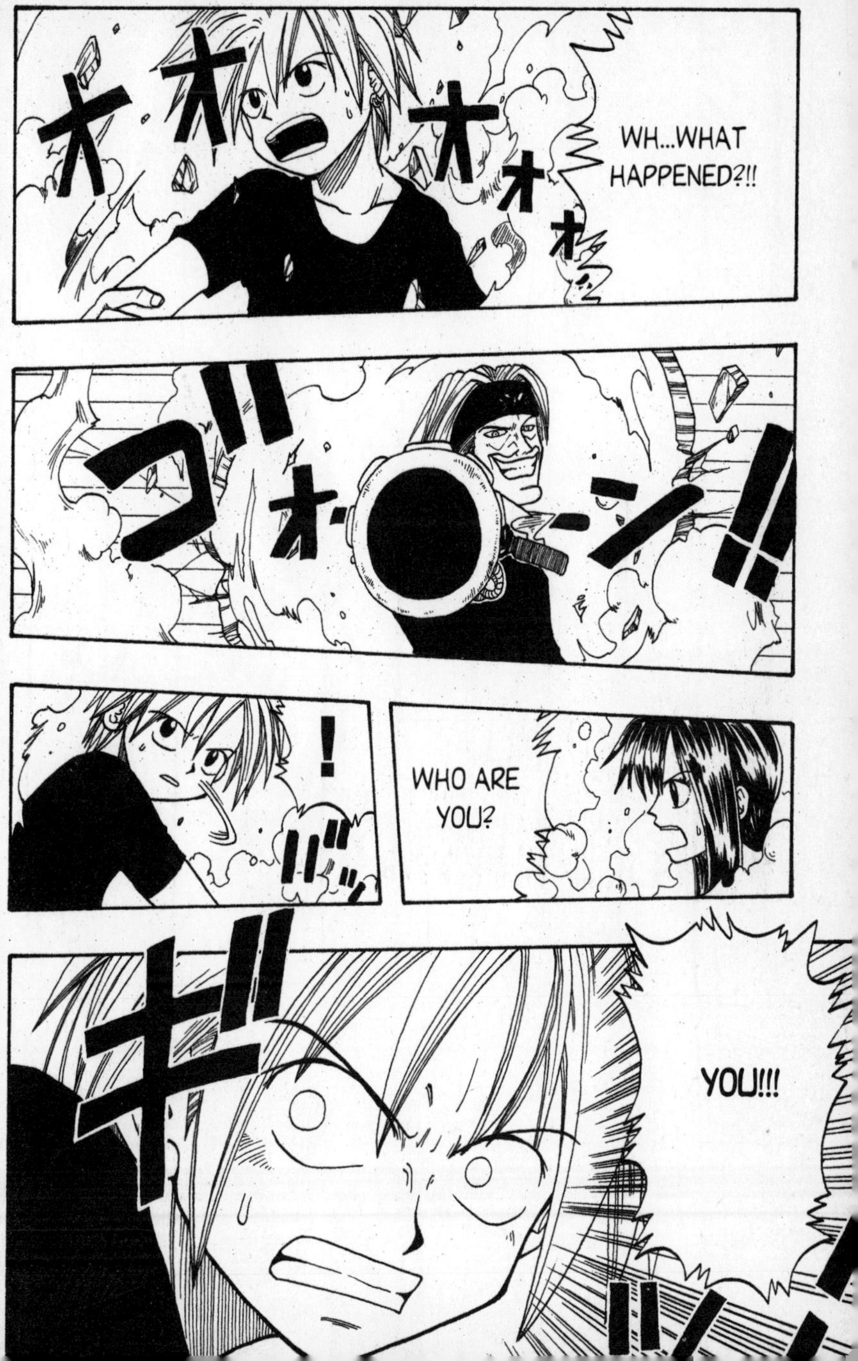
WH...WHAT HAPPENED?!!
!
WHO ARE YOU?
YOU!!!

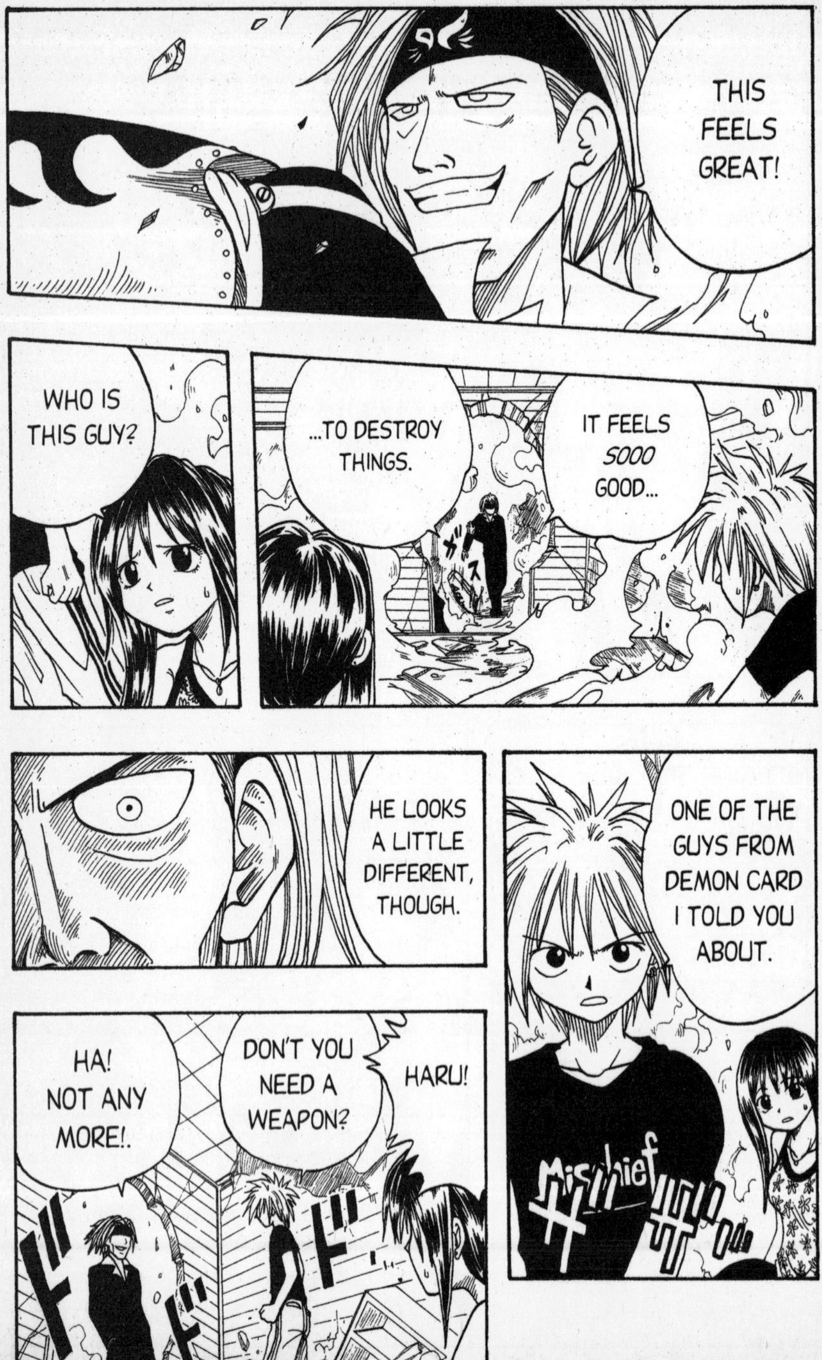
THIS FEELS GREAT!
IT FEELS *SOOO* GOOD...
...TO DESTROY THINGS.
WHO IS THIS GUY?
ONE OF THE GUYS FROM DEMON CARD I TOLD YOU ABOUT.
HE LOOKS A LITTLE DIFFERENT, THOUGH.
HARU!
DON'T YOU NEED A WEAPON?
HA! NOT ANY MORE!.

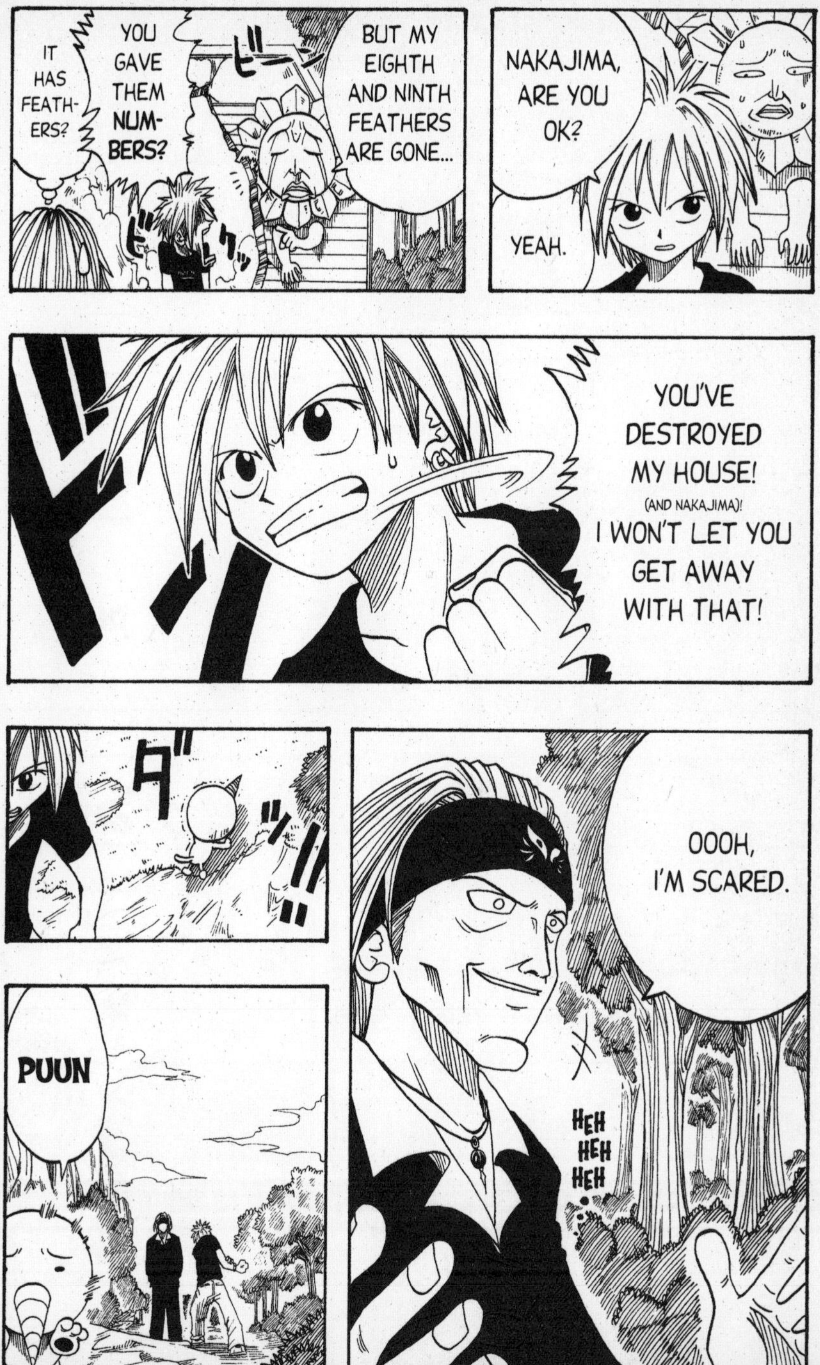
NAKAJIMA, ARE YOU OK?
YEAH.
BUT MY EIGHTH AND NINTH FEATHERS ARE GONE...
YOU GAVE THEM NUMBERS?
IT HAS FEATHERS?
YOU'VE DESTROYED MY HOUSE! (AND NAKAJIMA)! I WON'T LET YOU GET AWAY WITH THAT!
OOOH, I'M SCARED.
HEH HEH HEH
PUUN

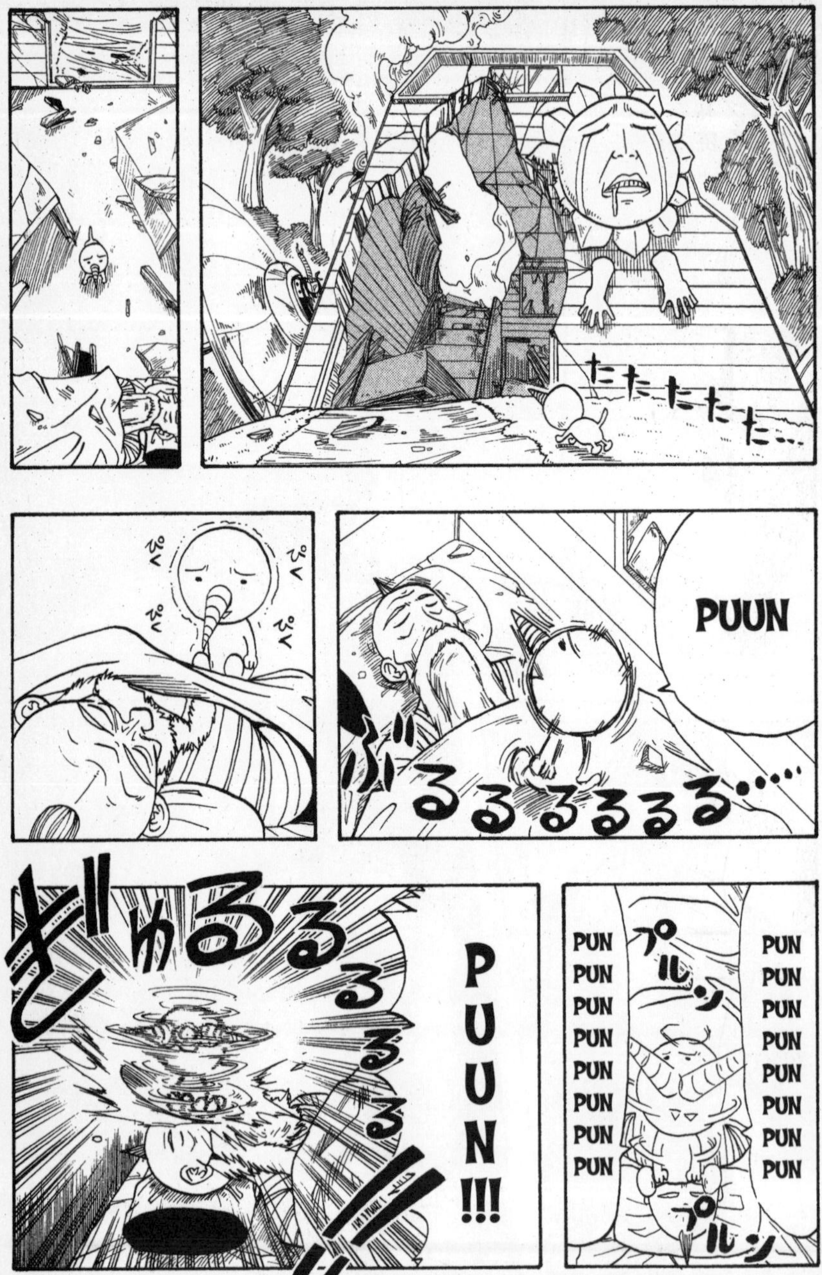
たたたたた…
ぶるるるるるる……
PUUN
ぴく ぴく
ぴく ぴく
PUN PUN PUN PUN PUN PUN PUN PUN
プルン
プルン
PUN PUN PUN PUN PUN PUN PUN PUN
ぎゅるるるるるる!!!
PUUN!!!

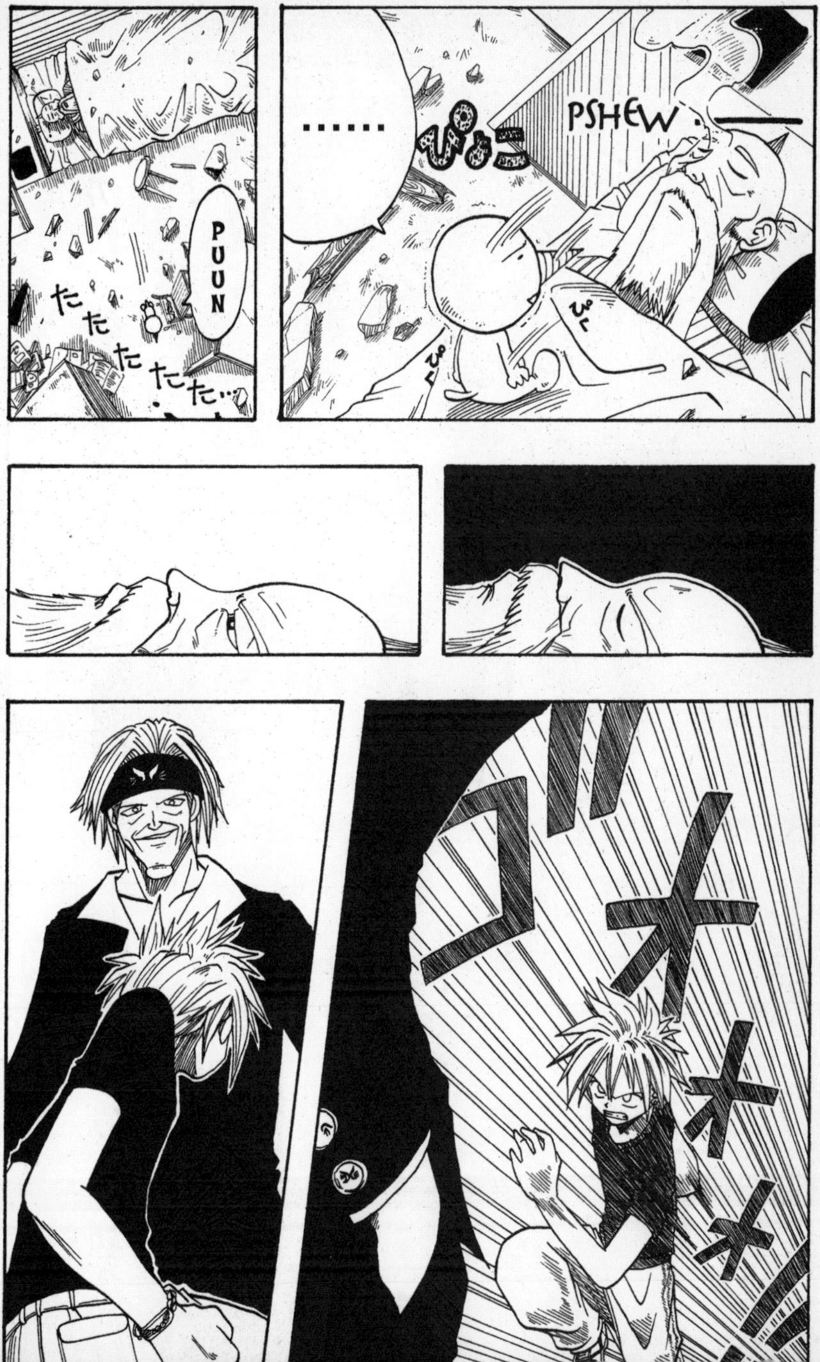
PSHEW
ぴょこ
ぴく
ぴく
......
PUUN
たたたたた…

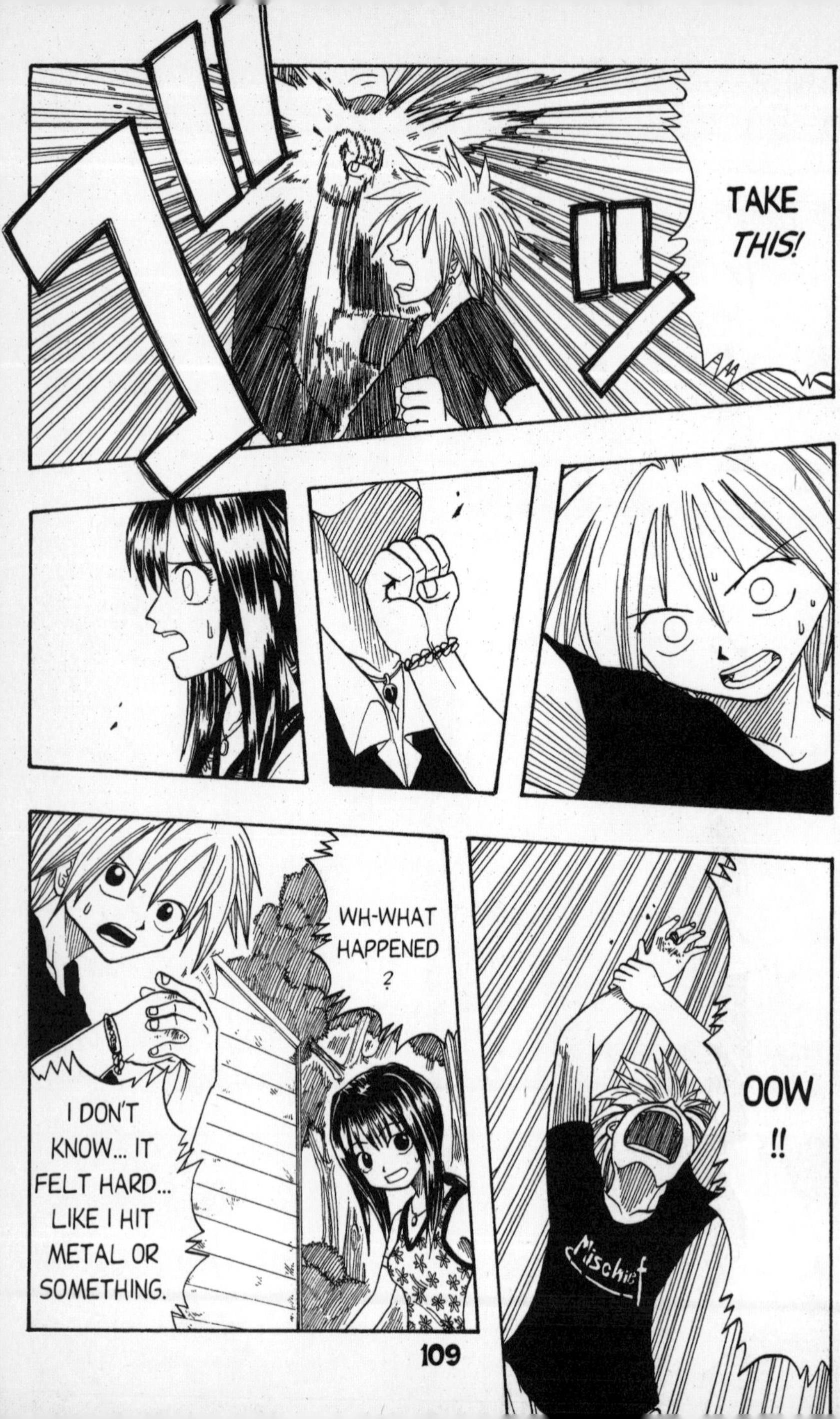
TAKE THIS!
OOW !!
WH-WHAT HAPPENED ?
I DON'T KNOW... IT FELT HARD... LIKE I HIT METAL OR SOMETHING.

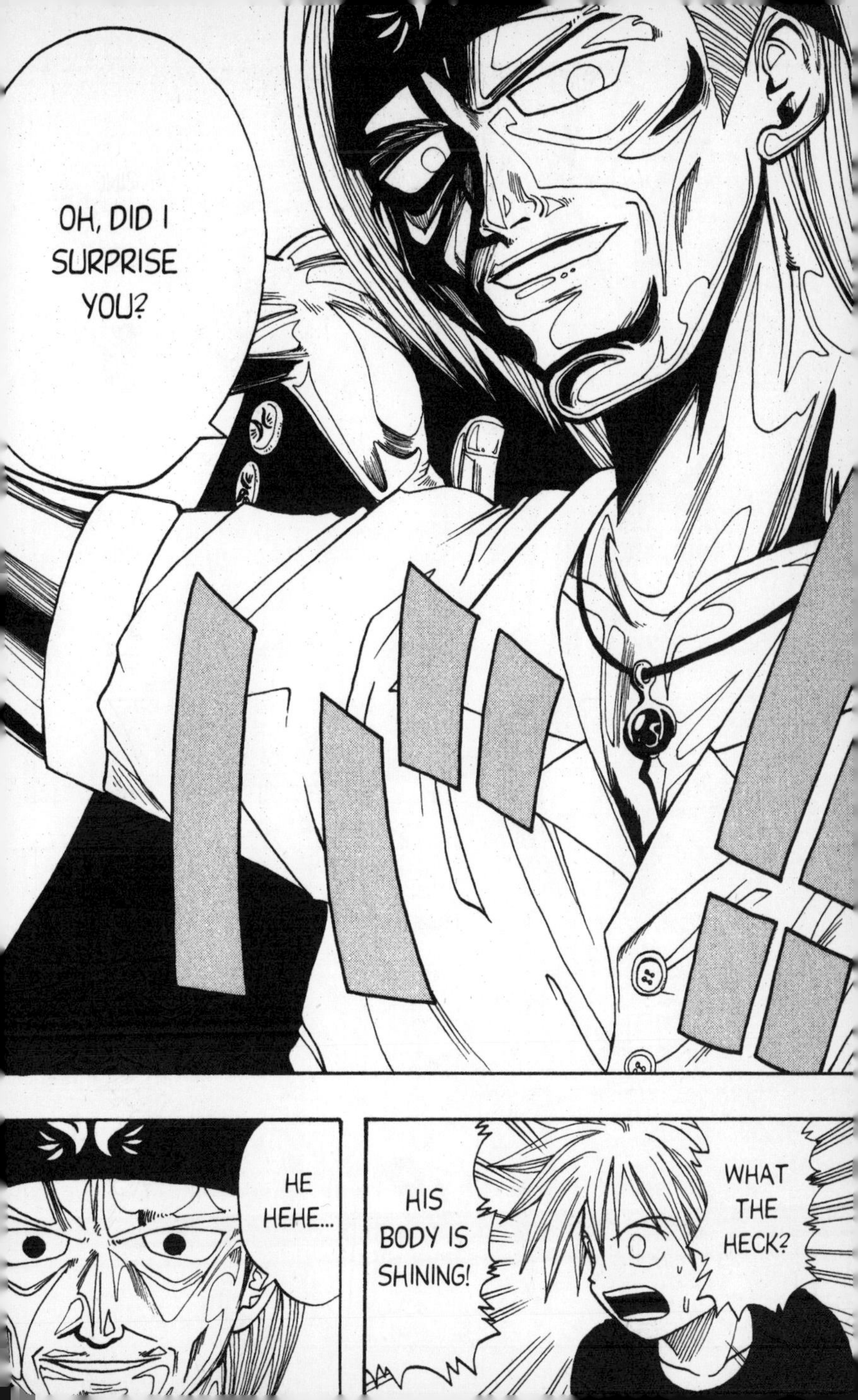
OH, DID I SURPRISE YOU?
WHAT THE HECK?
HIS BODY IS SHINING!
HE HEHE...

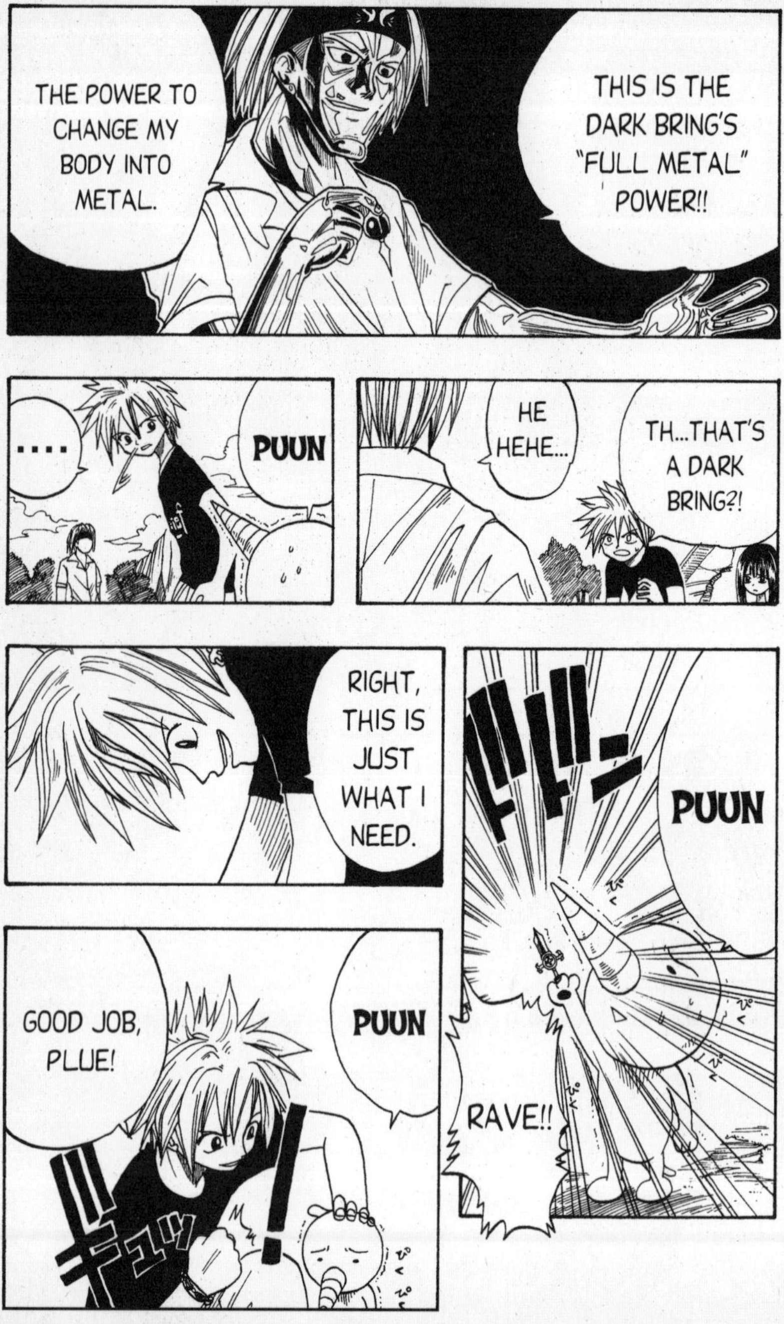
THIS IS THE DARK BRING'S "FULL METAL" POWER!!
THE POWER TO CHANGE MY BODY INTO METAL.
TH...THAT'S A DARK BRING?!
HE HEHE...
PUUN
....
PUUN
RAVE!!
RIGHT, THIS IS JUST WHAT I NEED.
PUUN
GOOD JOB, PLUE!

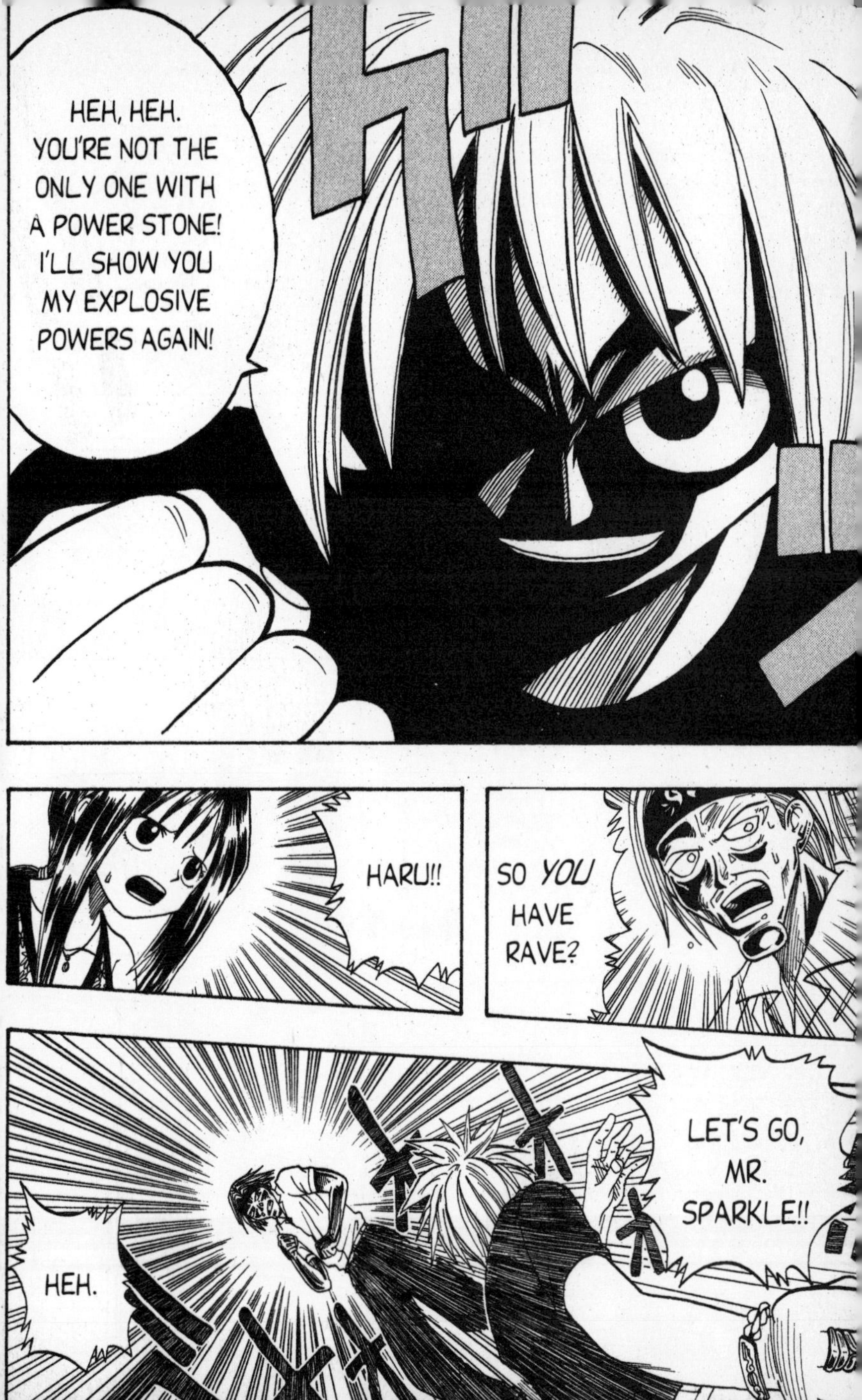
HEH, HEH. YOU'RE NOT THE ONLY ONE WITH A POWER STONE! I'LL SHOW YOU MY EXPLOSIVE POWERS AGAIN!
SO *YOU* HAVE RAVE?
HARU!!
LET'S GO, MR. SPARKLE!!
HEH.

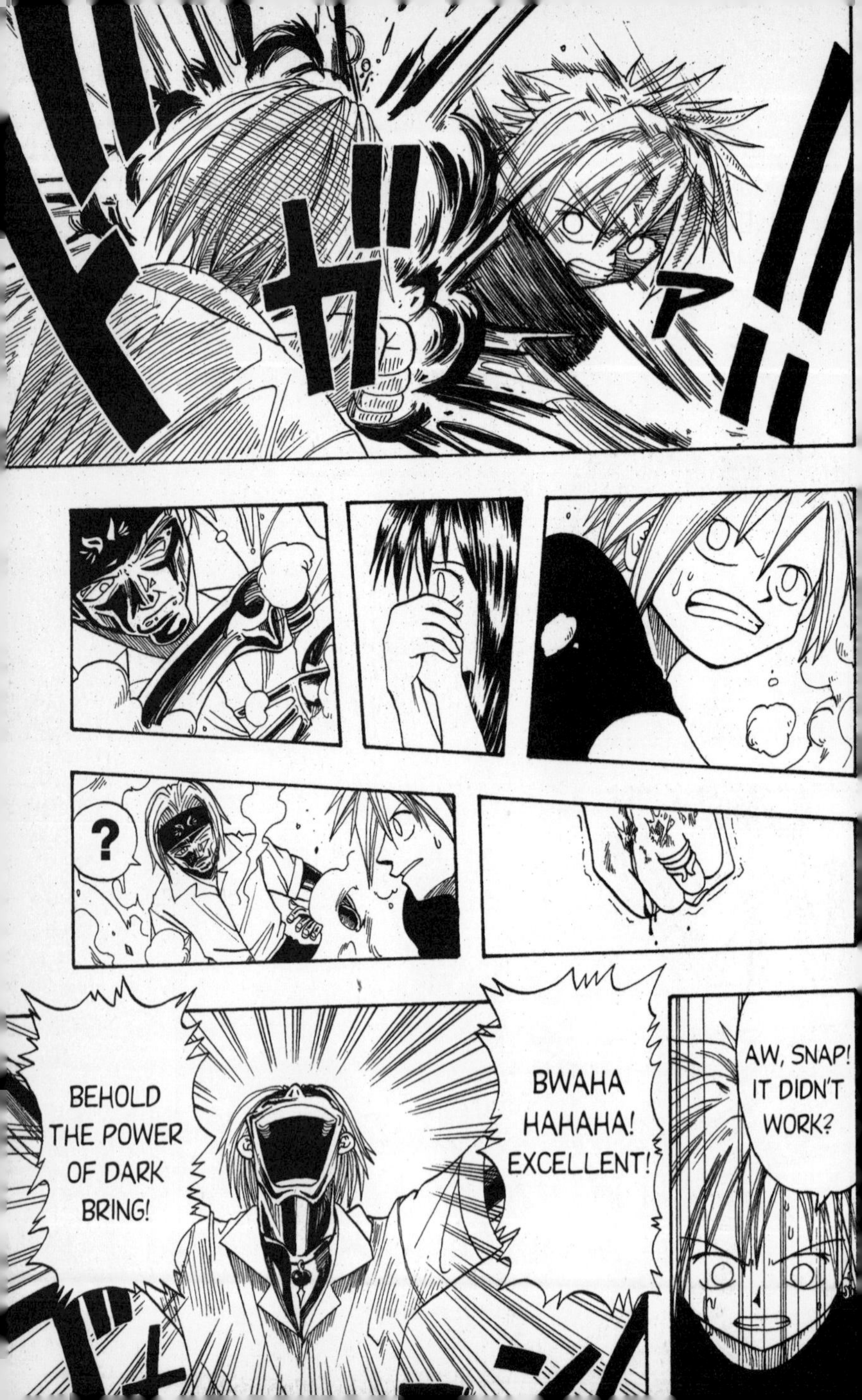
?
AW, SNAP! IT DIDN'T WORK?
BWAHA HAHAHA! EXCELLENT!
BEHOLD THE POWER OF DARK BRING!

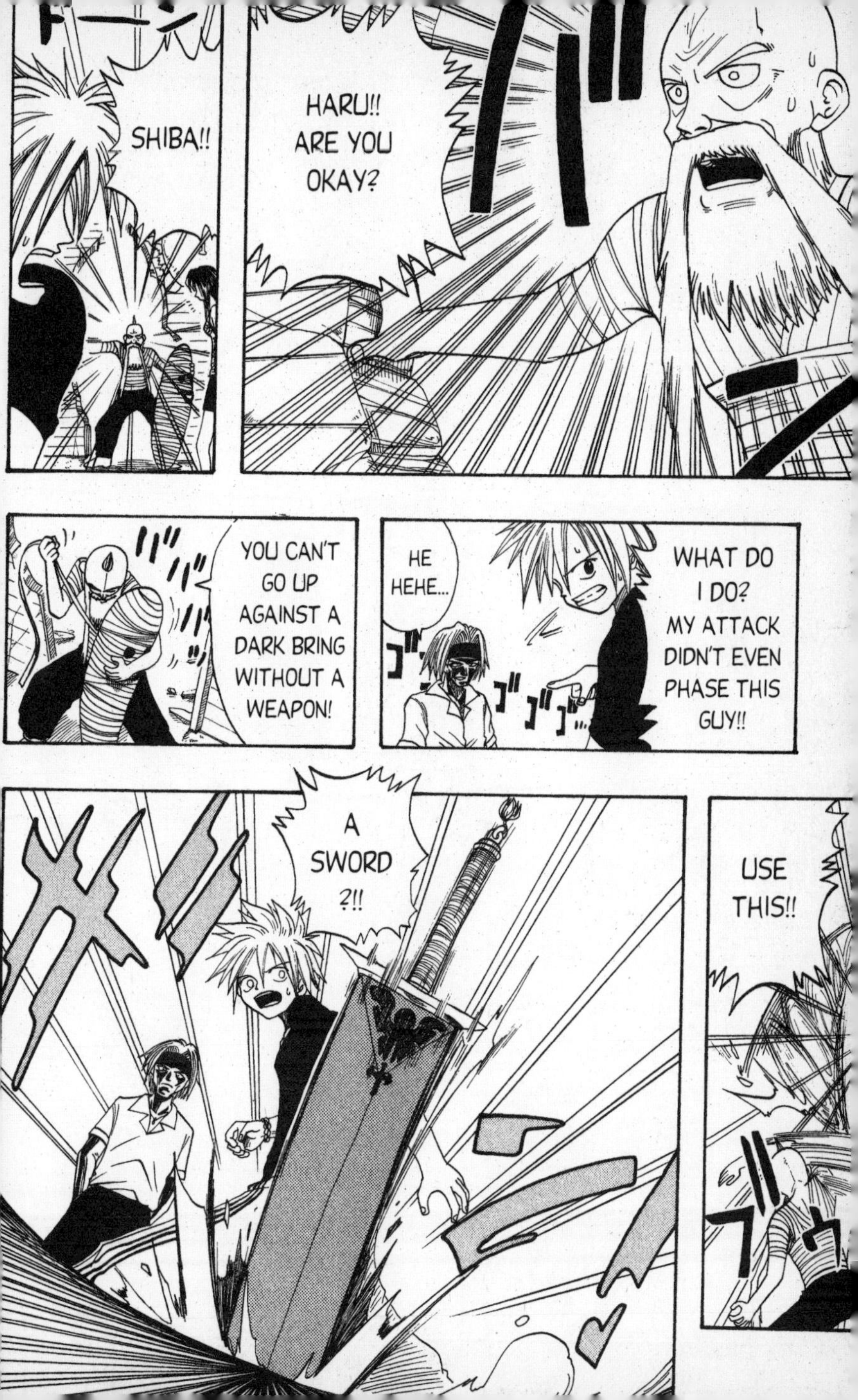
HARU!! ARE YOU OKAY?
SHIBA!!
WHAT DO I DO? MY ATTACK DIDN'T EVEN PHASE THIS GUY!!
HE HEHE...
YOU CAN'T GO UP AGAINST A DARK BRING WITHOUT A WEAPON!
USE THIS!!
A SWORD?!!

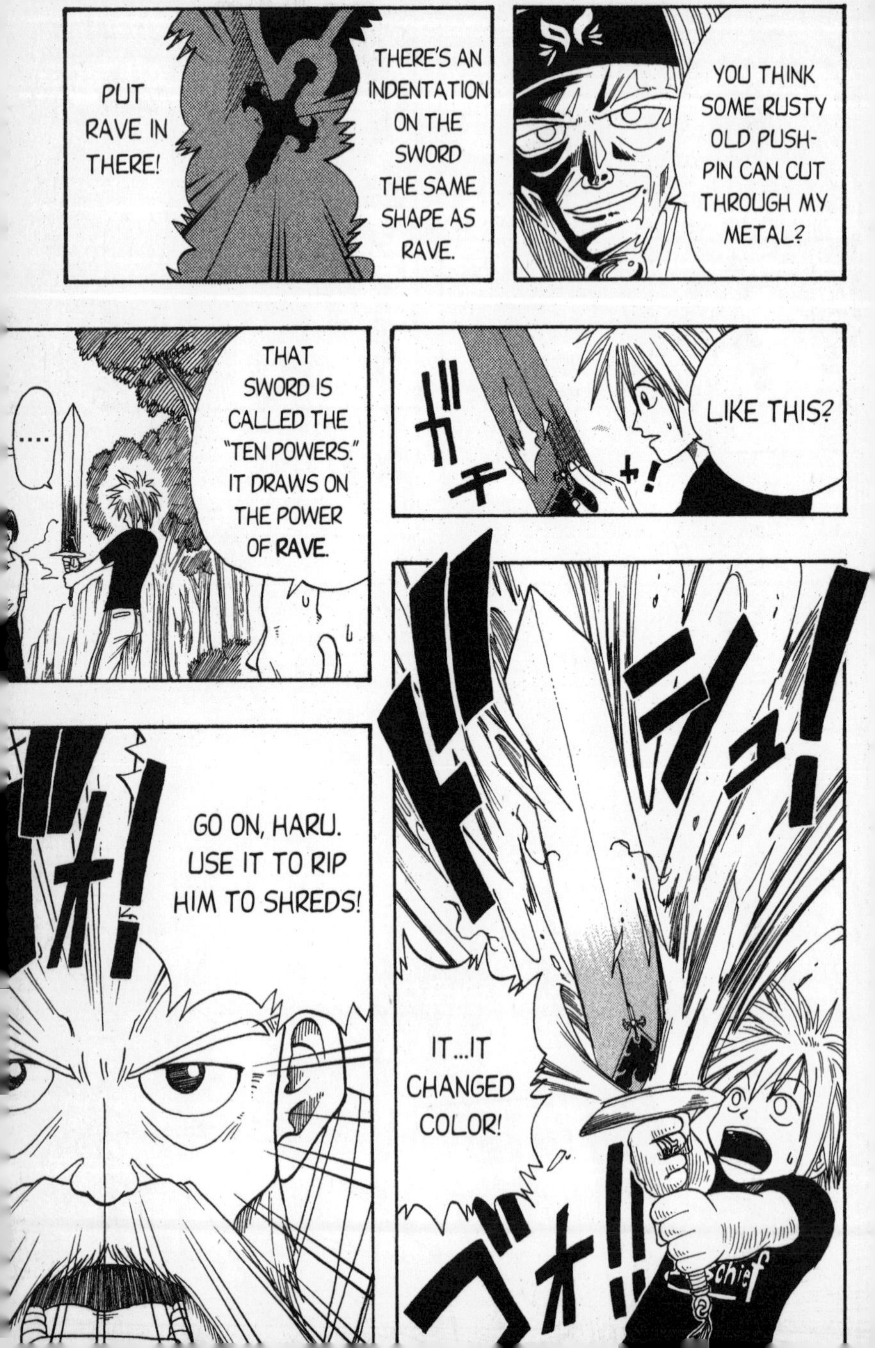
YOU THINK SOME RUSTY OLD PUSH-PIN CAN CUT THROUGH MY METAL?
THERE'S AN INDENTATION ON THE SWORD THE SAME SHAPE AS RAVE.
PUT RAVE IN THERE!
LIKE THIS?
IT...IT CHANGED COLOR!
THAT SWORD IS CALLED THE "TEN POWERS." IT DRAWS ON THE POWER OF **RAVE**.
.....
GO ON, HARU. USE IT TO RIP HIM TO SHREDS!

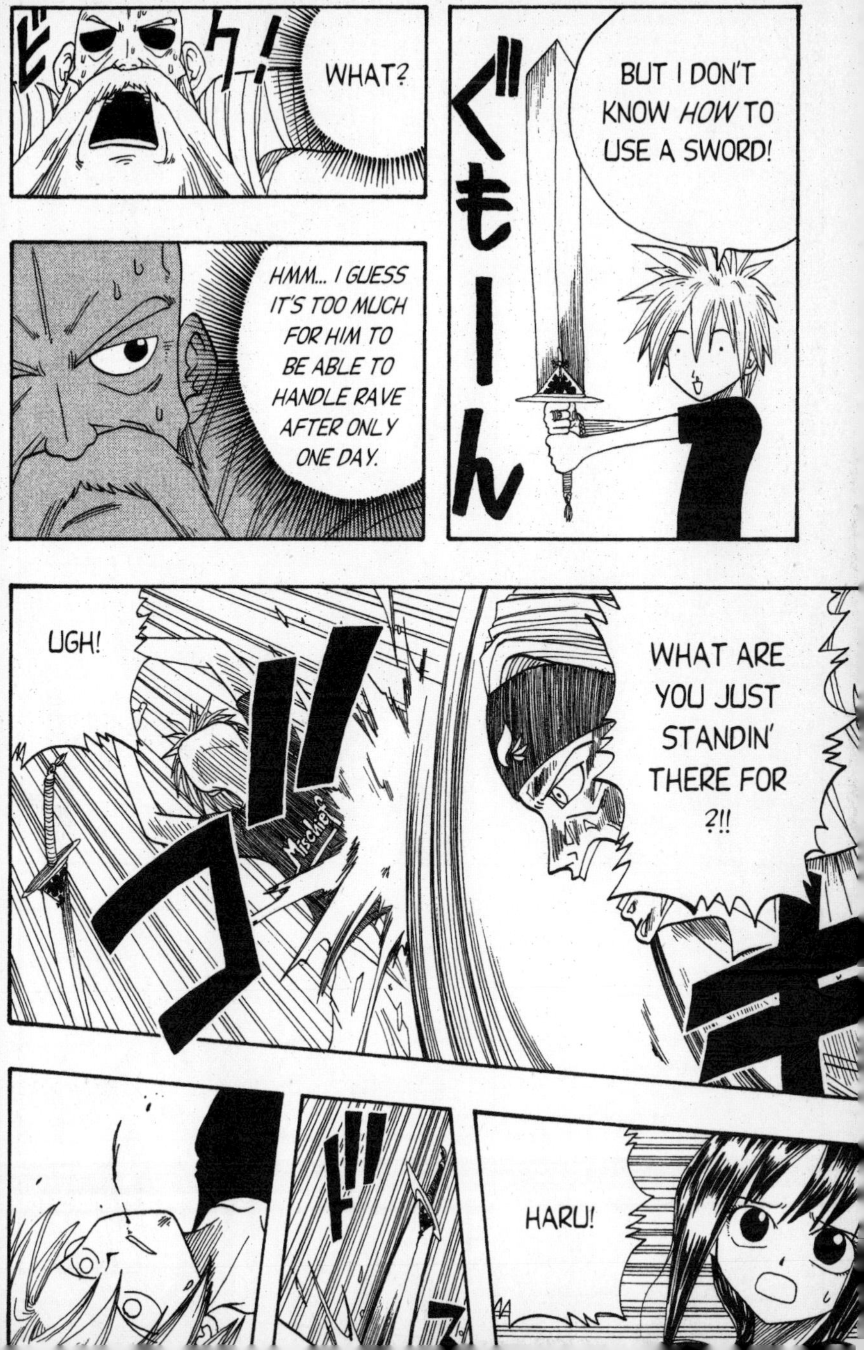
BUT I DON'T KNOW *HOW* TO USE A SWORD!
ぐもーん
WHAT?
HMM... I GUESS IT'S TOO MUCH FOR HIM TO BE ABLE TO HANDLE RAVE AFTER ONLY ONE DAY.
WHAT ARE YOU JUST STANDIN' THERE FOR ?!!
UGH!
Mischief
HARU!

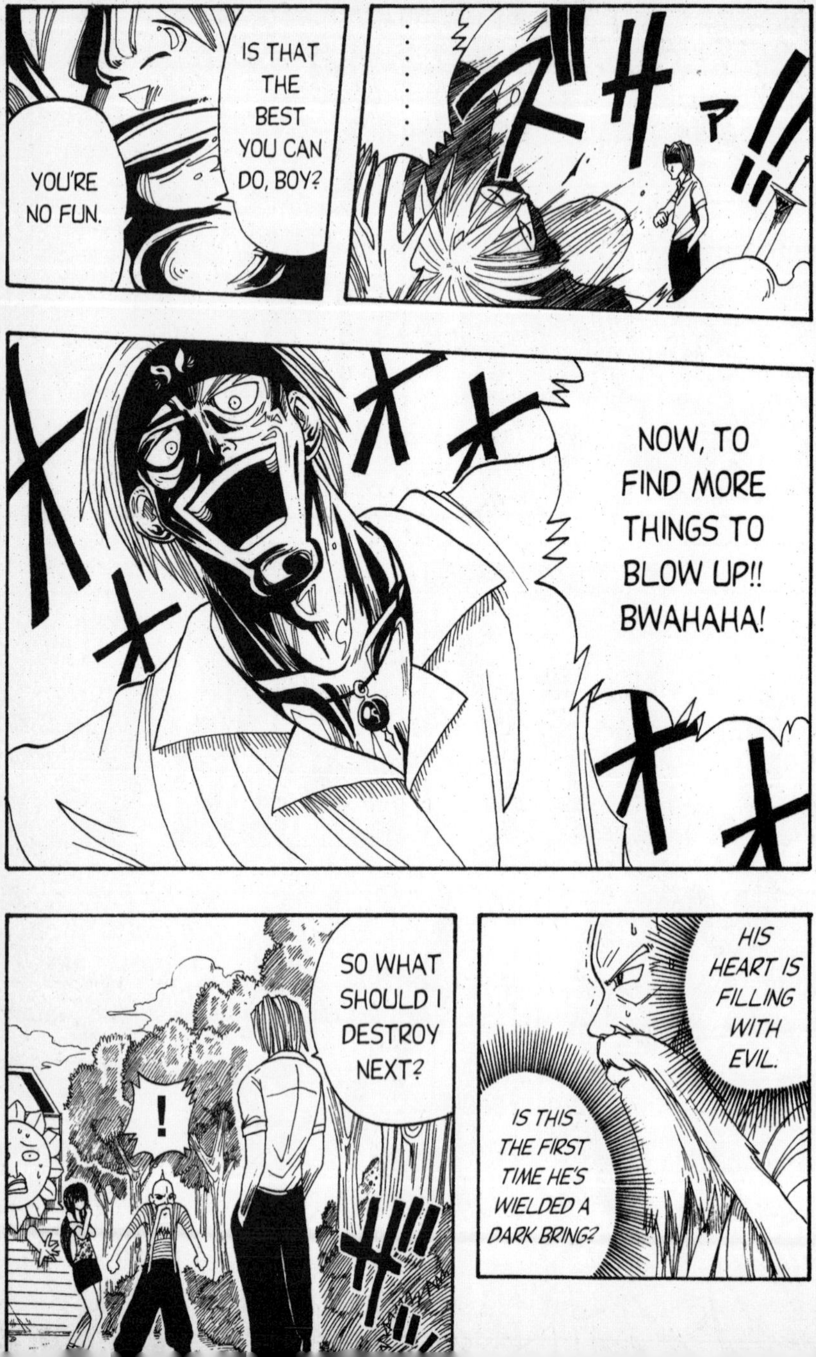
......
IS THAT THE BEST YOU CAN DO, BOY?
YOU'RE NO FUN.
NOW, TO FIND MORE THINGS TO BLOW UP!! BWAHAHA!
HIS HEART IS FILLING WITH EVIL.
IS THIS THE FIRST TIME HE'S WIELDED A DARK BRING?
SO WHAT SHOULD I DESTROY NEXT?
!

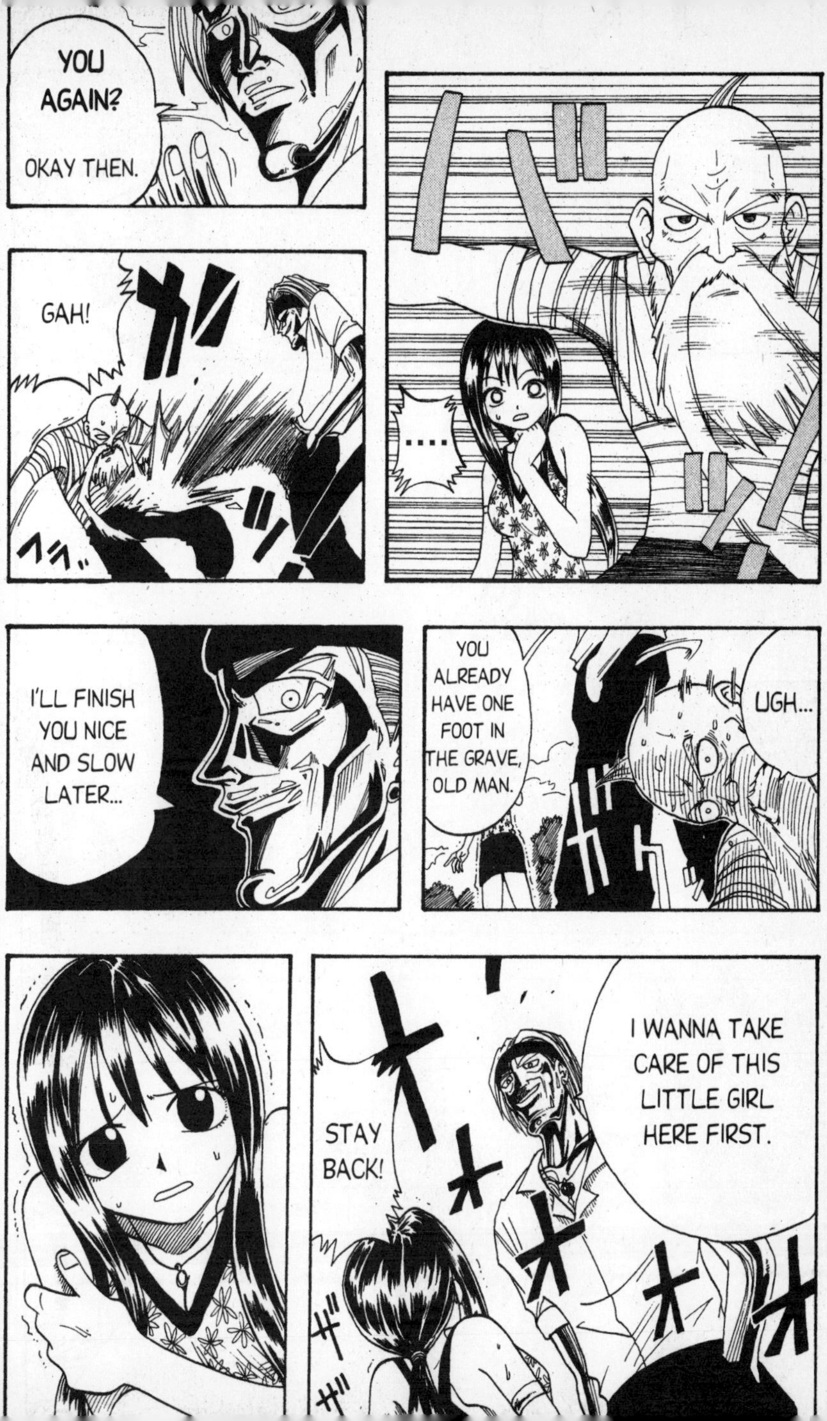
....
YOU AGAIN?
OKAY THEN.
GAH!
UGH...
YOU ALREADY HAVE ONE FOOT IN THE GRAVE, OLD MAN.
I'LL FINISH YOU NICE AND SLOW LATER...
I WANNA TAKE CARE OF THIS LITTLE GIRL HERE FIRST.
STAY BACK!

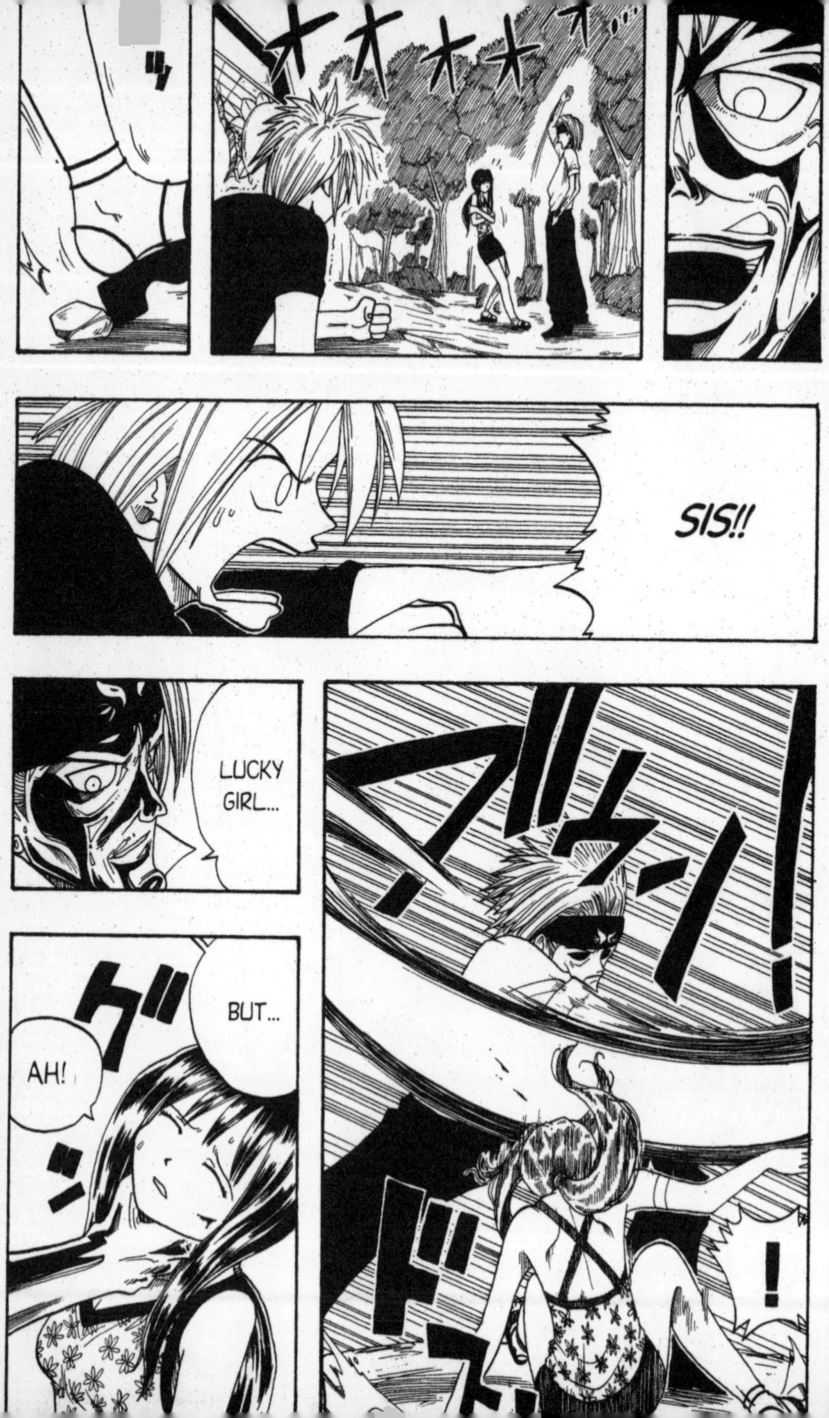
SIS!!
LUCKY GIRL...
BUT...
AH!
!

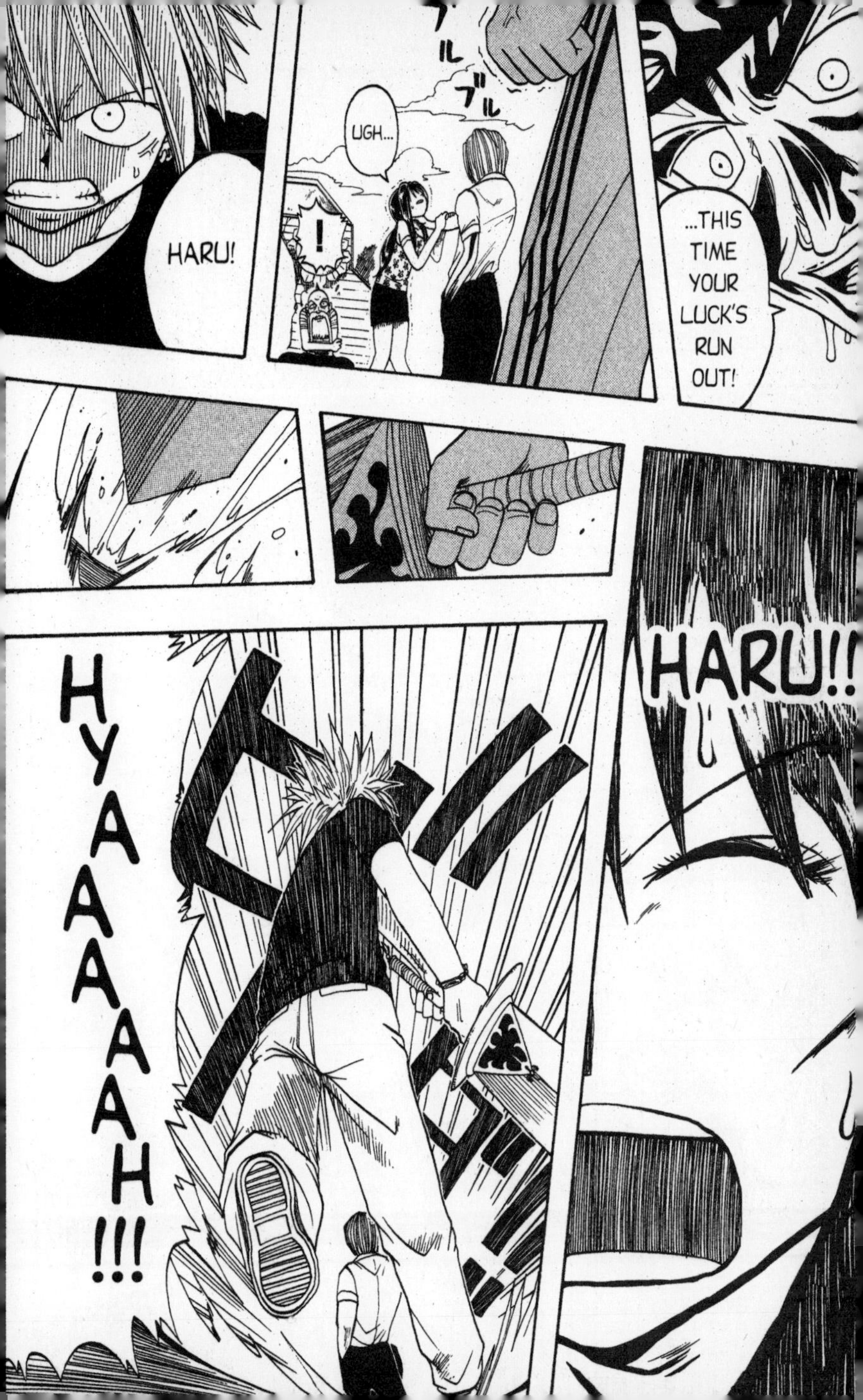
...THIS TIME YOUR LUCK'S RUN OUT!
ブル
ブル
UGH...
!
HARU!
HARU!!
HYAAAAAH!!!

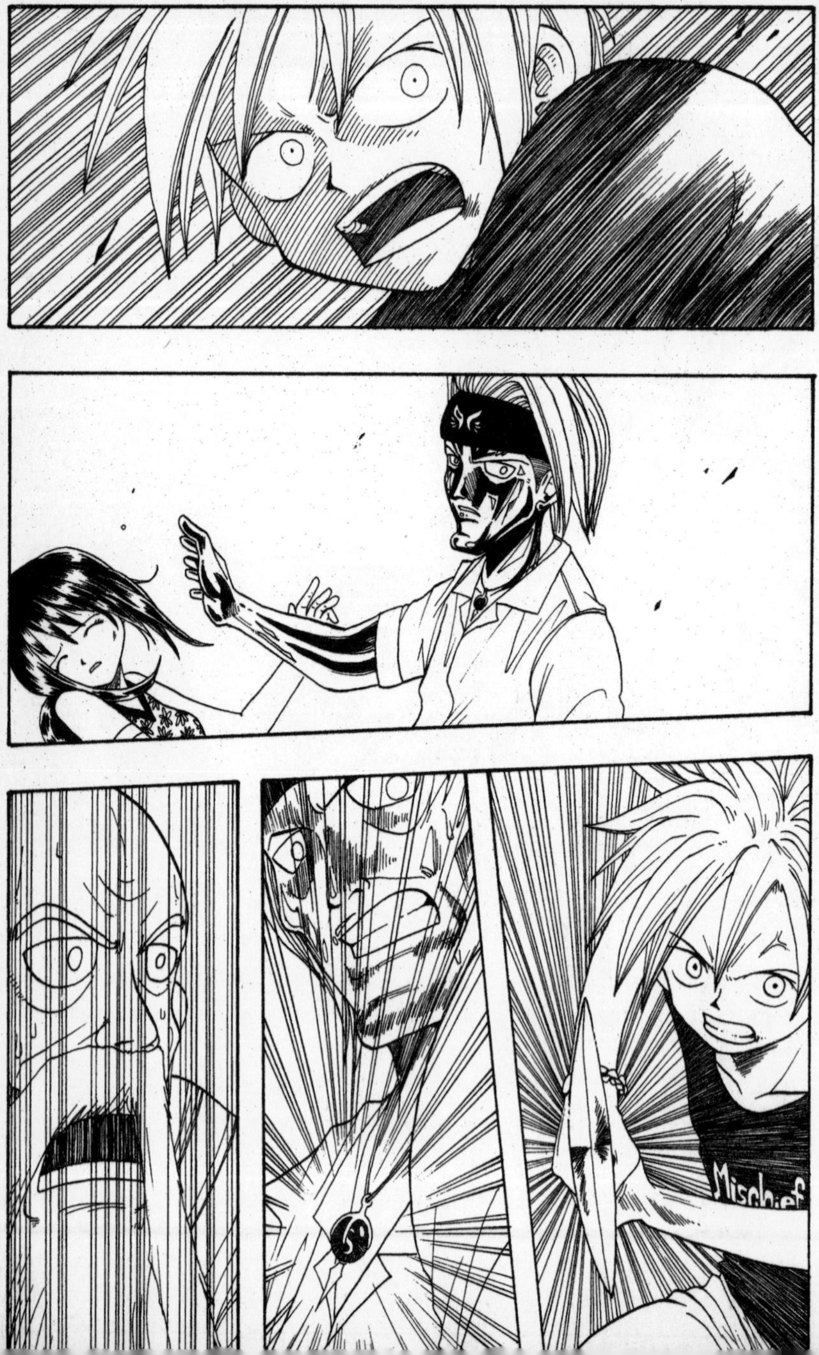
Mischief

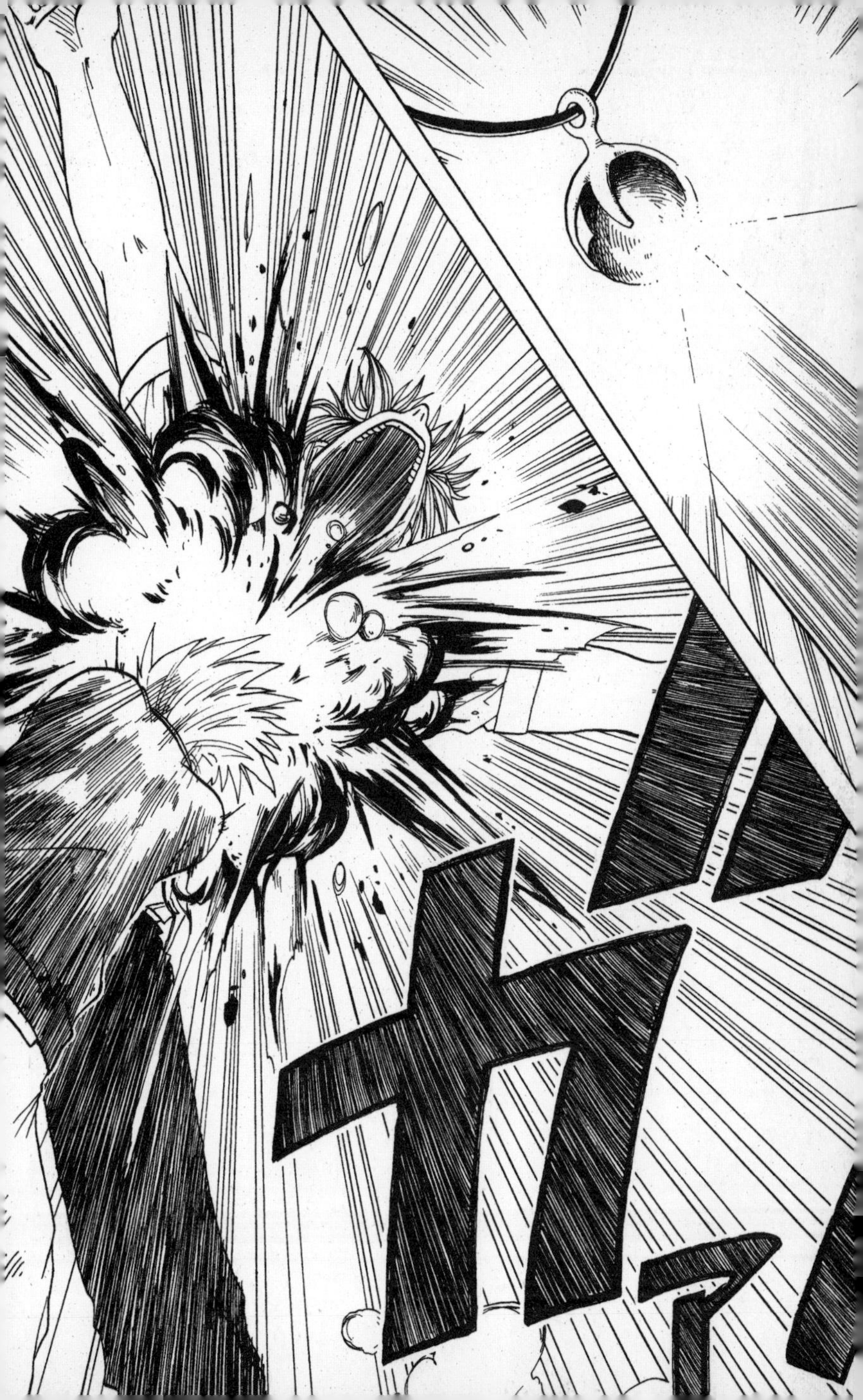

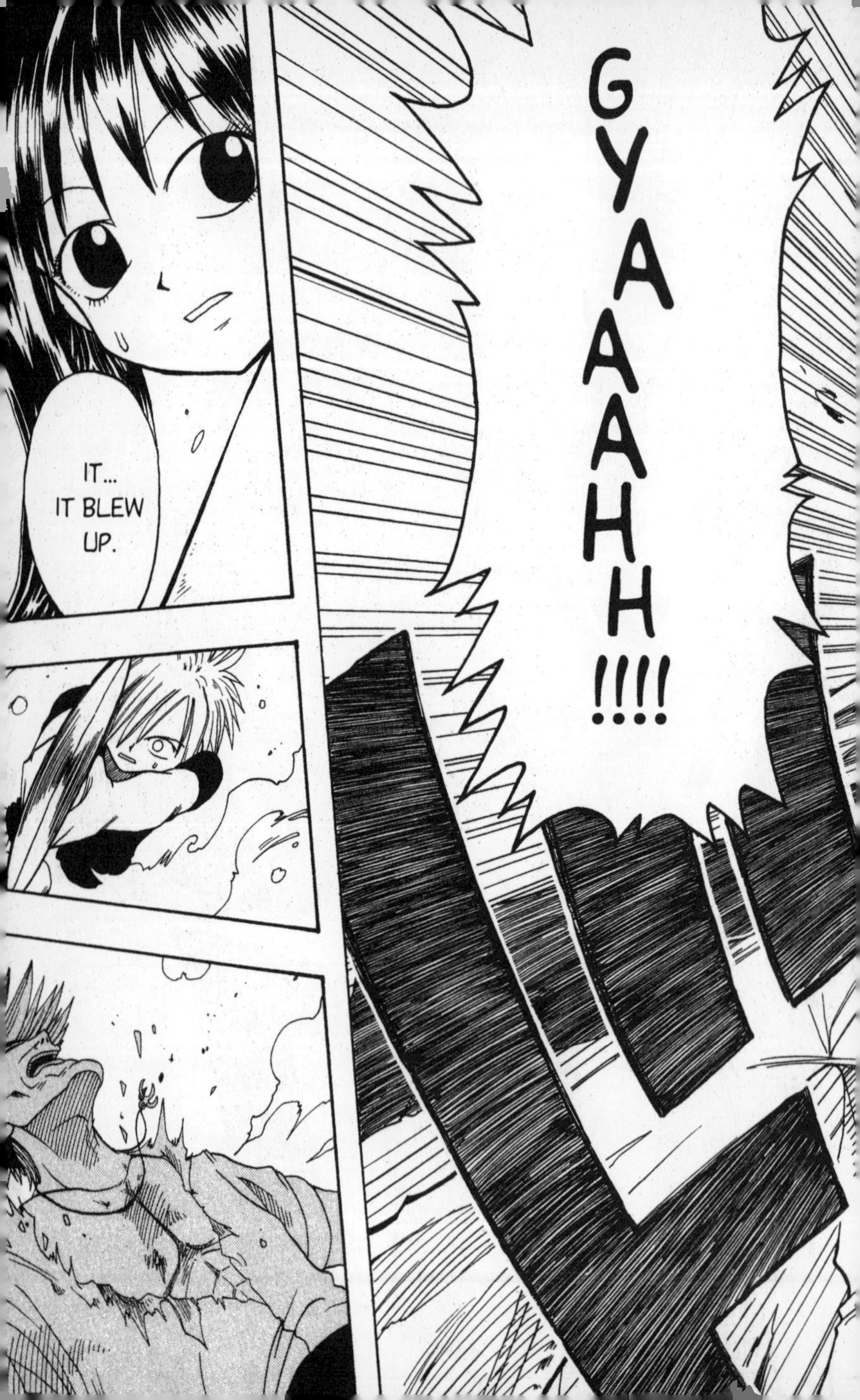
GYAAAH!!!!
IT... IT BLEW UP.

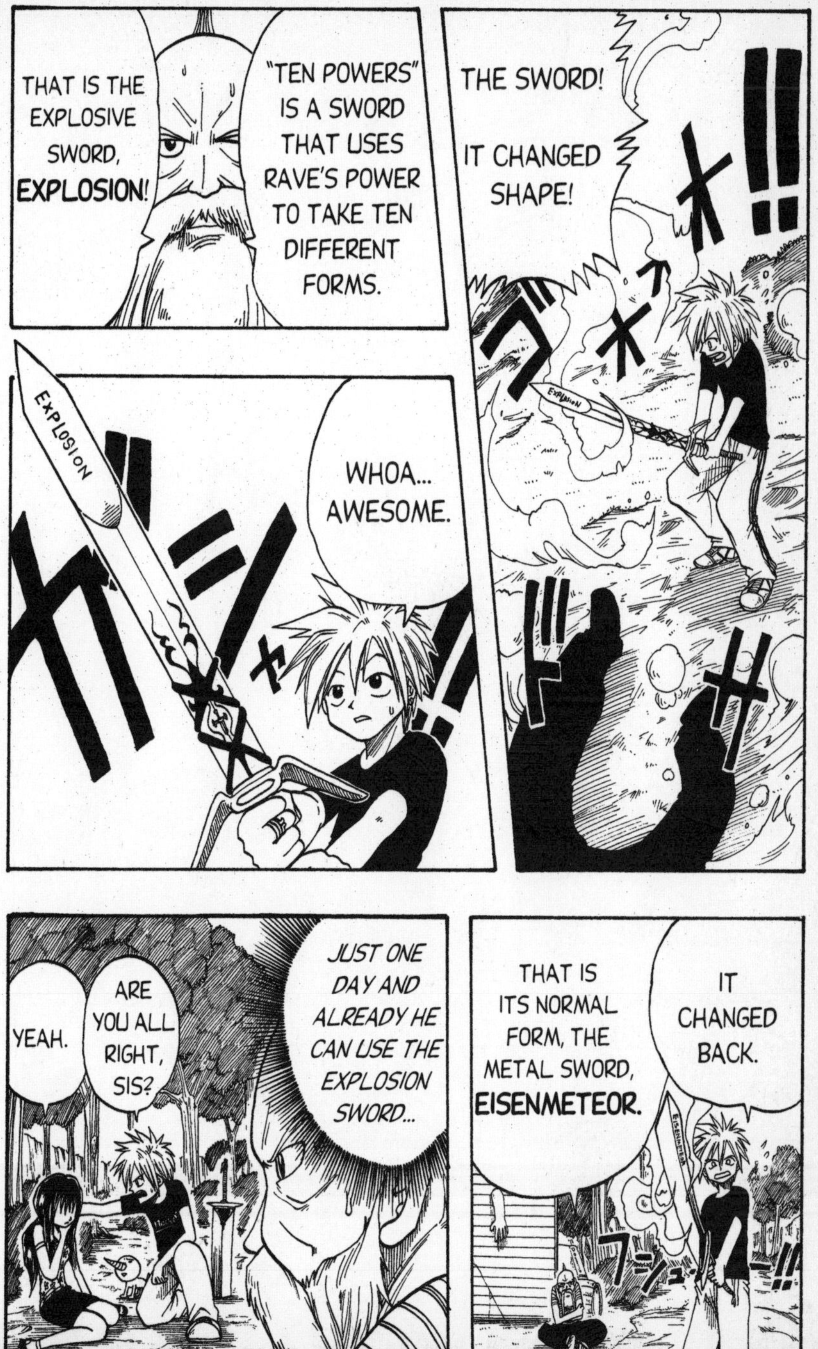
THE SWORD!
IT CHANGED SHAPE!
"TEN POWERS" IS A SWORD THAT USES RAVE'S POWER TO TAKE TEN DIFFERENT FORMS.
THAT IS THE EXPLOSIVE SWORD, **EXPLOSION**!
EXPLOSION
WHOA... AWESOME.
IT CHANGED BACK.
THAT IS ITS NORMAL FORM, THE METAL SWORD, **EISENMETEOR.**
JUST ONE DAY AND ALREADY HE CAN USE THE EXPLOSION SWORD...
ARE YOU ALL RIGHT, SIS?
YEAH.

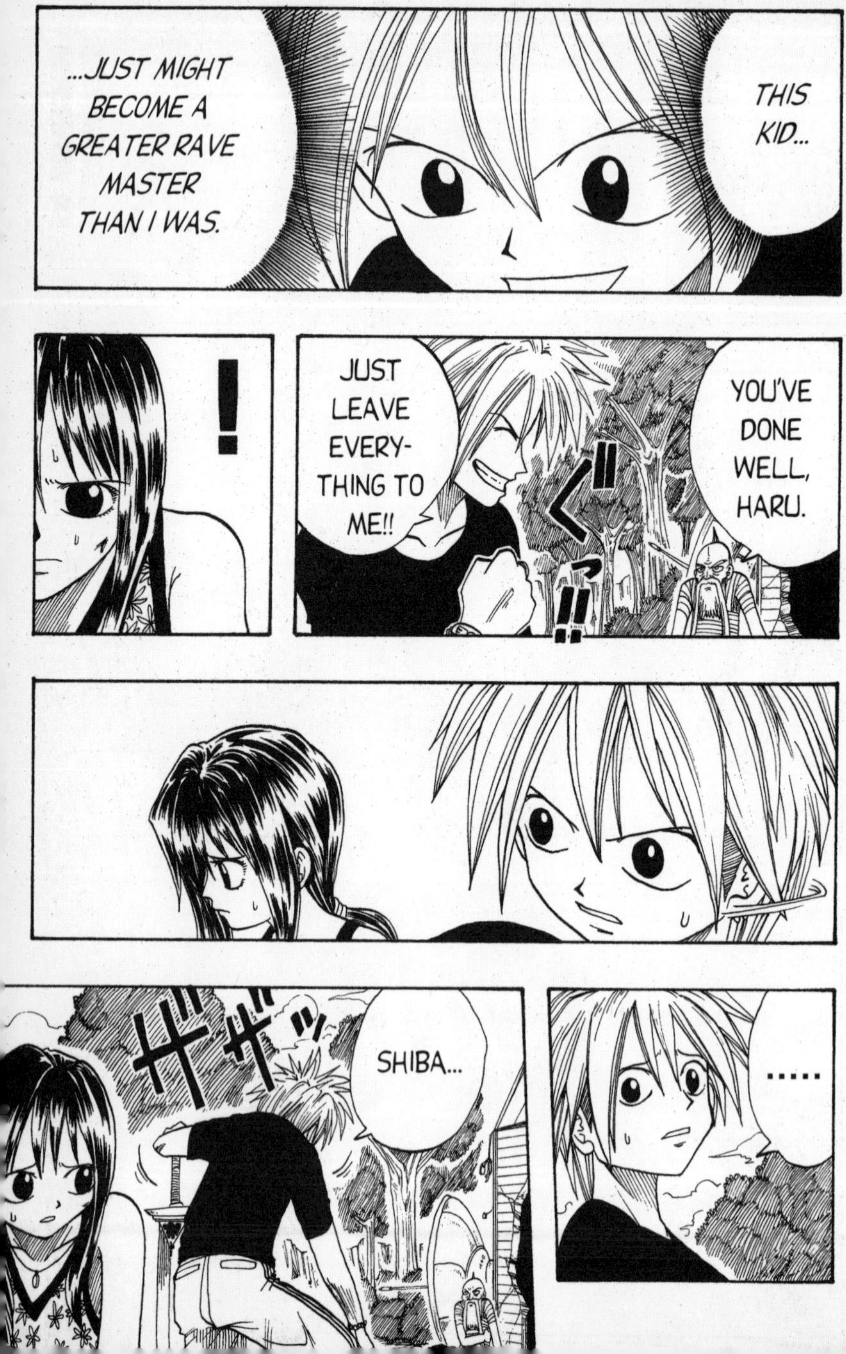
THIS KID...
...JUST MIGHT BECOME A GREATER RAVE MASTER THAN I WAS.
YOU'VE DONE WELL, HARU.
JUST LEAVE EVERY-THING TO ME!!
!
.....
SHIBA...

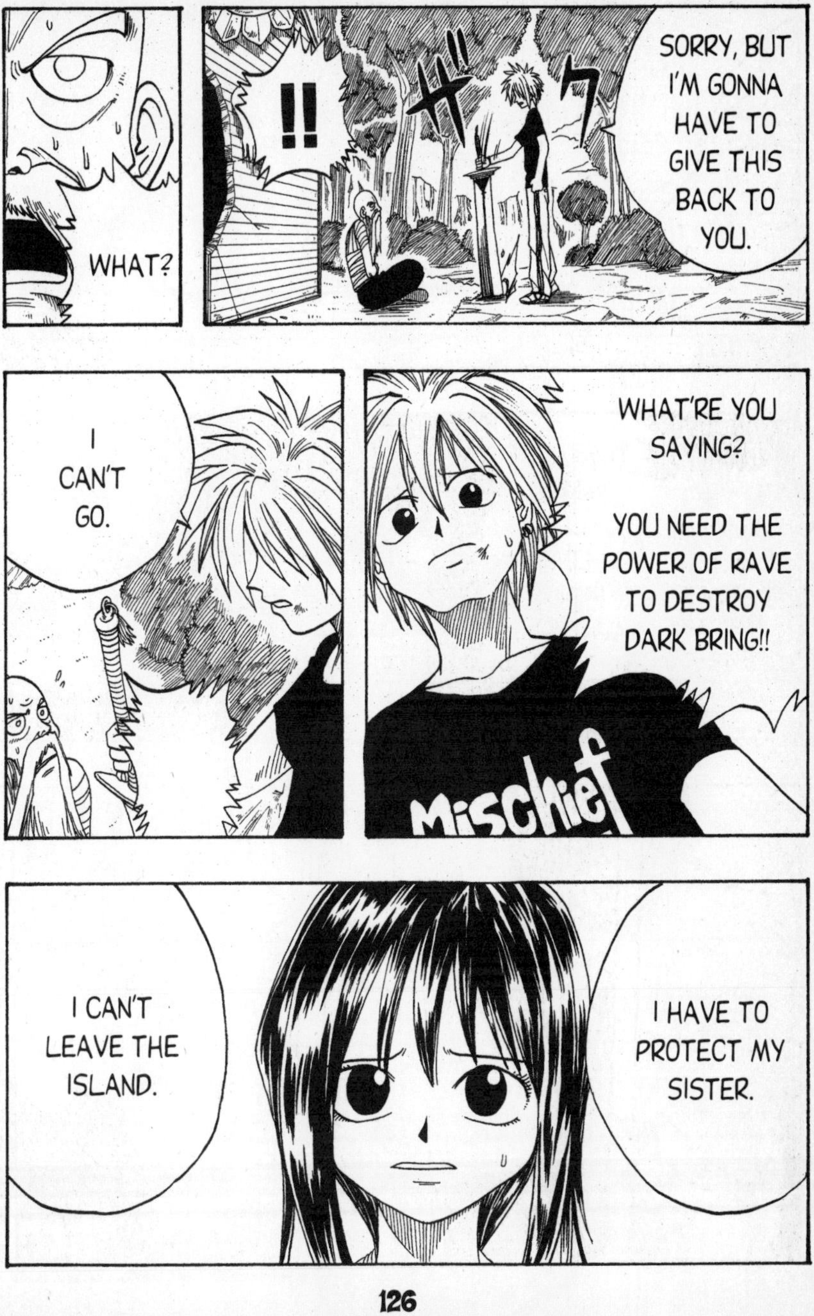
SORRY, BUT I'M GONNA HAVE TO GIVE THIS BACK TO YOU.
ザッ
!!
WHAT?
WHAT'RE YOU SAYING?
YOU NEED THE POWER OF RAVE TO DESTROY DARK BRING!!
Mischief
I CAN'T GO.
I HAVE TO PROTECT MY SISTER.
I CAN'T LEAVE THE ISLAND.

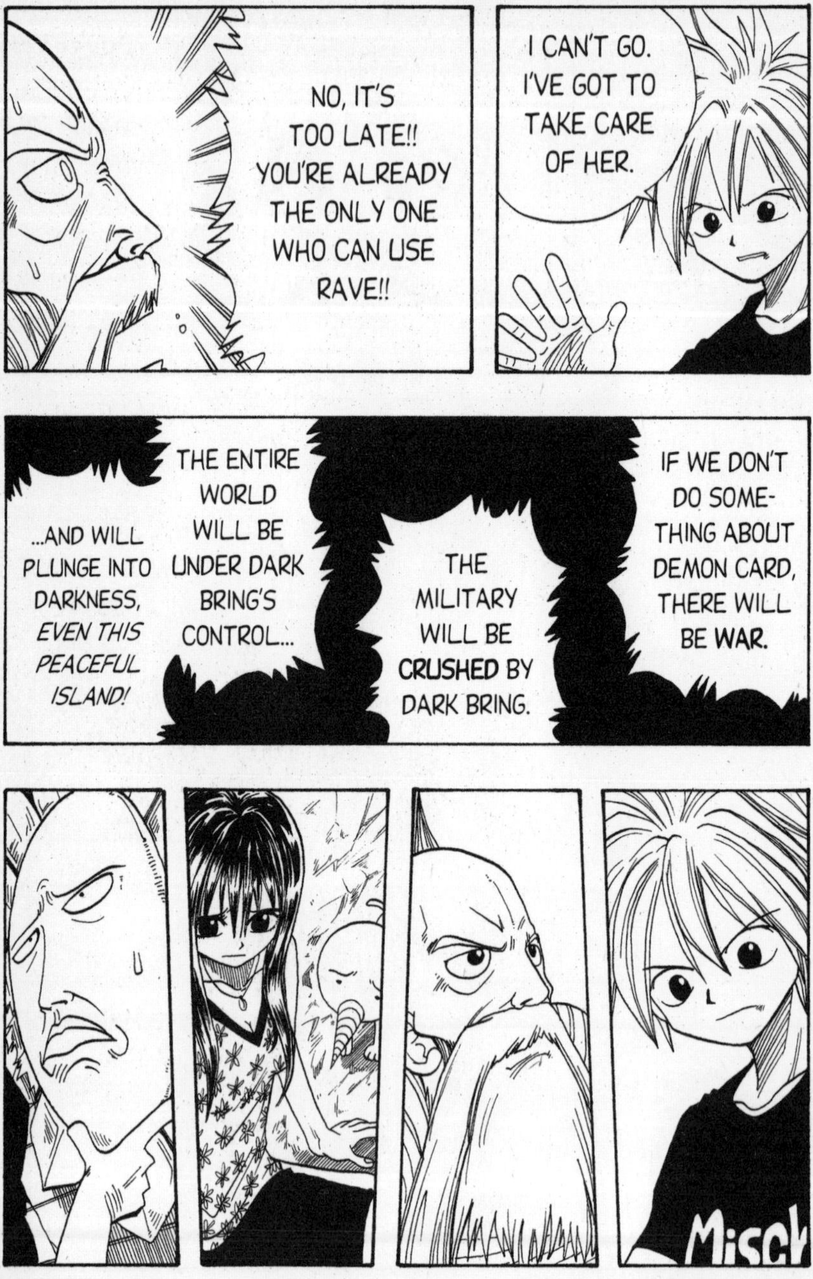
I CAN'T GO. I'VE GOT TO TAKE CARE OF HER.
NO, IT'S TOO LATE!! YOU'RE ALREADY THE ONLY ONE WHO CAN USE RAVE!!
IF WE DON'T DO SOME-THING ABOUT DEMON CARD, THERE WILL BE **WAR.**
THE MILITARY WILL BE **CRUSHED** BY DARK BRING.
THE ENTIRE WORLD WILL BE UNDER DARK BRING'S CONTROL...
...AND WILL PLUNGE INTO DARKNESS, *EVEN THIS PEACEFUL ISLAND!*
Misch

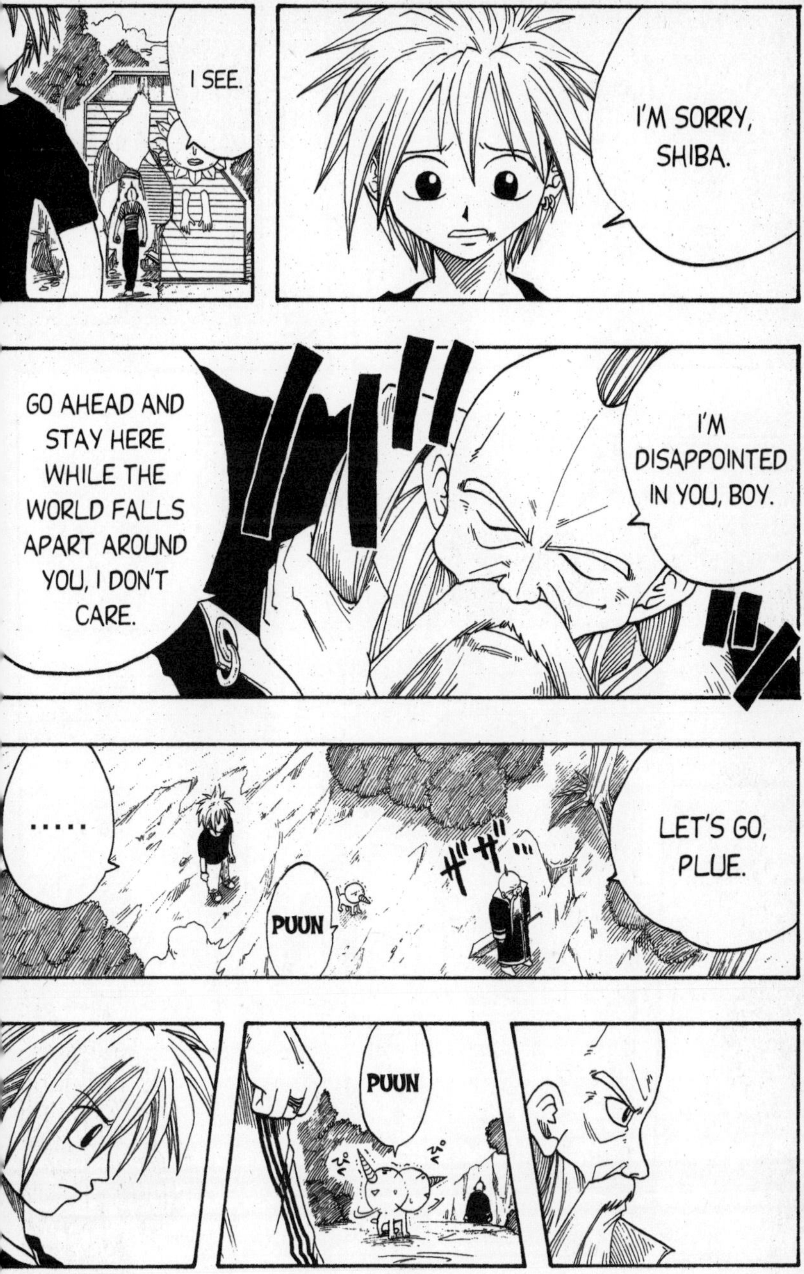
I'M SORRY, SHIBA.
I SEE.
I'M DISAPPOINTED IN YOU, BOY.
GO AHEAD AND STAY HERE WHILE THE WORLD FALLS APART AROUND YOU, I DON'T CARE.
LET'S GO, PLUE.
PUUN
.....
PUUN

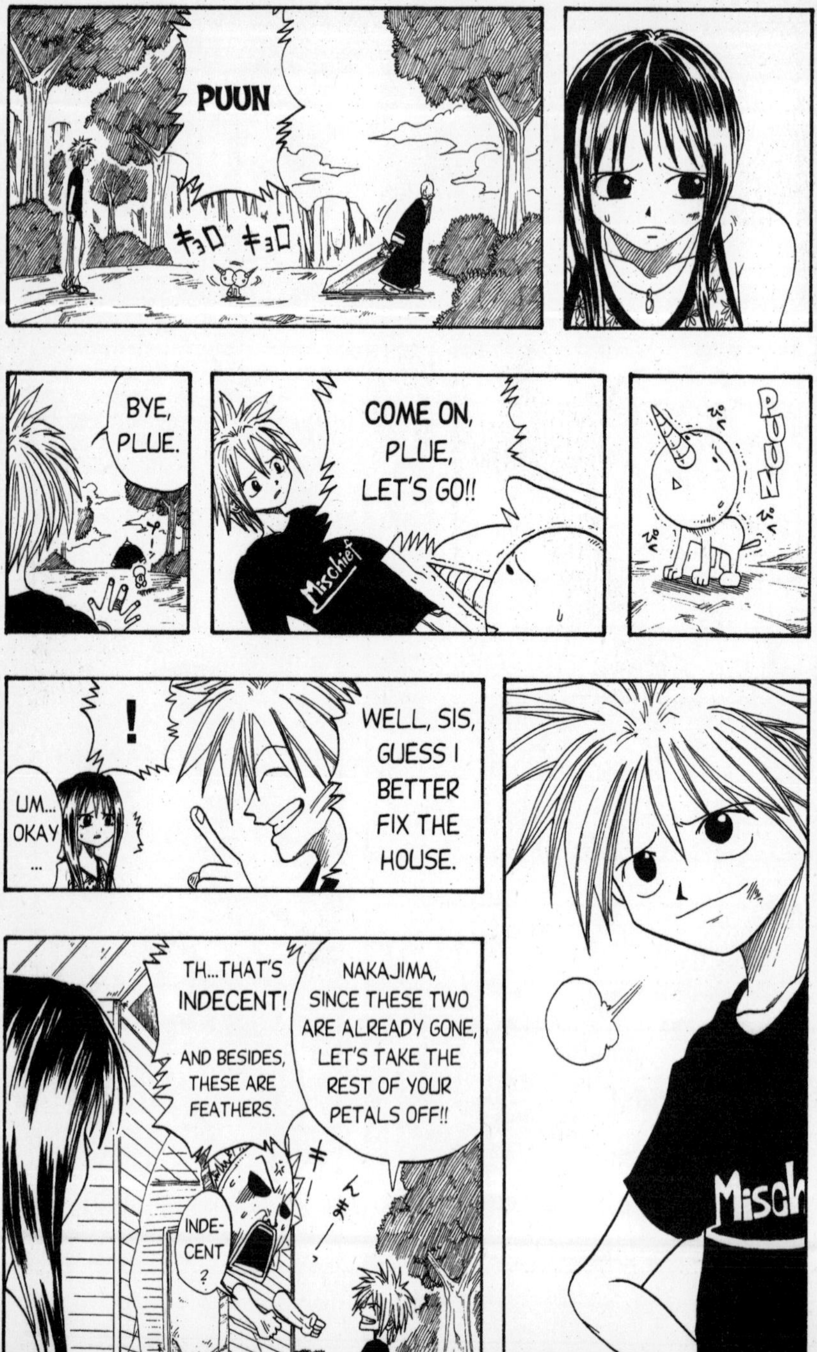
PUUN
キョロ キョロ
PUUN
COME ON, PLUE, LET'S GO!!
Mischief
BYE, PLUE.
Misch
WELL, SIS, GUESS I BETTER FIX THE HOUSE.
!
UM... OKAY ...
NAKAJIMA, SINCE THESE TWO ARE ALREADY GONE, LET'S TAKE THE REST OF YOUR PETALS OFF!!
TH...THAT'S INDECENT!
AND BESIDES, THESE ARE FEATHERS.
INDE-CENT?

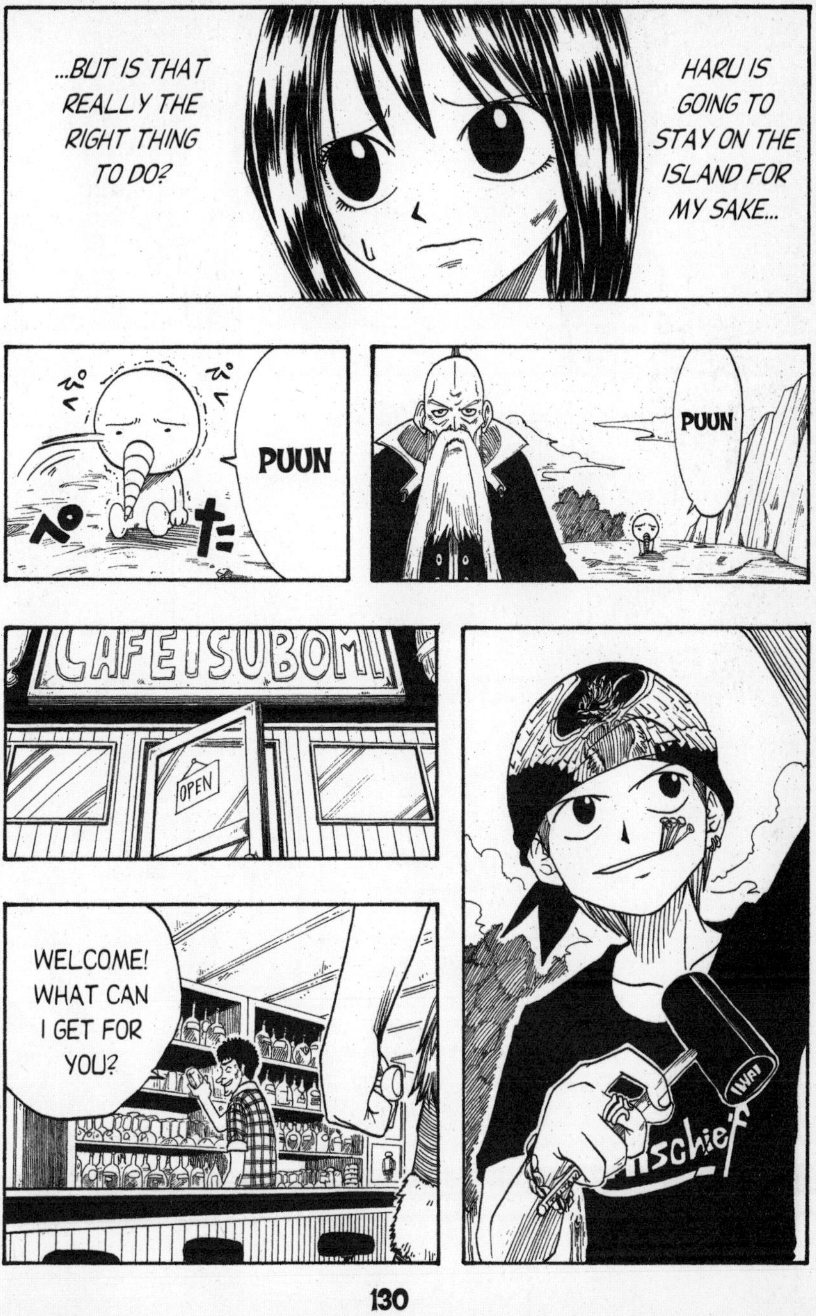
HARU IS GOING TO STAY ON THE ISLAND FOR MY SAKE...
...BUT IS THAT REALLY THE RIGHT THING TO DO?
PUUN
PUUN
ぴく
ぴく
ぺ
た
CAFE TSUBOMI
OPEN
WELCOME! WHAT CAN I GET FOR YOU?

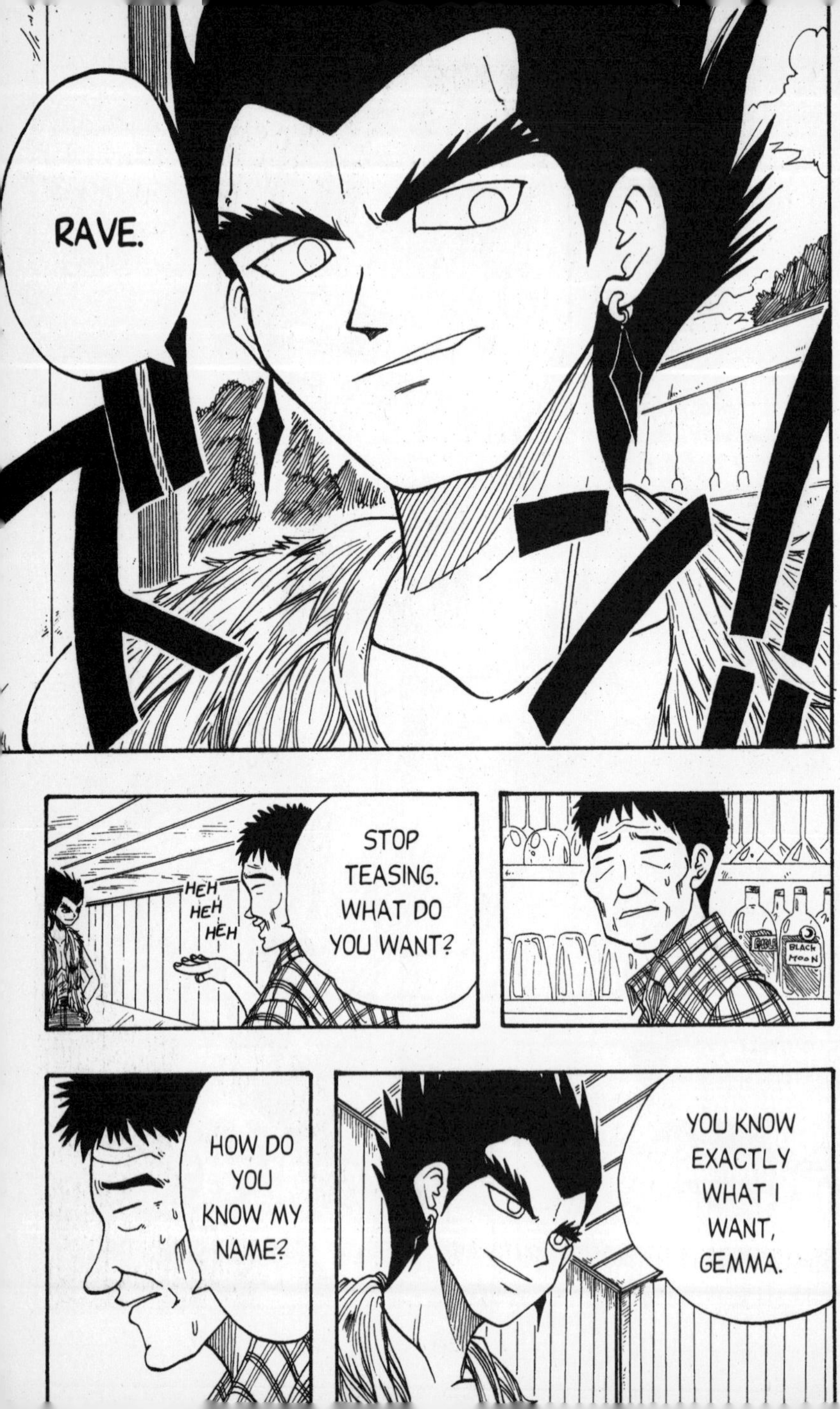
RAVE.
HEH HEH HEH
STOP TEASING. WHAT DO YOU WANT?
BLACK MOON
YOU KNOW EXACTLY WHAT I WANT, GEMMA.
HOW DO YOU KNOW MY NAME?

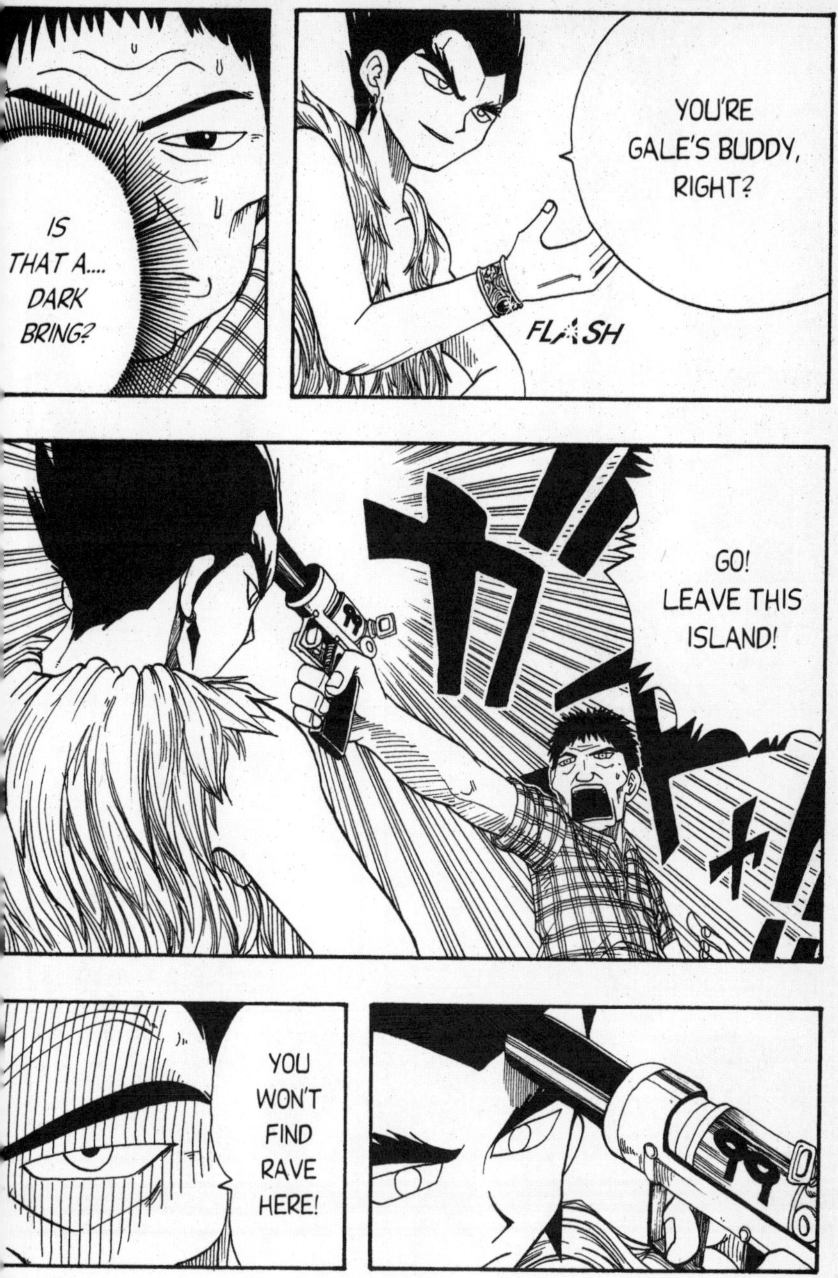
YOU'RE GALE'S BUDDY, RIGHT?
FLASH
IS THAT A.... DARK BRING?
GO! LEAVE THIS ISLAND!
YOU WON'T FIND RAVE HERE!

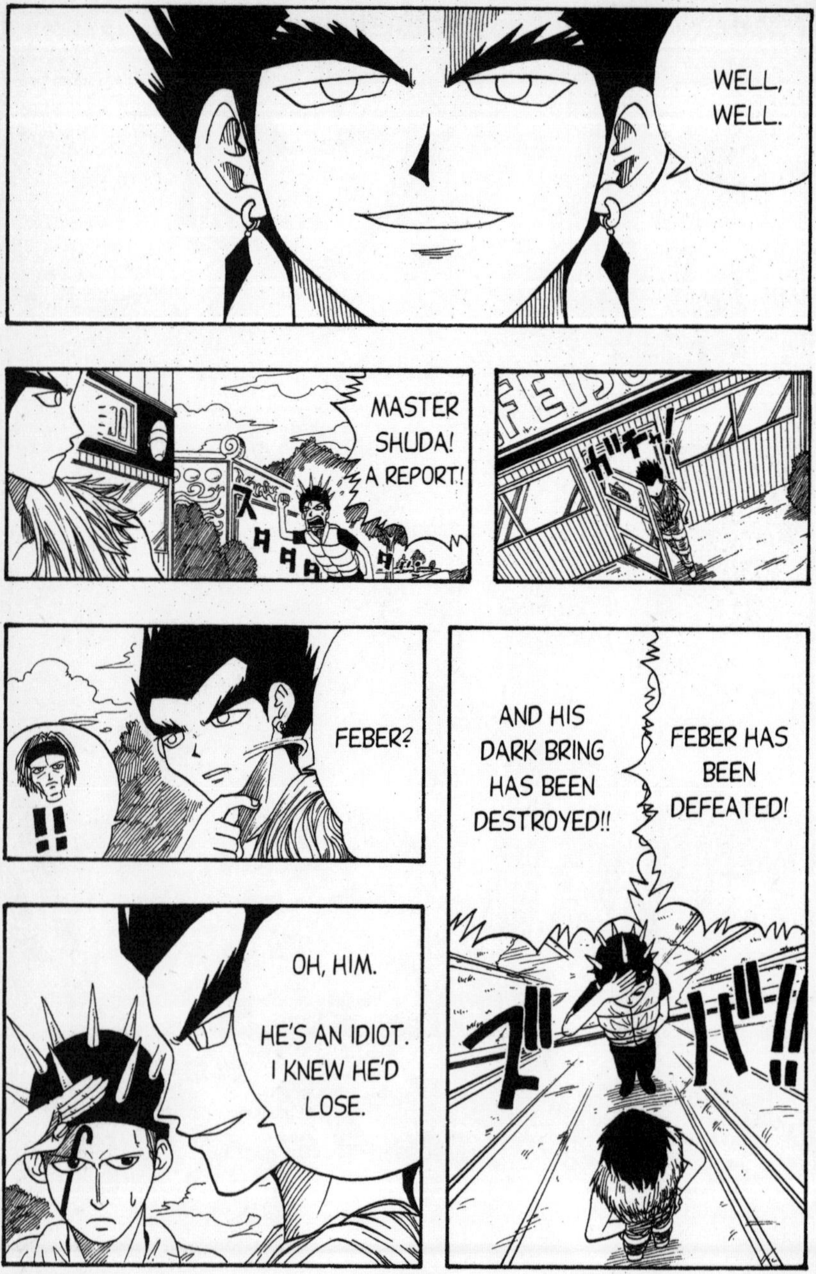
WELL, WELL.
MASTER SHUDA! A REPORT!
FEBER HAS BEEN DEFEATED!
AND HIS DARK BRING HAS BEEN DESTROYED!!
FEBER?
OH, HIM.
HE'S AN IDIOT. I KNEW HE'D LOSE.

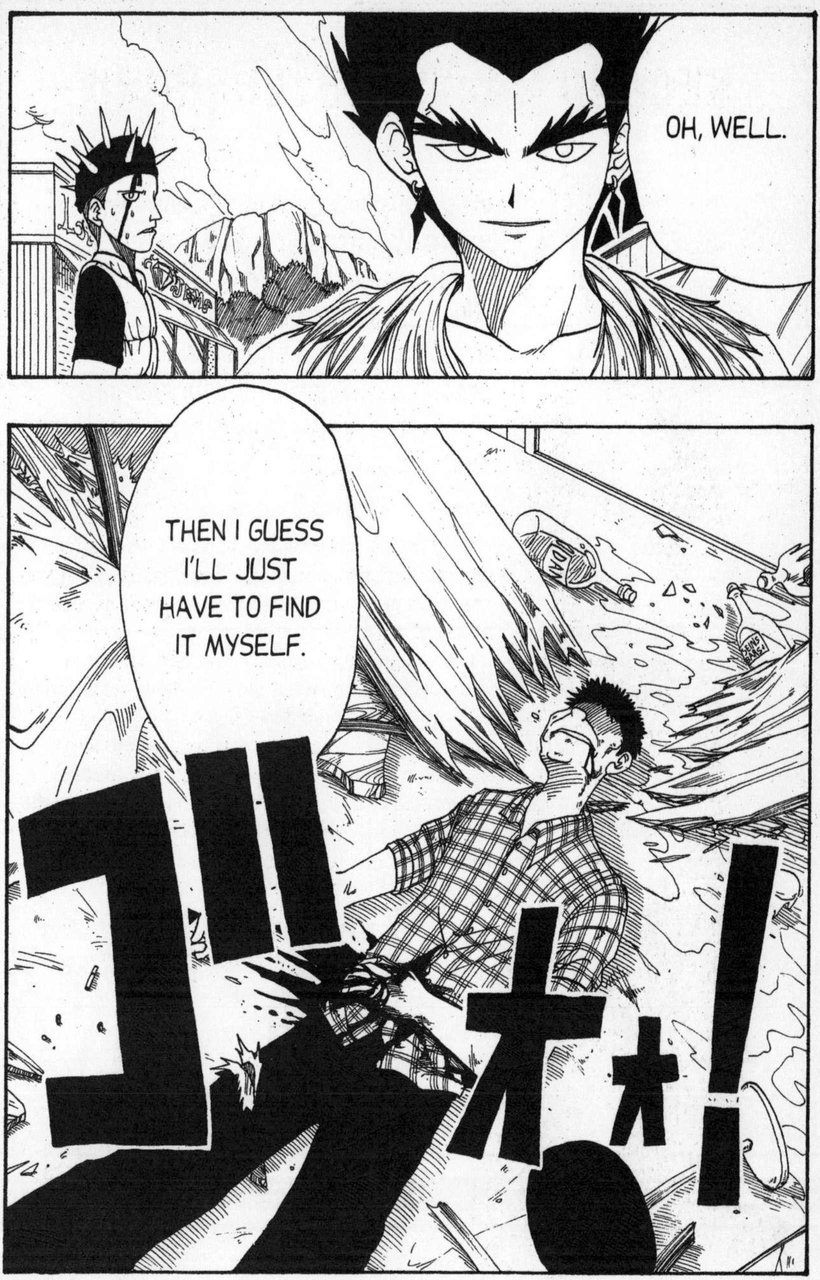
OH, WELL.
THEN I GUESS I'LL JUST HAVE TO FIND IT MYSELF.
ゴオォ!

SECOND RAVE MASTER: HARU

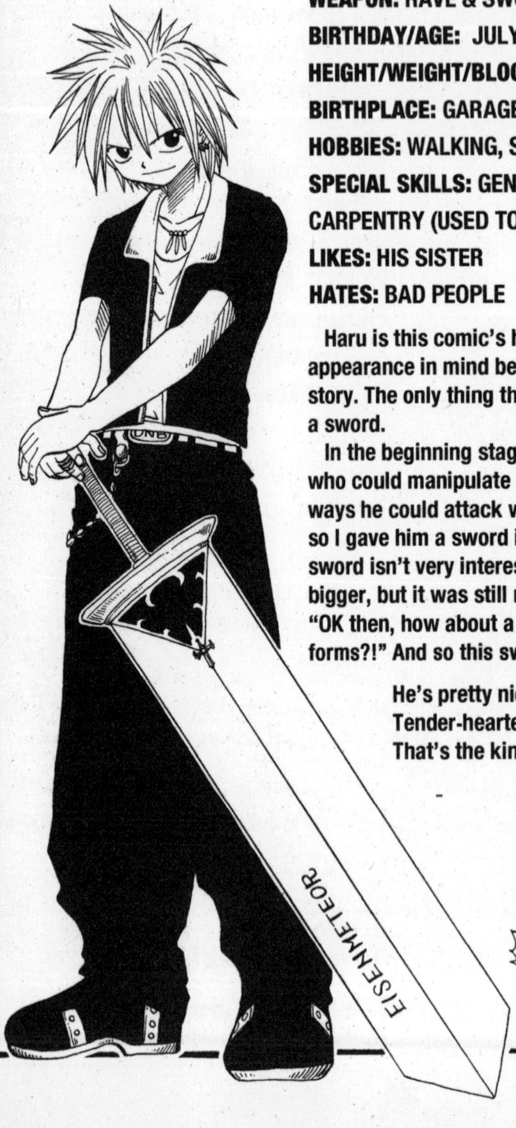
EISENMETEOR

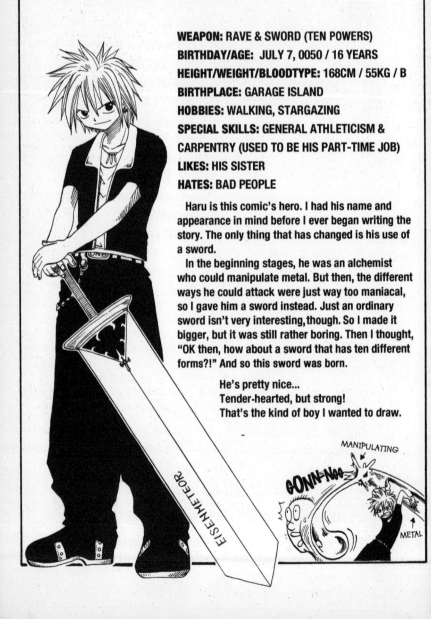

WEAPON: RAVE & SWORD (TEN POWERS)
BIRTHDAY/AGE: JULY 7, 0050 / 16 YEARS
HEIGHT/WEIGHT/BLOODTYPE: 168CM / 55KG / B
BIRTHPLACE: GARAGE ISLAND
HOBBIES: WALKING, STARGAZING
SPECIAL SKILLS: GENERAL ATHLETICISM & CARPENTRY (USED TO BE HIS PART-TIME JOB)
LIKES: HIS SISTER
HATES: BAD PEOPLE

Haru is this comic's hero. I had his name and appearance in mind before I ever began writing the story. The only thing that has changed is his use of a sword.

In the beginning stages, he was an alchemist who could manipulate metal. But then, the different ways he could attack were just way too maniacal, so I gave him a sword instead. Just an ordinary sword isn't very interesting, though. So I made it bigger, but it was still rather boring. Then I thought, "OK then, how about a sword that has ten different forms?!" And so this sword was born.

He's pretty nice...
Tender-hearted, but strong!
That's the kind of boy I wanted to draw.

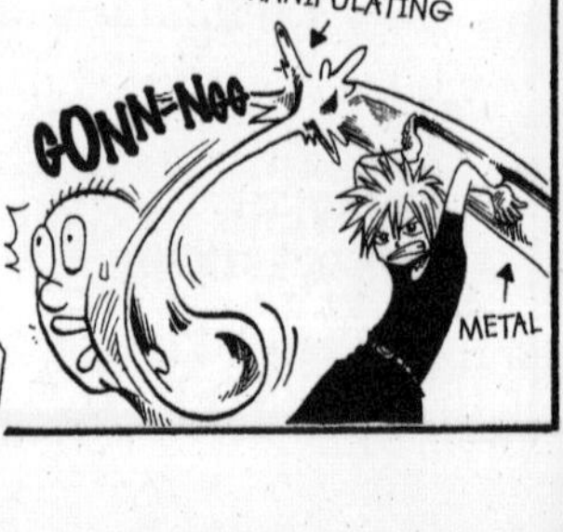
MANIPULATING
GONN-NOO
METAL

RAVE'S BEARER: PLUE

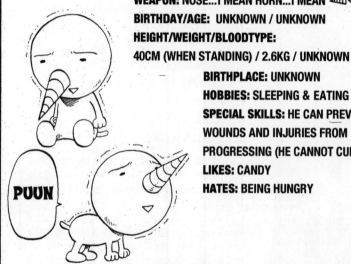

WEAPON: NOSE...I MEAN HORN...I MEAN ◁▥ ←THIS
BIRTHDAY/AGE: UNKNOWN / UNKNOWN
HEIGHT/WEIGHT/BLOODTYPE:
40CM (WHEN STANDING) / 2.6KG / UNKNOWN

BIRTHPLACE: UNKNOWN
HOBBIES: SLEEPING & EATING
SPECIAL SKILLS: HE CAN PREVENT
WOUNDS AND INJURIES FROM
PROGRESSING (HE CANNOT CURE THEM)
LIKES: CANDY
HATES: BEING HUNGRY

PUUN

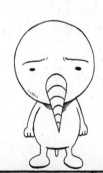

This character I thought up while doodling in
middle school, but I never thought he would appear
in my comic.
Even I don't remember if I modeled him after a
dog or what, so he's kinda mysterious. Incidentally,
he may appear simple, but he's actually hard to draw.

ANSWERS
TO YOUR QUESTIONS
ABOUT **RAVE**
MASTER

Q. How many Raves are there?
A. Five, including Shiba's

Q. Why is Plue always shaking?
A. It's a secret!

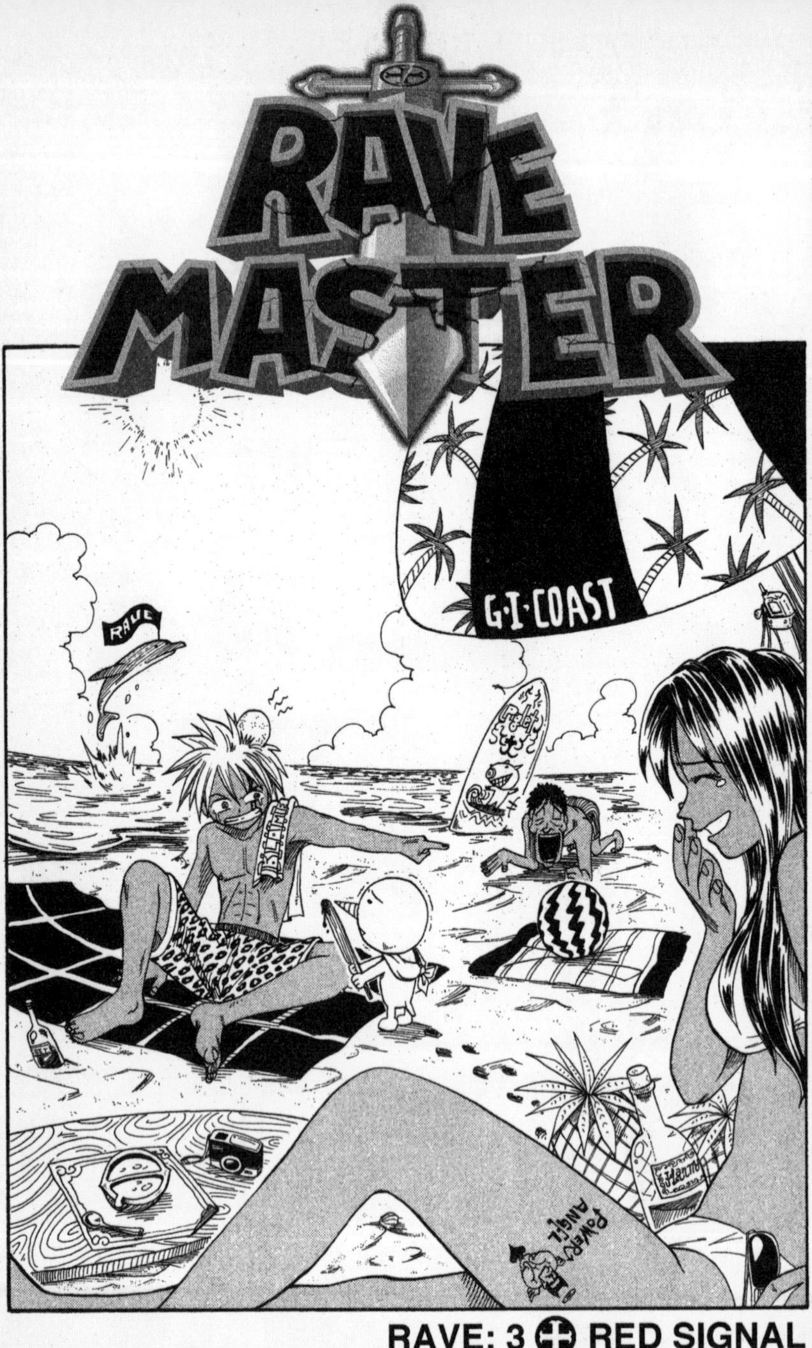
RAVE MASTER
G·I·COAST
RAVE
POWER ANGEL

RAVE: 3 RED SIGNAL

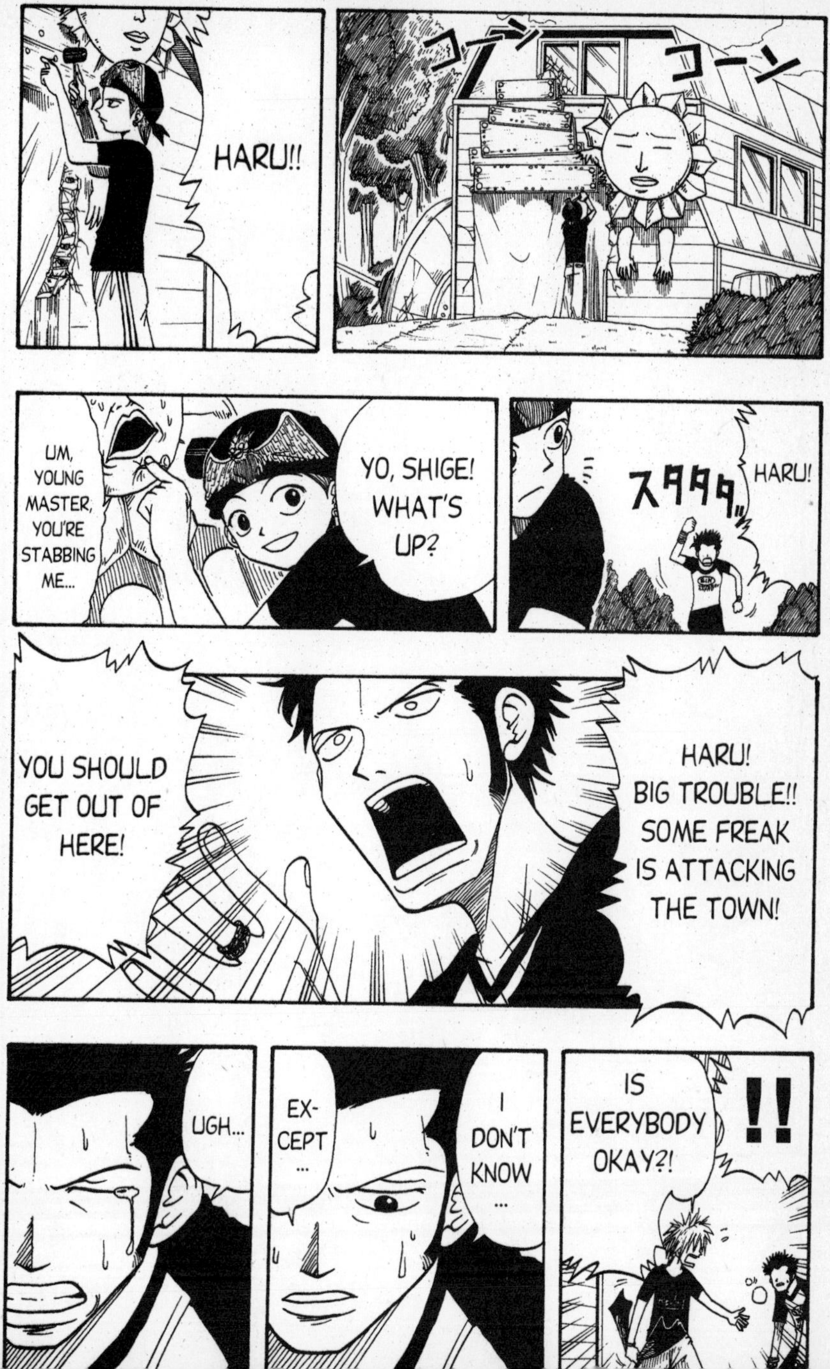
コーン
コーン
HARU!!
HARU!
スタタタ
YO, SHIGE! WHAT'S UP?
UM, YOUNG MASTER, YOU'RE STABBING ME...
HARU! BIG TROUBLE!! SOME FREAK IS ATTACKING THE TOWN!
YOU SHOULD GET OUT OF HERE!
!!
IS EVERYBODY OKAY?!
I DON'T KNOW...
EX-CEPT...
UGH...

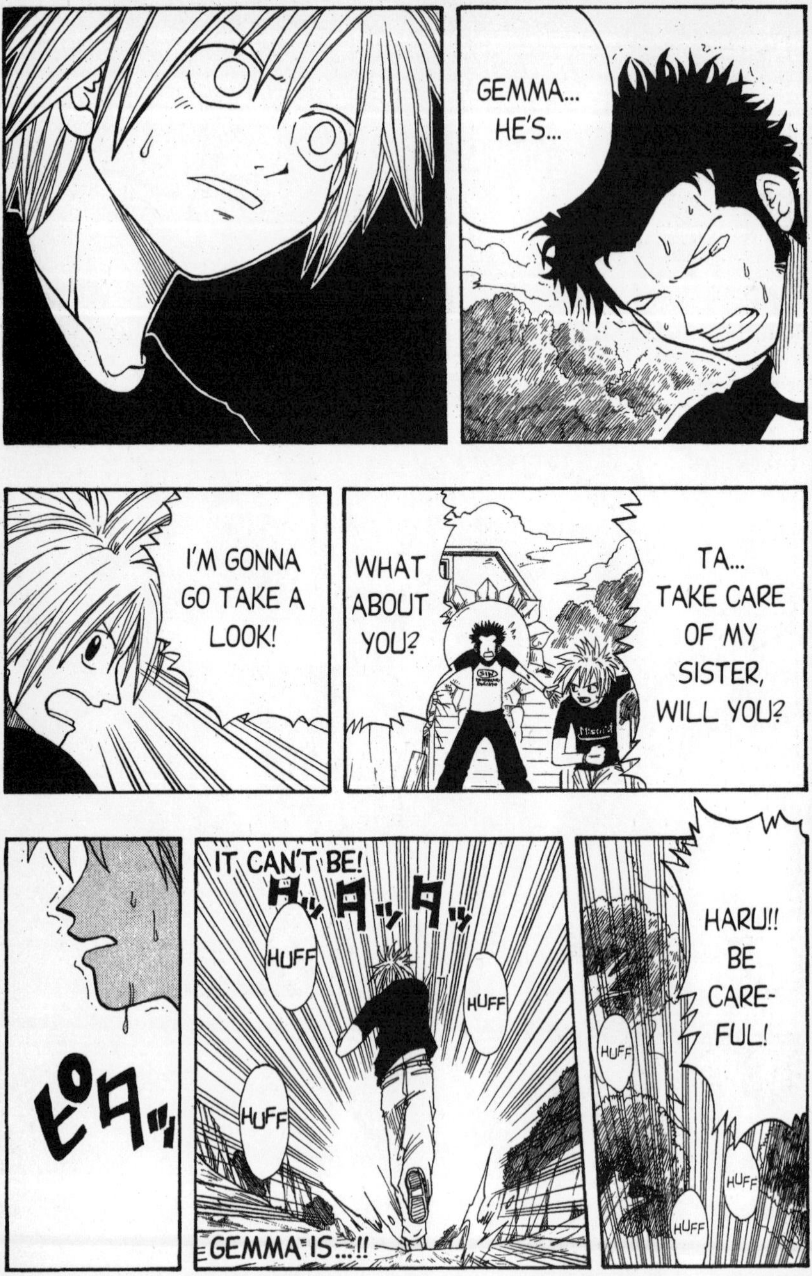
GEMMA... HE'S...
TA... TAKE CARE OF MY SISTER, WILL YOU?
WHAT ABOUT YOU?
I'M GONNA GO TAKE A LOOK!
HARU!! BE CARE-FUL!
HUFF
HUFF
HUFF
IT CAN'T BE!
ダッダッダッ
HUFF
HUFF
HUFF
GEMMA IS...!!
ピタッ

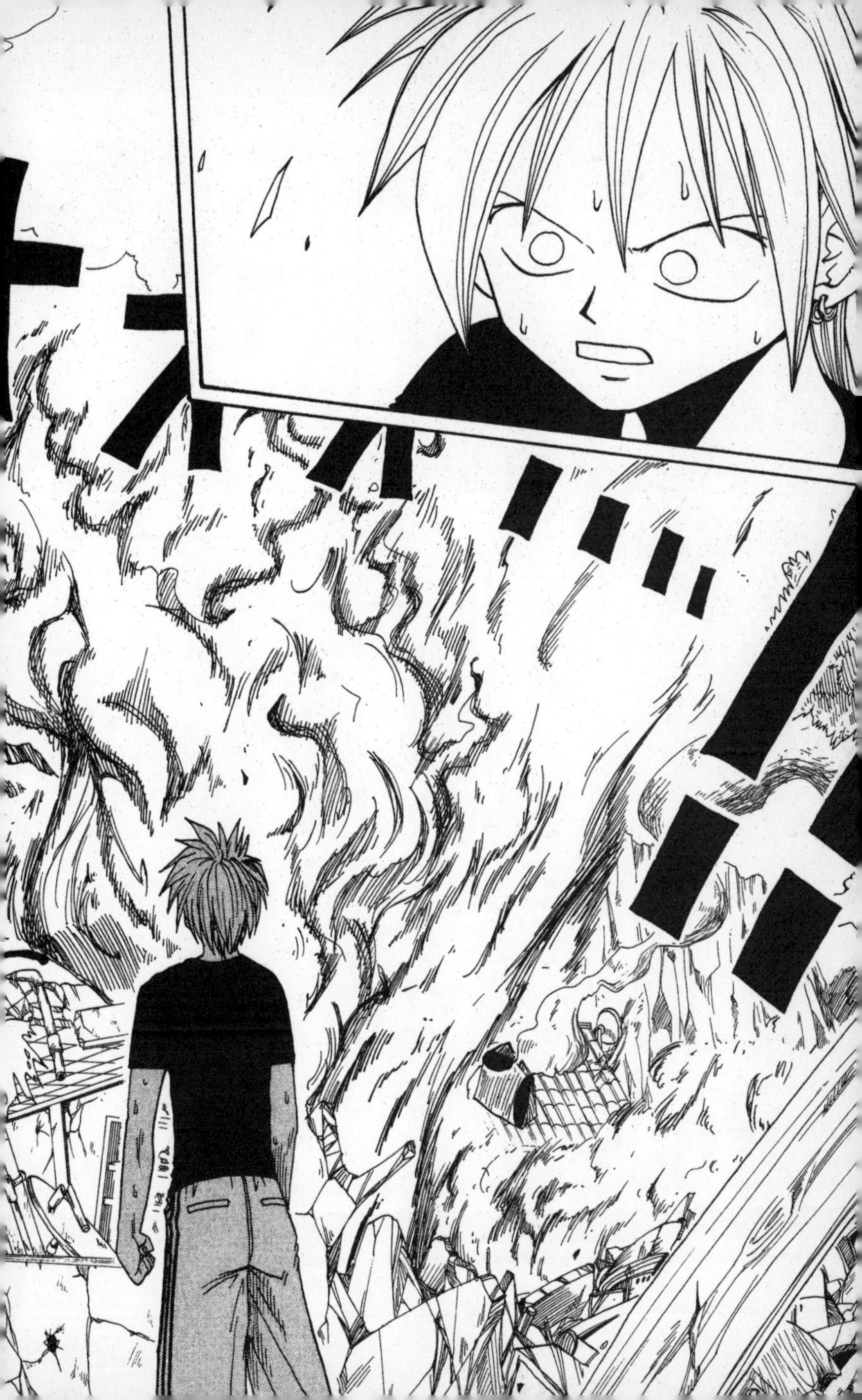

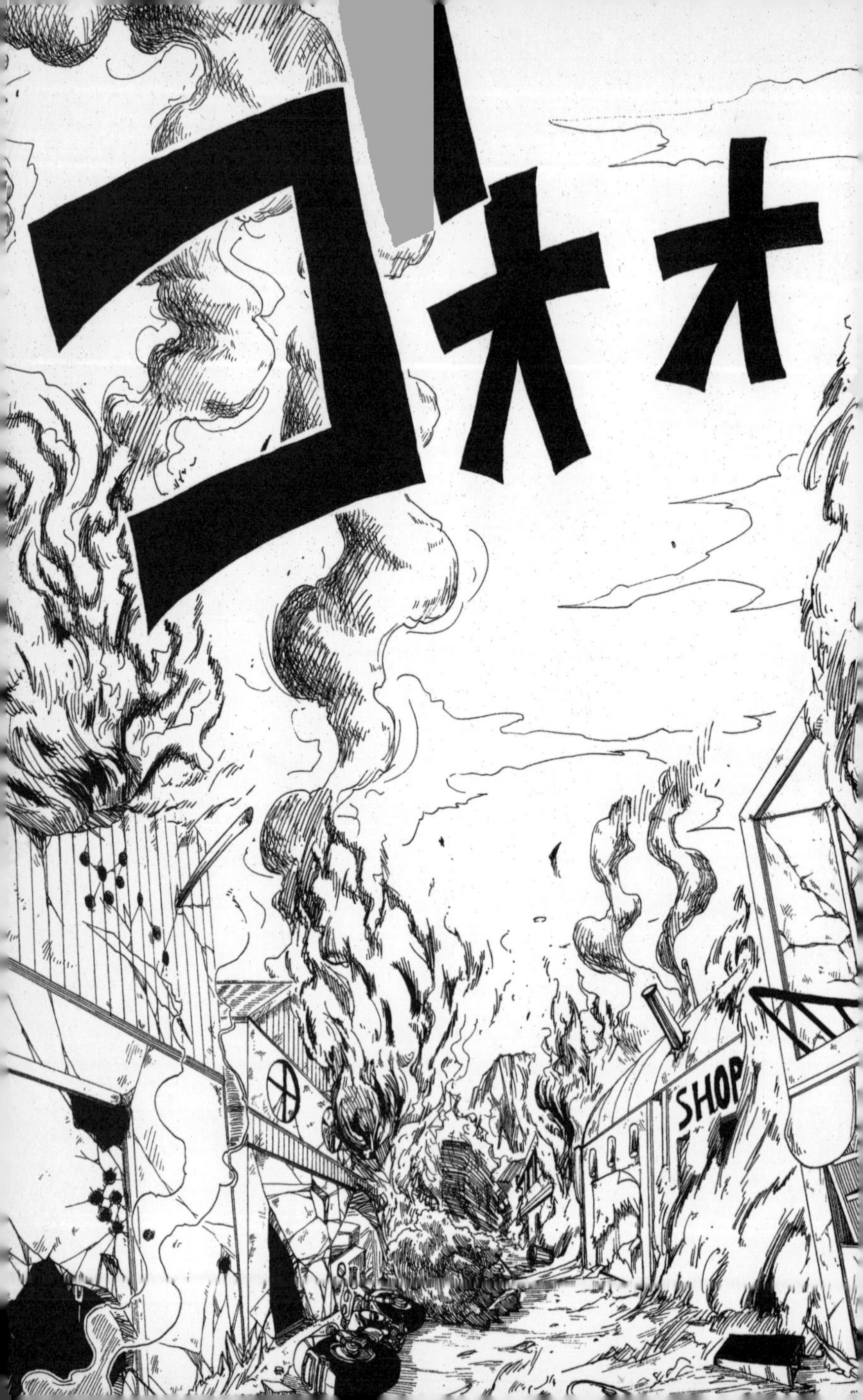
コオオ
SHOP

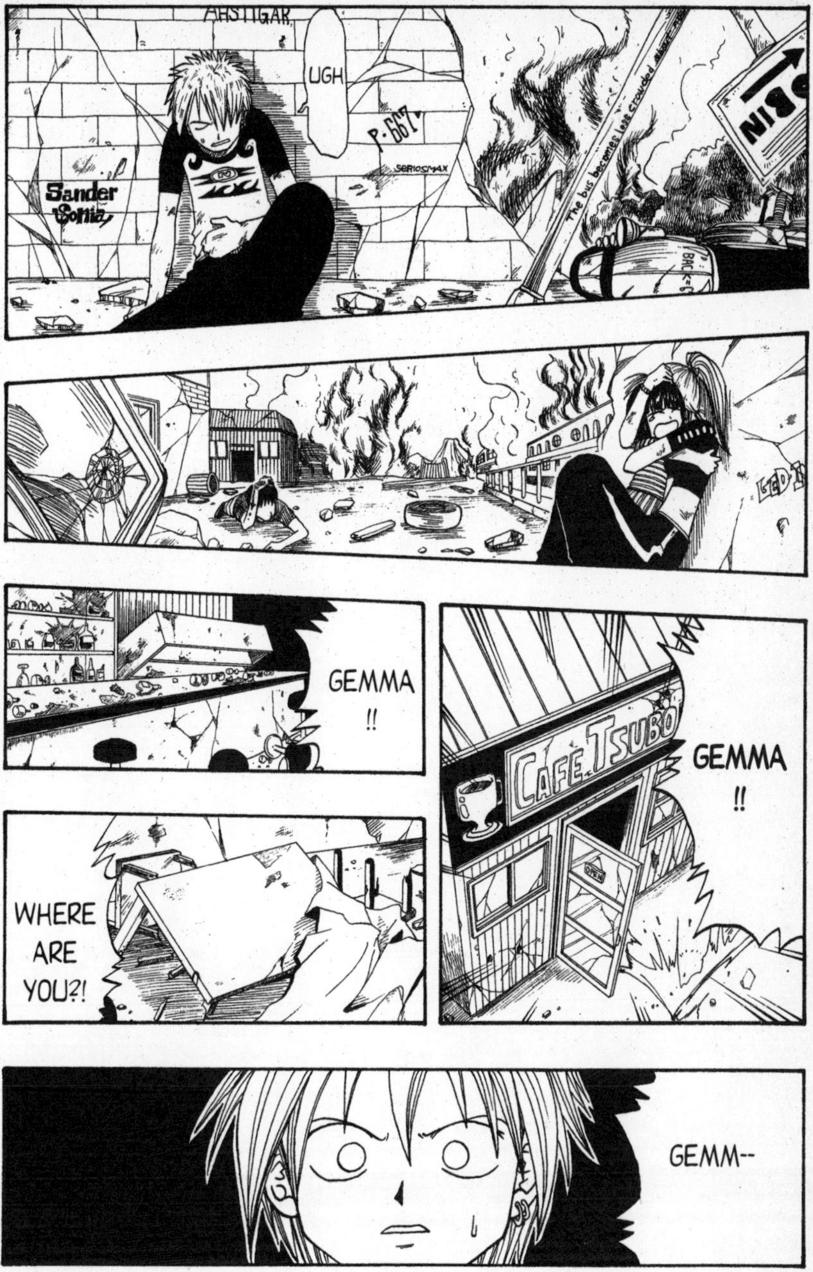
UGH
CAFE TSUBO
GEMMA !!
GEMMA !!
WHERE ARE YOU?!
GEMM--

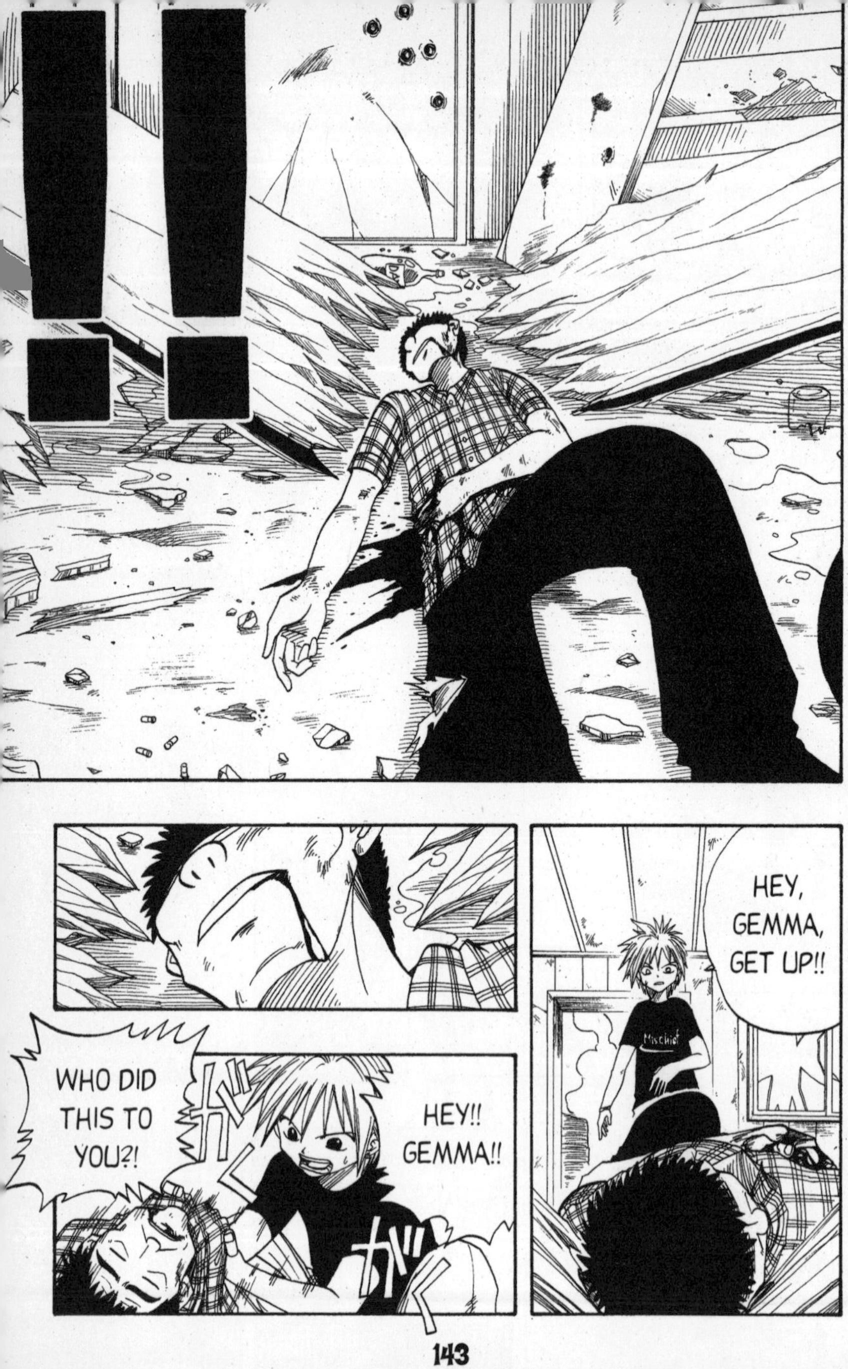
!!
HEY, GEMMA, GET UP!!
HEY!! GEMMA!!
WHO DID THIS TO YOU?!

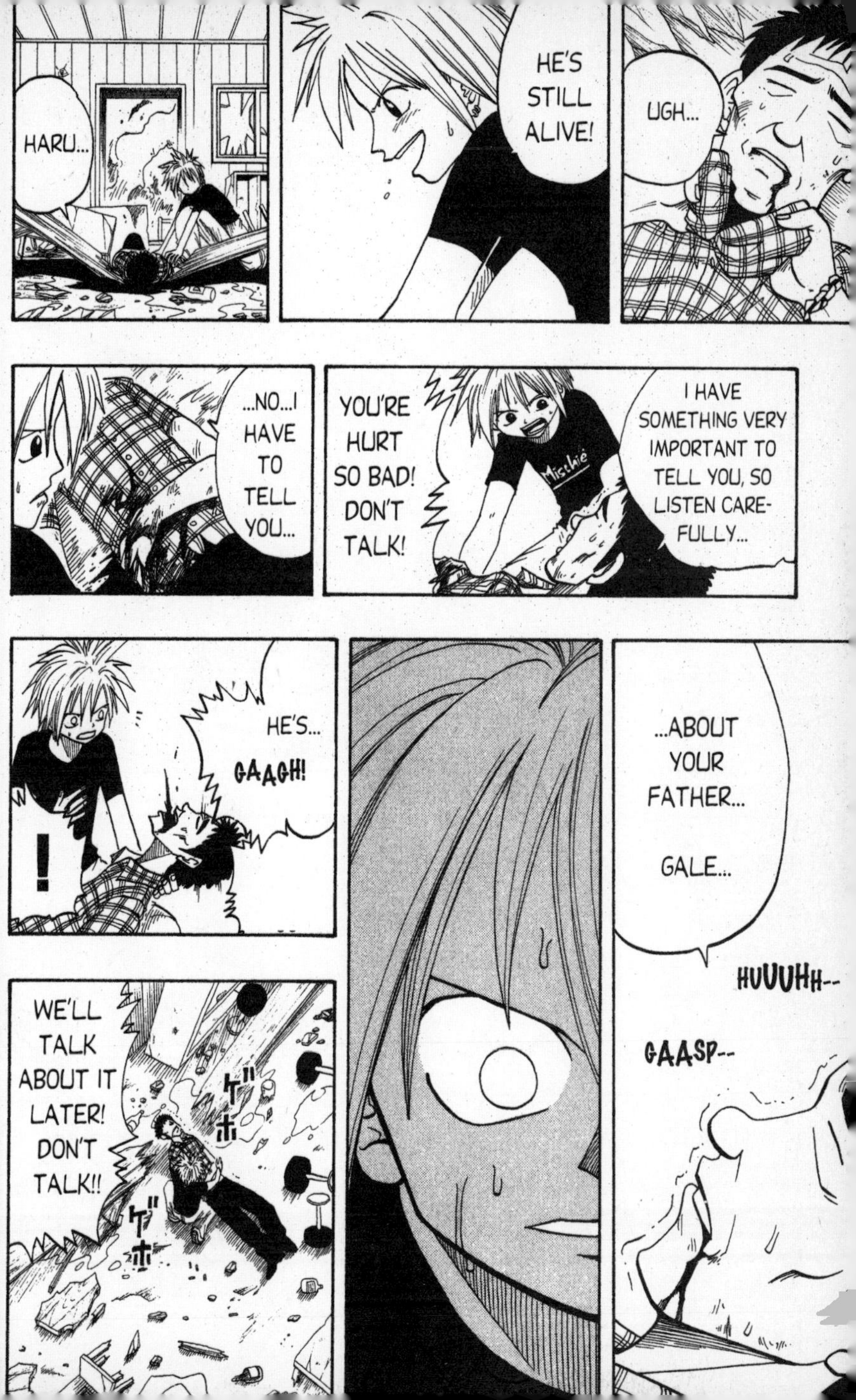
UGH...
HE'S STILL ALIVE!
HARU...
I HAVE SOMETHING VERY IMPORTANT TO TELL YOU, SO LISTEN CARE-FULLY...
YOU'RE HURT SO BAD! DON'T TALK!
...NO...I HAVE TO TELL YOU...
...ABOUT YOUR FATHER...
GALE...
HUUUHH--
GAASP--
HE'S...
GAAGH!
!
WE'LL TALK ABOUT IT LATER! DON'T TALK!!
ゲホ
ゲホ

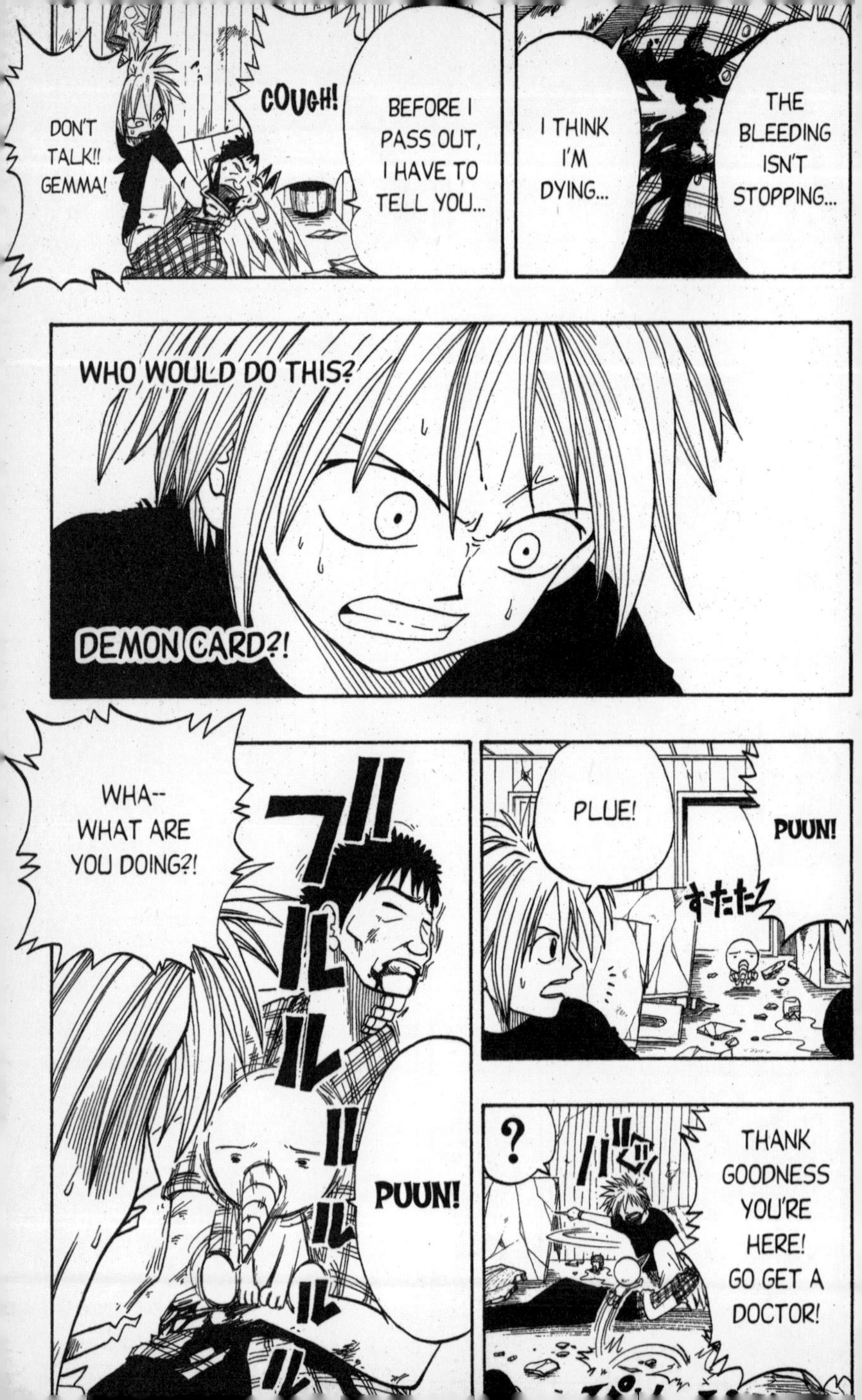
THE BLEEDING ISN'T STOPPING...
I THINK I'M DYING...
BEFORE I PASS OUT, I HAVE TO TELL YOU...
COUGH!
DON'T TALK!! GEMMA!
WHO WOULD DO THIS?
DEMON CARD?!
PLUE!
PUUN!
THANK GOODNESS YOU'RE HERE! GO GET A DOCTOR!
?
WHA-- WHAT ARE YOU DOING?!
PUUN!

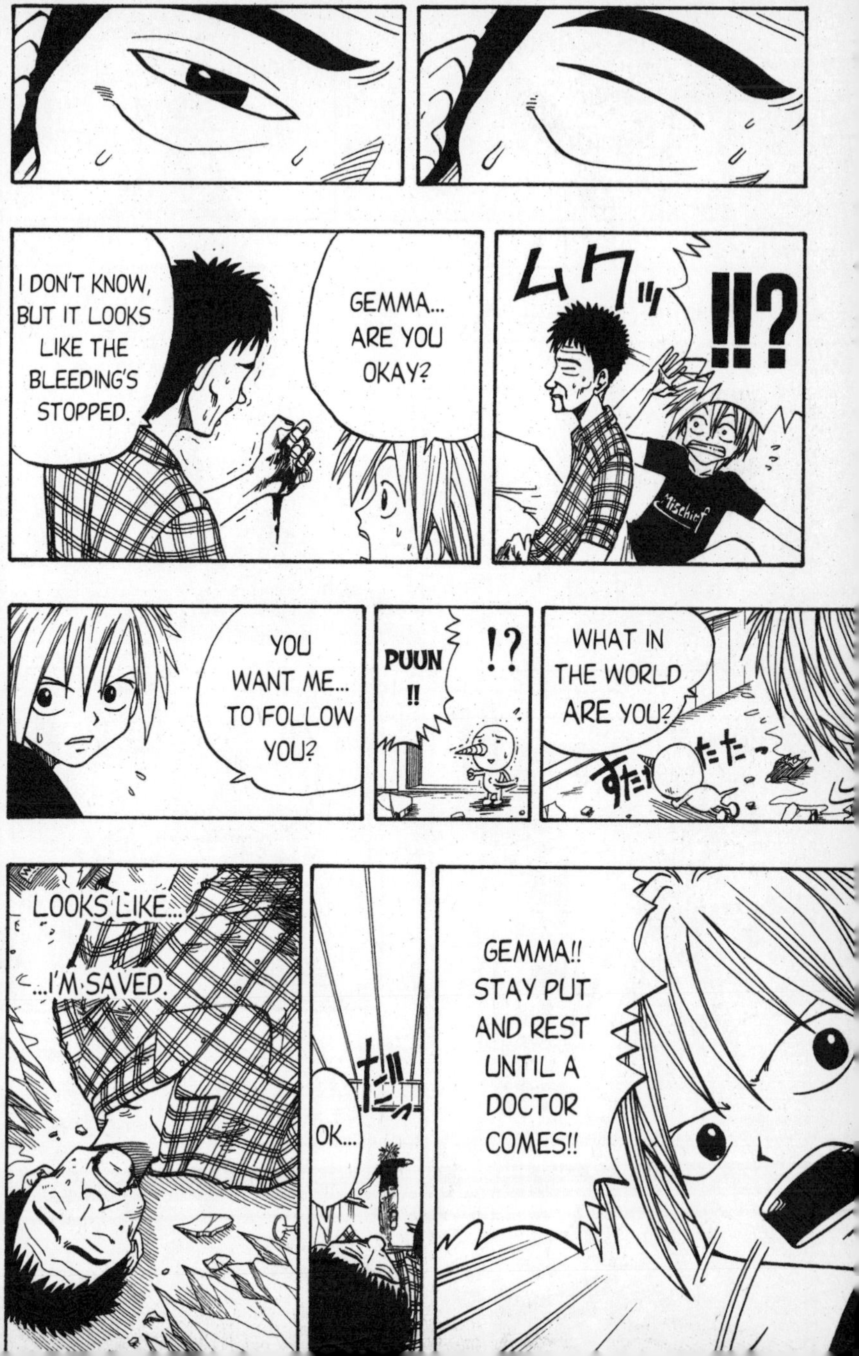
ムクッ
!!?
GEMMA... ARE YOU OKAY?
I DON'T KNOW, BUT IT LOOKS LIKE THE BLEEDING'S STOPPED.
WHAT IN THE WORLD ARE YOU?
すたっ
たたっ
PUUN !!
!?
YOU WANT ME... TO FOLLOW YOU?
GEMMA!! STAY PUT AND REST UNTIL A DOCTOR COMES!!
OK...
だっ
LOOKS LIKE...
...I'M SAVED.

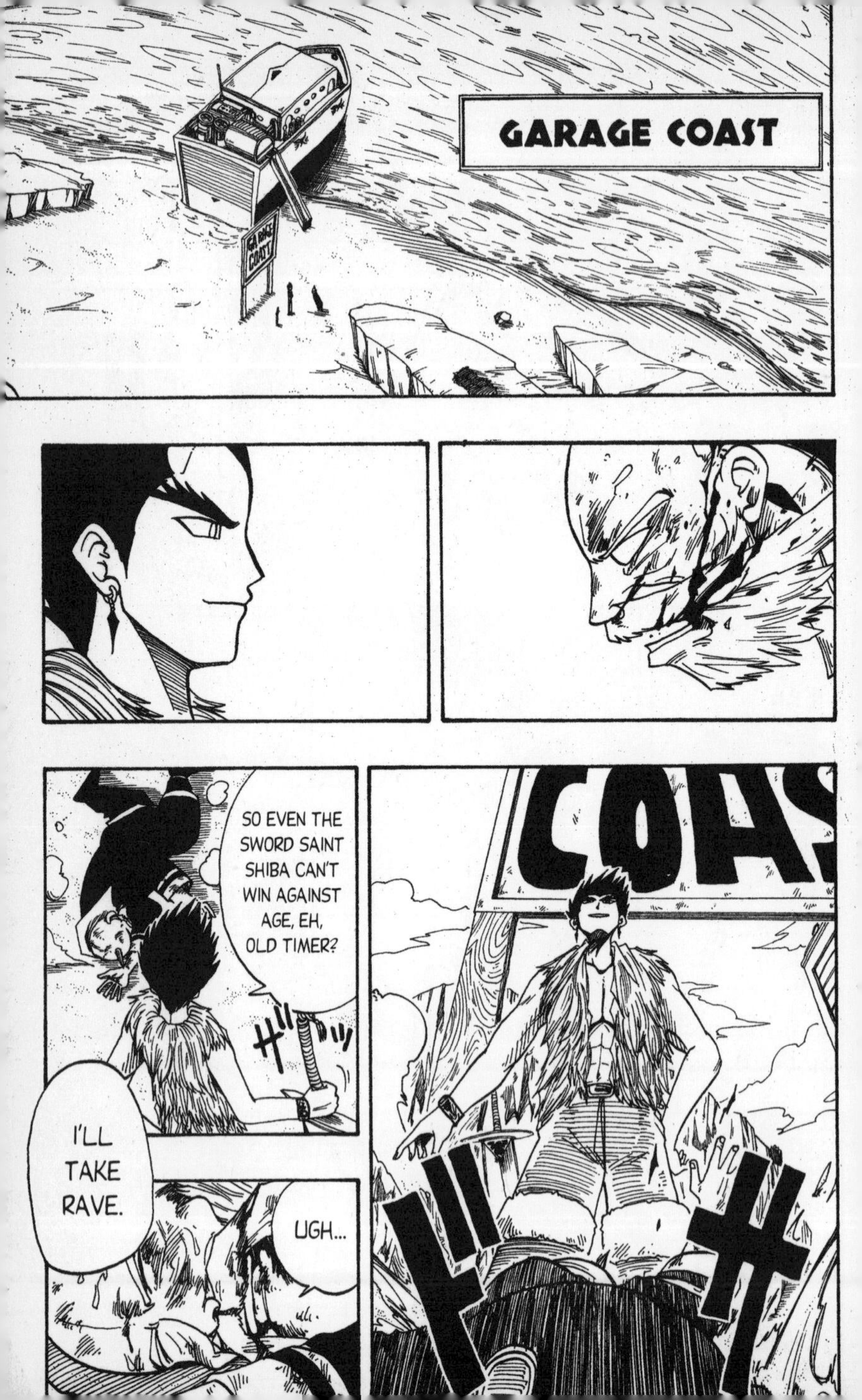
GARAGE COAST
GARAGE COAST
COAS
SO EVEN THE SWORD SAINT SHIBA CAN'T WIN AGAINST AGE, EH, OLD TIMER?
I'LL TAKE RAVE.
UGH...

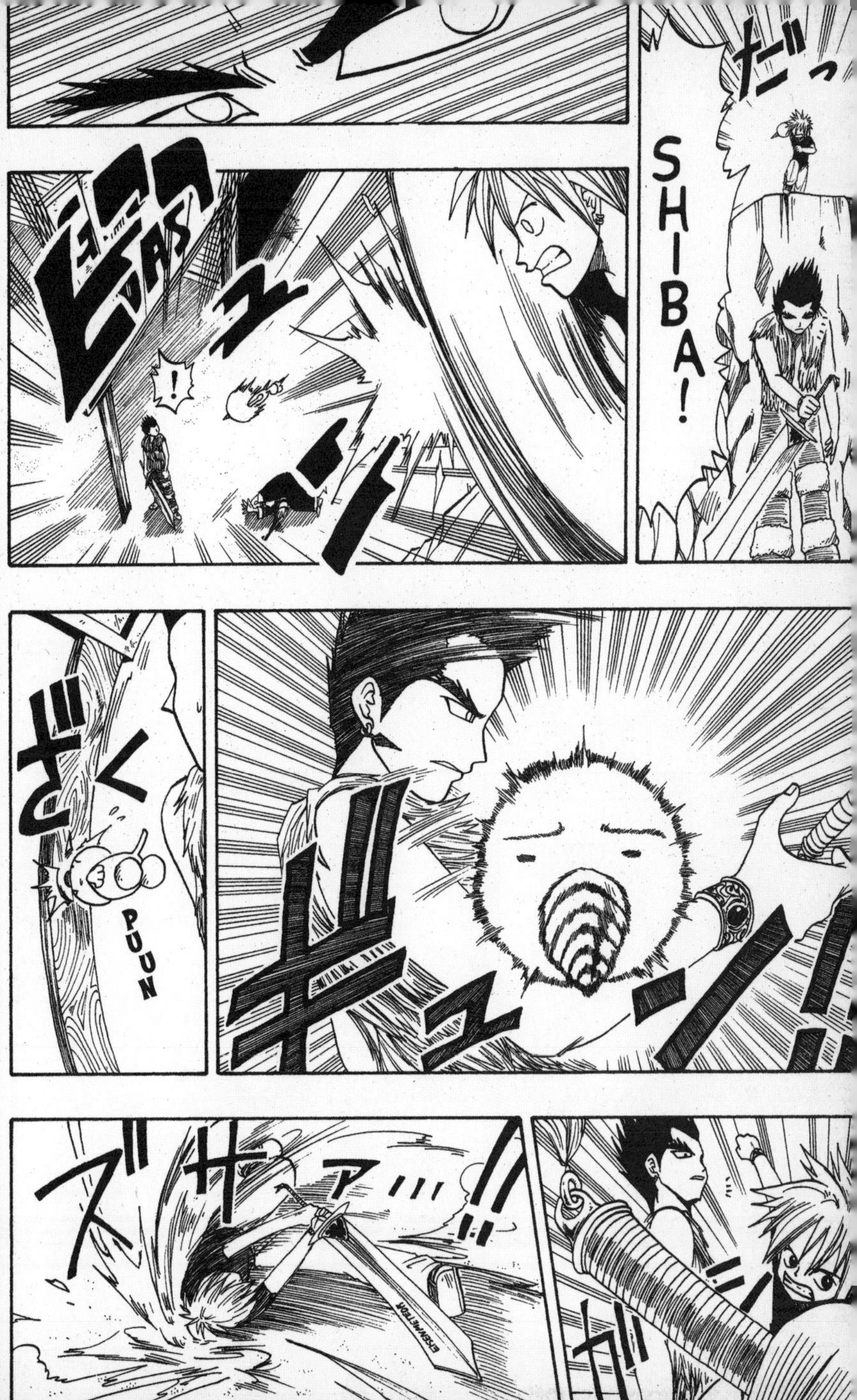

だっ
SHIBA!
DAS
!
PUUN
ズザァ…!!

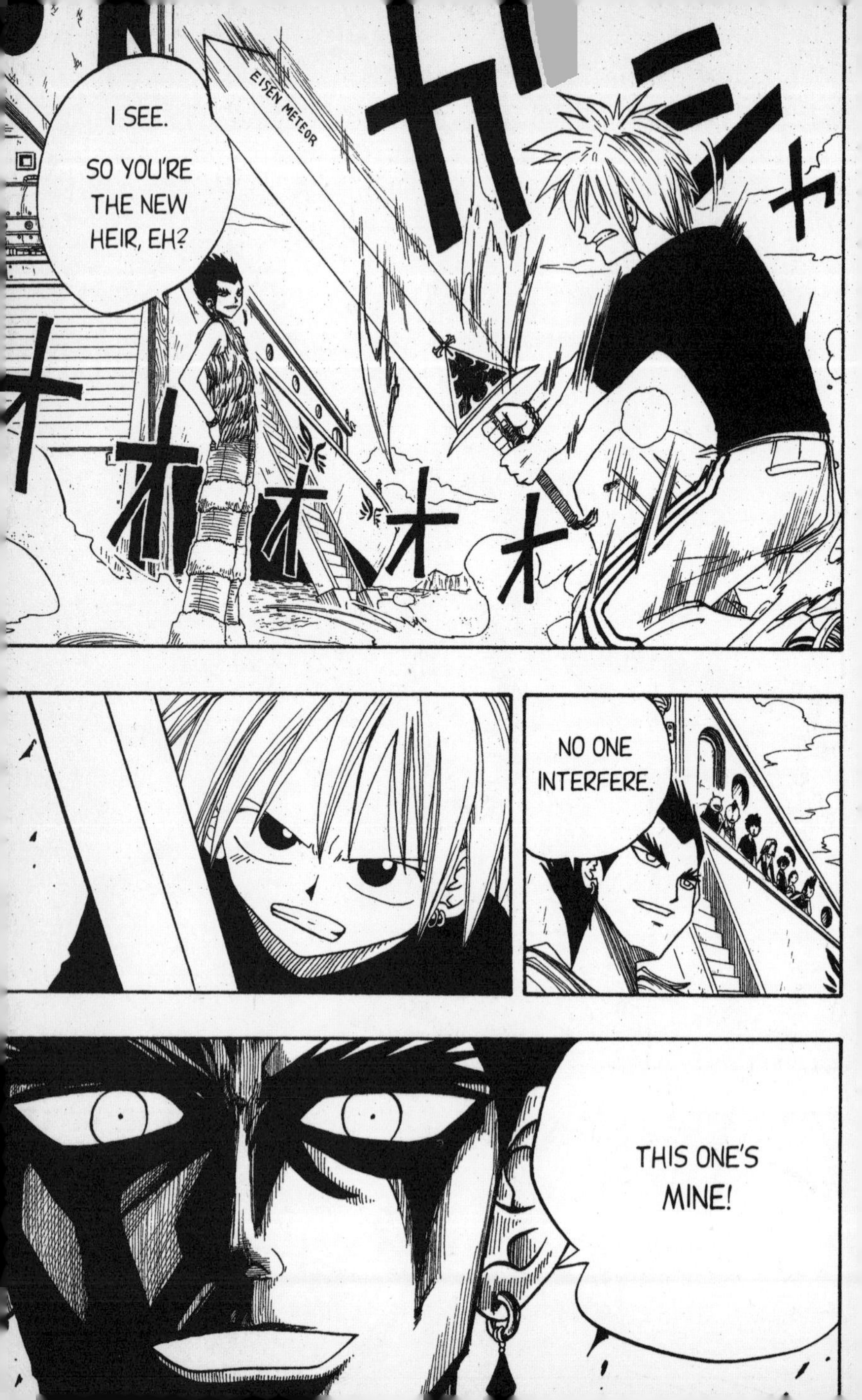

ガシャ
EISEN METEOR
I SEE. SO YOU'RE THE NEW HEIR, EH?
オオオオオ
NO ONE INTERFERE.
THIS ONE'S MINE!

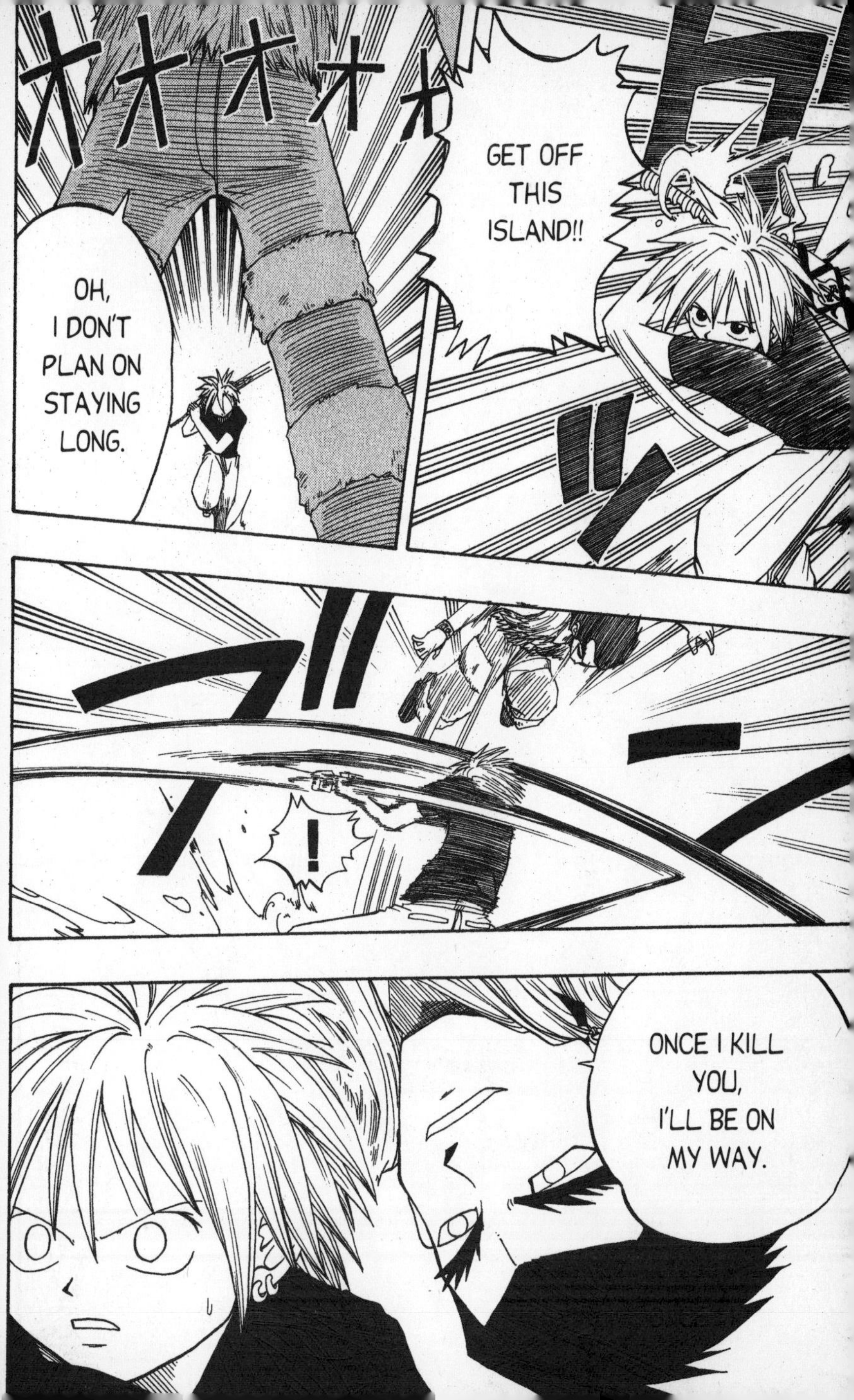

GET OFF THIS ISLAND!!
OH, I DON'T PLAN ON STAYING LONG.
!
ONCE I KILL YOU, I'LL BE ON MY WAY.

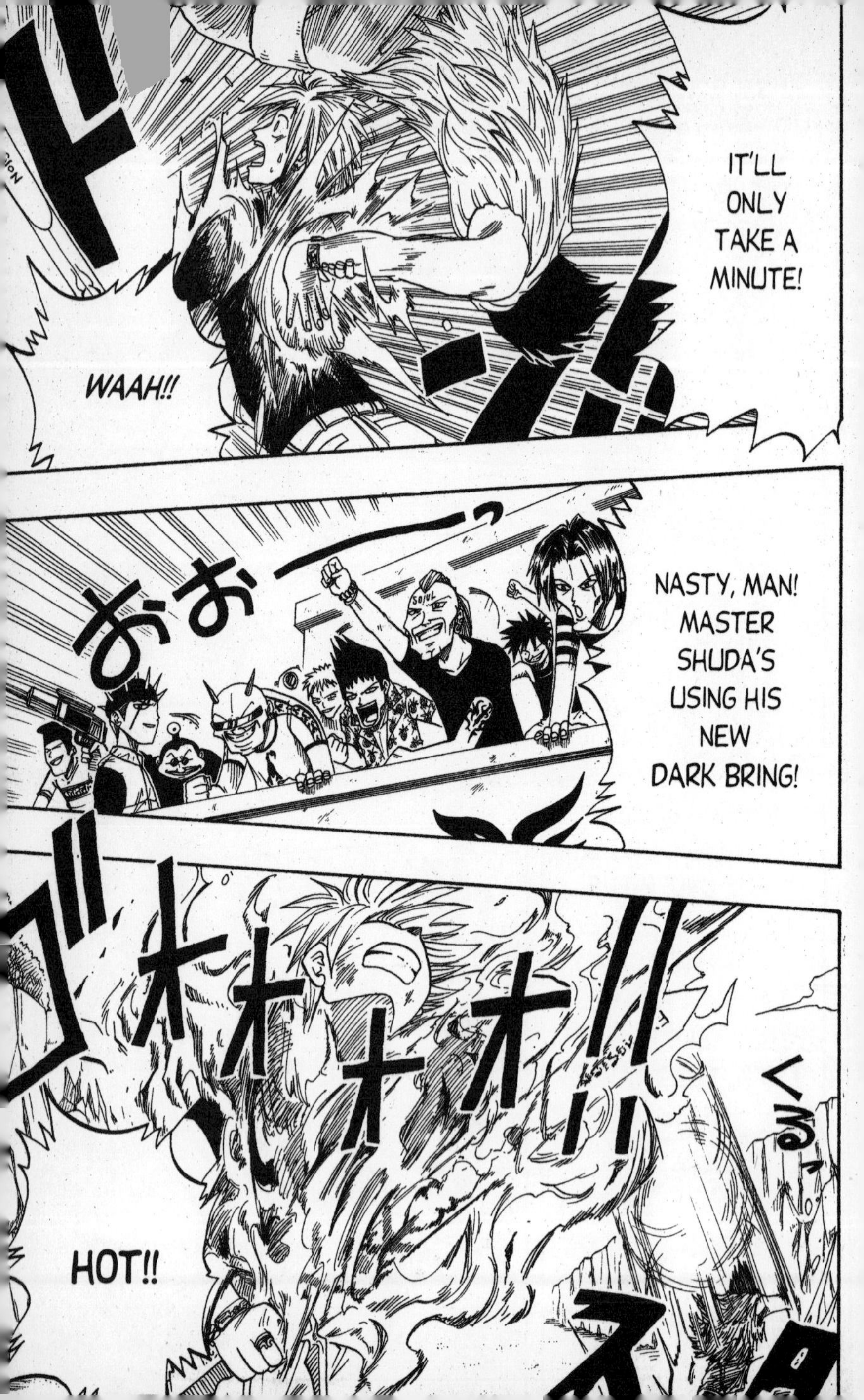
IT'LL ONLY TAKE A MINUTE!
WAAH!!
おおーーっ
NASTY, MAN! MASTER SHUDA'S USING HIS NEW DARK BRING!
ゴオオオ!!
くるっ
HOT!!

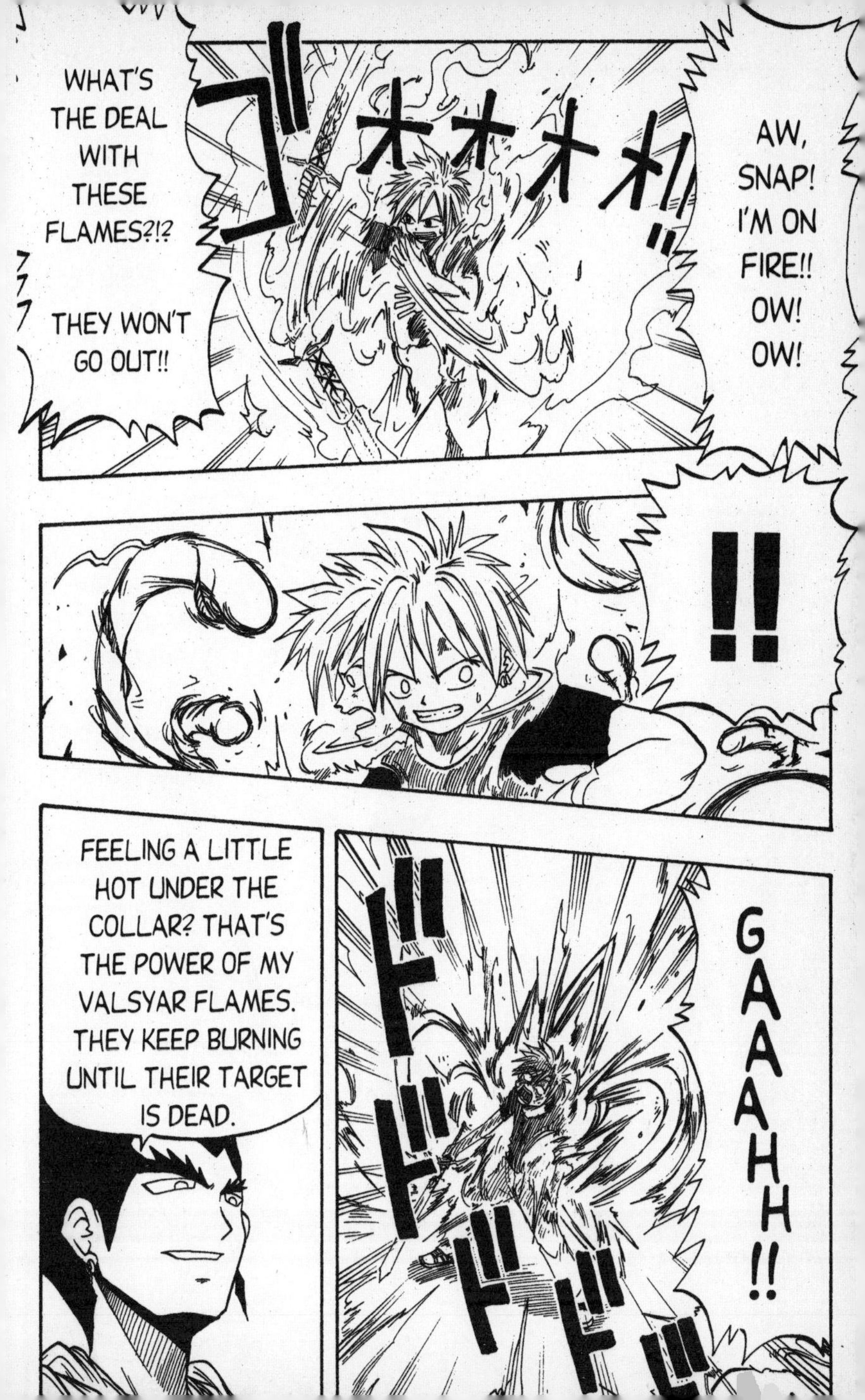
AW, SNAP! I'M ON FIRE!! OW! OW!
WHAT'S THE DEAL WITH THESE FLAMES?!?
THEY WON'T GO OUT!!
!!
GAAAAHH!!
FEELING A LITTLE HOT UNDER THE COLLAR? THAT'S THE POWER OF MY VALSYAR FLAMES. THEY KEEP BURNING UNTIL THEIR TARGET IS DEAD.

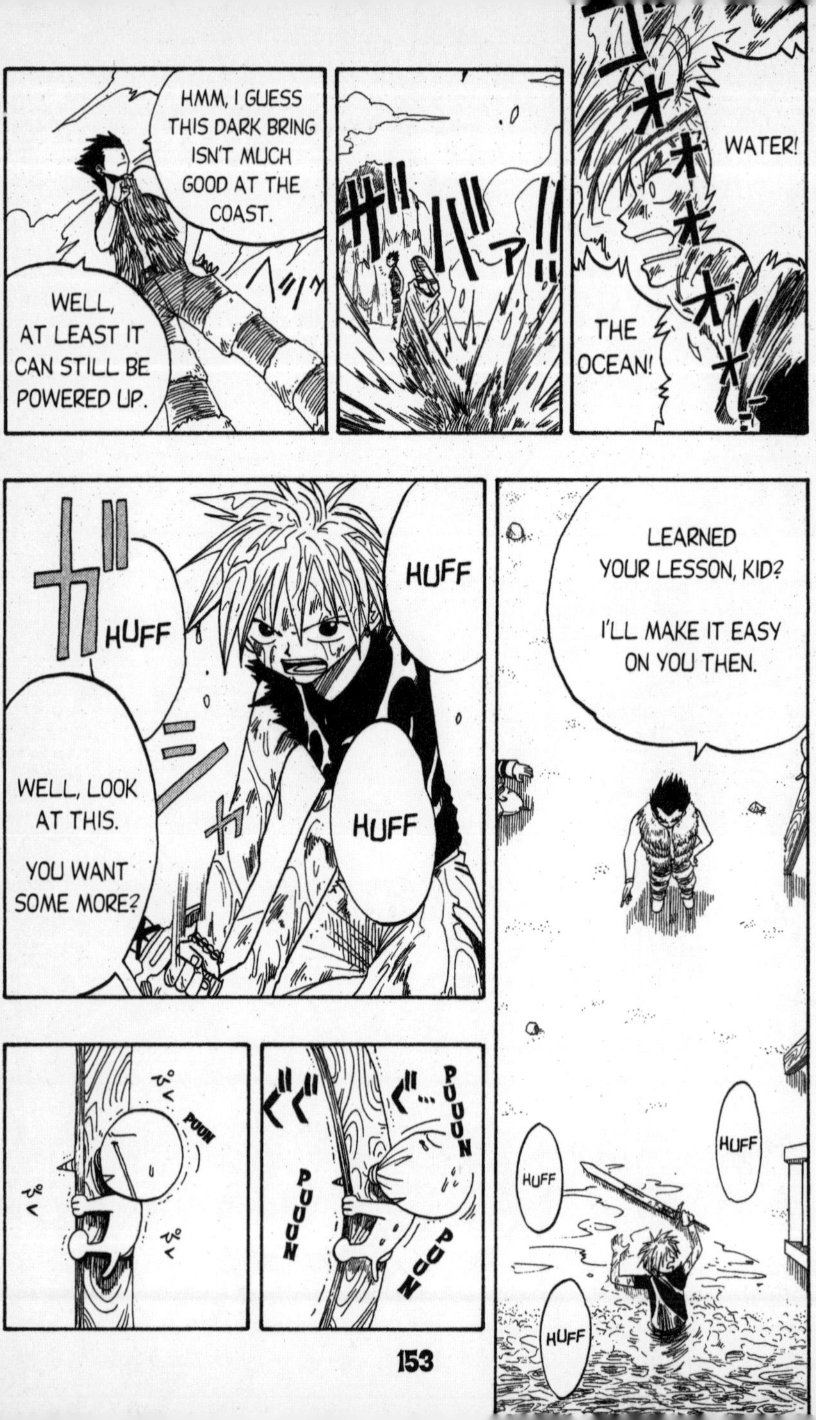
WATER!
THE OCEAN!
HMM, I GUESS THIS DARK BRING ISN'T MUCH GOOD AT THE COAST.
WELL, AT LEAST IT CAN STILL BE POWERED UP.
LEARNED YOUR LESSON, KID?
I'LL MAKE IT EASY ON YOU THEN.
HUFF
HUFF
HUFF
HUFF
HUFF
HUFF
WELL, LOOK AT THIS.
YOU WANT SOME MORE?
PUUUN
PUUUN
PUUN
PUUN

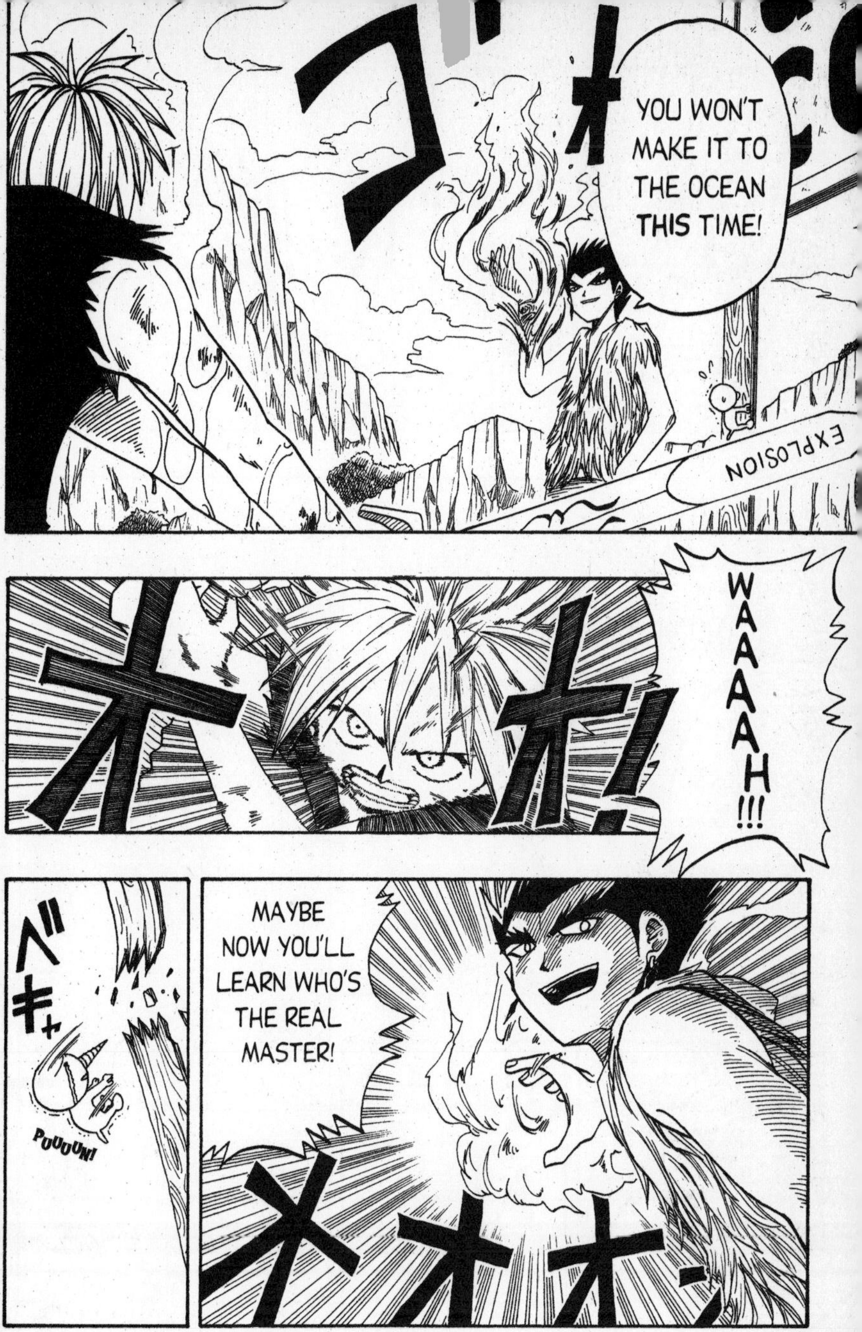
YOU WON'T MAKE IT TO THE OCEAN THIS TIME!
EXPLOSION
WAAAAAH!!!
MAYBE NOW YOU'LL LEARN WHO'S THE REAL MASTER!
PUUUUN!

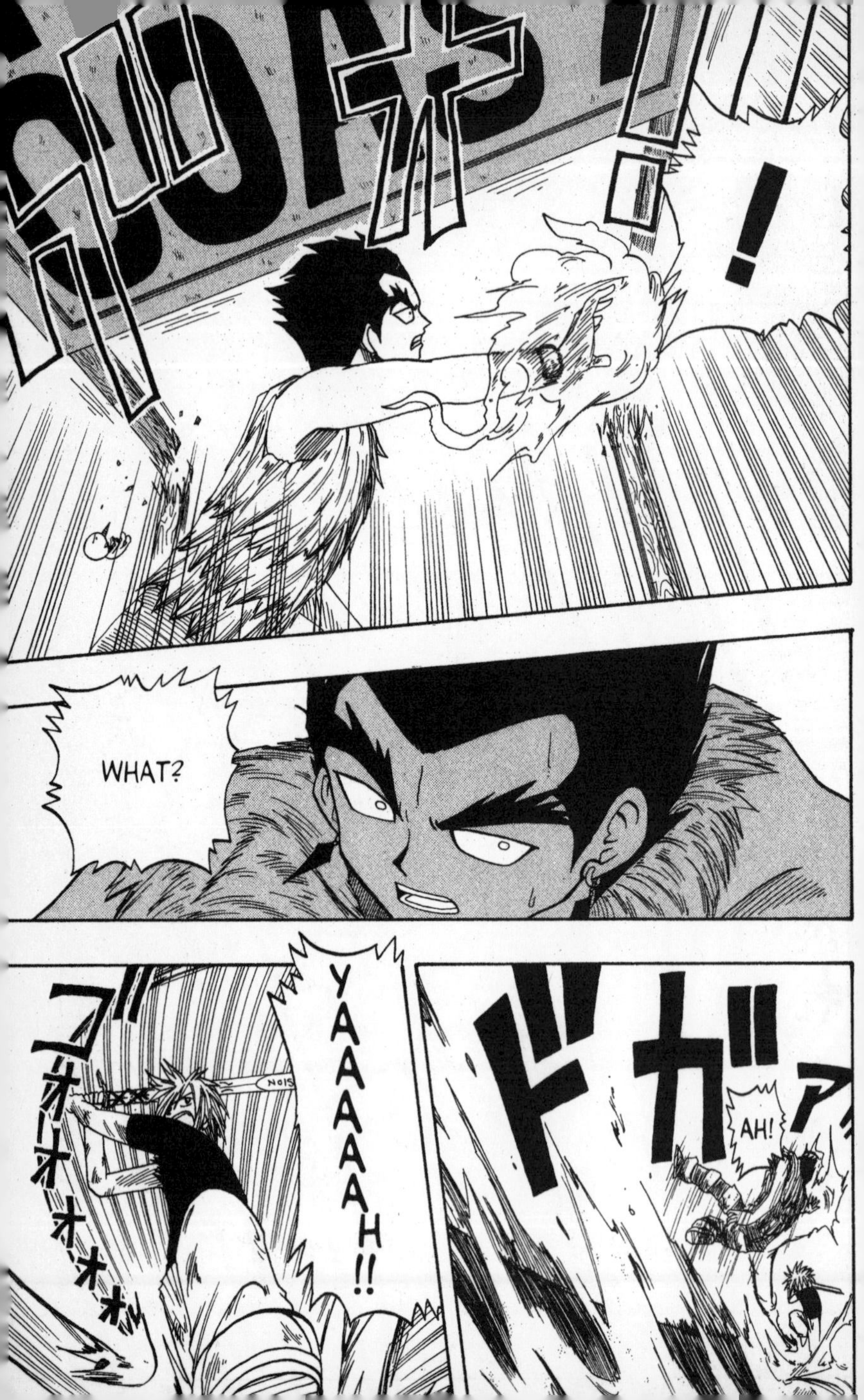
WHAT?
ドガァ
AH!
YAAAAAH!!

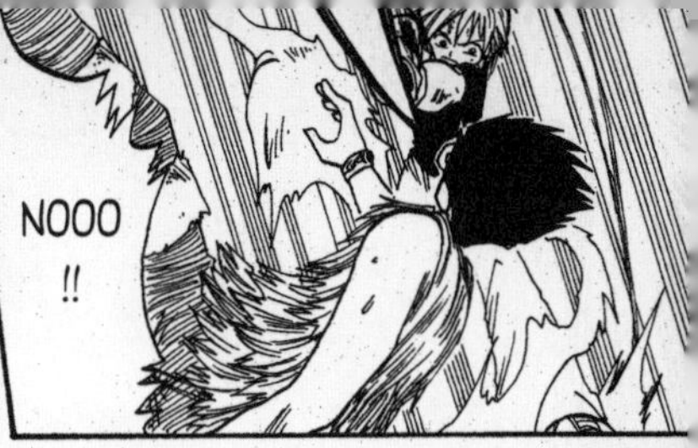
NOOO
!!

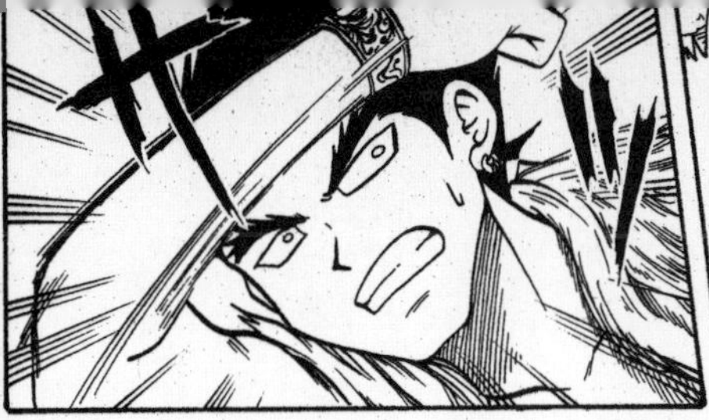

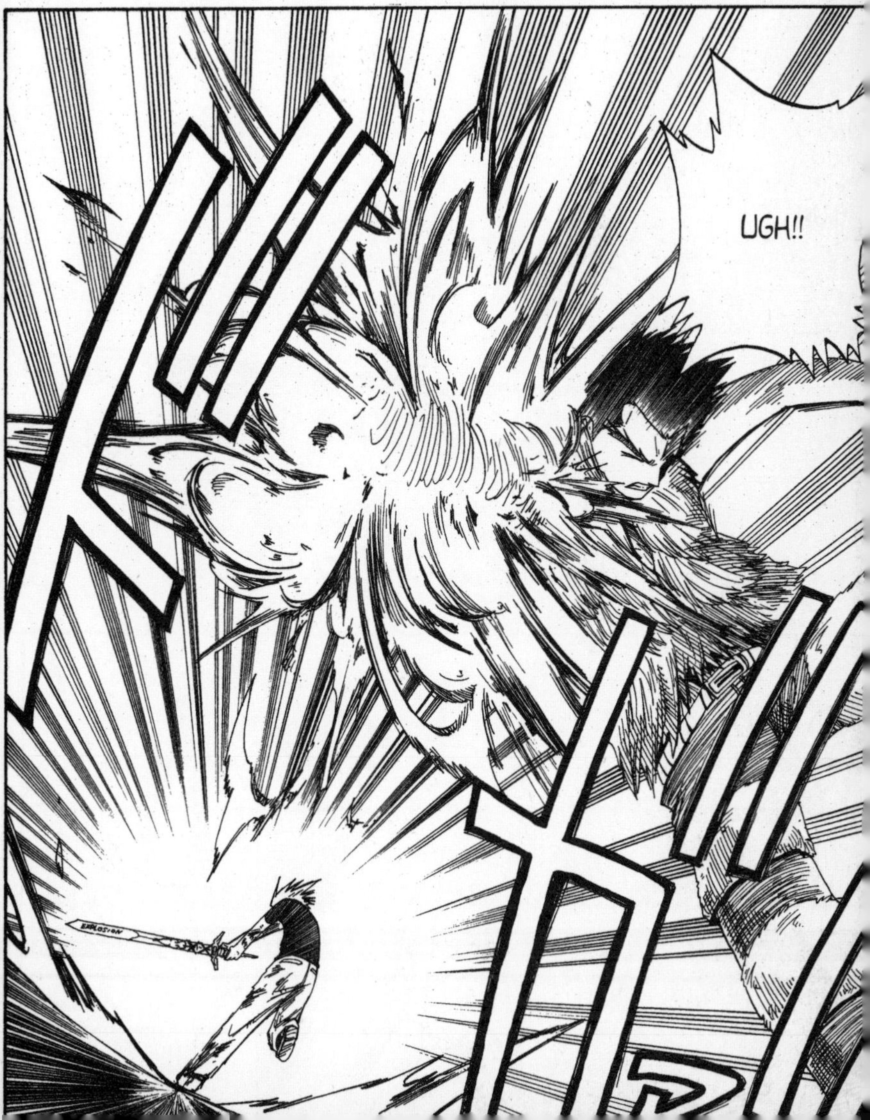
UGH!!

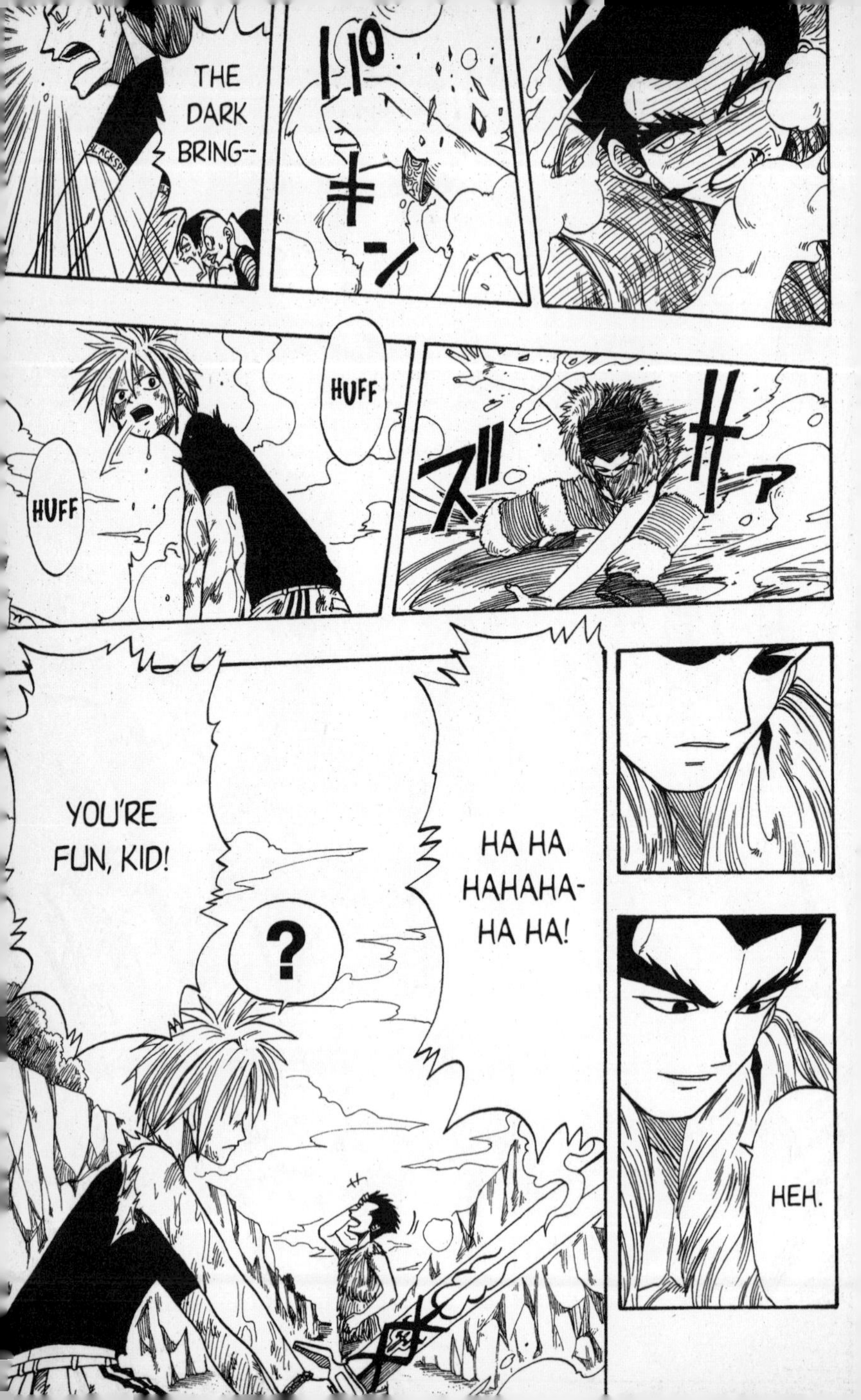
パキーン
THE DARK BRING--
ズザァ
HUFF
HUFF
HEH.
HA HA HAHAHA-HA HA!
YOU'RE FUN, KID!
?

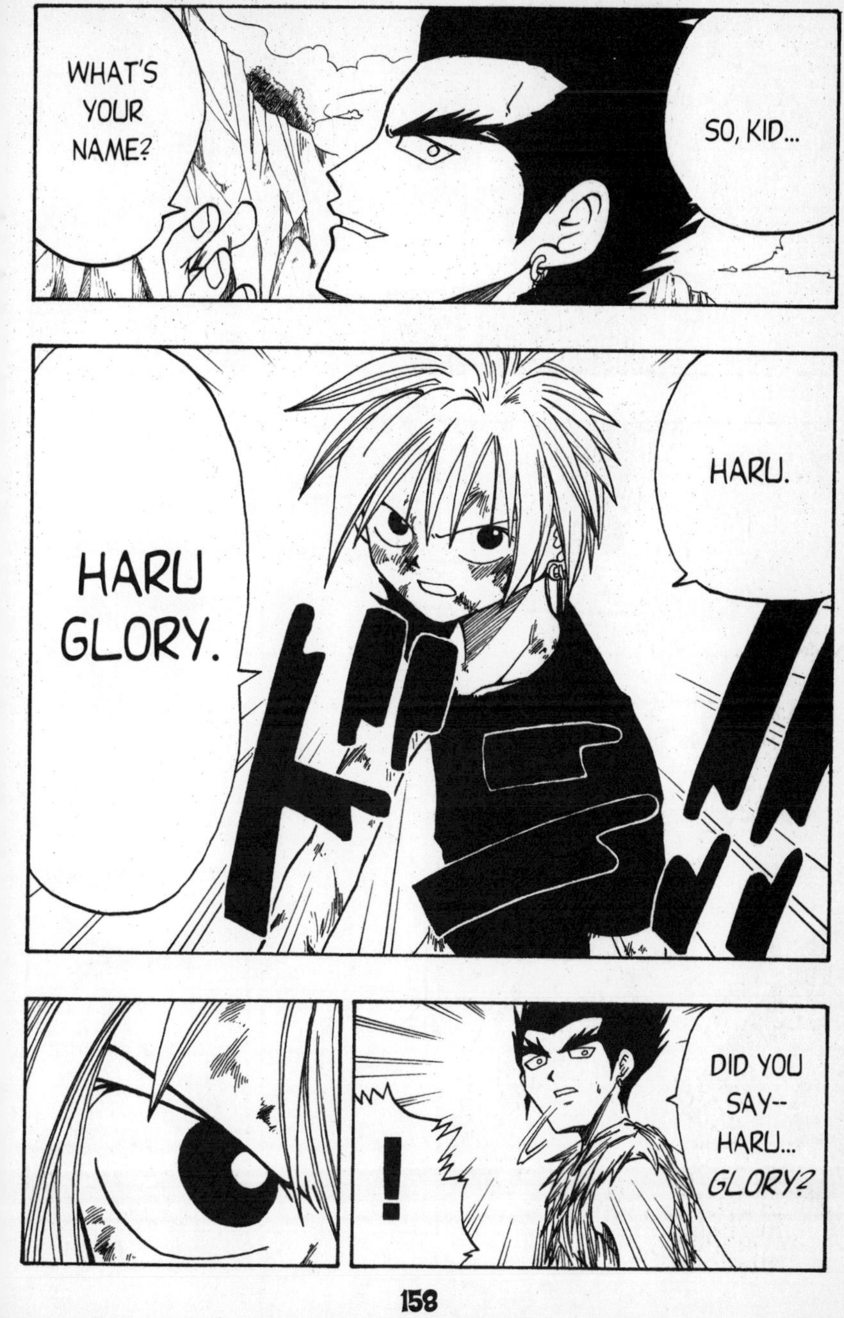
SO, KID...
WHAT'S YOUR NAME?
HARU.
HARU GLORY.
!
DID YOU SAY-- HARU... GLORY?

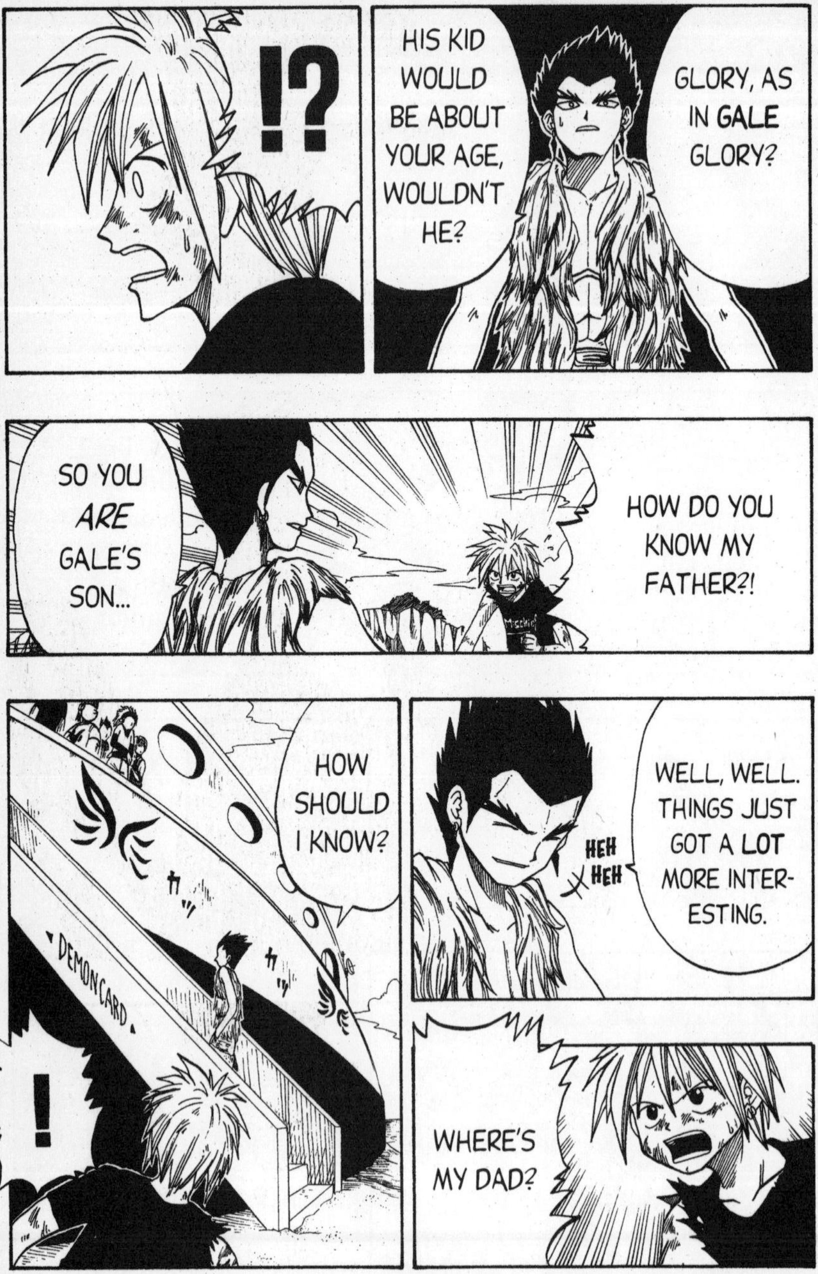
GLORY, AS IN GALE GLORY?
HIS KID WOULD BE ABOUT YOUR AGE, WOULDN'T HE?
!?
HOW DO YOU KNOW MY FATHER?!
SO YOU ARE GALE'S SON...
HEH HEH
WELL, WELL. THINGS JUST GOT A LOT MORE INTER-ESTING.
WHERE'S MY DAD?
HOW SHOULD I KNOW?
DEMONCARD
!

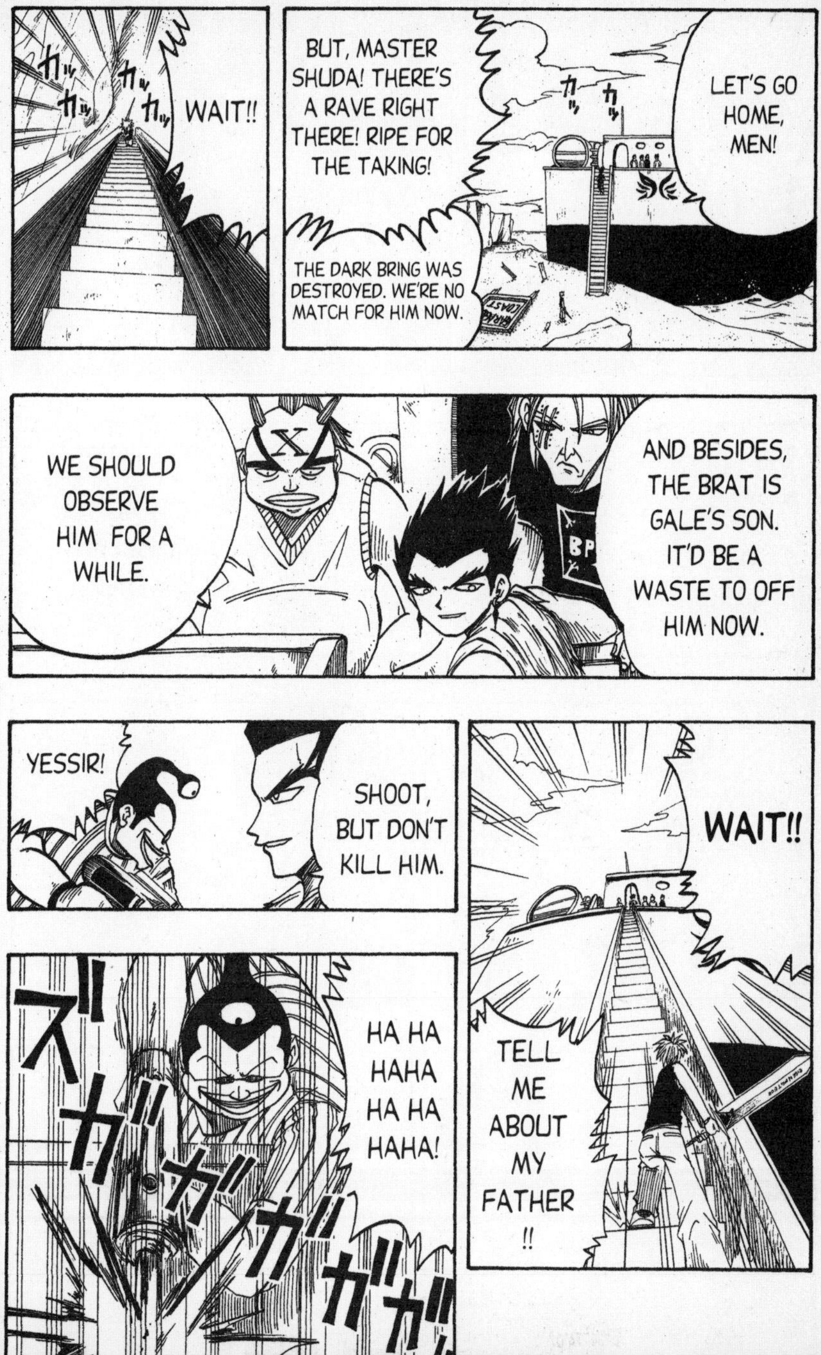
LET'S GO HOME, MEN!
BUT, MASTER SHUDA! THERE'S A RAVE RIGHT THERE! RIPE FOR THE TAKING!
THE DARK BRING WAS DESTROYED. WE'RE NO MATCH FOR HIM NOW.
WAIT!!
AND BESIDES, THE BRAT IS GALE'S SON. IT'D BE A WASTE TO OFF HIM NOW.
WE SHOULD OBSERVE HIM FOR A WHILE.
WAIT!!
TELL ME ABOUT MY FATHER !!
SHOOT, BUT DON'T KILL HIM.
YESSIR!
HA HA HAHA HA HA HAHA!

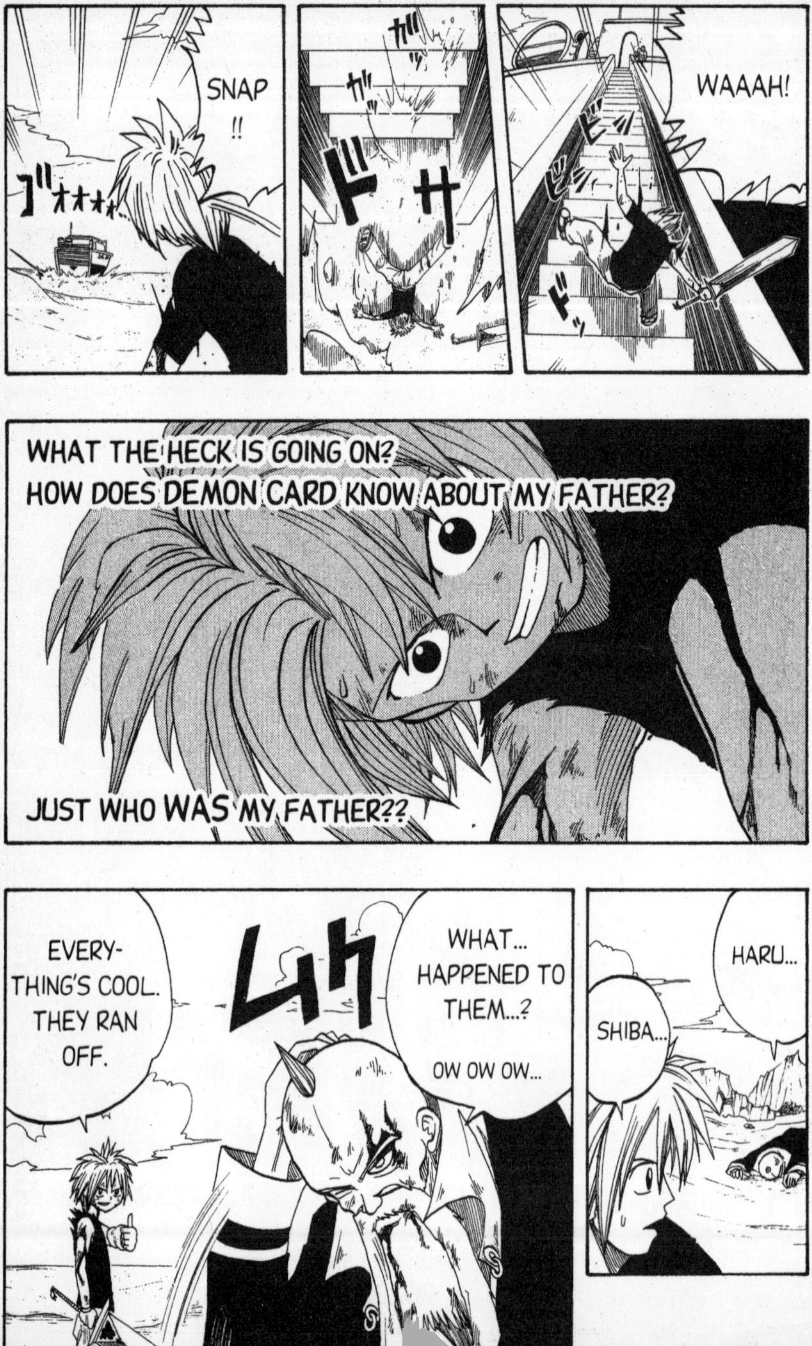
WAAAH!
ドサ
SNAP !!
WHAT THE HECK IS GOING ON? HOW DOES DEMON CARD KNOW ABOUT MY FATHER?
JUST WHO WAS MY FATHER??
HARU...
SHIBA...
WHAT... HAPPENED TO THEM...?
OW OW OW...
ムク
EVERY-THING'S COOL. THEY RAN OFF.

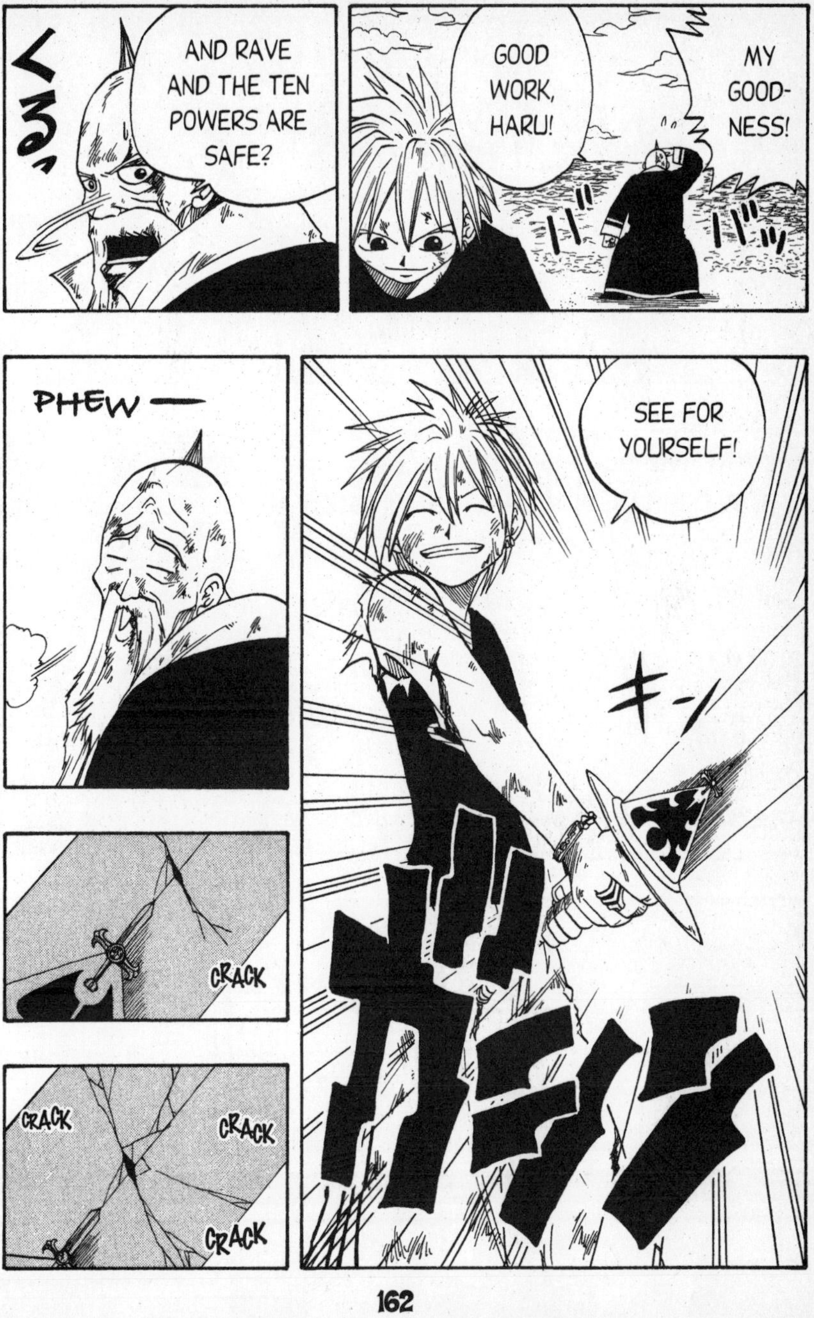
MY GOODNESS!
GOOD WORK, HARU!
AND RAVE AND THE TEN POWERS ARE SAFE?
SEE FOR YOURSELF!
PHEW—
CRACK
CRACK
CRACK
CRACK

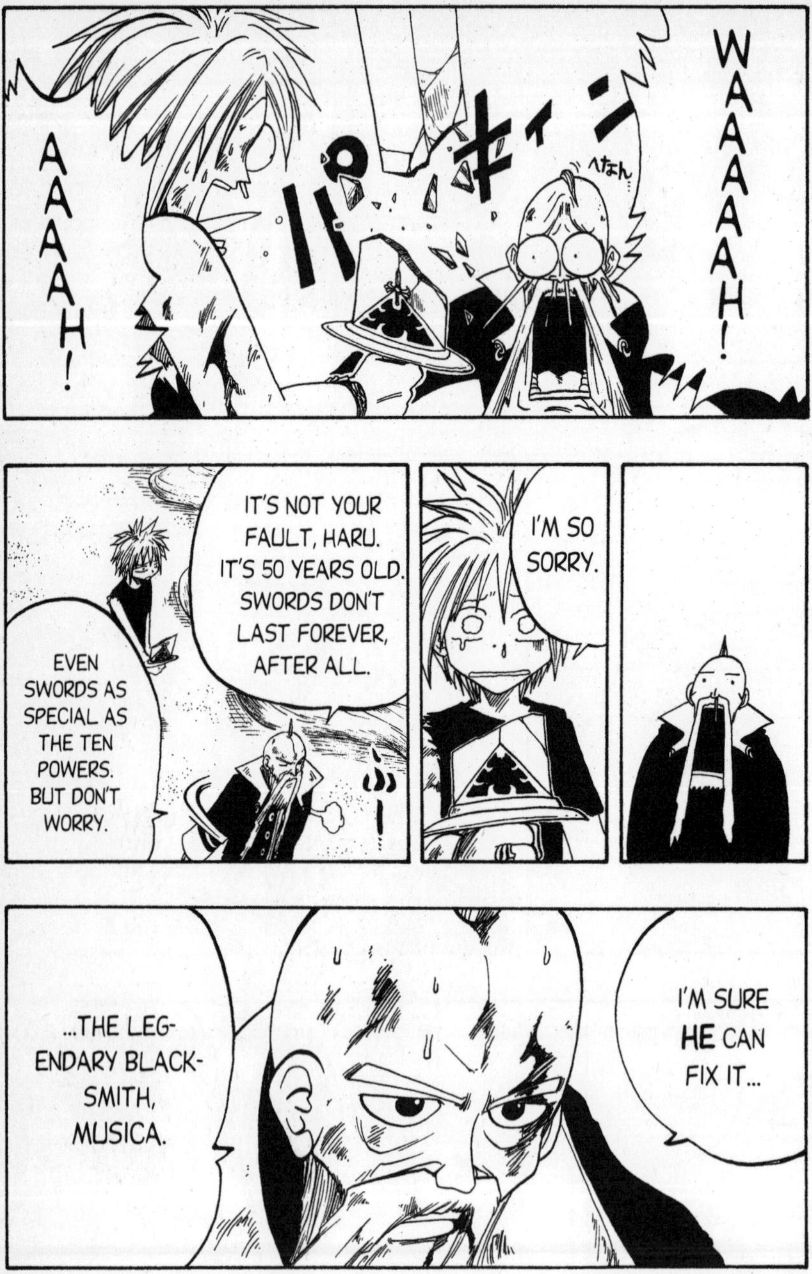
WAAAAAH!
パキィン
へなん
AAAAH!
I'M SO SORRY.
IT'S NOT YOUR FAULT, HARU. IT'S 50 YEARS OLD. SWORDS DON'T LAST FOREVER, AFTER ALL.
EVEN SWORDS AS SPECIAL AS THE TEN POWERS. BUT DON'T WORRY.
ふー…
I'M SURE **HE** CAN FIX IT...
...THE LEG-ENDARY BLACK-SMITH, MUSICA.

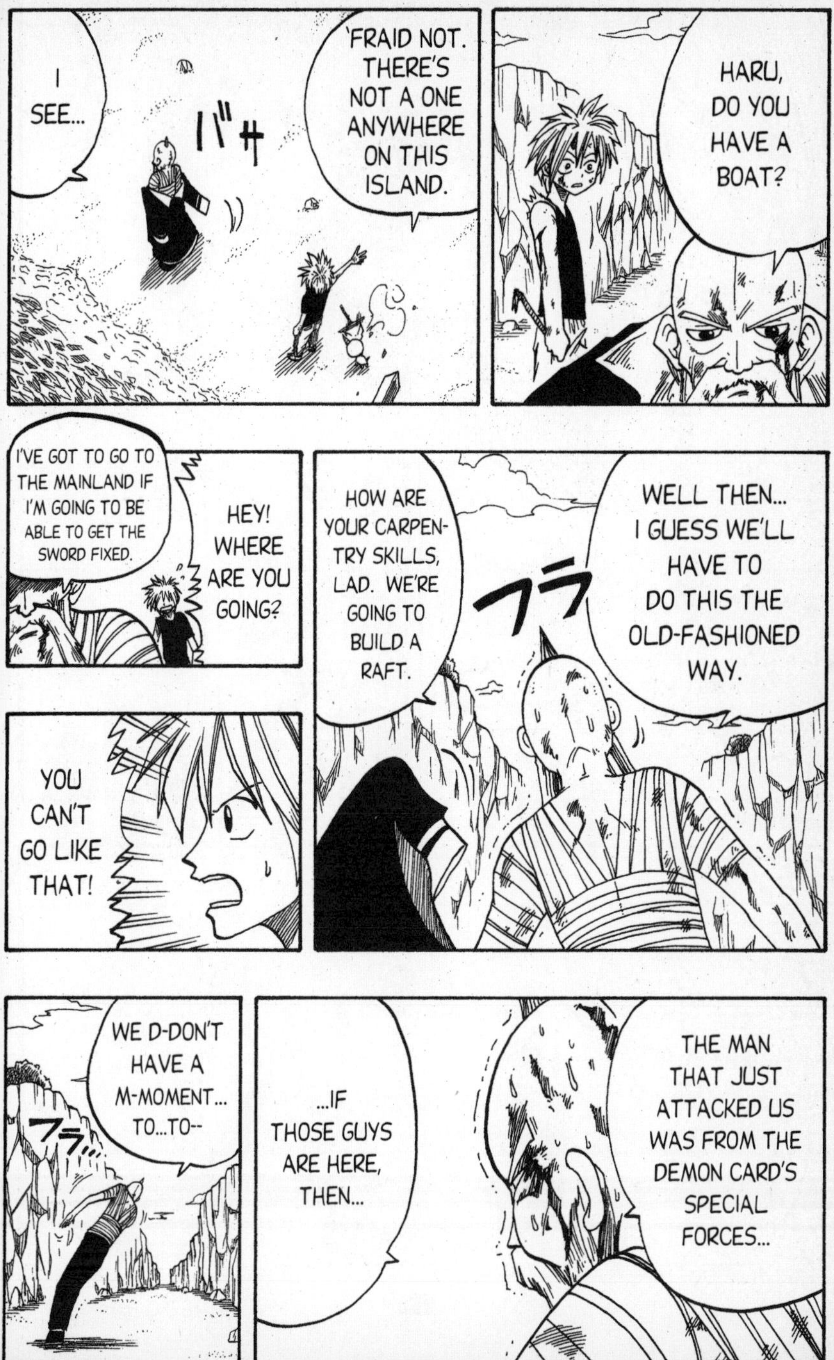
HARU, DO YOU HAVE A BOAT?
'FRAID NOT. THERE'S NOT A ONE ANYWHERE ON THIS ISLAND.
バッ
I SEE...
WELL THEN... I GUESS WE'LL HAVE TO DO THIS THE OLD-FASHIONED WAY.
フラ
HOW ARE YOUR CARPENTRY SKILLS, LAD. WE'RE GOING TO BUILD A RAFT.
HEY! WHERE ARE YOU GOING?
I'VE GOT TO GO TO THE MAINLAND IF I'M GOING TO BE ABLE TO GET THE SWORD FIXED.
YOU CAN'T GO LIKE THAT!
THE MAN THAT JUST ATTACKED US WAS FROM THE DEMON CARD'S SPECIAL FORCES...
...IF THOSE GUYS ARE HERE, THEN...
WE D-DON'T HAVE A M-MOMENT... TO...TO--
フラ...

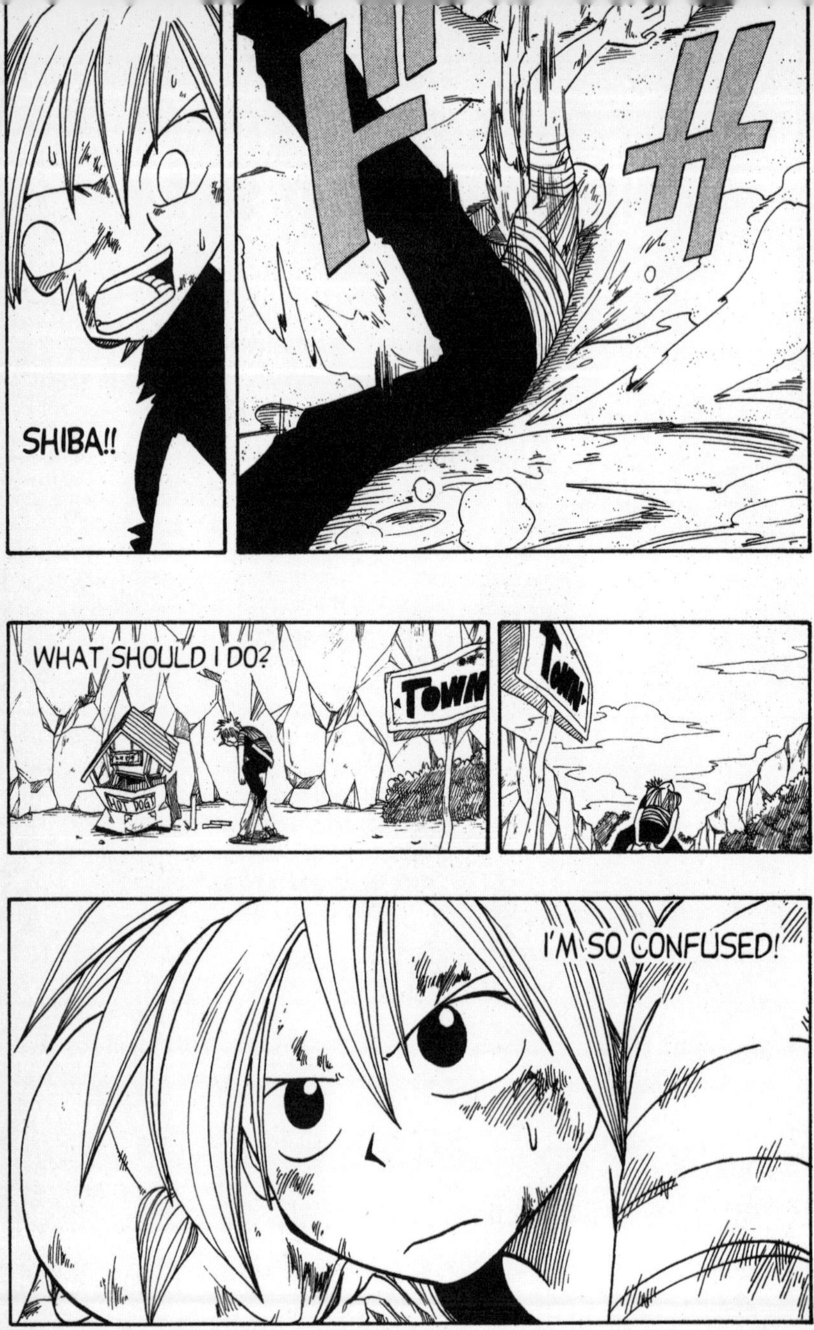
ドサ
SHIBA!!
TOWN
WHAT SHOULD I DO?
TOWN
HOT DOG
I'M SO CONFUSED!

FIRST RAVE MASTER: THE SWORD SAINT SHIBA

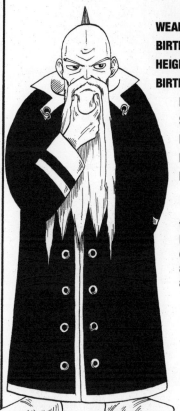

WEAPON: RAVE & SWORD (TEN POWERS)
BIRTHDAY/AGE: NOVEMBER 11, 9992 / 74 YEARS
HEIGHT/WEIGHT/BLOODTYPE: 155CM / 50KG / AB
BIRTHPLACE: GARAGE ISLAND
HOBBIES: READING & WRITING
SPECIAL SKILLS: WILL CRY ANYWHERE & EVERYWHERE
LIKES: HIS HOMELAND (GARAGE ISLAND)
HATES: DARK BRING

Shiba, the coward. He's the character with the most variety of appearance and attitude. Initially, he was supposed to have died, but even with Haru and Plue going off on a fun adventure, his death would have left a bad aftertaste. So he was reborn!

Look forward to his reappearance!!

SHIBA, AS HE FIRST LOOKED
HE WAS SET UP AS A PROPHET.

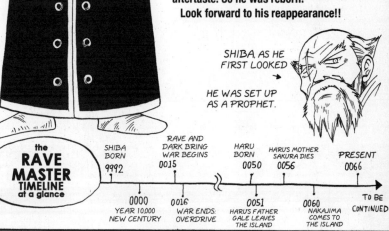

the RAVE MASTER TIMELINE at a glance
SHIBA BORN 9992
0000 YEAR 10,000 NEW CENTURY
RAVE AND DARK BRING WAR BEGINS 0015
0016 WAR ENDS: OVERDRIVE
HARU BORN 0050
0051 HARU'S FATHER GALE LEAVES THE ISLAND
HARU'S MOTHER SAKURA DIES 0056
0060 NAKAJIMA COMES TO THE ISLAND
PRESENT 0066
TO BE CONTINUED

RAVE MASTER

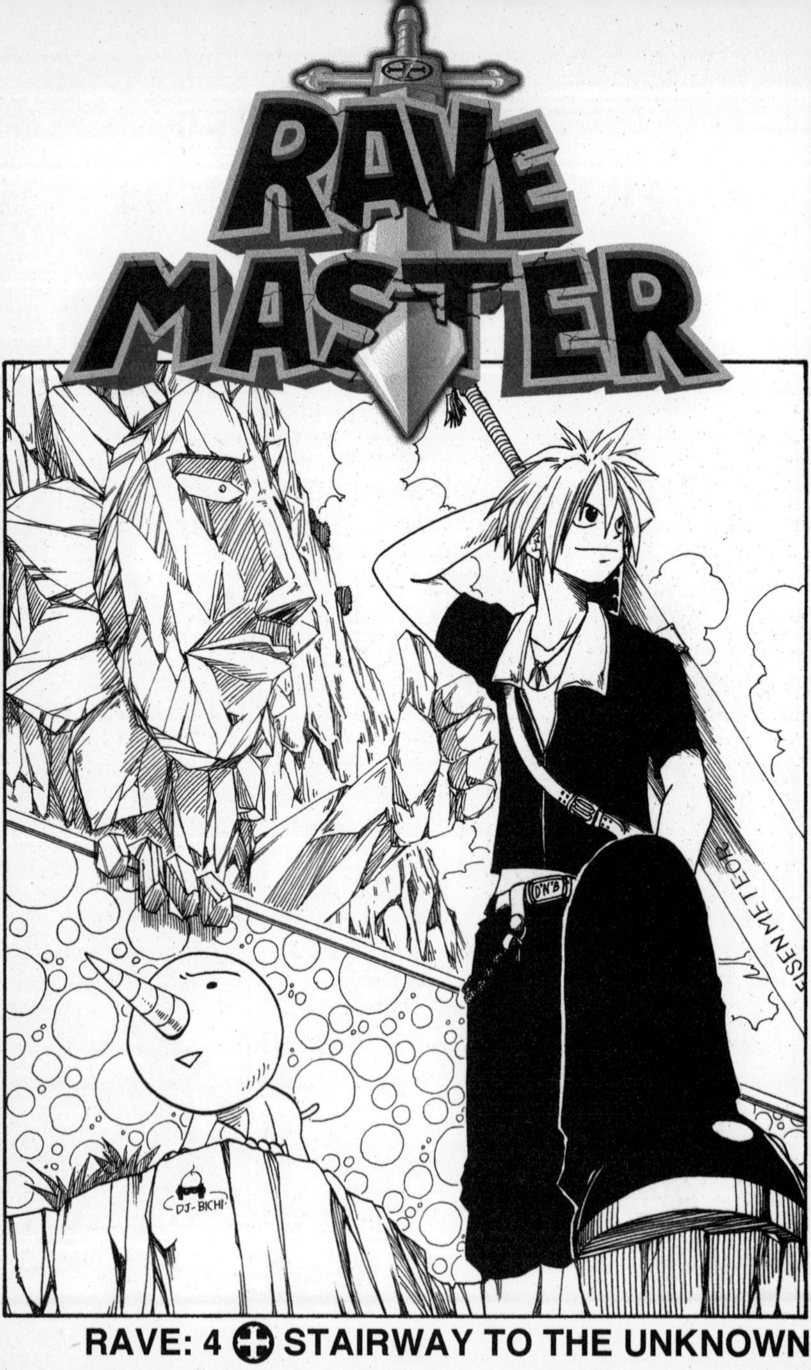
EISENMETEOR
D'N'B
DJ-BICHI

RAVE: 4 ✠ STAIRWAY TO THE UNKNOWN

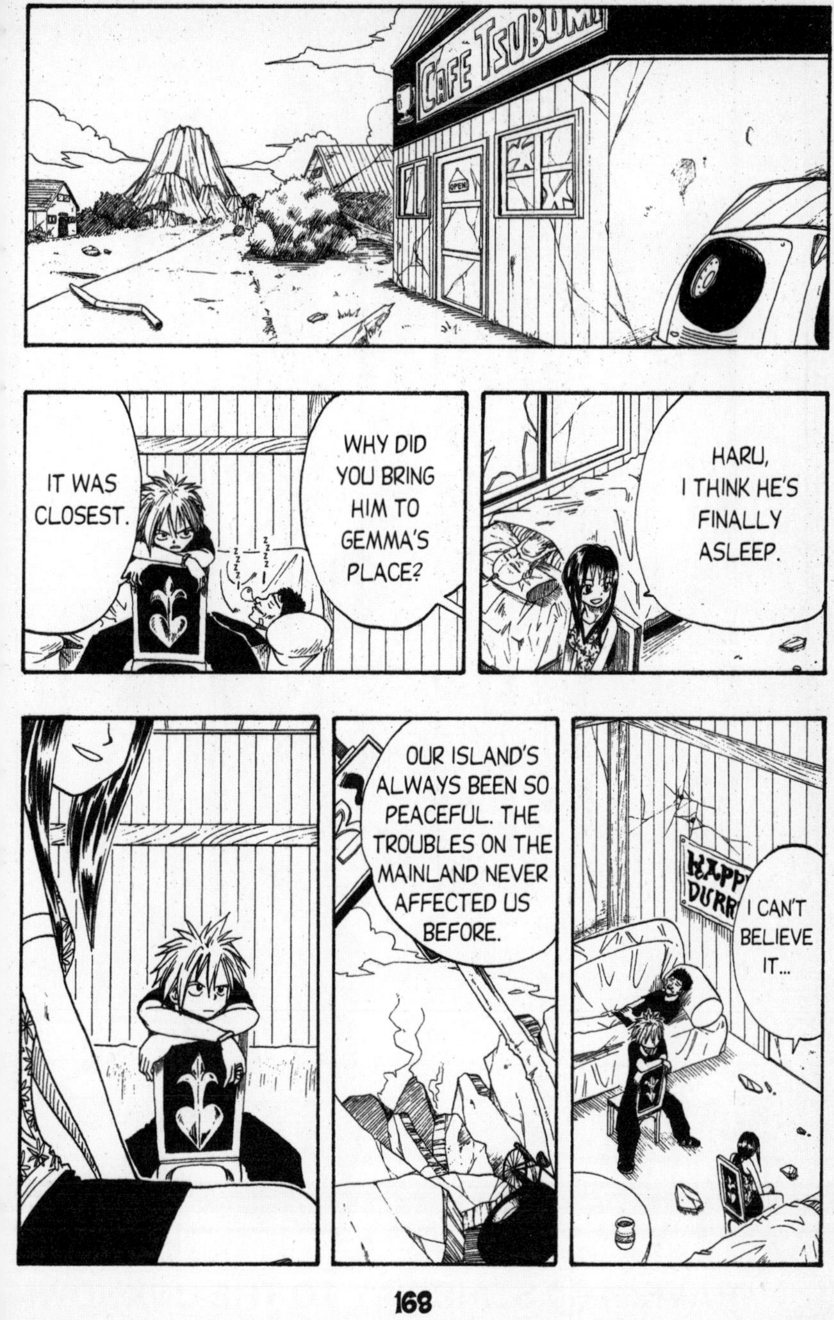
CAFE TSUBOMI
OPEN
HARU, I THINK HE'S FINALLY ASLEEP.
WHY DID YOU BRING HIM TO GEMMA'S PLACE?
IT WAS CLOSEST.
I CAN'T BELIEVE IT...
OUR ISLAND'S ALWAYS BEEN SO PEACEFUL. THE TROUBLES ON THE MAINLAND NEVER AFFECTED US BEFORE.

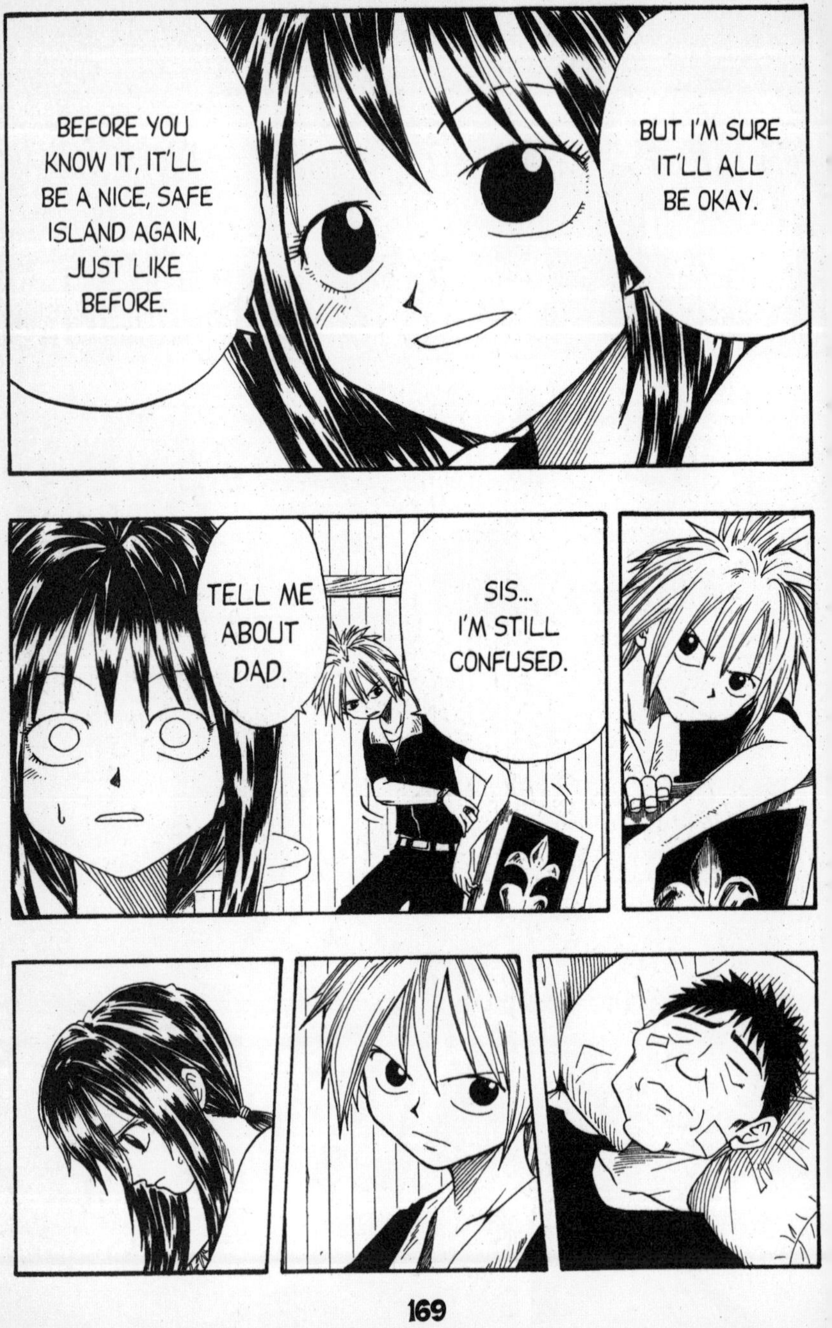
BUT I'M SURE IT'LL ALL BE OKAY.
BEFORE YOU KNOW IT, IT'LL BE A NICE, SAFE ISLAND AGAIN, JUST LIKE BEFORE.
SIS... I'M STILL CONFUSED.
TELL ME ABOUT DAD.

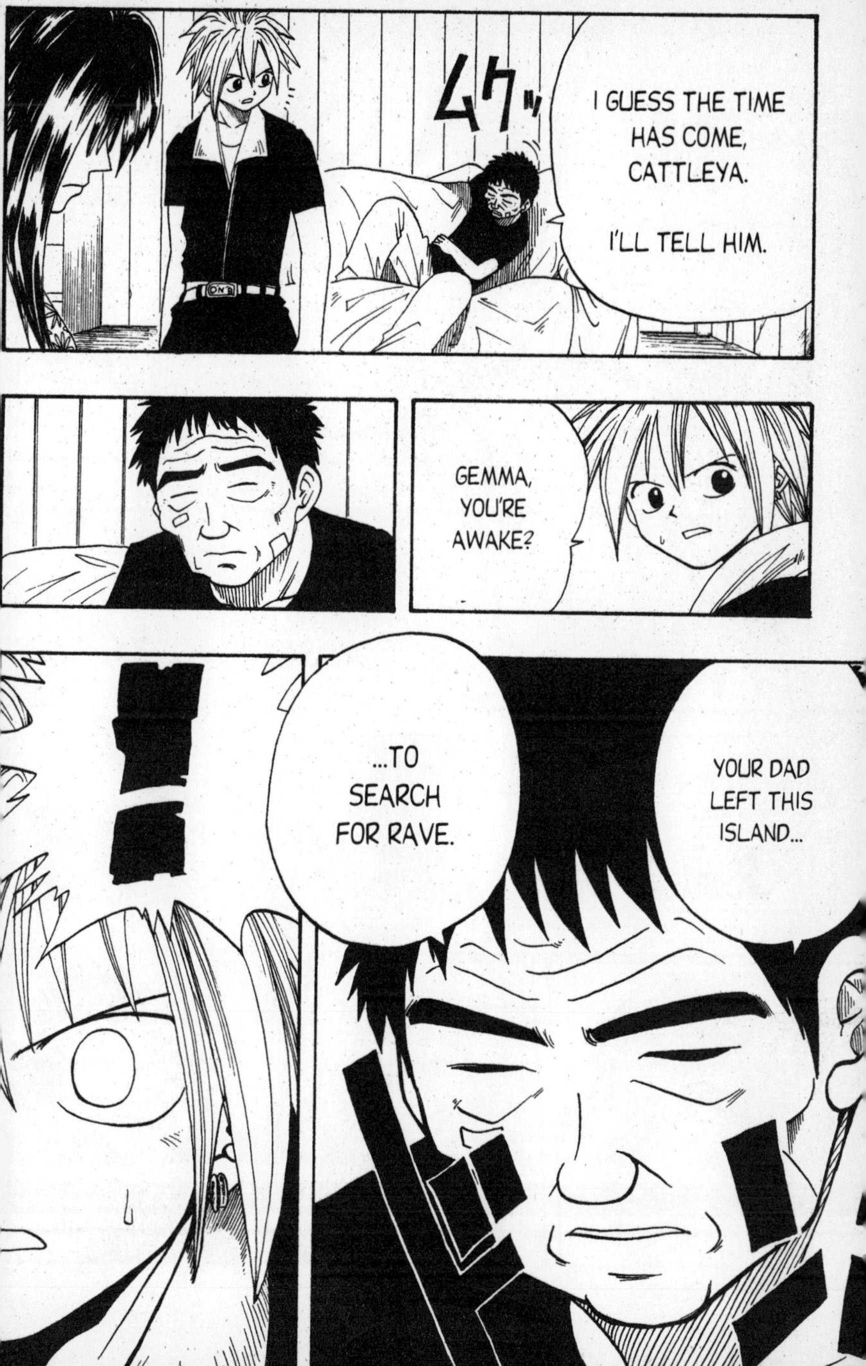
I GUESS THE TIME HAS COME, CATTLEYA.
I'LL TELL HIM.
ムクッ
GEMMA, YOU'RE AWAKE?
YOUR DAD LEFT THIS ISLAND...
...TO SEARCH FOR RAVE.

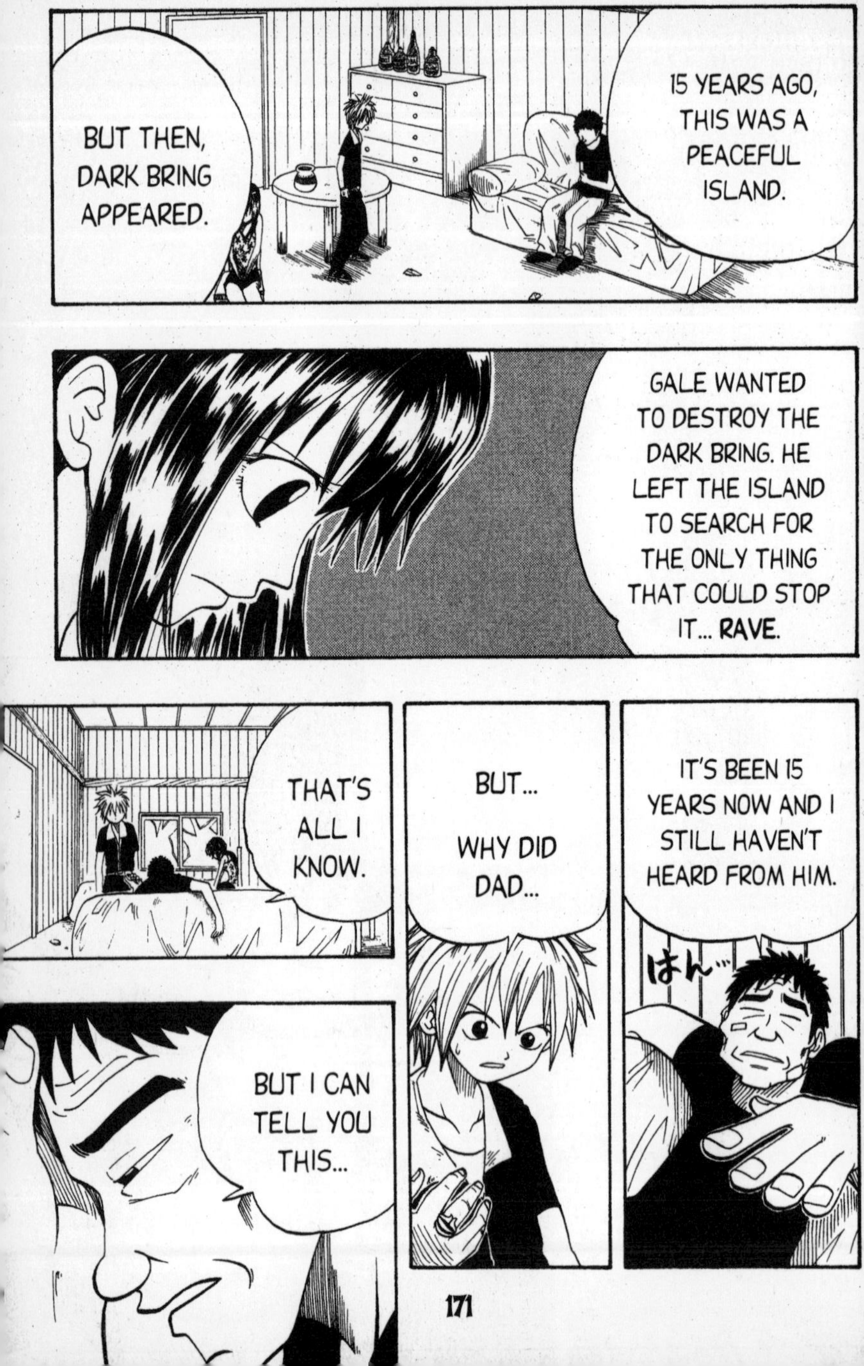
15 YEARS AGO, THIS WAS A PEACEFUL ISLAND.
BUT THEN, DARK BRING APPEARED.
GALE WANTED TO DESTROY THE DARK BRING. HE LEFT THE ISLAND TO SEARCH FOR THE ONLY THING THAT COULD STOP IT... **RAVE**.
IT'S BEEN 15 YEARS NOW AND I STILL HAVEN'T HEARD FROM HIM.
はん゛
BUT...
WHY DID DAD...
THAT'S ALL I KNOW.
BUT I CAN TELL YOU THIS...

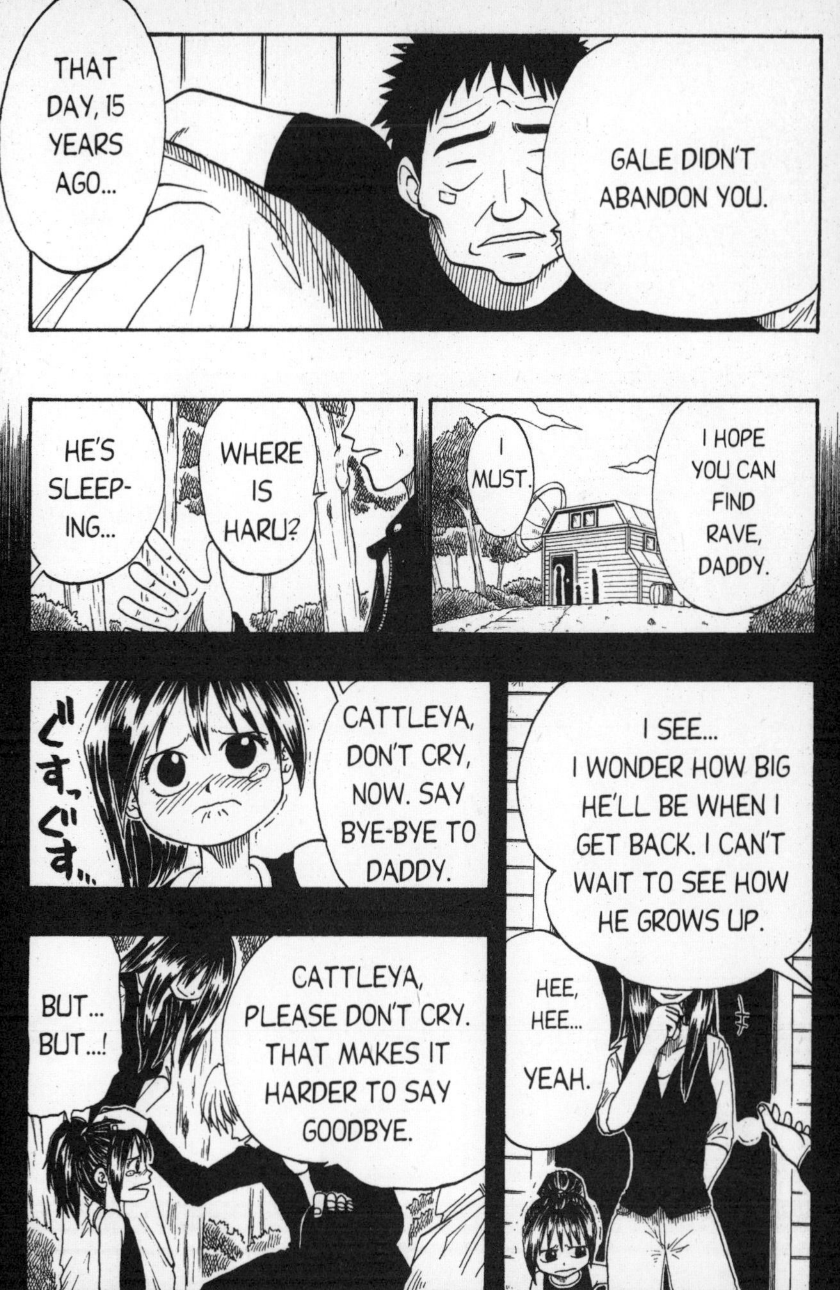
GALE DIDN'T ABANDON YOU.
THAT DAY, 15 YEARS AGO...
I HOPE YOU CAN FIND RAVE, DADDY.
I MUST.
WHERE IS HARU?
HE'S SLEEPING...
I SEE... I WONDER HOW BIG HE'LL BE WHEN I GET BACK. I CAN'T WAIT TO SEE HOW HE GROWS UP.
HEE, HEE...
YEAH.
CATTLEYA, DON'T CRY, NOW. SAY BYE-BYE TO DADDY.
ぐすっぐす…
CATTLEYA, PLEASE DON'T CRY. THAT MAKES IT HARDER TO SAY GOODBYE.
BUT... BUT...!

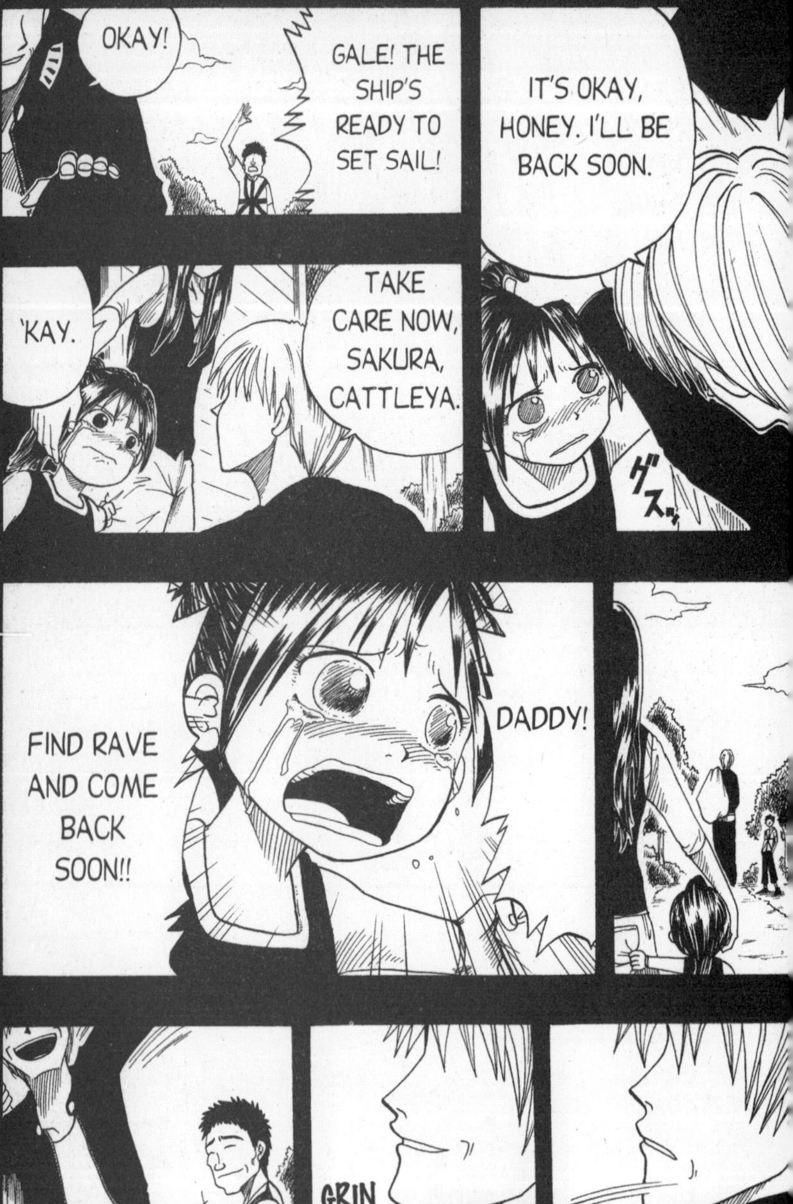
IT'S OKAY, HONEY. I'LL BE BACK SOON.
グスッ
GALE! THE SHIP'S READY TO SET SAIL!
OKAY!
TAKE CARE NOW, SAKURA, CATTLEYA.
'KAY.
DADDY!
FIND RAVE AND COME BACK SOON!!
GRIN

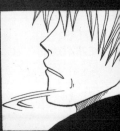

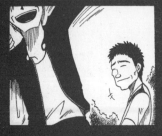

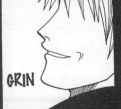

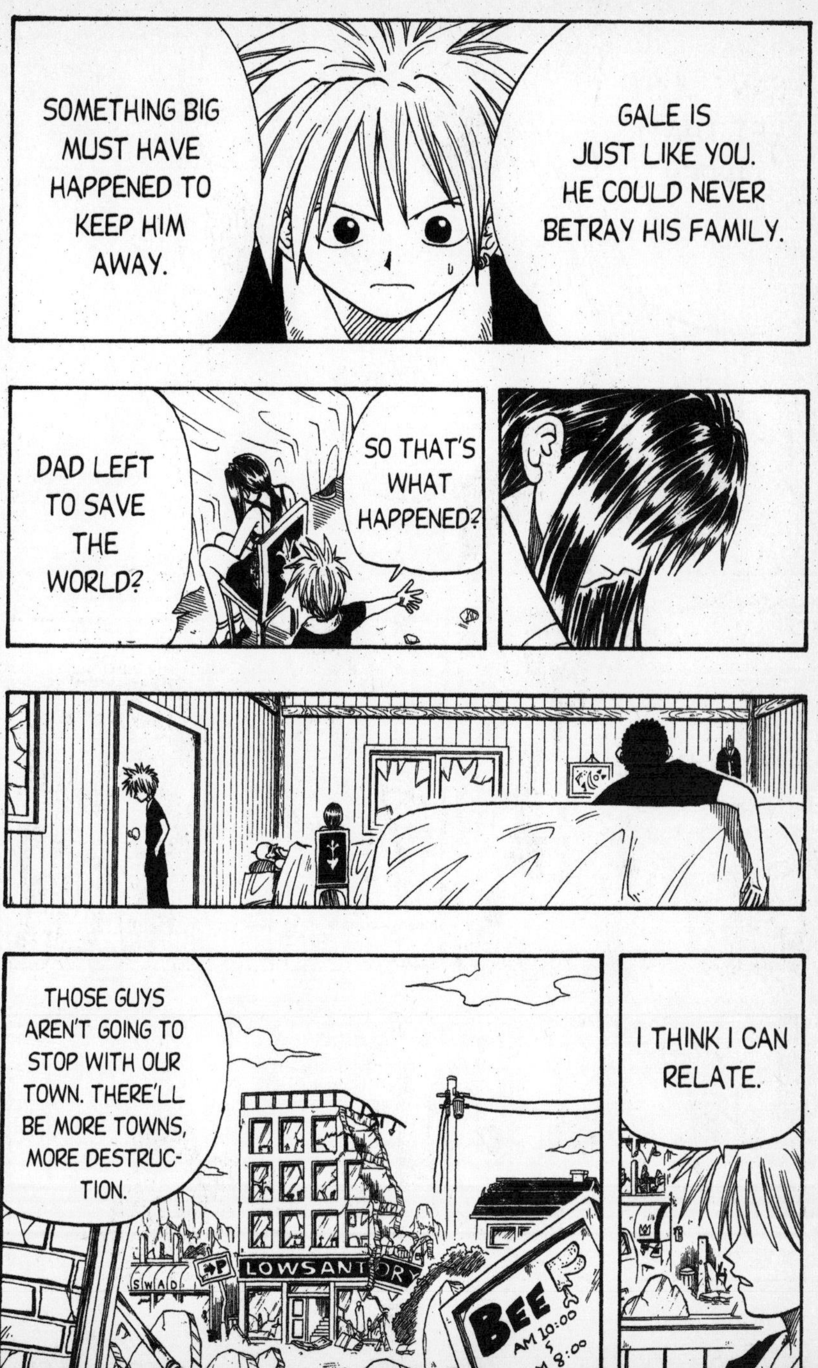
GALE IS JUST LIKE YOU. HE COULD NEVER BETRAY HIS FAMILY.
SOMETHING BIG MUST HAVE HAPPENED TO KEEP HIM AWAY.
SO THAT'S WHAT HAPPENED?
DAD LEFT TO SAVE THE WORLD?
I THINK I CAN RELATE.
THOSE GUYS AREN'T GOING TO STOP WITH OUR TOWN. THERE'LL BE MORE TOWNS, MORE DESTRUC-TION.

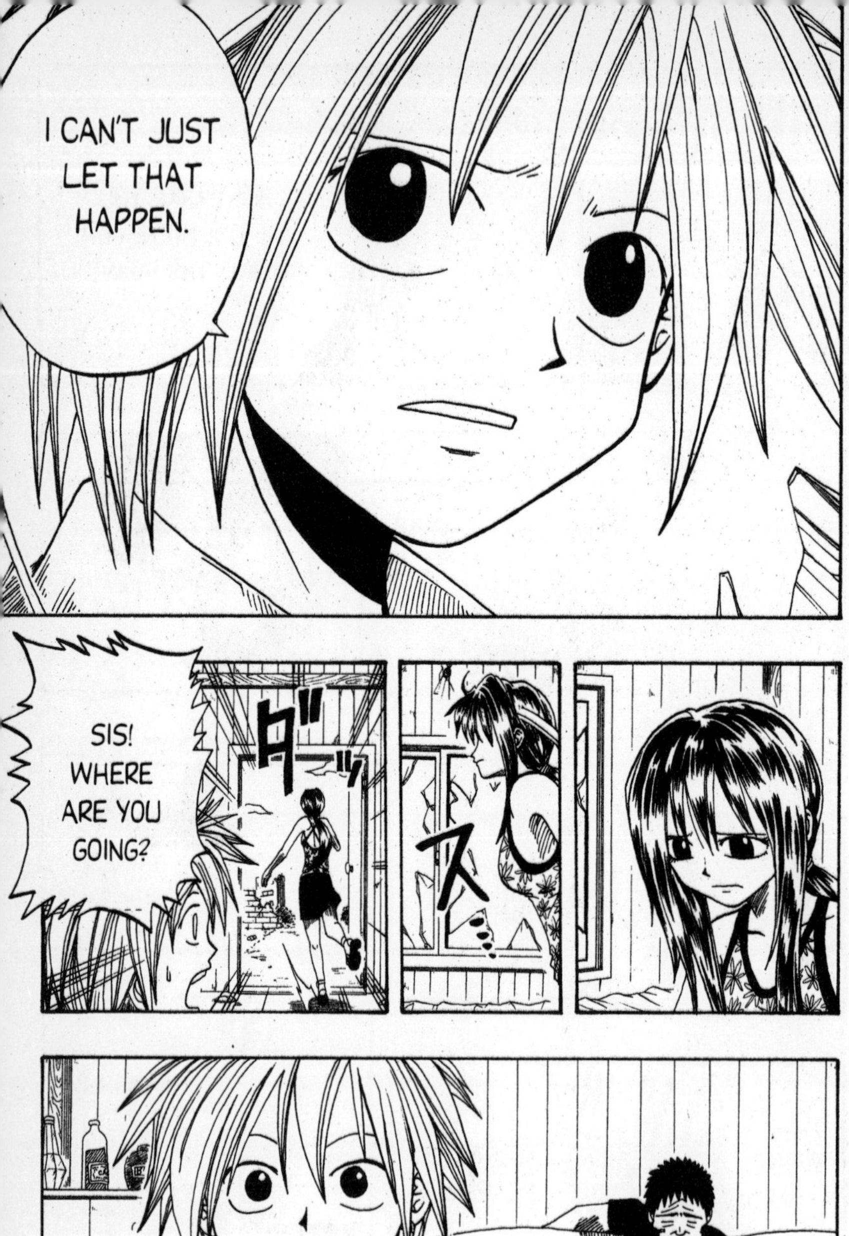
I CAN'T JUST LET THAT HAPPEN.
ス…
ダッ
SIS! WHERE ARE YOU GOING?

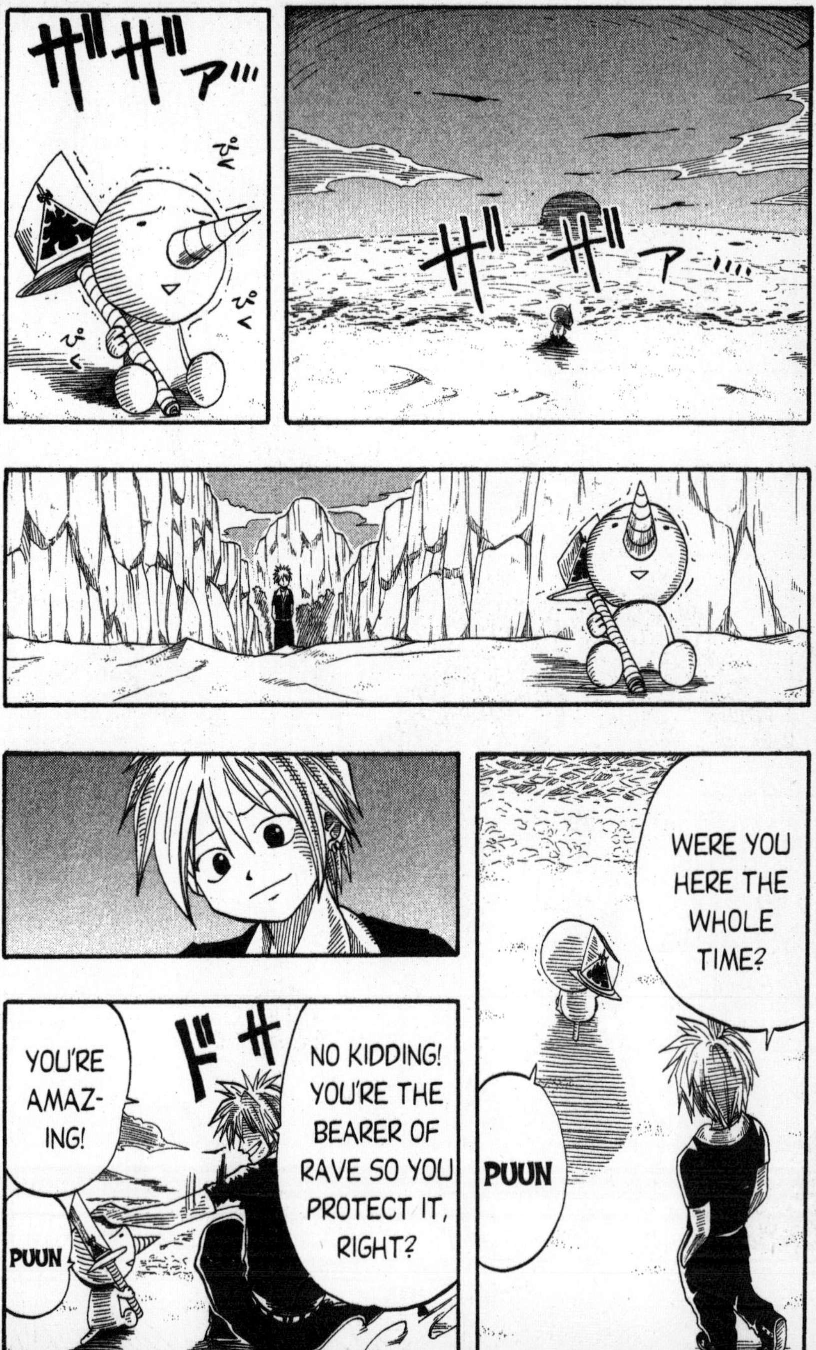
ザザァ…
ザザァ
ぴく
ぴく
ぴく
WERE YOU HERE THE WHOLE TIME?
PUUN
ドサ
NO KIDDING! YOU'RE THE BEARER OF RAVE SO YOU PROTECT IT, RIGHT?
YOU'RE AMAZ-ING!
PUUN

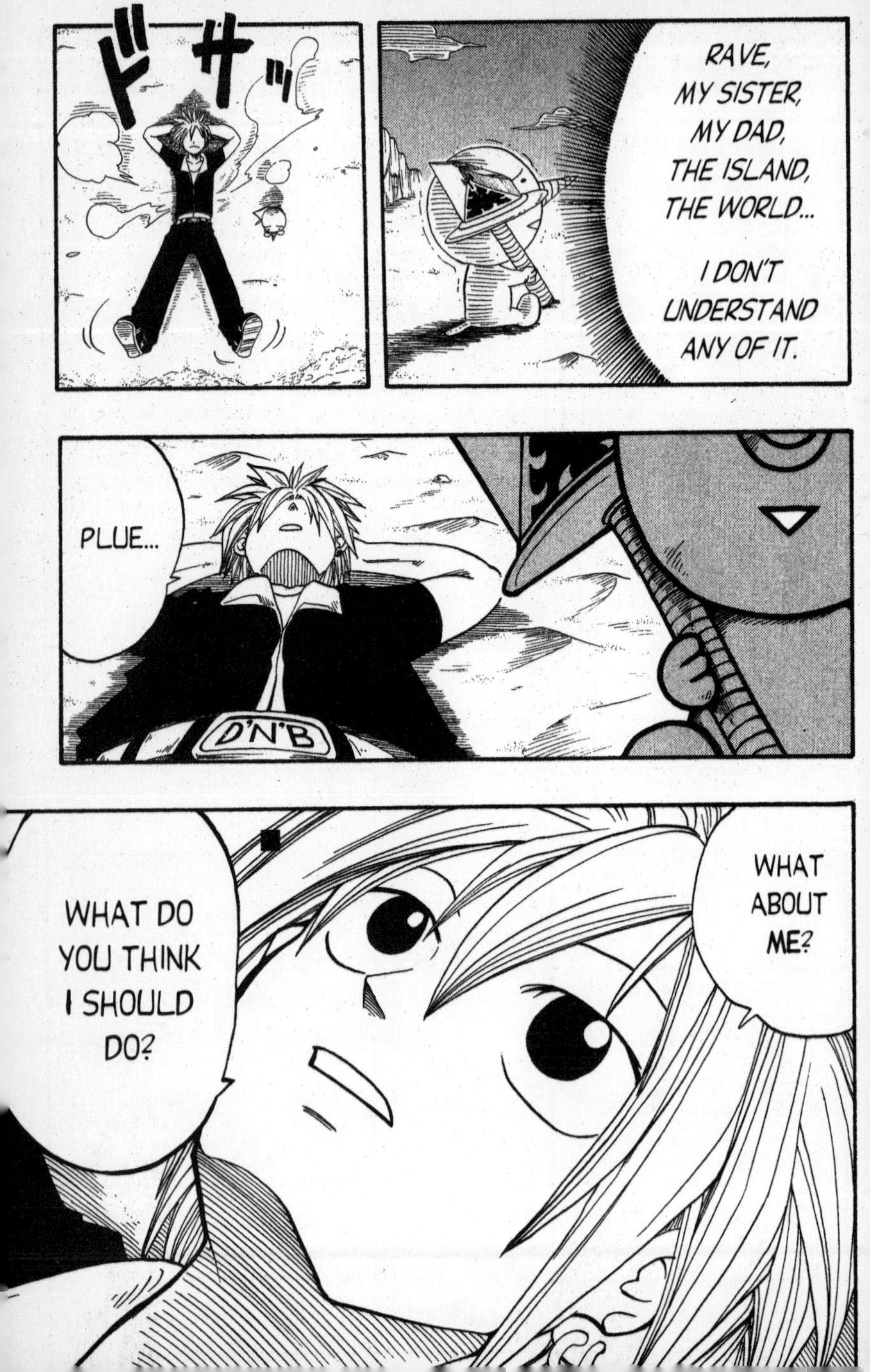
RAVE, MY SISTER, MY DAD, THE ISLAND, THE WORLD...
I DON'T UNDERSTAND ANY OF IT.
ドザッ
PLUE...
WHAT ABOUT ME?
WHAT DO YOU THINK I SHOULD DO?

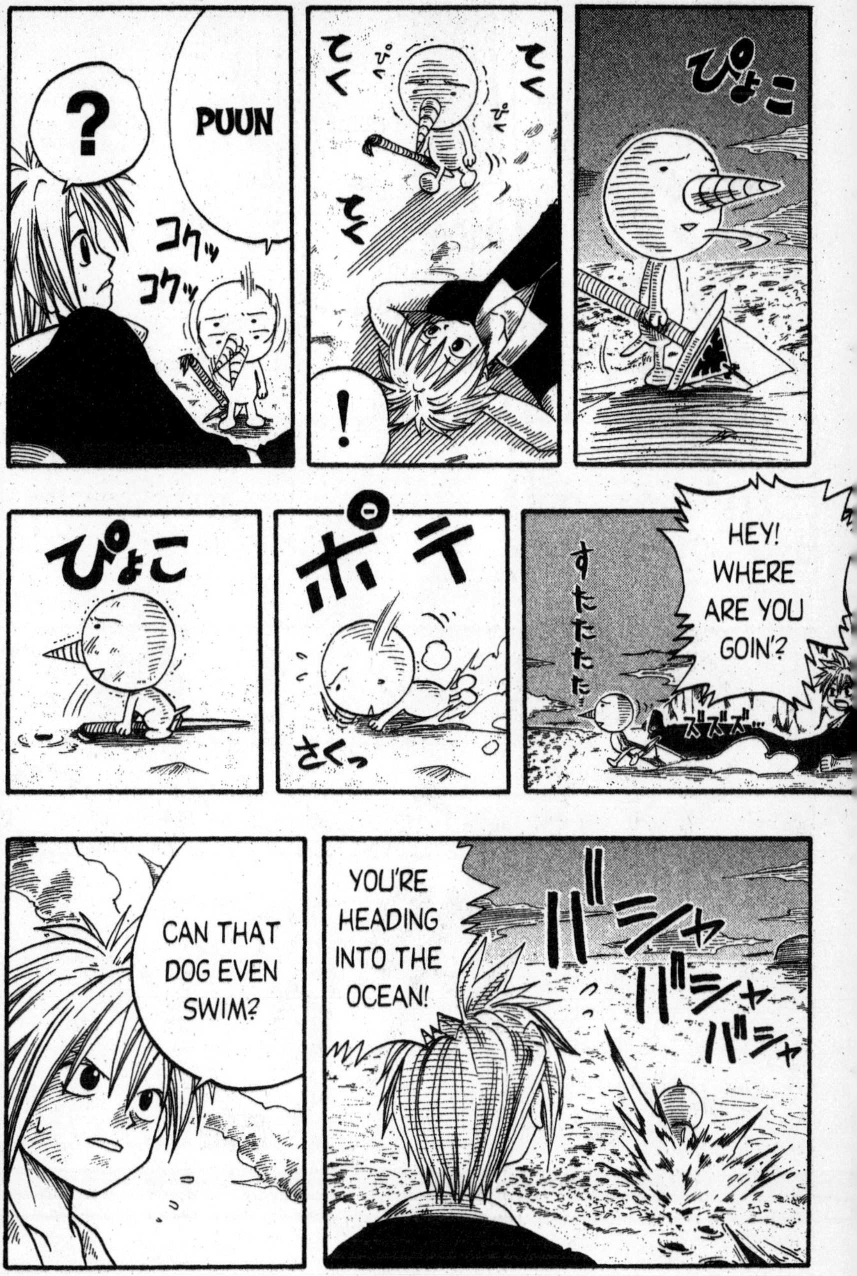
?
PUUN
コクッ
コクッ
てく
てく
ぴく
ぴく
てく
てく
!
ぴょこ
ぴょこ
ポテ
さくっ
すたたた
ズズズ
HEY! WHERE ARE YOU GOIN'?
CAN THAT DOG EVEN SWIM?
YOU'RE HEADING INTO THE OCEAN!
バシャ
バシャ
バシャ

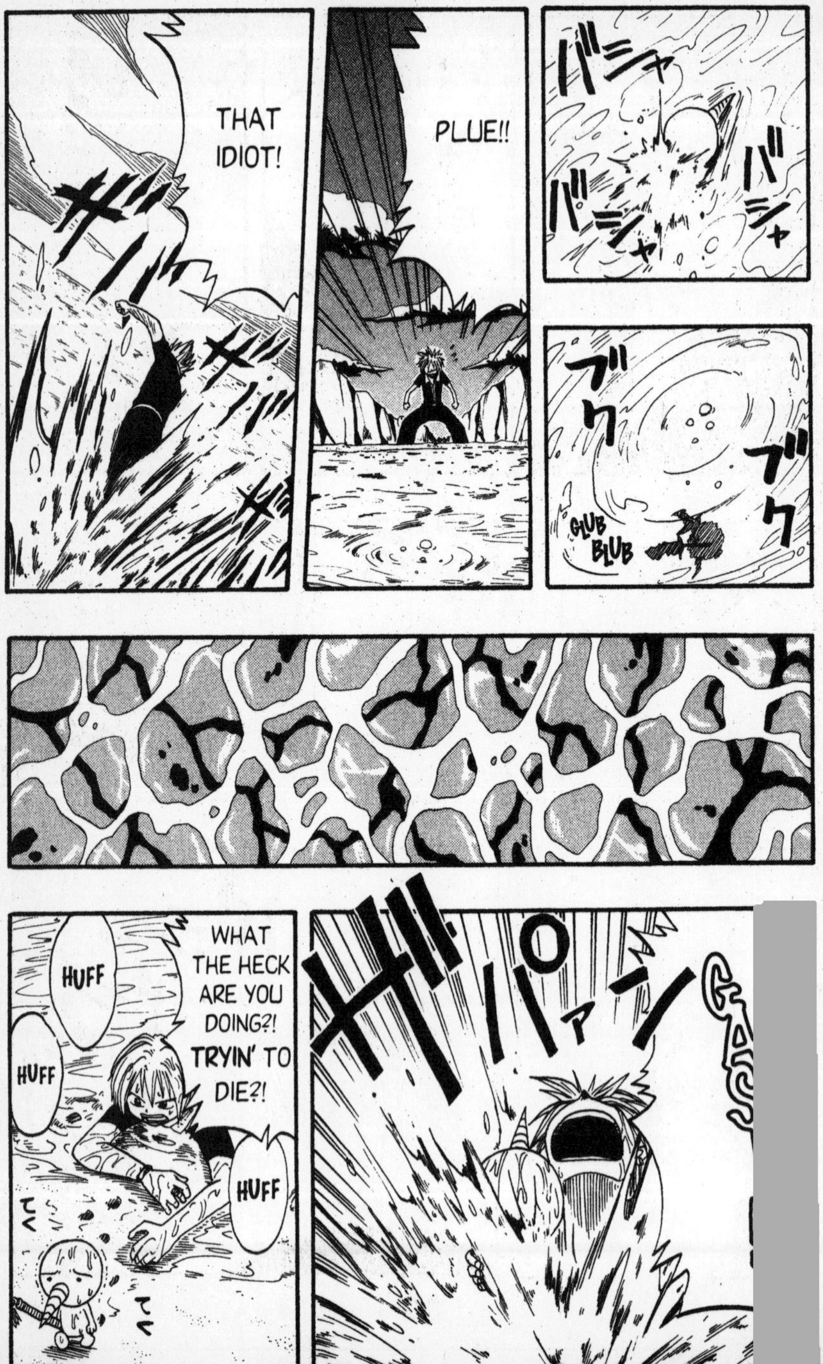
バシャ
バシャ
バシャ
ブク
ブク
GLUB BLUB
PLUE!!
THAT IDIOT!
ザパァーン
WHAT THE HECK ARE YOU DOING?! TRYIN' TO DIE?!
HUFF
HUFF
HUFF
てく
てく

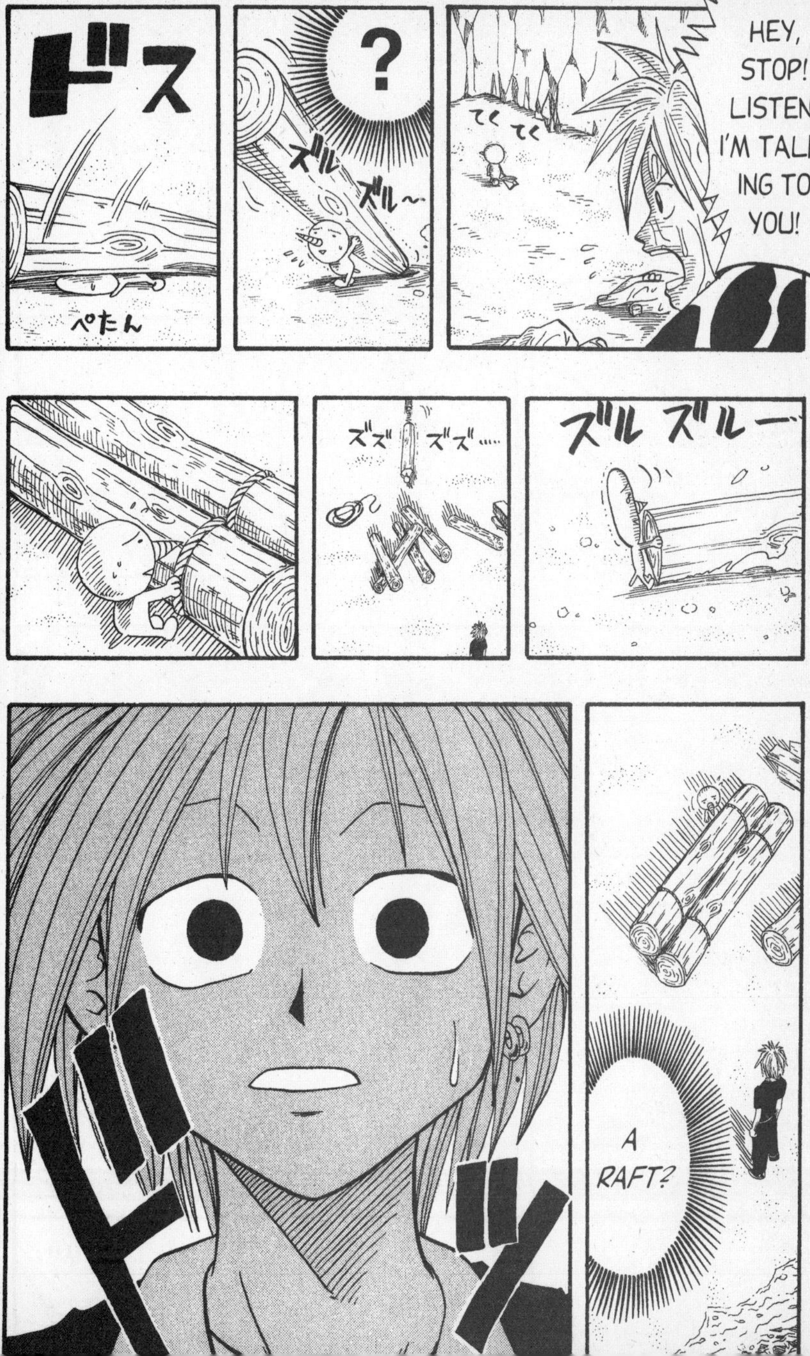
HEY, STOP! LISTEN! I'M TALKING TO YOU!
てく てく
?
ズル ズル～
ドス
ぺたん
ズル ズルー
ズズ ズズ……
A RAFT?

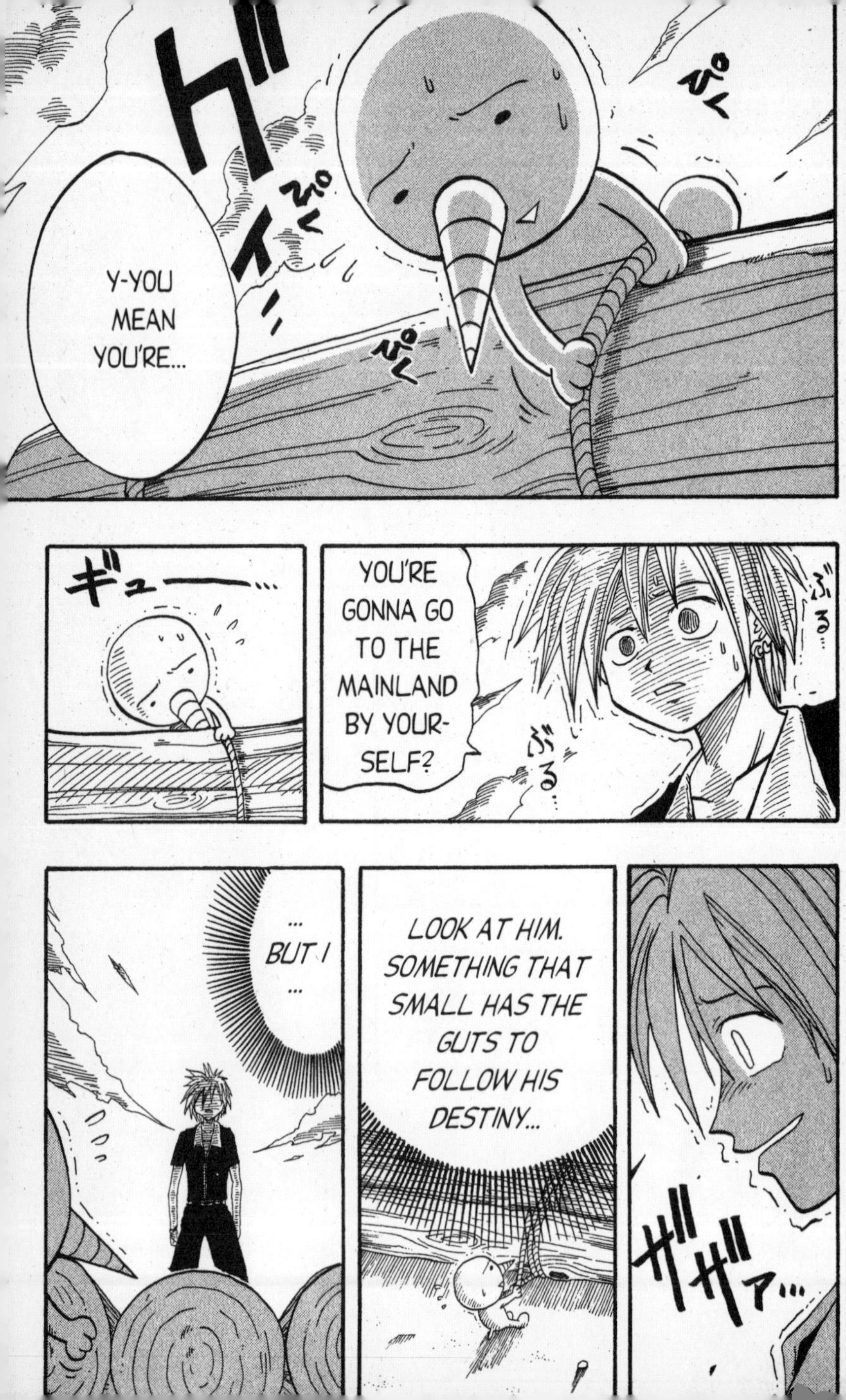
ぴく
ぴく
Y-YOU MEAN YOU'RE...
ぴく
YOU'RE GONNA GO TO THE MAINLAND BY YOUR-SELF?
ぶる…
ぶる…
ギュー…
ザザア…
LOOK AT HIM. SOMETHING THAT SMALL HAS THE GUTS TO FOLLOW HIS DESTINY...
... BUT I ...

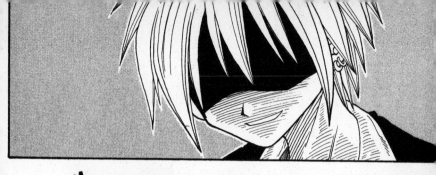

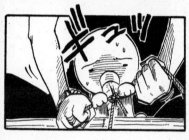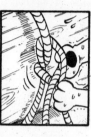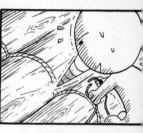

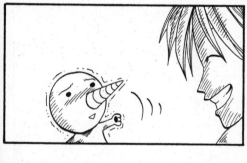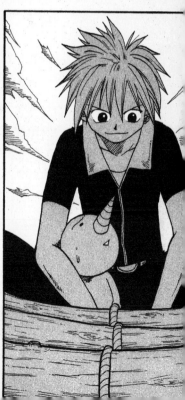

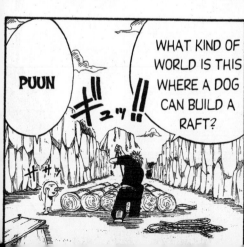

WHAT KIND OF WORLD IS THIS WHERE A DOG CAN BUILD A RAFT?

PUUN

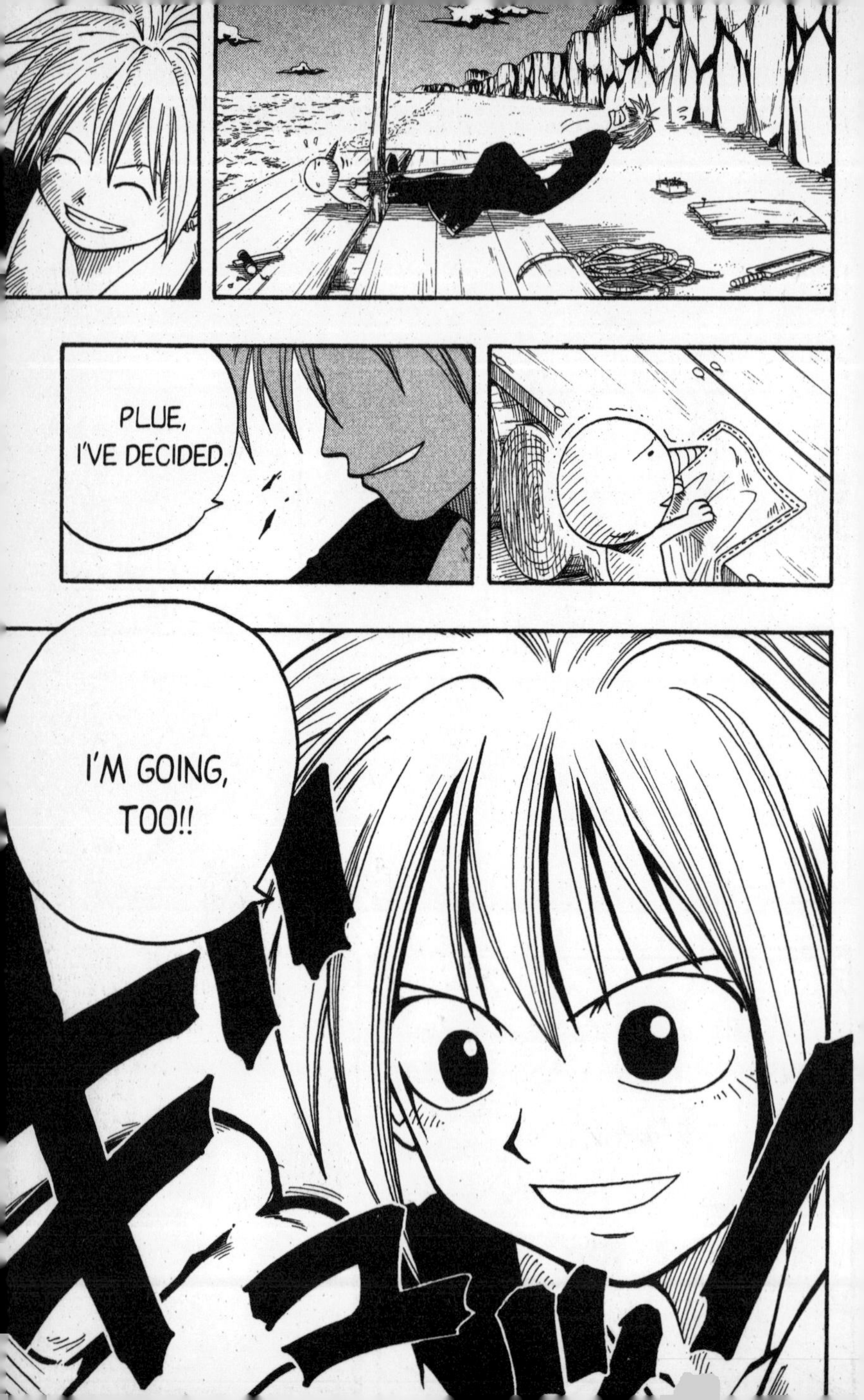
PLUE, I'VE DECIDED.
I'M GOING, TOO!!

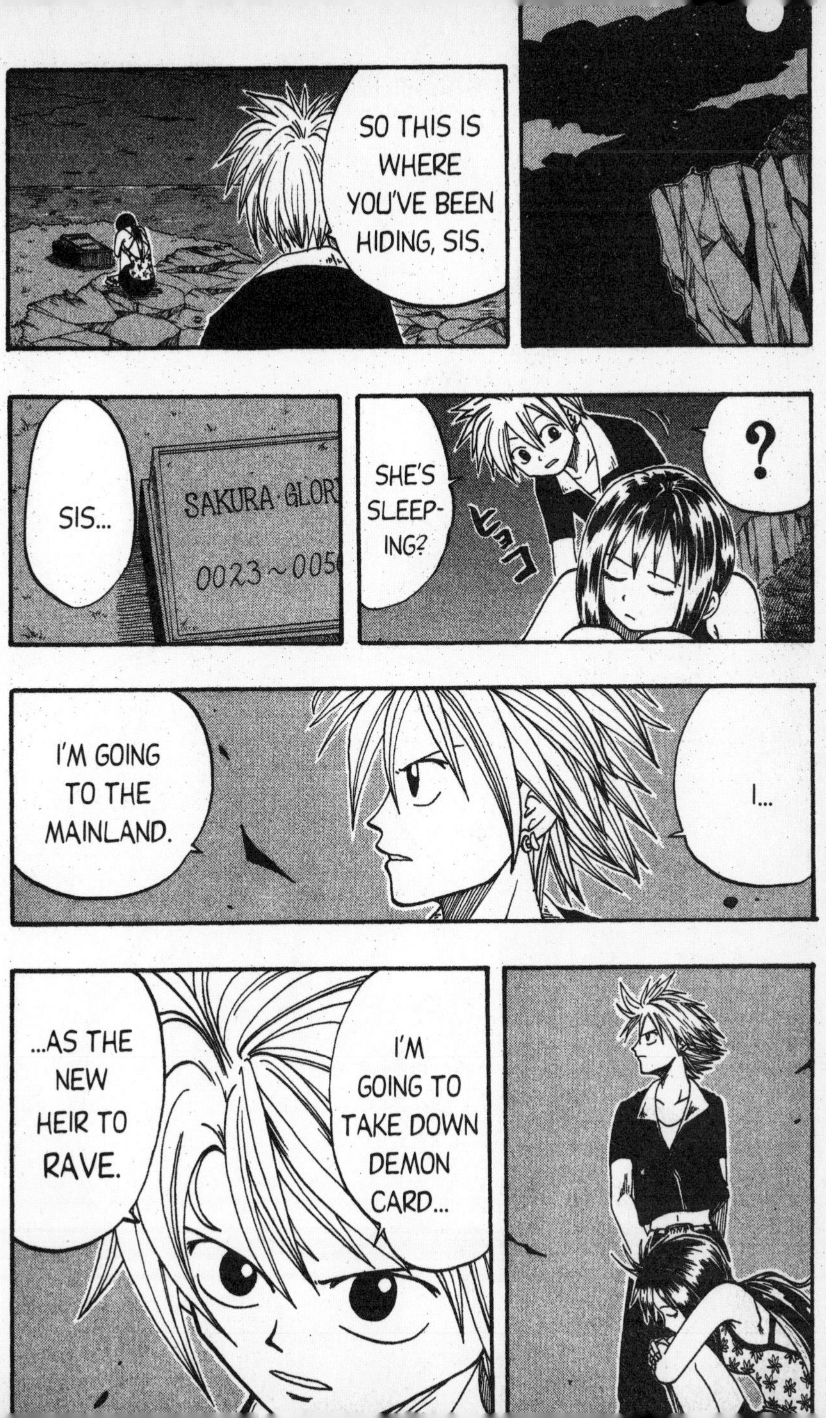
SO THIS IS WHERE YOU'VE BEEN HIDING, SIS.
?
SHE'S SLEEP-ING?
SIS...
SAKURA·GLORI
0023~005
I...
I'M GOING TO THE MAINLAND.
I'M GOING TO TAKE DOWN DEMON CARD...
...AS THE NEW HEIR TO RAVE.

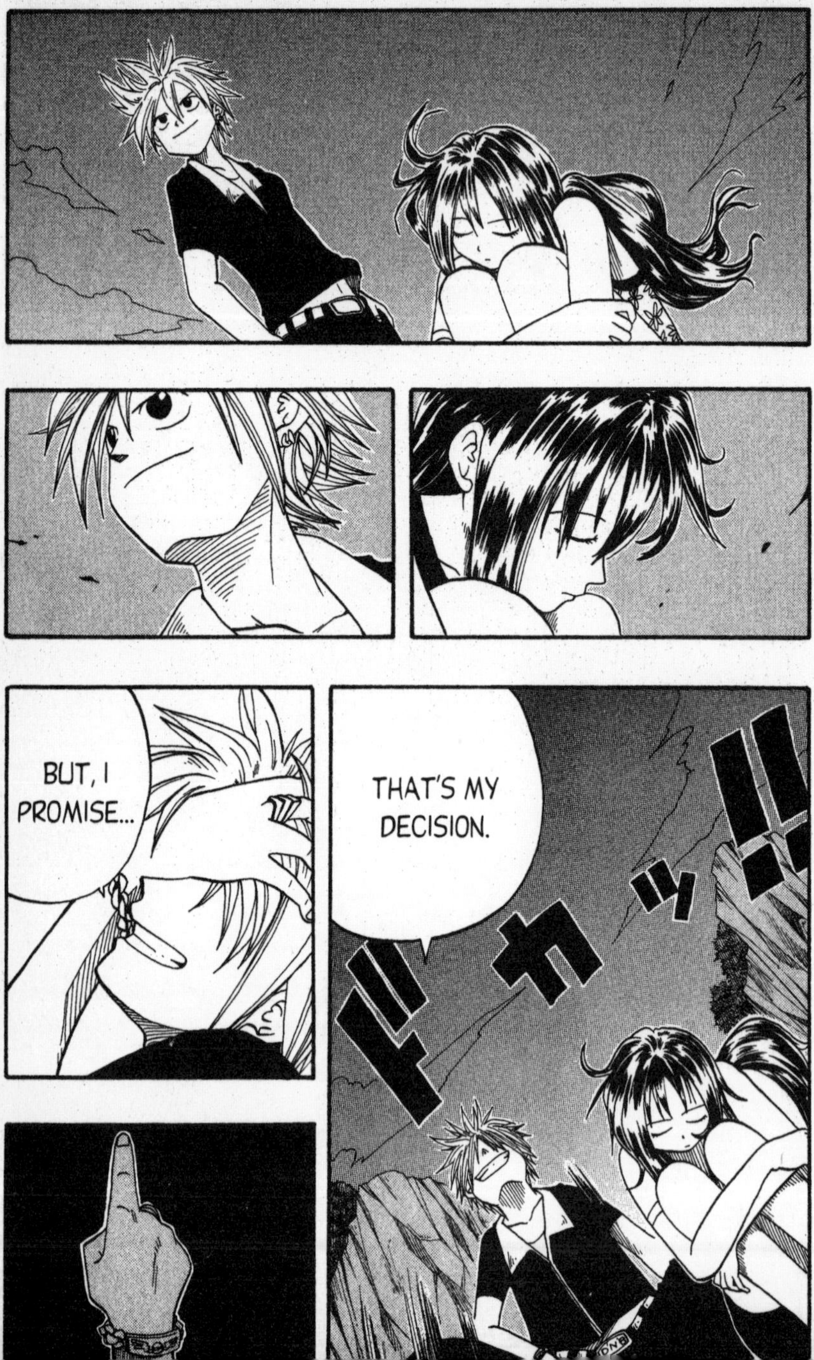

BUT, I PROMISE...
THAT'S MY DECISION.
ドカッ!!

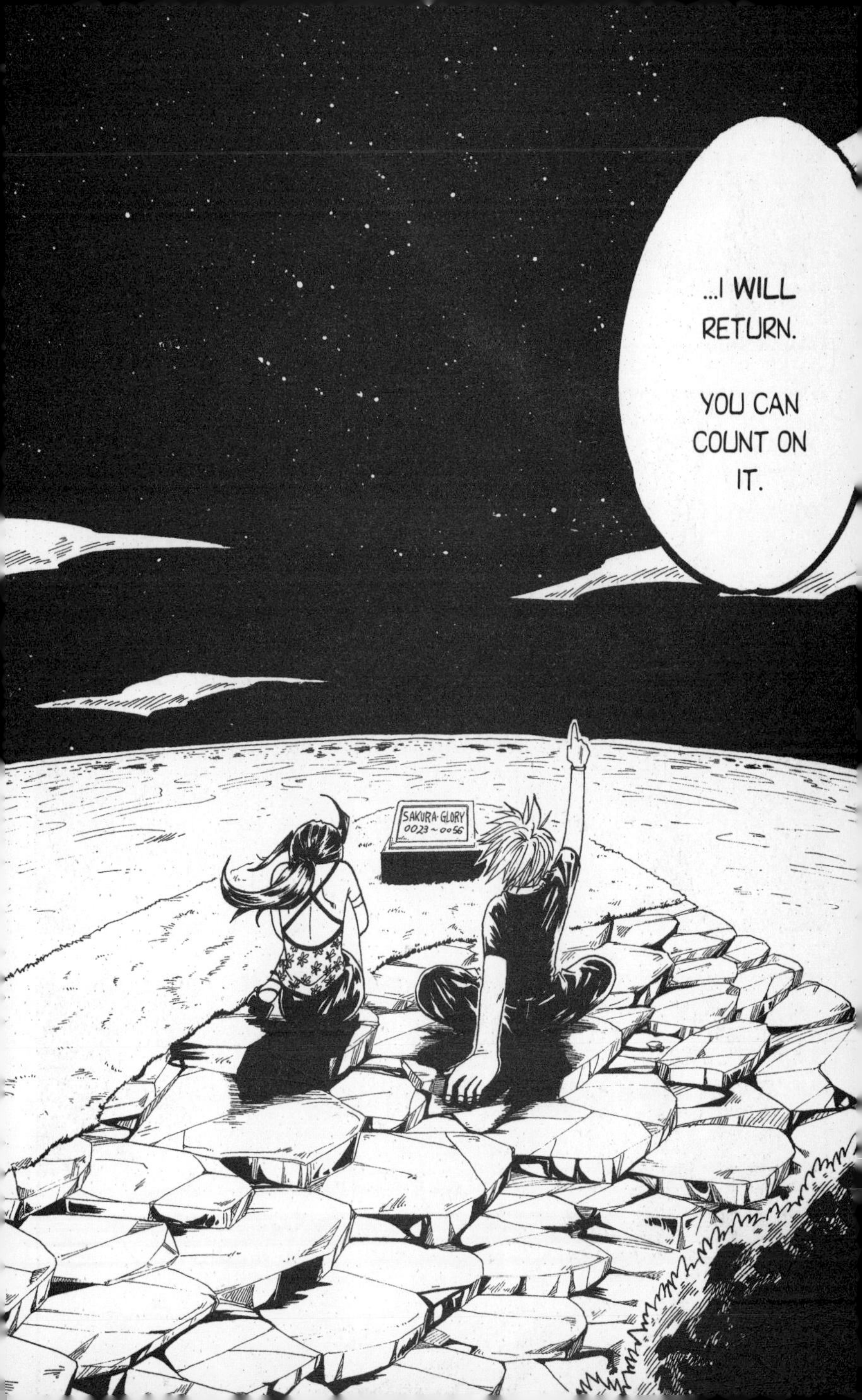
...I WILL RETURN.
YOU CAN COUNT ON IT.
SAKURA GLORY
0023 ~ 0056

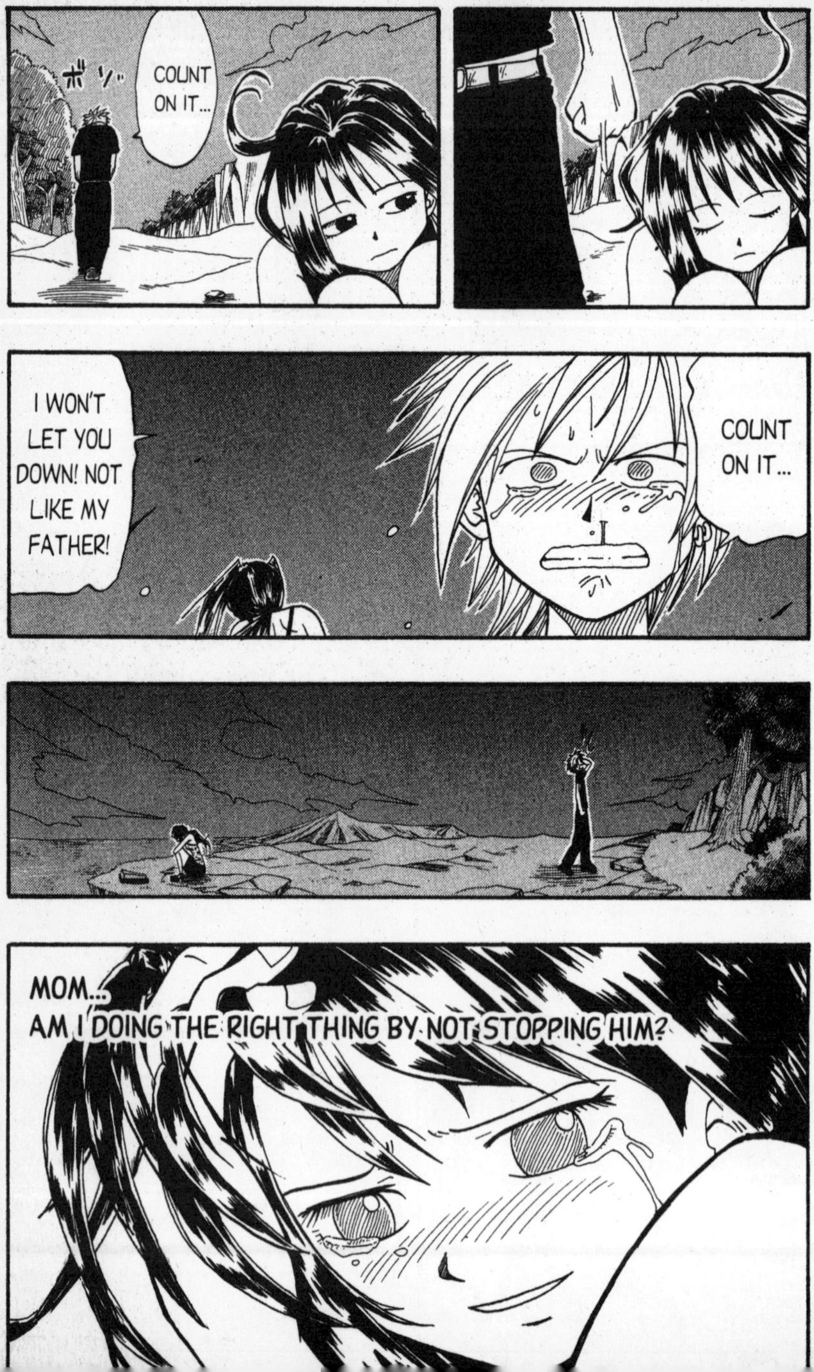
ボソッ
COUNT ON IT...
COUNT ON IT...
I WON'T LET YOU DOWN! NOT LIKE MY FATHER!
MOM...
AM I DOING THE RIGHT THING BY NOT STOPPING HIM?

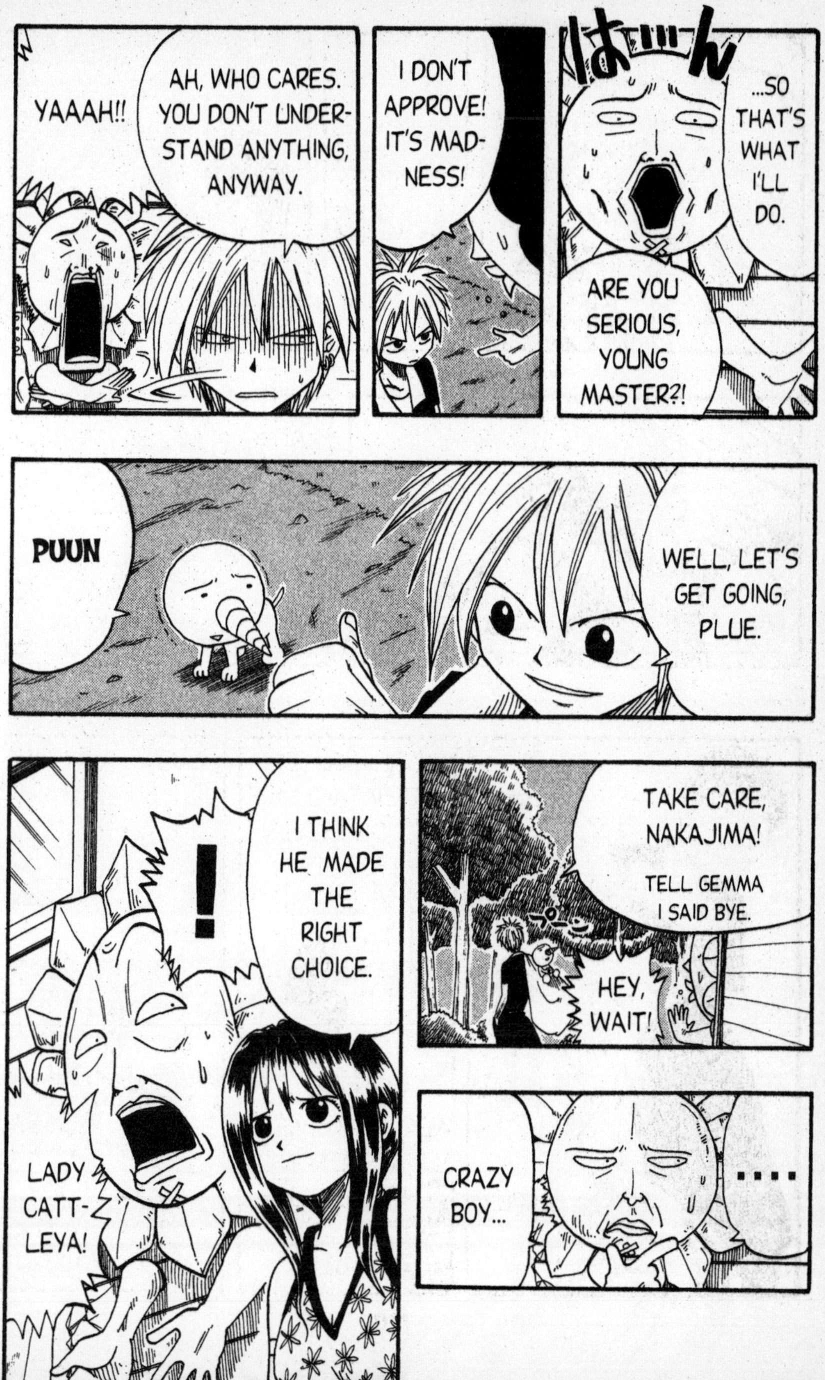
...SO THAT'S WHAT I'LL DO.
ARE YOU SERIOUS, YOUNG MASTER?!
I DON'T APPROVE! IT'S MADNESS!
AH, WHO CARES. YOU DON'T UNDERSTAND ANYTHING, ANYWAY.
YAAAH!!
WELL, LET'S GET GOING, PLUE.
PUUN
TAKE CARE, NAKAJIMA!
TELL GEMMA I SAID BYE.
HEY, WAIT!
....
CRAZY BOY...
I THINK HE MADE THE RIGHT CHOICE.
!
LADY CATTLEYA!

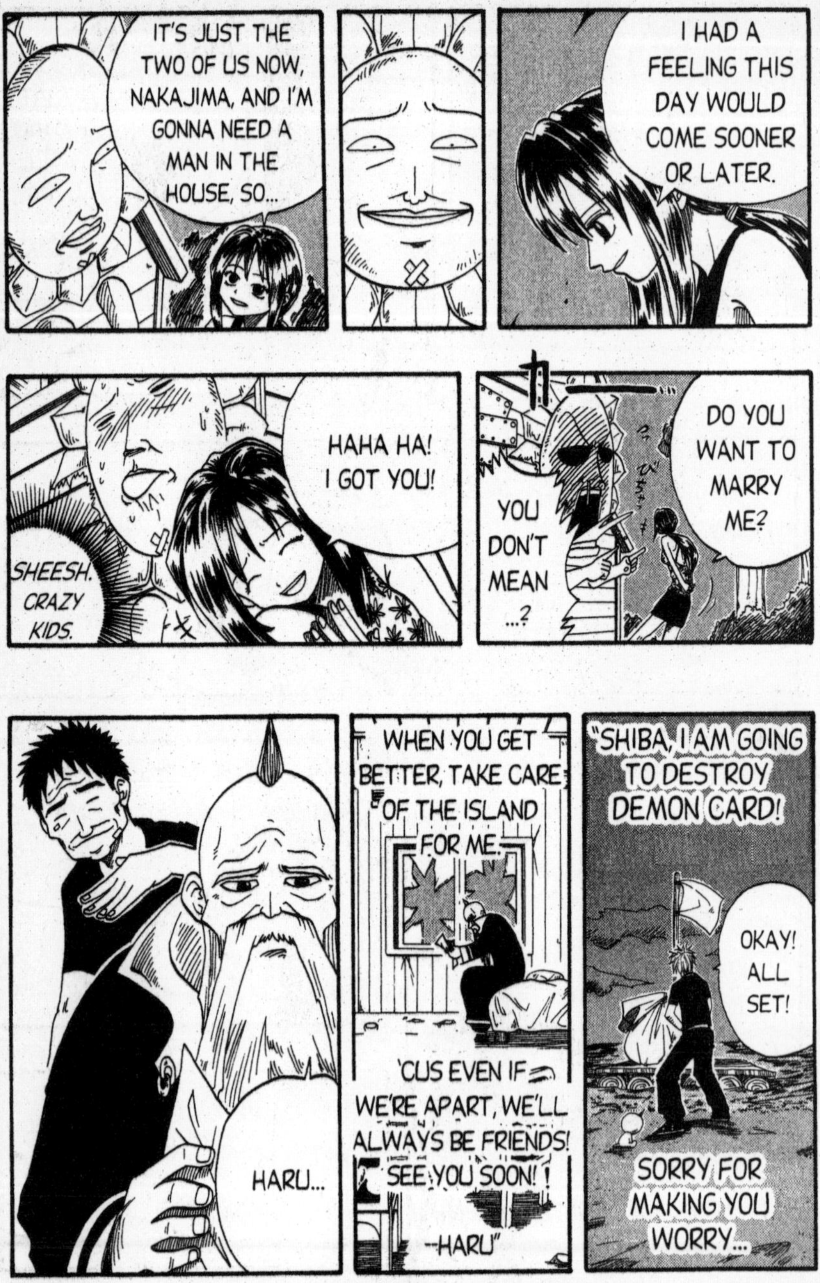
I HAD A FEELING THIS DAY WOULD COME SOONER OR LATER.
IT'S JUST THE TWO OF US NOW, NAKAJIMA, AND I'M GONNA NEED A MAN IN THE HOUSE, SO...
DO YOU WANT TO MARRY ME?
YOU DON'T MEAN ...?
HAHA HA! I GOT YOU!
SHEESH. CRAZY KIDS.
"SHIBA, I AM GOING TO DESTROY DEMON CARD!
OKAY! ALL SET!
SORRY FOR MAKING YOU WORRY...
WHEN YOU GET BETTER, TAKE CARE OF THE ISLAND FOR ME.
'CUS EVEN IF WE'RE APART, WE'LL ALWAYS BE FRIENDS! SEE YOU SOON!
--HARU"
HARU...

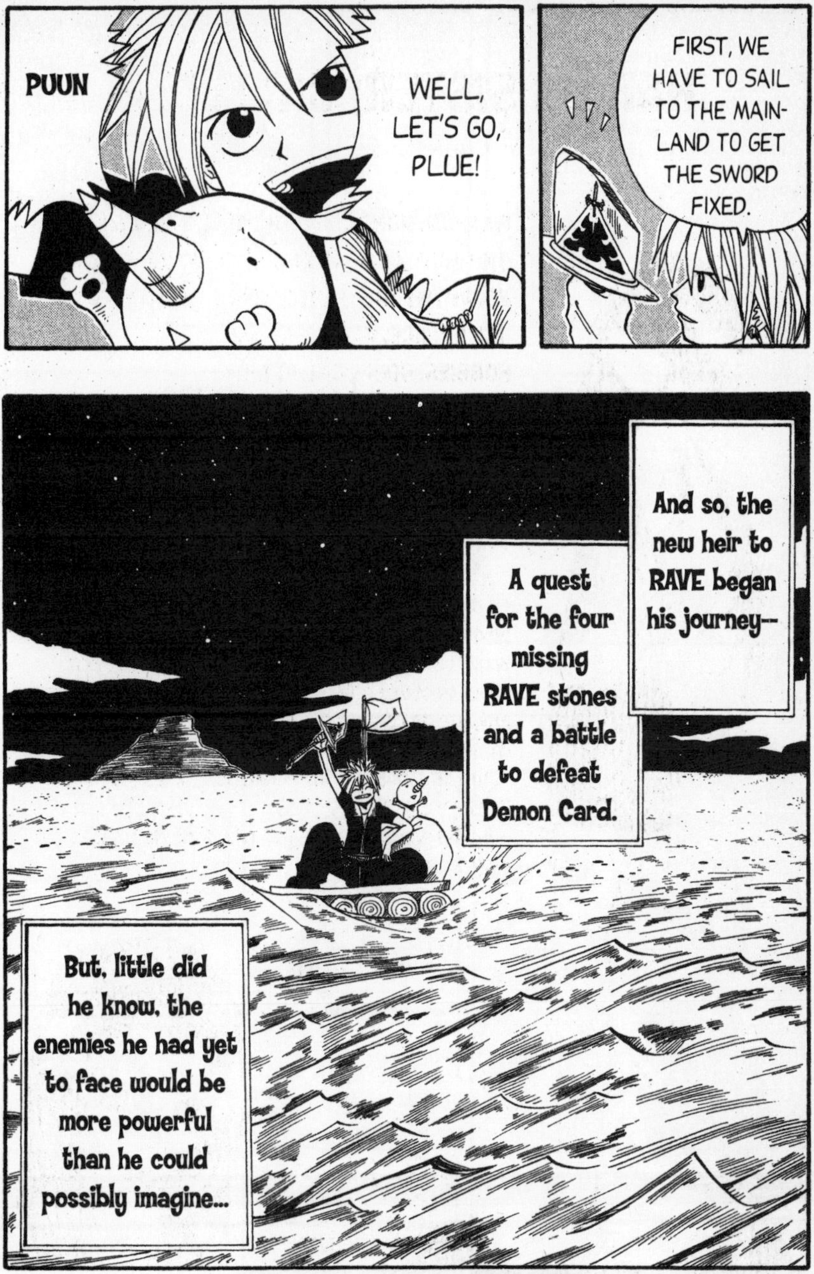
PUUN
WELL, LET'S GO, PLUE!
FIRST, WE HAVE TO SAIL TO THE MAIN-LAND TO GET THE SWORD FIXED.
And so, the new heir to RAVE began his journey--
A quest for the four missing RAVE stones and a battle to defeat Demon Card.
But, little did he know, the enemies he had yet to face would be more powerful than he could possibly imagine...

TO BE CONTINUED

HARU'S SISTER: CATTLEYA

WEAPON: NONE (USED TO DO A LITTLE KENDO)
BIRTHDAY/AGE: AUGUST 5, 0046 / 20 YEARS
HEIGHT/WEIGHT/BLOODTYPE: 166CM / 46KG / A
BIRTHPLACE: GARAGE ISLAND
HOBBIES: COOKING, LAUNDRY
SPECIAL SKILLS: KARAOKE (SELF-DESCRIBED "BEST ON THE ISLAND")
LIKES: HER FAMILY
HATES: HER EX-BOYFRIEND

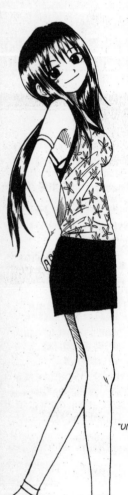

I decided from the very beginning that there would be one other person in Haru's family. Initially, it wasn't a sister, it was an uncle. I changed it to a sister because otherwise there wouldn't have been any female characters until the 4th chapter, and THAT would've been tacky (laugh).

And so I thought, "Ah, I'll make it a sister!" and Cattleya was born!

By the way, that was also when the Nakajima character was born, too (laugh).

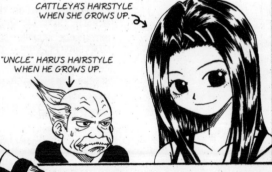

CATTLEYA'S HAIRSTYLE WHEN SHE GROWS UP.

"UNCLE" HARU'S HAIRSTYLE WHEN HE GROWS UP.

CAFE TSUBOMI'S SECOND OWNER GEMMA

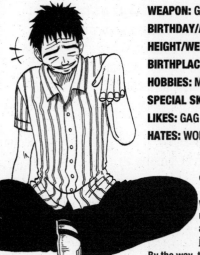

WEAPON: GUN (99 MAGNUM)

BIRTHDAY/AGE: JUNE 13, 0016 / 51 YEARS

HEIGHT/WEIGHT/BLOODTYPE: 175CM / 60KG / A

BIRTHPLACE: GARAGE ISLAND

HOBBIES: MAKING GREAT COFFEE

SPECIAL SKILLS: LAUGHING NON-STOP FOR 24 HOURS

LIKES: GAG COMICS

HATES: WORRYING

Gemma ended up a more important character than initially planned.

He's the spitting image of one of my friends, who was the model for the character. His hand movements were awkward, and he would always burst out laughing. Tame (22) and I are just showing our age (laugh).

By the way, the name "Gemma" means "flower bud" in Latin, just like "Tsubomi" means "flower bud" in Japanese.

THE MYSTERIOUS LIFEFORM: NAKAJIMA

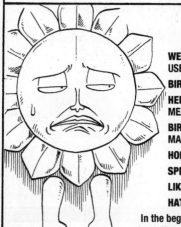

WEAPON: NONE (BUT ACCORDING TO HIM, HE CAN USE HIS FEATHERS AS WEAPONS IF NEED BE)

BIRTHDAY/AGE: UNKNOWN / UNKNOWN

HEIGHT/WEIGHT/BLOODTYPE: (IT'S UNCERTAIN HOW TO MEASURE THESE) UNKNOWN / UNKNOWN / N-DUCK

BIRTHPLACE: AKAPERA ISLAND (THERE SEEM TO BE MANY SUCH CREATURES ON THAT ISLAND)

HOBBIES: STUDYING

SPECIAL SKILLS: CATCHING INSECTS

LIKES: TULIPS

HATES: RAIN AND SNOW

In the beginning, he was the character I got the most questions about. He seemed more popular than I would have thought, so I decided to let him reappear.

BONUS COMIC

RAVE0077

LEVIN MINDS THE HOUSE

#1: Hanging with Nakajima

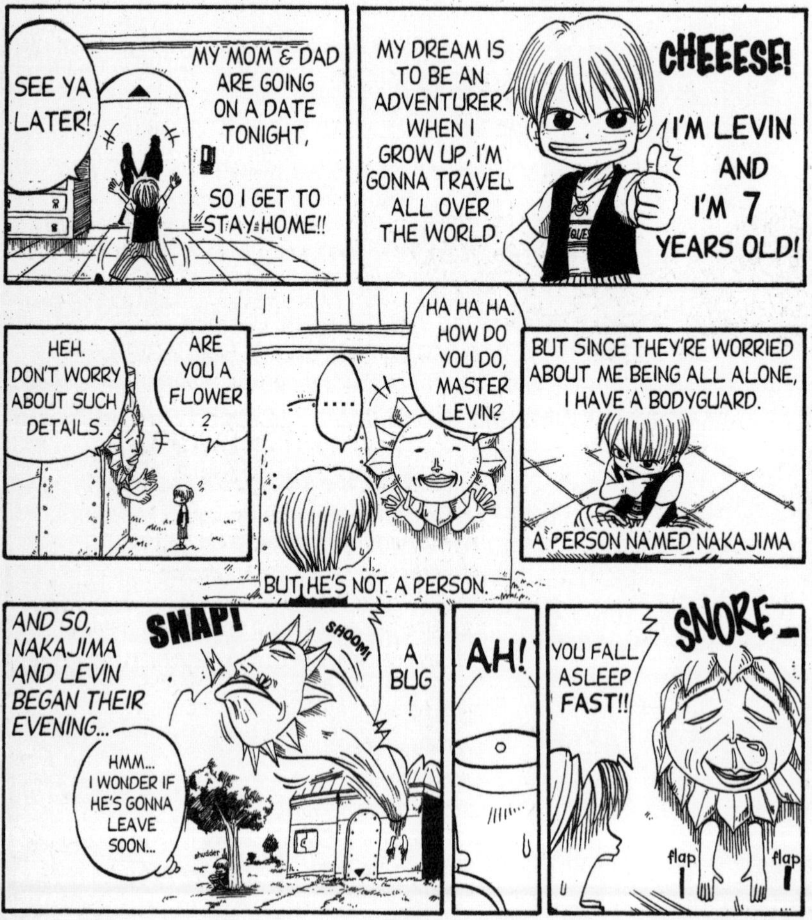
CHEEESE!
I'M LEVIN AND I'M 7 YEARS OLD!
MY DREAM IS TO BE AN ADVENTURER. WHEN I GROW UP, I'M GONNA TRAVEL ALL OVER THE WORLD.
MY MOM & DAD ARE GOING ON A DATE TONIGHT,
SEE YA LATER!
SO I GET TO STAY HOME!!
BUT SINCE THEY'RE WORRIED ABOUT ME BEING ALL ALONE, I HAVE A BODYGUARD.
A PERSON NAMED NAKAJIMA
HA HA HA. HOW DO YOU DO, MASTER LEVIN?
....
BUT HE'S NOT A PERSON.
ARE YOU A FLOWER?
HEH. DON'T WORRY ABOUT SUCH DETAILS.
SNORE
YOU FALL ASLEEP FAST!!
flap
flap
AH!
A BUG!
SHOOM!
SNAP!
AND SO, NAKAJIMA AND LEVIN BEGAN THEIR EVENING...
HMM... I WONDER IF HE'S GONNA LEAVE SOON...
shudder

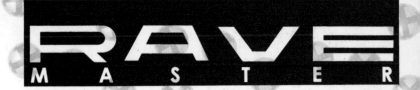

RAVE MASTER

BEFORE I BEGIN, I WANT TO SAY "THANK YOU, WITH ALL MY GRATI-
TUDE!!" TO ALL MY READERS. THE FIRST VOLUME OF RAVE IS FINALLY
ON SALE. IT'S MY FIRST GRAPHIC NOVEL EVER. IT MAKES ME SUPER
HAPPY!!

IN EACH VOLUME, I'LL USE THIS SPACE TO GIVE YOU THE INSIDE
STORY ON RAVE OR FOR OTHER THINGS I FEEL LIKE WRITING ABOUT.
FOR THIS FIRST VOLUME, I WOULD LIKE TO THANK EVERYONE WHO
HELPED ME OUT OR CHEERED ME ON AS I WORKED ON THIS SERIES.
(SORRY FOR SUDDENLY GETTING INTO MY OWN PERSONAL AFFAIRS.)

FIRST OFF, THANKS TO MATSUKI, MY MANAGER, WHO SUPPORTED MY
WORK FROM THE TIME I WAS JUST BEGINNING. TO YOSHIDA, THE VETER-
AN EDITOR WHO'S WORKED WITH ME SINCE THE PLANNING STAGES,
THANK YOU VERY MUCH! TO OGAWA, THE COVER DESIGNER FROM
KODANSHA COMICS AND ISHII, THE MANAGER FROM KODANSHA COMICS, I
AM TRULY THANKFUL. AND THANK YOU TO EVERYONE IN THE EDITORIAL
DEPARTMENT WHO CHEERED ME ON AND GAVE ME ADVICE. AND AS
ALWAYS, THANKS TO MY ASSISTANTS, NAKAMURA, YAMA AND YUKA!!
THANKS TO THE TWO "A" SISTERS, WHO HELPED ME OUT ON CHAPTER 3!
AND LOTS OF THANKS TO MY FAMILY AND FRIENDS! OH, AND TO THE
HIGH SCHOOL TEACHERS WHO LET ME GRADUATE (LAUGH)! TO ALL MY
READERS, THANK YOU!! AND FINALLY, THANK YOU TO THOSE AT WEEKLY
SHONEN MAGAZINE FOR LETTING THIS WORK BE SERIALIZED!!

I'LL KEEP TRYING MY BEST! PLEASE KEEP LENDING ME YOUR
SUPPORT, EVERYONE!!

MASHIMA.

RAVE MASTER

Volume 2 Preview

SMELLS LIKE ANOTHER TEEN HERO

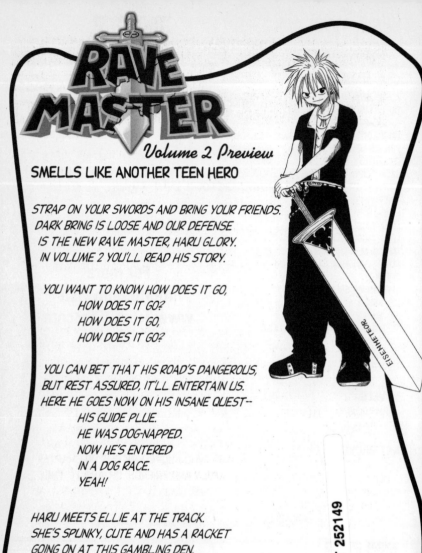

STRAP ON YOUR SWORDS AND BRING YOUR FRIENDS.
DARK BRING IS LOOSE AND OUR DEFENSE
IS THE NEW RAVE MASTER, HARU GLORY.
IN VOLUME 2 YOU'LL READ HIS STORY.

YOU WANT TO KNOW HOW DOES IT GO,
HOW DOES IT GO?
HOW DOES IT GO,
HOW DOES IT GO?

YOU CAN BET THAT HIS ROAD'S DANGEROUS,
BUT REST ASSURED, IT'LL ENTERTAIN US.
HERE HE GOES NOW ON HIS INSANE QUEST--
HIS GUIDE PLUE.
HE WAS DOG-NAPPED.
NOW HE'S ENTERED
IN A DOG RACE.
YEAH!

HARU MEETS ELLIE AT THE TRACK.
SHE'S SPUNKY, CUTE AND HAS A RACKET
GOING ON AT THIS GAMBLING DEN,
'TIL DEMON CARD COMES BARGING IN.

AND NOW SHE'LL GO,
SHE'LL GO, SHE'LL GO, SHE'LL GO WITH HARU.
SHE'LL GO, SHE'LL GO, SHE'LL GO WITH HARU.

EISENMETEOR

T 252149

ALSO AVAILABLE FROM TOKYOPOP®

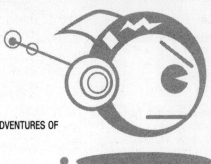

ALSO AVAILABLE FROM TOKYOPOP

MANGA

.HACK//LEGEND OF THE TWILIGHT
ANGELIC LAYER
BABY BIRTH
BRAIN POWERED
BRIGADOON
B'TX
CANDIDATE FOR GODDESS, THE
CARDCAPTOR SAKURA
CARDCAPTOR SAKURA - MASTER OF THE CLOW
CHRONICLES OF THE CURSED SWORD
CLAMP SCHOOL DETECTIVES
CLOVER
COMIC PARTY
CORRECTOR YUI
COWBOY BEBOP
COWBOY BEBOP: SHOOTING STAR
CRESCENT MOON
CULDCEPT
CYBORG 009
D.N. ANGEL
DEMON DIARY
DEMON ORORON, THE
DIGIMON
DIGIMON ZERO TWO
DIGIMON TAMERS
DRAGON HUNTER
DRAGON KNIGHTS
DREAM SAGA
DUKLYON: CLAMP SCHOOL DEFENDERS
ET CETERA
ETERNITY
FAERIES' LANDING
FLCL
FORBIDDEN DANCE
FRUITS BASKET
G GUNDAM
GATE KEEPERS
GIRL GOT GAME
GUNDAM SEED ASTRAY
GUNDAM WING
GUNDAM WING: BATTLEFIELD OF PACIFISTS
GUNDAM WING: ENDLESS WALTZ
GUNDAM WING: THE LAST OUTPOST (G-UNIT)
HARLEM BEAT
I.N.V.U.

INITIAL D
JING: KING OF BANDITS
JULINE
KARE KANO
KILL ME, KISS ME
KINDAICHI CASE FILES, THE
KING OF HELL
KODOCHA: SANA'S STAGE
LEGEND OF CHUN HYANG, THE
MAGIC KNIGHT RAYEARTH I
MAGIC KNIGHT RAYEARTH II
MAN OF MANY FACES
MARMALADE BOY
MARS
MINK
MIRACLE GIRLS
MODEL
ONE
PEACH GIRL
PEACH GIRL: CHANGE OF HEART
PITA-TEN
PLANET LADDER
PLANETES
PRINCESS AI
PSYCHIC ACADEMY
RAGNAROK
RAVE MASTER
REALITY CHECK
REBIRTH
REBOUND
RISING STARS OF MANGA
SAILOR MOON
SAINT TAIL
SAMURAI GIRL REAL BOUT HIGH SCHOOL
SEIKAI TRILOGY, THE CREST OF THE STARS
SGT. FROG
SHAOLIN SISTERS
SHIRAHIME-SYO: SNOW GODDESS TALES
SKULL MAN, THE
SUIKODEN III
SUKI
THREADS OF TIME
TOKYO MEW MEW
VAMPIRE GAME
WISH
WORLD OF HARTZ
ZODIAC P.I.

01.09.04Y

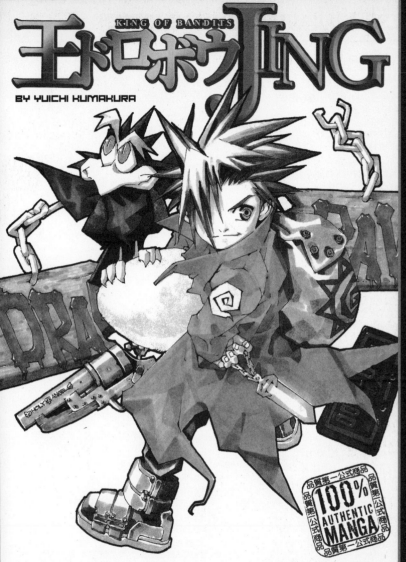

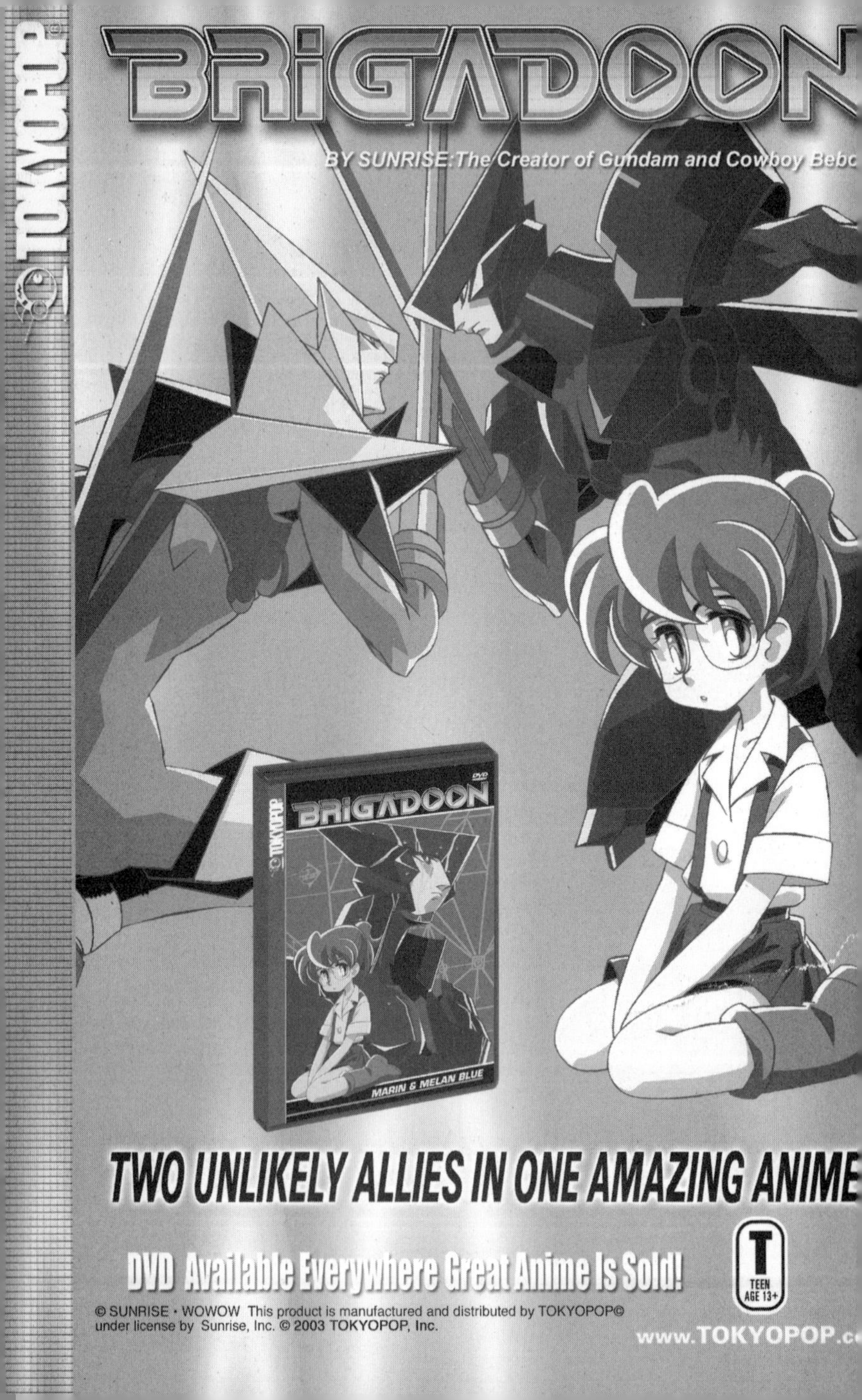
TOKYOPOP
BRIGADOON
BY SUNRISE: The Creator of Gundam and Cowboy Beb
BRIGADOON
DVD
TOKYOPOP
MARIN & MELAN BLUE
TWO UNLIKELY ALLIES IN ONE AMAZING ANIME
DVD Available Everywhere Great Anime Is Sold!
T
TEEN AGE 13+
© SUNRISE · WOWOW This product is manufactured and distributed by TOKYOPOP© under license by Sunrise, Inc. © 2003 TOKYOPOP, Inc.
www.TOKYOPOP.c

W9-AHI-276

STOP!

This is the back of the book.
You wouldn't want to spoil a great ending!

This book is printed "manga-style," in the authentic Japanese right-to-left format. Since none of the artwork has been flipped or altered, readers get to experience the story just as the creator intended. You've been asking for it, so TOKYOPOP® delivered: authentic, hot-off-the-press, and far more fun!

DIRECTIONS

If this is your first time reading manga-style, here's a quick guide to help you understand how it works.

It's easy... just start in the top right panel and follow the numbers. Have fun, and look for more 100% authentic manga from TOKYOPOP®!

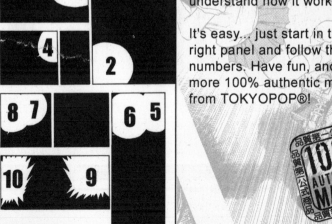

100% AUTHENTIC MANGA